BOY COLONEL OF
THE CONFEDERACY

They shall grow not old as we that are left grow old. Age shall not weary them nor the years condemn. At the going down of the sun and in the morning we shall remember them.

The Scottish War Memorial to
the Dead, 1914–1918 War,
Edinburgh Castle, Edinburgh, Scotland

BOY COLONEL OF THE CONFEDERACY

THE LIFE AND TIMES OF
HENRY KING BURGWYN, JR.

ARCHIE K. DAVIS

The University of North Carolina Press

Chapel Hill and London

© 1985 The University of North Carolina Press
All rights reserved
Manufactured in the United States of America
01 00 99 98 97   10 9 8 7 6
Library of Congress Cataloging in Publication Data
Davis, Archie K.
Boy colonel of the Confederacy.
Includes index.
1. Burgwyn, Henry King, 1841–1863. 2. Confederate States of America. Army—Biog-
raphy. 3. Soldiers—North Carolina—Biography.
4. North Carolina—Biography. I. Title.
E467.1.B79D38   1985   973.7'456'0924   84-26958
ISBN 0-8078-1647-7 (cloth : alk. paper)
ISBN 0-8078-4709-7 (pbk. : alk. paper)

The publisher gratefully acknowledges the
assistance of the Kellenberger Historical Trust
toward the publication of this volume.

FRONTISPIECE
Colonel Henry King Burgwyn, Jr. (courtesy Burgwyn family)

To Arch, Bonnie, Haywood, and Tom

CONTENTS

ILLUSTRATIONS

MAPS

ACKNOWLEDGMENTS

My long journey into the life and times of Harry Burgwyn has been a richly rewarding experience, made easier by the support and assistance of countless friends and acquaintances.

I am especially indebted to Professors H. G. Jones, Frank W. Klingberg, John R. Nelson, William S. Powell, and Frank W. Ryan at the University of North Carolina at Chapel Hill, whose encouragement and professional guidance have provided invaluable and sustained support all along the way. And I shall always be grateful to the members of the distinguished Burgwyn family, who have made available a wealth of original source material, particularly John Alveston Burgwyn Baker, John G. Burgwyn, W. H. S. Burgwyn, Jr., the late W. H. S. Burgwyn, Sr., and Maria Hunter.

The generous support afforded me by a number of institutions could not have been more thorough and accommodating. To the directors and able staff members of the Southern Historical Collection, the North Carolina Collection, the Jamaica Plain Tuesday Club, the Moravian Archives, the Moravian Music Foundation, the New England Genealogical Society, and the North Carolina Department of Archives and History I express my genuine appreciation. For valuable information and guidance, I particularly thank Colonel John G. Barrett, Virginia Military Institute; Kathleen R. Georg, Gettysburg National Military Park; Josephine L. Harper, State Historical Society of Wisconsin; Warren W. Hassler, Jr., Pennsylvania State University; D. Tennant Bryan and Margaret Lechner, *Richmond Times-Dispatch*; Stephen Riley, Massachusetts Historical Society; and Clyde N. Wilson, University of South Carolina.

In addition, I have been privileged to have the helpful assistance of many friends who have made available old letters, newspapers, and diaries, have provided introductions to valuable sources of information, and have accompanied me on battlefield inspections in search of old landmarks and long-forgotten fieldworks. Among them I am particularly grateful to Thomas C. Boushall, Joseph Bryan III, Beth Crabtree, Cortlandt Preston Creech, Virginius Dabney, Burke Davis, Mary Ellen Gadski, Edward B. Hanify, the late Margaret Mackay Jones, Albert S. Kemper, Jr., Clay M. Kirkman, Jr., Clarence T. Leinbach, Jr., Henry W. Lewis, Margaret Lilly, Fred M. Mallison, the late

Acknowledgments

Francis Manning, Bishop Edward T. Mickey, Laura Jones Millender, Elizabeth Moore, Jane Morrison Moore, the late Dr. Alfred Mordecai, Edmund Randolph Preston, Jr., Julia Jackson Christian Preston, Anna Preston Shaffner, Dr. Louis deS. Shaffner, Frederick M. Tate, and David L. Ward.

I wish my wife, Mary Louise, to know that without her generous spirit of indulgence, thoughtful understanding, and encouragement over many years this study would not have been possible. Nor could it have been successfully concluded without the faithful, patient, and dedicated contribution of Katherine Shore. Her task of preparing a seemingly endless manuscript was monumental. The work of my copyeditor, Trudie Calvert, has been characterized by a remarkable facility for simplification and clarification without compromising meaning or style.

Finally, three poignant memories will always remain with me: of the day that The Very Reverend Canon, Robert Rawsthorne, and I knelt before the old safe in St. Mary's Church, Thornbury, Gloucestershire, England, as he read to me the account of the baptismal ceremony for Harry's grandfather, John Fanning Burgwyn; of the day that the late Henry King Burgwyn IV, Harry's great-nephew, and Robert E. Lee DeButts, the great-grandson of General Robert E. Lee, walked with me along the historic route taken by the Twenty-sixth North Carolina through McPherson's woods to Seminary Ridge on the first day at Gettysburg and almost to the crest of Cemetery Ridge on the third; and of a cold, frost-laden, November morning that I walked alone down the old dirt road leading to where Thornbury, the Burgwyn homeplace, once stood. It was down this road, past a giant sentinel tree still standing today, that a sorrowing, faithful friend, Kincian, brought Harry's two horses and a few personal belongings after a lonely trek from Gettysburg.

BOY COLONEL OF
THE CONFEDERACY

CHAPTER 1

THE IRONY AND THE TRAGEDY

On 15 September 1865 Assistant Marshal James M. Drennan of Worcester, Massachusetts, most recently a captain in the Twenty-fifth Massachusetts Infantry Volunteers, sent the following letter from that city to Henry King Burgwyn, Sr., in Boston:

> Sir, I have just been informed in a note from Gov Holden of N.C. "that you were staying in Boston Mass." I sent a letter of enquiry to him to find where the Father of Col Burgwin late of the 26th N.C.S.T. could be found hence the reply as above.
>
> My reasons for wishing to communicate with you are these. At the Battle of New Bern March 14/62, where your son took an active part was found his private Diary, which I have kept with much care ever since with a view of returning it to him if he had lived, or to you or his Relations if he was taken away.
>
> The time has arrived when I trust we shall have peace everlasting, and all our sectional difference and prejudices may be buried up in the past.
>
> Your Son I am shure had he lived (although bitter against the Yankees) would not hesitate to take me by the hand at this time as a Country man and a Brother and I sir should be the last to utter ought against his memory.
>
> This Diary comprises facts and a great many things connected with his every day life from the time he entered the Service untill the Battle of NB.
>
> Should you feel like taking a trip to this place, only 45 miles, I shall be glad to see you, or if you will enform me where to send to you by express I shall cheerfully do so. I am Sir very respt. Your obt. Servt.[1]

Henry K. Burgwyn, Sr., was not in Boston to receive this message. On 11 September he had sailed from New York for Europe and would be gone for almost a year. He and his family had only recently arrived in Boston from North Carolina and were staying at Mrs. Putnam's in Pemberton Square. It was his wife, Anna Greenough Burgwyn, who first read Captain Drennan's note. She apparently invited the captain to visit the family in Boston, for she later recorded that on 16 October "Captain Drennan came to see me and kindly brought Harry's Diary which he had found at New Berne, N.C. and carefully preserved."[2] This visit could only have evoked sad and poignant memories as Anna talked about her beloved son Henry ("Harry") King Burgwyn, Jr., who had been killed at Gettysburg on 1 July 1863.

He had died a hero's death leading the Twenty-sixth North Carolina Regiment into action. The Twenty-sixth was virtually destroyed on that fateful first day at Gettysburg in its fight with Brigadier General Solomon Meredith's famed Iron Brigade. The gallantry of that assault and the sheer courage of sustained attack in the face of almost hopeless odds have few, if any, counterparts in military history. Out of 800 effectives, 584 were killed or wounded in less than an hour in driving the enemy out of McPherson's woods.[3]

Harry Burgwyn, the "Boy Colonel," fell in his twenty-first year. He was one of the youngest colonels in the Confederate service.[4] His death was mourned by all who knew him. That his loss to the regiment was severe is unquestioned. He enjoyed the respect and admiration of the men but probably not their abiding affection until after his death. He was a strict disciplinarian and a trained military man, but his comparative youth forced him to earn the allegiance of his men and their respect for his leadership.

As the story unfolds, it will be seen that he did just that—in the first major engagement of the Twenty-sixth at the battle of New Bern on 14 March 1862. He was then a lieutenant colonel. In August of that year, when Colonel Zebulon B. Vance resigned after being elected governor, the men of the Twenty-sixth elected Burgwyn to succeed him. Brigadier General Robert Ransom thought he was too young and reportedly indicated that he wanted no boy colonels in his brigade. The men petitioned for removal to another brigade, and thus the Twenty-sixth was transferred to the command of Brigadier General James Johnston Pettigrew.

In this manner, the lives of two remarkable young North Carolinians were brought together. They quickly developed an abiding respect for each other, and they died within two weeks of each other on "foreign" soil. Both were born into North Carolina's aristocracy, had considerable wealth, were highly educated, and were not provincial in the usual sense. Pettigrew, at thirty-four, had lived and studied abroad. Burgwyn, at twenty, had studied in the North and was an honor graduate of the University of North Carolina as well as of the Virginia Military Institute. Both Pettigrew and Burgwyn were fearless in combat and were apparently motivated by the highest patriotic instincts in defending what they firmly believed was their country. They shared the same respect for military discipline, and both were living examples of self-discipline.

They were admirable men. A state or region could ill afford the loss of such potential leadership. They were but two of thousands, however. In the fratricidal conflict of the American Civil War the losses were unprecedented in military history, and no state bore a proportionately greater loss than did North Carolina. Of 600,000 troops committed to the Confederacy, it is estimated that more than 125,000 were North Carolinians, including the Home Guard. North Carolina lost in killed and from wounds and disease approximately 40,000 men, resulting in a mortality rate, not casualty, of about 32 percent. The use of the term "flower of manhood" applied to none more than to these lost North Carolinians.[5]

It is in this context that one is prompted to inquire into the causes of the Civil War, why this frightful waste of men and material in a nation so young, so rich in natural wealth and in hope. Of course, the existence of slavery in the South, and its extension as the nation expanded westward, was one of the major sources of sectional bitterness and political antagonism. It does not explain, however, the Confederate capability to wage war so long with such limited resources. Slaveowners constituted but a small fraction of the population in the South, and the Southern cause could not have been solely the defense of slavery. But the release of several million Negroes from bondage, constituting one-third of the total population in the slave states in 1860, was fearful to contemplate; "for the 'typical' Southerner was not only a small farmer but also a non-slaveholder." Nor did the average Southerner ever forget the Nat Turner rebellion of late August 1831. This was neither the first nor last of the slave insurrections, and the fear of one was ever-present.[6]

At the outbreak of the war, the South was essentially agrarian and virtually untouched by the industrial revolution. An agricultural economy had long since established a political climate in which the South felt at odds with the tariff-sheltered, industrial North. Otherwise, there would have been no John C. Calhoun or doctrine of nullification. The people of the South were deeply rooted to the land. There were no highly urbanized areas to attract thousands of uprooted foreign immigrants.

Southerners, tied to the soil, were independent by nature and tradition, proud of their heritage, and loyal defenders. They shared a common bond of provincial distinctiveness, and, for the average Southerner, after Abraham Lincoln's call for troops, the transfer of allegiance from the United States of America to the Confederate

States of America was not a difficult choice; how could one fail to defend his homeland against willful aggression? In many quarters the decision was made with enthusiasm, but not in the state of North Carolina. She was loath to leave the Union and was the last to cut the tie. Hot heads did not precipitate the dissolution in North Carolina. After Lincoln's call for troops there was little choice left, with or without enthusiasm. It is against this background of reluctant withdrawal that one must measure the magnitude of their sacrificial effort and staying power.

Colonel Harry Burgwyn was one of those North Carolinians. To single out this young man for special consideration is no disparagement of those other thousands who gave their lives for a cause and for their country. Rather, it is to study him as a young man, well-educated and with every prospect of future promise, with a heritage as much Northern as Southern, suddenly catapulted into a catastrophic national conflict. He was personally ambitious but did not shrink from battle. He combined high intelligence and great energy into a brief but remarkably successful career by virtue of a strongly disciplined character. Fortunately, he was a prolific writer. His letters span a period of only seven years, from his fourteenth to his twenty-first, but they reveal a maturity of judgment and character far beyond his years. He was indeed the personification of noblesse oblige. In examining his life we honor all those who dignified their lives and their times with such patriotic devotion and sacrifice.

One is tempted to say that Burgwyn's fate in battle was predetermined. His every act and thought bore witness to his will not only to succeed but to excel in life. His school years were characterized by a diligent pursuit of learning. Highly intelligent, he was quick to learn; and his innate abilities were more than matched by an inquiring mind and a positive attitude toward life.

His and his father's ambition was for the boy to enroll in the United States Military Academy, but he never made it. At the age of fifteen he was tutored for one year at West Point but was considered too young for admission. He then enrolled at the University of North Carolina as a special student in the summer of 1857, from which he was graduated two years later. Again failing to receive an appointment to the academy, he applied and was admitted to the Virginia Military Institute in August 1859. There he excelled in both scholarship and leadership and graduated in the class of 1861.

The knowledge that he was born into a family of affluence and distinction early manifested itself; but his pride of ancestry was not so self-centered that he failed to recognize the duties and responsibilities associated with his privileged station in life. Letter after letter to members of his family, particularly to his mother, reveal a remarkable character in development during the brief span of only seven years. From beginning to end there is the indelible mark of maturity in one so young. As the eldest son he was concerned with the problems and cares of every member of his family. He constantly admonished his mother in the care of her health. Nor was he above advising his father on farming and economic matters, but always in a suggestive and deferential manner. He was concerned with the academic performance of his younger brothers and strongly emphasized to them the need for purposeful commitment. He practiced what he preached. He commanded no one more than himself.

Perhaps the most revealing part of his written record lies in his deep attachment to his mother. While away at school he wrote to her almost weekly, to his father less frequently. It is evident that he wrote to please her. His letters were informal, newsy, and self-revealing, whereas his letters to his father were more formal and less personal. His mother was a dominant but not a dominating personality. Highly intelligent, reflective, deeply religious, and purposeful, she undoubtedly had a strong influence upon all the members of her family but especially upon young Harry. His being her oldest son could have led to this close relationship. His letters written between early fall 1856 and mid-1863 represent the only substantial body of family correspondence extant for that period. These letters were carefully preserved by his mother and later by his older sister, Maria.[7]

A number of his mother's letters have recently come to light. They were presented to the Southern Historical Collection at the University of North Carolina at Chapel Hill in 1974. They cover the period 1838 to 1843 in the life of a young Bostonian, Anna Greenough, who was married to Henry King Burgwyn of North Carolina on 29 November 1838.[8] Almost immediately the newlyweds moved to their new home in New Bern, and with equal immediacy she began writing her mother, Mrs. William Hyslop Sumner—at times almost daily. These letters not only provide the same self-revealing characterizations as do her son's correspondence in later years but also serve as a perceptive commentary on the life and times of antebellum eastern North Carolina, as seen through the eyes of a talented and sophisticated young woman born and bred in New England aristocracy and culture.

Harry's father was born into both Southern and English aristocracy, was well-educated, had lived "at the North" for seven years, and would shortly inherit substantial wealth. The melding of these influences piques the imagination. For the first time, Anna was exposed to the life and society of a small Southern town, in a state that had just emerged from a long sleep, where slavery was both condoned and defended, where dancing was considered sinful in some quarters, where Unitarianism was more than heretical, where neither Jew nor Catholic could hold office legally, at least before amendment of the state constitution in 1835.[9]

And for the first time, Henry King Burgwyn was directly confronted by the question of slavery within his own family. The beauty of the story is that both husband and wife, with devotion and understanding, accommodated to each other and to the situation in which they found themselves.

Harry Burgwyn was born on 3 October 1841. His short life was destined to coincide with the end of an era for the South. In contemplating his life and the times in which he lived, one might readily conclude that he was born to tragedy; but an early death did not necessarily connote a tragic end for Harry Burgwyn. The meaning of his life is to be found both in the manner in which he lived it and the manner in which he met its end. The same might be said of his mother and father. Both irony and tragedy marked their lives. But, again, it was the manner in which they bore questionable fortune and unquestionable ill fortune that set them apart as people of character.

Henry and Anna Burgwyn came of uncommonly good stock. Many of their forebears and relations distinguished themselves in private and public life. They were both Northern and Southern in background. Their ancestors were patriots in the colonial and antebellum periods of American history. And their relations were equally and truly patriotic in a nation divided. If precept and example are meaningful to posterity, one may study their lives with profit. Fortunate is the present that certain members of the Burgwyn family confided so much of their personality and thought to the written word. They wrote with feeling and candor.

CHAPTER 2

THE LADY FROM BOSTON

It all began in New York City one evening in late May 1838 while she visited with her relatives. In a letter to General William Hyslop Sumner, her stepfather, Anna Greenough confided:

> In the evening we went to the Chatham St. Chapel to hear the Creation. Mr. and Mrs. Griffin accompanied us, which made it very pleasant, as I like Mrs. G. In gazing around the house, before the performance commenced, who should I spy but our Astor House acquaintance, Mr. Burgwyn. He instantly recognized me and joined our party, where he played the equable all the evening, presented me with a book containing the order of performances, and last of all escorted me home. Pray give Mother this information, as it will doubtless be reviving to her. Mr. G. asked him to visit us the next evening, but whether he accepted or not I was too agitated to understand. I should not consider this circumstance worthy of relation, did I not know your particular interest in such affairs. I advise you by all means to send for me immediately, as New York is a dreadful place for *romantic* young ladies.[1]

This chance meeting led to their marriage at Jamaica Plain, Massachusetts, on 29 November 1838. Almost immediately they left for their new home in North Carolina, traveling by land and water. At Baltimore they boarded the steamer *Albemarle* for an overnight trip down Chesapeake Bay to Portsmouth, Virginia. On the *Albemarle* Anna had her first exposure to Southern people in the South.

"This was the first time," she wrote her mother, "that I had really felt away from home. But here everything was Southern. Not a white person of the serving description to be seen, and the ladies with their blackies and Southern accents and manners, to say nothing of crying children, not at all interesting. However, Henry introduced to me a Mr. Collins of N.C., the first gentleman from that state I had ever known I believe, whom I found to be extremely conversable, intelligent and agreeable. He told the old stewardess of the boat who I was, and I can assure you, Dear Mother, I never knew the force of that

Anne (Anna) Greenough Burgwyn (courtesy Burgwyn family)

expression 'what's in a name' before. The old blacky and her daughters treated me like a child."[2]

Mr. Collins was undoubtedly alluding to her Greenough and her husband's Burgwyn connections. As the daughter of David Stoddard Greenough (second of that name) of Boston and Maria Foster Doane of Cohasset, she bore the names of some of the most distinguished families in New England history.[3] Anna's father had died in 1830, and in 1836 her mother married General Sumner, son of Governor Increase Sumner, a distinguished lawyer and jurist who was three times elected governor of Massachusetts and died in that office.[4] Anna had married into a family with equally strong claims to a distinguished past, involving such family names as Burgwyn, Pollok, and Devereux in North Carolina and Jonathan Edwards in Massachusetts. Anna's great-grandfather was Deacon Thomas Greenough, a member of the Ancient and Honorable Artillery Company of Boston and a highly successful manufacturer of precise mathematical instruments. Henry King's great-grandfather, on his mother's side, was Jonathan Edwards, the distinguished eighteenth-century theologian.[5] Henry's father (John Fanning Burgwyn) and grandfather (John Burgwin) had both been born and reared in England, the elder migrating to America in 1751, the younger in 1801. Both had engaged in international trade and banking and had developed close family and business ties in England and in the North over two generations. Henry King had, in fact, been born in New York City in 1811. His paternal grandfather, John Burgwin, as private secretary to Governor Arthur Dobbs and as clerk of the council during the administrations of Governors Dobbs, William Tryon, and Josiah Martin, had enjoyed political favor in the years just before the revolutionary war.[6] But these ancestral details were not uppermost in Anna's mind as she journeyed South for the first time.

Arriving at Portsmouth early Tuesday morning, 4 December, they took "the cars" for a short journey to the Blackwater River, where they boarded the little steamer *Fox* that would carry them down the Blackwater into North Carolina, then down the Chowan River and across the western end of Albemarle Sound to Plymouth. At Plymouth they took the stage for New Bern by way of Washington, North Carolina, for what should have been a day's journey, but, because of heavy rains and muddy roads, the newlyweds did not reach their destination until Thursday evening, 6 December.

A warm family welcome awaited Anna at New Bern. "It was very dark," she wrote, "and when we drove to the door the house looked like an illumination. There were lights in almost all the windows, and Mr. Burgwyn and Thomas ran down to meet us and caught me in their arms most affectionately. Oh mother, I am delighted with Southern manners thus far." This letter was written on 7 December from the "Cottage on the Neuse." Although commodious, the Burgwyn house was referred to as the "cottage"; Anna was delighted with it, especially with her own apartments. "They are fitted out altogether by Henry's taste," she added, "and he has not omitted the slightest article which could conduce to my pleasure or comfort."[7] She shared her residence with a number of in-laws: Henry's father, John Fanning Burgwyn; Henry's sister, Julia; and his two brothers, Thomas Pollok and Collinson. On occasions, other relatives were welcomed for brief visits, and Anna proved to be a competent hostess.

Anna bore the crowded domestic circumstances with equanimity. She promoted tranquillity by accepting Henry's sister Julia as the lady of the house. "I sometimes question in my own mind," she wrote, "whether I ought not to offer Julia my assistance, for she frequently gives me hints that she would most willingly relinquish all care to me, if I should like it; but then the knowledge of my own deficiency in such matters, and a firm determination to preserve neutral ground in all matters relating to a residence here, added to the satisfactory nature of my own pursuits, decide me at once."[8]

The expression "to preserve neutral ground in all matters relating to a residence here" indicates Anna's determination to return to Boston with Henry. Whether they had tentatively reached agreement on this point earlier is not known, but during their first few months together in New Bern the subject was constantly on her mind. On 25 January 1839 she addressed her mother plaintively but with resignation: "Would you not like to know of the air castles I build when alone? It is to be at housekeeping in a neat little house in Boston, and to have you and the Gen'l with the rest of the family come to see me as often as you would. . . . I know he [Henry] hates the idea of living in Boston and from my soul do I regret it, for he is so kind and affectionate to me here, that I cannot ask it of him." But on 10 February Anna was more emphatic: "I believe were I to live here a thousand years I should always feel like a stranger and a sojourner in the land; but such, Dear Mother, is not my intention. My thoughts are bent upon spending my days in the land of my birth and among those I love, and if I do not carry my point it will be the first time I ever failed."[9]

There was no question as to Anna's domestic happiness, for she was beloved by all in her new home. But she was a stranger in a strange land and felt it deeply. Time and again in her correspondence she refers to herself as a "yankee" or a "Northerner" and, as such, felt out of place. She believed most Southerners were prejudiced against the North; but she was fair enough—a characteristic trait—to recognize that she might have been at fault by virtue of her own misconceptions. At any rate, the following letter clearly reveals her state of mind within a few weeks after her arrival in New Bern:

> I enjoy myself much more at parties now, than I did at first, as I begin to feel more acquainted with the guests. We meet almost always the same persons, and I begin to feel more interested in them. At first it was horribly irksome to me to go out, as I was a total stranger; not that I felt any diffidence on the subject, but because I cared not a straw for any one present, and supposed they had the same feeling toward me. But now that I become more acquainted they seem to me much more sociable. . . . I believe Southerners have a great prejudice to all Northerners, & very likely at first they were disposed to think somewhat unfavorably of any one from that clime; but now they appear to like me well enough. Perhaps I was a little stiff, from my invincible indifference towards them. I dare say it might have been so though I endeavored not to be. Oh, Dear Mother, I do so rejoice that I am a Yankee. I am more & more proud of it every day.[10]

Anna's first Christmas in the South was a delight. She wrote her mother,

> The guests assembled about eight o'clock, being invited to tea. The ladies here dress remarkably well, as much so as any young ladies in Boston, and are for the most part good looking. The Gentlemen were in abundance also. After a tea a band of music arrived, consisting of 2 flutes and two drums, and we commenced dancing, which we followed up very closely I can assure you. We commenced with our Virginia reel, which the New Bernites call a scamper down, from thence we proceeded to cotillions and waltses, having refreshments and a little piano music interspersed by way of variety. The Boston wedding cake was cut upon the occasion and proved to be very nice, and its merits were appreciated. Syllibub is used here, to supply the deficiency of Ice creams and I like it very much. We were so agreable that out guests stopt to wish us a merry Christmas first, and then to make it so, for they did not leave until half past two o'clock—The next morning we breakfasted at ten, and then went to church.[11]

The next day Anna reasserted her determination not to yield to Southern blandishments, writing her brother David: "I strive earnestly to keep up my habits of New England industry as I would not on any account lose one of my yankee traits of character. I am every day more and more proud of New England, and in no danger whatsoever of becoming a Southerner at heart."[12] It is not to be inferred that Anna failed to make every effort to accommodate to her new surroundings. She and Henry were instrumental in organizing among their friends a musical group that met weekly. She and Julia dutifully made their social calls together. Anna often accompanied Henry to the field on his hunting expeditions, and she developed a close friendship with some of the young women of the town. But New Bern was not Boston. In her heart Anna never fully adjusted, but in her manner she was always a lady.

Although claiming that "I shall never become a Southerner, or ever like to live among them," she had previously written General Sumner that "it [is] my ambition and pride to support the character of a lady, whether in the 'dismal swamp,' or in the 'polished circle' at Putnam's."[13] The truth is that New Bern in the late 1830s had little to offer in the way of professional entertainment, little to offer in the way of community conveniences except dirt streets and a few nice houses, and very little excitement except that created by numerous stray animals and an occasional fire.

In a letter to her mother on 12 March 1839 Anna provided a refreshingly humorous account of the normal hazards to be encountered in making social calls:

> I always think of you when I set out on such a disagreeable expedition as we have so often been companions in distress at such times. My trouble here is fear of the cows. I am told they will never attack me but a cow is a cow and as such is terrific to me. And, then the dogs are another nuisance. I should think upon the average that there were three dogs to every house in the town. The pigs I do not mind at all, nor the horses much. I seldom glean anything new on such expeditions, for we are much more ceremonious in the length of time we devote to the business than in cities. Five minutes is ample most time for one place.[14]

Anna felt that her "vital existence" was somewhat inhibited. No wonder she wanted to return to Boston with Henry. Wistfully she wrote her mother, after about three months in New Bern, "You never need have doubted, Dear Mother, that I should forget my home, and ever for a moment cease to wish to return to it again. I would relinquish everything earthly except my husband's love, it appears to me, for the sake of being settled once more amongst you all."[15]

Henry always responded with patience and sympathetic understanding, for both he and the members of his family were broadly traveled and were not so provincial-minded as most of their fellow townsmen. On the subject of dancing, a sore issue in many homes, Anna was outspoken, at least in the privacy of her correspondence. On 4 February 1839 she wrote: "We had a very pleasant evening. There was no party, and we amused ourselves with talking and music. We have very few games here, such as we have been accustomed to, but the ladies, generally speaking, do not seem to be fond of frolicking as we are. There are a great many who from religious motives think it a sin to dance and do not seem to enjoy gaiety in any way. But it does not make much difference with me."[16]

Anna found solace for her frustrations among members of the Burgwyn family. None found fault with her Unitarian beliefs, although she felt that "the Unitarians, are considered worse than heretics at the South" and that she was "past redemption." She unburdened herself to Henry's uncle, George Burgwyn of Wilmington, and with no little satisfaction reported to her mother:

> At dinner we had, as is very frequently the case, a dissertation upon the sin of dancing. Now I am always as silent as the grave whenever this question is discussed, as I do not wish to have any altercation upon the subject. When Mr. George Burgwyn turned to me and asked me my opinion on the matter, I told him candidly that I was more of an Unitarian than anything else in the world, that dancing was conducive to my health and consequently to my happiness; therefore I highly approved of it. He did not by any means object to it.[17]

Undoubtedly, slavery was the most perplexing problem that faced Anna Burgwyn in the early months of her sojourn in the South. In her mind there was no justification for it. On 4 February 1839 she wrote: "If I were not in Carolina I think I would be an open abolitionist, for I would rather have one white servant than sixteen blacks. But the trouble is to be relieved of such a curse. I believe every slave holder in the union would be glad to abolish them if he could. But thus and so it is. I have no fancy for Southern institutions." Again in early March she was constrained to say, "I grow more opposed to slavery every day and think I would rather be reduced to *poverty* than I would have anything to do with it."[18]

In the summer of 1839, Anna and Henry returned to her home at Jamaica Plain, Massachusetts, where the Greenoughs had lived for more than fifty years.[19] Their first child, Maria Greenough Burgwyn, was born there on 21 September. They returned to New Bern in the fall, and beginning about that time one can discern a change in Anna's outlook. A new element had entered their lives that precluded any hope of ever living in the North. Henry and other members of his family had fallen heir to a fortune in land and slaveholdings through the death of their uncle, George Pollok, a bachelor who died intestate. This inheritance gave them a permanent home on the Roanoke River near the Virginia border. For Henry, it meant substantial agricultural responsibilities. For Anna, it meant a life she thought she abhorred and for which she was never trained. For them both, it meant Southern plantation life based on slave culture. She was a woman of immense fortitude. He was a man of diligence and understanding. The record reveals that they played their roles accordingly.

Little did they realize at the time that this change of fortune had cast them in a role that would lead to ultimate tragedy. Their new way of life was doomed almost before it started, for it was predicated on slavery, which was becoming increasingly intolerable as the century progressed. Anna and Henry Burgwyn undertook their new responsibilities with the best of intentions but with misgivings. Anna felt that slavery was wrong but only vaguely comprehended the fear, shared by practically all Southerners, of the consequences that might result from the release of three million blacks from involuntary servitude.

George Pollok's vast land and slaveholdings were distributed to his Devereux and Burgwyn kin, although not without some family bitterness arising from disputes over property division and valuation. "The conclave at last dissolved," wrote Anna to her mother on 9 February 1840, "and its members are fast scattering to the four winds of heaven." She continued:

> The great business of division has been concluded, and each one is now beginning to look out for himself. . . . A portion of the Negroes have already been removed to [the] Roanoke. On Monday evening seventy slept on the lot. There was one large baggage wagon with five horses to convey their clothes and implements, and a covered cart, with their food. They came in indian file, and looked like a little army. The weather was very cold at the time, and we had a large fire kindled in the yard, and

The Loring-Greenough House, Jamaica Plain, Massachusetts (courtesy Jamaica Plain Tuesday Club, Jamaica Plain, Massachusetts)

those who could not get into the office kept themselves warm about that. They cooked their own provisions and were very quiet and orderly. I went out to see them after tea, and every one came and shook hands with me. As I did not expect it I had no gloves on and it was severe enough, but still it must be done. I had one or two of Henry's in my chamber, making for them warm tea etc. as the case required. Collinson says, he believes that in six months Henry might go over the plantation and get every one of the Negroes to say they wished to live with him, for he takes as much care of them as if they were his children.[20]

A few weeks later, Anna, Henry, and their daughter, Maria ("Minnie"), were on their way to the Roanoke. But for the fateful passing of George Pollok, Anna might have prevailed and they could have been on their way to Boston. Instead, for the next twenty years, they were destined to live the lives of the Southern landed aristocracy. By any standard of measurement in that day, they were exceedingly fortunate. No material inheritance in that part of the country could match the substantial land and slaveholdings in the rich alluvial valley of the Roanoke. The irony of their situation was that neither was suited by temperament or training for this new way of life. Anna detested slavery. Henry had never been engaged in agriculture. Both were more Northern than Southern. The tragedy of their situation, unknown to them then, was that there was no escape from the inevitable collapse of a system that would not be permitted to die peacefully. The Southern way of life was destined for destruction. The young Burgwyn family was swept with the tide, but they played out their role with courage, good humor, family solidarity, pride, prayer, and surprisingly patriotic devotion to the Southern cause.

CHAPTER 3

ON THE ROANOKE

The Burgwyns were hardly settled in their temporary quarters at White's Hotel in Jackson, the county seat of Northampton County, before Anna was busily engaged in preparing for a wedding of a slave couple at the plantation:

> One of Henry's boys asked permission to marry the other day, which was granted of course, and then the next request was that "He might be married out of the book," which was also granted, and we are to have our landlord's carriage and horses tomorrow, and Marianne, the baby and myself, go to witness Henry's debut as Matrimoniser. I have prepared for the bride a new calico dress, and a white cape with a flaming red ribbon around it, and he gives the bridegroom a "fit out" also. I shall not fail to write you how "the match comes off" if I am enabled to witness it.[1]

Anna and little Maria would be leaving in early June for Boston, where they would remain until mid-October and would be joined by Henry around the first of July. This annual trek North was planned to escape the malarial infection (generally described as bilious fever) common to the Roanoke River country during the summer months. "I do not think we shall reach Boston," Anna wrote, "until after the first of June, as I am very desirous to have Henry remain at his plantation as long as it is expedient. His presence there effects a great deal I can assure you. He has the reputation in this part of the country of being truly a 'driving man' which I think he deserves. Unlike most of the planters he works with his own hands as well as head, when it is necessary and the good effect of this is very visible."[2]

She should have had no concern, for Henry had immersed himself immediately in the myriad details incident to developing his plantation, which additionally involved the care and handling of more than one hundred slaves. Boundaries had to be surveyed and corners established. A great variety of farming equipment had to be acquired, lands cleared and grubbed of stumps, and existing fields plowed and planted. A start had to be made on their plantation house (the Hillside). Farm buildings and fencing were also a part of the new construction program, as well as roads, dikes, and drainage ditches. Several times a year the low grounds near the river were inundated, providing a mixed blessing because the floodwaters often destroyed crops but improved the soil in the process.

The first year on the plantation was heavily demanding of Henry's skills and energies. At twenty-nine, he was beginning his career as a planter, and it was obviously a year of testing. He was both owner and, in a way, overseer, both doctor and disciplinarian to the laborers, and both engineer and builder. In subsequent years he would demonstrate his capacity for experimentation and innovation in agricultural practices. Anna was busily engaged in addressing herself to training and presiding over household domestics. She possessed the same qualities of managerial self-involvement as did Henry. She, too, was a concerned mistress. She was an immaculate housekeeper, and her preoccupation with cleanliness and tidiness would later be remarked on in jest by the members of her family. But all was not work in that first year on the Roanoke. Christmas was pleasant, and the workers were not overlooked. Anna reported to General Sumner that "I have been very busy the last week in preparing Christmas presents for all my negroes. Henry and I went down early in the morning with the carriage loaded and gave each one something. It would have amused Mother very much to have seen the collars and scarfs I prepared, decorated with bows and tassels of the brightest colors— Henry gave them the substantial and I the ornamental."[3]

On 28 May 1841 Anna and little Maria, in company with Anna's brother John Greenough, left for Boston. It was there, in Jamaica Plain, on 3 October, that Henry King Burgwyn, Jr. (Harry), was born. His father was in Northampton County at the time and did not learn of his birth until 15 October, when he "went to Post Office & found several letters among others one from D.S.G. [David Stoddard Greenough, Anna's brother] with the joyous acct of the birth of my first born son."[4] On 27 October, in a letter to her sister, Anna reported Henry's reaction: "I had a letter from Henry last eve'g. He was very well & you can hardly conceive how delighted he is with the Baby as it is a boy but he says that he thinks he loves Maria even better than before."[5] In December, Henry went to Boston to bring his family back South, but because Mrs. Sumner was ill, they remained in Boston. It is likely that little Harry spent the better part, if not all, of his first year "at the North."

The antebellum life of the Burgwyn family on the Roanoke was hectic. For Henry, reputedly one of the South's most successful planters, it was twenty years of intense preoccupation and labor. There

Henry King Burgwyn, Sr. (courtesy Burgwyn family)

are neither diaries nor letters to attest to Anna's role, for with the death of her mother in 1843 she lost the one correspondent with whom she shared the joys and sorrows of her new life in the old South. But one can assume that she presided over her household with dedication and understanding. There can be no doubt that loving care and discipline were the twin attributes of her parental concern and hard work a necessity. Probably no better description of Anna's role can be had than that given by another young Yankee girl who had married a well-to-do North Carolina planter. Writing in 1853, she characterized her mother-in-law: "Mother Williams works harder than any Northern farmer's wife I know. She sees to everything."[6]

Henry King Burgwyn's diaries for the years 1840–48, reveal certain basic characteristics in his preoccupations and performance. Litigation over the Pollok estate was deeply troublesome but not all-consuming. His love of horses and modest interest in politics did not interfere with his driving determination to succeed at farming. Among his brothers he was clearly the leader. His West Point experience undoubtedly sharpened his disciplinary and engineering capabilities. But he was also a religious and humane person. Although he was a slave master and Anna a slave mistress, both were motivated by a high sense of responsibility in adjusting to a system they could not escape. They worked in tandem. They raised a fine family. In their letters and diaries, it is apparent that Anna enjoyed a deeply personal and openly affectionate relationship with her children. Not that Henry was denied the same degree of affection, but it is likely that his penchant for discipline evoked a more formal and respectful relationship. His son Harry, for instance, deeply respected his father, and they seemed to enjoy a fine relationship; yet seldom can one find more than a cursory and cryptic reference by their father to Harry or the other boys.

Ahead of his time in applying engineering and scientific technology to agriculture, Henry accomplished much. His diary notations are filled with countless questions and observations about the quality of the soil, drainage problems, and methods of cultivation. For three days in early March 1845, Henry was host to two visitors from Virginia, John A. Selden of Westover plantation and Robert B. Bolling of Petersburg, successful planters whose suggestions and criticisms he had sought. Their reactions were critical but undoubtedly constructive.

After this visit of the Virginians it is not surprising to find the following diary notation dated 4 April 1845: "I visited Mr. Batts,

Editor of the Southern Farmer & left with him samples of the Marle Limeston from Ravenswood, & soil from the Pocosin, he pronounced the Marl of the very best quality & the soil very rich, and of the kind to be benefited by Marl. I gave him an order for a McCormick Reaper which he is to have [in] Petersb'g by 1st May."[7]

This was Henry's first reference to a mechanical reaper. On 7 June, he wrote that "My Wheat Reaper has come, been tried to answer well thus far, but it was only for about 1/2 an acre & under the management of McCormick himself." On 16 June 1847, he referred to the arrival of a Hussey reaper by steamer, the *Loper*. On 23 June Henry reported, "Harvesting, both Reapers at work & doing good work. McCormick's fails where the wheat is very thick or too low, & often gets out of order."[8]

But the principle of mechanical reaping worked so well that the Burgwyns continued and expanded its use. In the early years, competition between McCormick and Hussey for regional and national markets was intense. Henry's first reaper was a McCormick, purchased in 1845, and it was probably the second McCormick reaper sold in North Carolina or anywhere in the South except Virginia.[9] Following the later purchase of a Hussey reaper, it seems that the Burgwyns increasingly favored the Hussey and proclaimed its competitive virtues as being "vastly superior in execution and durability."[10]

In the June 1853 issue of the *American Farmer*, Henry Burgwyn branded the McCormick reaper as being among "the miserable failures." This was a challenge that Cyrus McCormick could not ignore, for the Burgwyns were among the leading planters of North Carolina. They were also recognized nationally, and Henry had served as vice-president of the United States Agricultural Society in 1852. So McCormick decided to meet his two principal competitors, Hussey and Burrall, in field tests on Burgwyn's plantation in 1854. He selected A. D. Hager, a Yankee from Vermont, to serve as his agent in an area in which the McCormick reaper had not enjoyed even modest acceptance. His selection of Hager may have been a mistake, for the Burgwyns had recently manifested sectional bias by saying that "Southerners were growing suspicious of all 'Yankee wares,' particularly those marked 'built for the Southern market.'" The Hussey reaper, built in Baltimore, was not considered a Northern product. Hager was determined to capture the North Carolina market for McCormick. Although his mission to the Roanoke was a failure, it was not for want of Yankee shrewdness, persistence, and, thankfully, a keen sense of humor.[11]

The Burgwyns' preoccupation with the mechanical reaper, however, did not preclude attention to the problems of inadequate transportation. If they were to improve and expand their farming operations, adequate means of transportation for inbound supplies and for moving products to market would be essential. They were not far from the Wilmington and Weldon Railroad, but the Roanoke River provided access to the cheapest and best water routes to Norfolk, Charleston, and New York. The river was navigable up to the Burgwyn plantations, but modern loading docks and facilities had to be provided. The Burgwyns wasted no time after arriving on the Roanoke in getting this project under way.

On 14 December 1843 Henry recorded in his diary: "I return'd home & found the Sch [Schooner] Jno. C. Demarest, which had been chartered by Williams & Wortham of N. York to come out and bring me 2000 bush. lime & take a cargo of corn to N.Yk. at 10¢ freight & 50 $ bonus. She is the first seagoing vessel that has ever been this high up the Roanoke alongside my Snowden Barn discharging her lime. She had arrived last evening & began discharg' this morn'g. The Steamboat Chieftan was also along side & Mr. B. Maitland on board her."[12]

Several days later, referring to the steamer *Pilot*, 79.6 feet in length, 13.3 feet in breadth of beam, 5.6 feet depth of hold, 20 horsepower, he wrote, "She came from Norfolk in 50 hours & 28 hours up the river only. The Captain expressed himself much pleased with the River. Said it had been represented to him as far worse than it turned out. He found no difficulty in running at night."[13] Henry Burgwyn's keen interest and support undoubtedly spurred navigation on the Roanoke.

His active participation in the work of the United States Agricultural Society and his contributions to national farm journals were also calculated to bring him some degree of national prominence. It should not be surprising, therefore, in the mid-1850s, to read the following account of his plantation activities, told by a traveling reporter:

> Henry Burgwyn alone had nine hundred acres in wheat, four hundred and fifty in corn and five hundred in clover, not to speak of minor crops. His wheat yielded twenty-three thousand bushels, and brought $2.25 per bushel when sold at Petersburg. For 1856 his cast of clover was nine hundred acres, part of it intended as meadow, part as pasture, and part as fallow to be turned under for soiling. The numerous horses, mules and cattle were well kept; and as to the Negroes the sojourning

Yankee said after a week's observation that the master "provides so well for the animal happiness of the slave that it necessitates one to continually summon up his principle to resist falling in with it and heartily approving the whole system." [14]

All the evidence testifies to Henry Burgwyn's innovativeness as a farmer. With his engineering background, he understood the mechanical and appreciated the scientific. He made every effort to improve the quality and condition of the land and to improve harvesting methods. But his field hands were not hired hands. They were Negro slaves.

When Henry and his brothers took possession of their estate on the Roanoke, their intention was to manumit the slaves when a suitable plan could be worked out. Whether for reasons of humanitarianism or efficiency, they imported a number of Irish workers from New York and Boston for specialized work. On 3 January 1848 Henry concluded arrangements to this end with a Mr. Doane, a cousin of Anna's. The experiment proved a costly failure, but it demonstrates their desire to ameliorate, if not escape, conditions beyond their control. [15]

This abortive effort apparently ended any hope, or even desire, of substituting white for slave labor. But the Burgwyns' concern for the spiritual and physical welfare of their Negroes never wavered. As early as 1843, the Reverend Cameron MacRae reported that "at the request of the late J. Collinson Burgwyn he had been to Alveston plantation in Northampton County and baptized thirty-two colored children." In 1848 the rector of St. Paul's, Edenton, and his assistant "reported the baptism of twelve adults and four infants 'at Mr. T. P. Burgwyn's plantation on the Roanoke.'" And, on the third Sunday after Easter 1849 Bishop Levi Silliman Ives "officiated at the house of Henry K. Burgwyn, Esq., and confirmed 7 colored persons." Bishop Ives concluded that "Mr. Burgwyn is making very laudable efforts to Christianize his slaves which thus far have proved eminently successful." [16]

The Burgwyns were instrumental in establishing the Church of the Saviour in Jackson, the county seat of Northampton County. It was consecrated on 4 May 1851. On the day following, friends of the church met at Henry Burgwyn's rented house (the Nicholas house) on the outskirts of the town to petition the diocese for admission as a parish. Henry was elected to serve as one of the eight vestrymen and as one of the four delegates to the Diocesan Convention of 1851. From that day forward, Anna and Henry were veritable pillars of their little church. At about this time, their new plantation home, known as Thornbury, was completed (Hillside had burned), and the young rector, Frederick Fitzgerald, was asked to live with them at Thornbury. Three Sundays a month the rector held services in Jackson; the fourth was reserved for Thornbury, where "a plain chapel" had been erected for the Negroes.[17]

In March 1854 Thomas Atkinson, bishop of North Carolina, reported: "On Friday, the 10th, at a little chapel on his [H. K. Burgwyn's] estate, after Evening Prayer, I preached to his slaves, who attended most numerously and with a gratifying appearance of interest and devotion. The Rev. Mr. Fitzgerald who lives at Mr. Burgwyn's, gives much of his time and labor to this important and often neglected part of our population; and with the efficient aid which he receives from Mr. [Daniel] Morrell, now a candidate for Orders, who resides as a Tutor in the family, and from the excellent mistress of the household, the good work seems to make gratifying progress." To the Burgwyns, concern for the spiritual welfare of their people meant concern for their general welfare as well. According to one observer, it was not surprising that "visitors were particularly struck with the provisions made for the comfort of the Negroes on the plantations. Their houses are all good framed buildings with a garden attached to each, and 'regular hospitals' were maintained for the sick."[18]

The Burgwyns did not live elegantly. At both Hillside and Thornbury plantations they were comfortably housed in attractive frame dwellings sufficiently commodious to accommodate family and guests. All the material conveniences of a prosperous farm family were available to them, as were the advantages of superior education and travel. But the Burgwyns' life should not be compared with that of the older and more established plantation families in the low country of the Carolinas and the Sea Islands of Georgia.

The romantic version of plantation life in the deep South—the Georgian home of soft-textured, handmade brick framed in a broad expanse of lawn and formal gardens, shrouded by magnolias and live oaks draped in Spanish moss, all creating an atmosphere of wealth and ease—should not be confused with that along the Roanoke. Those who farmed her rich, alluvial soil did so at considerable risk and expense. No amount of ditching and diking could contain her swollen waters during the great spring freshets, and the winters in northeastern North Carolina were generally cold and hard.

The plantation houses were not mansions. For the most part they were the winter homes of working planters. They were well built, generally of frame construction, and not unpleasing to the eye. Most of the large plantations along the Roanoke were, in effect, self-contained farm communities, including the overseer's house, the barns, the smokehouse, the storehouse, the ginhouse, the carpenter's shop, the blacksmith shop, generally a loomhouse, and, in the case of the Burgwyns, a powered mill for grinding corn and threshing wheat. The slave dwellings were located some distance from the "Great House" and were generally arranged in parallel rows with a road between and garden plots to the rear. This would be a fair description of Thornbury in the 1850s, and of other plantations of that period, such as Thomas Pollok Devereux's Conoconarra, Feltons, Looking Glass, Montrose, Polenta, and Barrows.[19]

The decade of the 1850s was undoubtedly a period of fruition for the Burgwyns. Henry and his brother Tom had labored manfully and with foresight. In the fifteen years since they had moved to the Roanoke, they had cleared hundreds of acres, drained and diked their lands, shifted from the traditional cotton production of the area to wheat and corn, promoted navigation on the Roanoke, and introduced the mechanical harvester and steam-powered threshing equipment. Henry spent the summer and fall of 1851 studying agricultural practices in Europe, and in August 1852 the *Farmers' Journal* summed up the Burgwyns' achievements: "They have done more to show what our State might be in an agricultural point, than any other gentlemen with whom we are acquainted. . . . Upon these farms we saw land that this year, even with the dry season, is estimated to average from ten to twelve barrels of corn, and twenty bushels of wheat per acre, which ten years since would not have made that of corn per acre, and scarcely any wheat." In 1855 their two plantations, Thornbury and Occoneechee Wigwam, were judged by one traveler and professional observer to be "the best plantations between Canada and Louisiana."[20]

The decade of the 1850s was the growing-up period for Henry and Anna's three older boys, Harry (Henry King, Jr.), Sumner or Will (William Hyslop Sumner), and Pollok (George Pollok). There is little information extant about their youthful activities at Hillside and Thornbury[21] except that gleaned by reference in later correspondence, especially between that of Harry and his mother. The boys were early sent off to school. On 10 May 1855 their grandfather, John Fanning Burgwyn, noted in his diary that Henry and Anna had left to place Harry and Sumner at Burlington College, near Philadelphia but in New Jersey. The following year, on 3 July 1856, their grandfather noted that the "Revd. Fd. [Fitzgerald] arrived last night at HK's & takes George [George Pollok] to school [Mr. Gibson's] at Chestnut

Hill" in Baltimore.[22] In early fall of that same year, Harry was sent to West Point for a year of tutoring in the hope that he might be enrolled as a cadet at the academy.

All was well at Thornbury and Occoneechee Wigwam in the 1850s. The Burgwyns were reaping the harvest. Their estate was flourishing and their growing family promising. And slave labor, properly handled and managed, had undoubtedly been profitable to them. For the Burgwyns, at least, Edmund Ruffin was probably right when he said, "It is true that *good farming* is rare here [speaking of Virginia]; and so it is elsewhere, but our best farming in lower and middle Virginia is always to be found in connection with [the] use of slave labor."[23] On 19 March 1856, according to John Fanning Burgwyn, that same Edmund Ruffin was visiting with Henry during the time that the "McCormick Reaper came over."[24]

Money had been a problem for the Burgwyns from the day they moved to the Roanoke. At the outset, lack of experience and overreliance on credit could easily have led to overexpansion. Undoubtedly, the protracted litigation with Thomas Pollok Devereux was costly in both legal expense and final settlements, the latter requiring the sale of land and slaves to raise approximately $60,000.[25]

In addition, the soundness and service of commercial banking in the 1840s and 1850s was a far cry from its twentieth-century counterpart. Following the expiration of the charter of the second Bank of the United States in 1836, there was no provision for chartering national banks until the enactment of the National Bank Act in 1864. In the meantime, state-chartered banks were generally permitted to issue currency without protecting its value with adequate reserves in specie. As a consequence, during the period of widespread "wildcat banking" and thereafter, bank failures were not uncommon, and currency values were seldom realized at par, varying between states and even between banks within a given state. In addition, there was little, if any, systemization for the clearance and collection of checks and drafts between banks.

Therefore, anyone engaged in extensive trade between distant points, such as the Burgwyns, had to rely not only upon banks but upon commercial factors and trading partners as well for the orderly handling of financial transactions. Only against this background can one appreciate the banking difficulties of the Burgwyns as they attempted to balance credits against debits in their expanding agricultural domain. The following diary entry is representative of one of Henry's banking days in Raleigh on 22 November 1843:

In Raleigh I arranged my business with the Cape Fear Bank, had my note replaced, gave a draft for $400 for 90 days from 21st on B. Dow, paid $250 cash & rec'd. $5.74, being balance due me. I gave a renewal note for $600 in Bank of State. I gave a draft for 90 days from 21st on H. K. B. for $680 payable in Petersburg. Paid T. P. B.'s execution in favor of Reardon $250.56; sent $412 to New Bern to Cashier, Bank of State, to pay instalment there & left a draft with W. H. Jones on H. K. B., payable in Merchants Bank, New York, to offer for discount in Bank of State.[26]

The nature of these transactions was normal, but their extent indicates an inordinate dependence upon credit on the part of Henry Burgwyn and perhaps his brother Tom. Their father had long been concerned, and it was not until 1 January 1856 that he seemed able to temper his apprehensions with a faint ray of hope: "And the worldly concerns of my Sons, thinking of which I have passed many an anxious & sleepless night, are improving. With due care, caution, prudence, *economy* & good management, they will be enabled to surmount the difficulties which have so long enthralled them— Amen—"[27]

Celebrating Christmas at Thornbury a few days earlier, with Harry and Sumner at home for the holidays, "Grandpa" was in a more cheerful mood when he wrote: "The children all in delight with their gifts—last Night between 9 & 10 Anna sent to Alveston after the trunks I had brought containing the gifts from Phida & busied herself until after 11 in selecting & fixing them in the stockings for St. Claus, & this morning long before day, George was down to examine & Uncle Tom came over afterwards & gave some for all— Harry had a handsome gold watch from his father—the people had their cloathes & presently all was happy & merry inside."[28]

On 31 December 1855 the following laconic entry appears in his grandfather's diary: "Harry left today, to return to his College at Burlington."[29]

CHAPTER 4

HARRY BURGWYN — HIS

FORMATIVE YEARS

It is difficult to portray the early years of Harry Burgwyn either at Hillside plantation or at Thornbury. With the exception of his father's diaries, 1840–48, and those of his grandfather, 1855–56, there are no documents that provide intimate glimpses into Harry's boyhood. And these diary entries were concerned primarily with farming and related problems and only casually with the informal and more pleasurable aspects of a growing family. One gets the impression that Harry's father spent little time with his children, not from choice but because of the responsibilities associated with developing his farming interests.

Then, too, the Burgwyns were ever on the move. Anna returned to Jamaica Plain for the birth of each of her first five children. Each summer the family moved to New England or to one of the popular resort areas in North Carolina or Virginia to escape the ever-present danger of malaria. They normally did not return to the plantation until late autumn. Their home at Hillside burned in September 1849. Temporary quarters were rented in nearby Jackson, and the Burgwyns did not move into their new plantation home, Thornbury, until January 1853.

Although the children were tutored at home, they were sent off to school at an early age. When only ten, Harry was sent to Mr. Gibson's school at Chestnut Hill in Baltimore; and for the next ten years he was destined to spend every school year away from home. His brothers, Will and George Pollok, were also sent away at about the same age and followed a similar pattern in their subsequent schooling. Their sister, Maria, at twelve, attended St. Mary's in Raleigh. The Civil War interrupted the preparatory schooling of the two youngest, Alveston and Collinson.

Although a governess[1] and tutors lived with the family, Harry was not exposed to a life of ease and financial security far removed from the normal vexations and uncertainties of rural life. His parents were building and adjusting to the vicissitudes of fortune, not enjoying the fruits of mature accomplishment. Because they required as much

Henry King (Harry) Burgwyn, Jr. (courtesy Burgwyn family)

of themselves as they did of others, it is not surprising to discover in young Harry such distinctive characteristics as steadfastness of purpose, a strong sense of self-discipline, ambition to achieve, and a genuine concern for the welfare of his family. Altogether he did not live for more than ten years on the Roanoke. Three of those years were spent in Jackson, and, at best, his plantation experiences were limited. As a farm boy, he had to learn to ride and hunt before he was ten years old. The influences of his home and family, however, early crystallized into a pattern of living remarkable for its purposeful commitment in one so young.

Indeed, that is the significance of his letters written from West Point during the academic year 1856–57. These letters are the earliest extant.[2] His father was determined that Harry should attend the United States Military Academy. Whether he wished to see his son and namesake achieve where he had failed or whether he anticipated war is not known. Nonetheless, although too young to be enrolled as a cadet, Harry was sent there in November 1856 for special tutoring in the hope that he might receive an appointment the following year.

The boy's letters to his mother and father contain no surprising revelations, but his purposeful outlook and determination are consistently apparent. Any mother would beam with satisfaction to read, "There are three churches in town, a Presbyterian, a Methodist & an Episcopalian, but of course I go to the latter & I intend to make it an invariable rule whenever the weather will permit to go to church at least once every Sunday, & I expect to go oftener if I have time." He replied to his mother's admonition on tobacco, "You caution me about the use of tobacco; I don't think there is much danger of my falling into its use for, of my three companions here, there is not one who chews & although they smoke they look upon chewing with as much disgust as I do; & as for smoking I have firmly resolved not to smoke until I am 25 years old, if I do then, & I hope I shall not." But perhaps most reassuring to his mother was his casual admission: "By the bye, I now wash all over in cold water every Sunday." Apparently this reassurance did not convey the certainty expected at home, for Harry felt compelled to mention the same subject again in April: "I am certain you will be glad to hear that I am to take a bath tonight. As a general thing I take a bath about once a week."[3]

In referring to his previous schooling at Burlington College, he wrote:

Strange as it may seem to you, My Dear Mother, I have not much more time now than I had at Burlington, but I will have learnt it in a little over a month. I expect to finish Davies Bourden in algebra, a volume of about 400 pages in 6 weeks & then I expect to finish geometry & trigonometry in 4 weeks & then go through descriptive or analytical geometry & finish them all by the 1st of April [1857], at which time I hope to go home, if only for a short time, & I will probably finish by that time all that is gone through West Point in the 1st year with the exception of a little history I take up at the same time as my algebra [and] English grammer; & I intend to, as the common saying is, put them "through a course of sprouts" which means to get them as thoroughly & as quickly as possible. I expect to study very hard this winter & in fact now I study about 8 hours & a half a day. I always study till 11 o'clock p.m. & generally till half past. I would prefer to get up in the morning & study half an hour or an hour before breakfast, but I cannot get my fire made before a certain time without paying the boy to make it earlier which I intend to do as soon as I receive an answer from father to my last letter.[4]

Harry not infrequently enlisted his mother's aid in asking his father to send him money. The sad condition of his clothing was a subject of considerable correspondence. He graphically depicted the condition of his shirts, socks, drawers, and shoes. But for the tongue-in-cheek descriptive powers of this young man, one would think his parents kept him under severe financial discipline. Of an old shooting coat given him by his father, he wrote, "If I possibly can find room in my trunk I intend to bring it home to demonstrate to any & everybody how many large and terrific tears a piece of cloth can sustain. I think if I were to dress myself in it & go in New York begging alms no one could have the hardness of heart to refuse me."[5] His letters indicate a deep attachment to his mother and great respect for his father. It is likely that his wishes were always granted, but references to items that he did or did not buy because of the price indicate that he handled money with great prudence.

His letters also reveal concern for all the members of his family, his mother's health, conditions at the farm (the size of the harvest and what had been planted), and his father's plans and interest in reports on his sister Maria and his brothers William Hyslop Sumner (sometimes referred to as Sumner, sometimes as Tupps or Will) and George Pollok, whom he always refers to as Pollok. The latter was the younger of the two and apparently did not apply himself in school as Harry thought he should.[6]

But in the winter of 1857, his principal concern, and that of his father, was that he receive an appointment to West Point. In this effort they failed, despite the assistance of a fellow North Carolinian, James C. Dobbins, secretary of the navy. On 10 February, the secretary wrote Harry's father: "I return your son's letter & really congratulate you as a father in being blessed with so affectionate, discreet & promising a son. Your disappointment in failing to secure the cadetship I can well appreciate. On receiving your very kind letter I saw the President & mentioned the case of your son. He said his selections had been made & his promises were of such a character as to prevent his qualifying you."[7]

Young Harry was undoubtedly disappointed, but he was not easily dissuaded. He considered every strategem. A presidential appointment was not the only road to West Point, so he presented other alternatives to his father. He had heard that it was possible to get an appointment through any member of Congress and wrote, "So if you could get introduced to some Western Representative & he would consent to apply for me, you could get me an appointment."[8] Whether Harry's father attempted to implement these proposals is not known. Undoubtedly, Harry's age was his greatest handicap. In July 1857, he left West Point and on 1 August enrolled as an "irregular" student at the University of North Carolina in Chapel Hill.[9]

Harry commenced his studies in sophomore and senior mathematics "in order to get along faster," he reported to his mother. He also took Latin, chemistry, and sophomore and junior French. In the same letter he expressed concern over the dissipation at Chapel Hill: "I think this place is fast improving in point of dissipation. The faculty are trying to put it down as much as possible & I hear that they caught twenty students last night either drunk or with liquor in their possession. I should think that, if the Trustees would make it incumbent on the faculty to expel every student who was caught in that state & have it carried out, they would soon have this college equal if not superior to the University of Virginia which stands second only to West Point."[10]

The problem of drinking and disorderly conduct had been brought to the attention of the board of trustees the previous fall, and the executive committee of that body had determined that "disorderly conduct among the students is daily increasing, for want of due execution of the ordinance of the University."[11] Apparently these problems were not new to the university in the pre–Civil War days, but President David L. Swain was quick to reply that "the allegations contained in the resolution are founded in misconceptions." He was unaware of any rule infractions and emphasized that alleged student disorders in Raleigh during vacation periods were beyond the jurisdiction of the university. Nor had any names of student offenders ever been proffered.[12]

Henry Francis Jones, a fellow student of Harry Burgwyn's, perhaps with more pleasurable surprise than concern, recorded in his diary: "Wednesday, October 7, 1857—Some of the students got on a slight bust last night. They took the College bell, weighing 973 pounds, and carried it off on a wagon by themselves about a quarter [of a mile] from the College and put it in a branch."[13] Such college pranks could normally be charged to youthful exuberance, but the university at Chapel Hill had grown rapidly under the leadership of President Swain. Between 1849 and 1857, student enrollment had increased from 191 to 456. In 1855, the existing dormitories could accommodate only 144 students, leaving 180 who had to rent rooms in the village. There were no accommodations for organized sports and no gymnasium on the campus.[14] These conditions undoubtedly had a deleterious effect upon student morale and might have induced those who did not like to hunt or explore the surrounding woods and hills to seek less wholesome diversions.

An informal relationship had developed between faculty and students as well as a conspicuous laxity in class attendance. Some professors were subjected to harassment such as catcalls, heckling, open defiance, throwing of acorns, and, at times, mass refusal to attend class. Although the students were severely censured by the faculty for some of these infractions they were seldom dismissed for offenses "other than duels or extreme and repeated drunkenness and disorderliness."[15]

The most celebrated case of faculty ridicule in Harry Burgwyn's day was perpetrated against the French instructor, Henry Harrisse. Initially students ridiculed his excitable French nature and foreign mannerisms. This and other developments soon led to a "battle royal," involving President Swain and the trustees, and his "stormy exit" two years later, before Burgwyn's appearance on the campus in August 1857. Of greater significance, however, was Harrisse's support of Professor Benjamin S. Hedrick, head of the newly created Department of Agricultural Chemistry, whose only indiscretion had been to support publicly John Charles Frémont and his free-soil doctrines in the heated presidential campaign against James Buchanan. The reaction of the North Carolina press was highly critical. Hedrick was burned in effigy by the students. He then published his defense in the newspapers. The faculty moved into the fray with two resolutions of censure, with Harrisse casting the only dissenting votes.

Professor Hedrick's position became so intolerable that he left the university in November 1856.[16]

Although these events occurred before Harry's arrival at Chapel Hill, they were indicative of the atmosphere on the campus in the late 1850s—one of evident progress but subjected to recurring student problems stemming from inordinate growth and inadequate funding. Scholarship undoubtedly suffered. One observer states that in the years before the Civil War, students at the university were little concerned with "scholarship in its strictest sense."[17] This judgment was substantiated in the report of the committee of trustees, appointed to attend the annual examination of the students, which was filed on 3 June 1858. Although the report was high in its praise of many students, "the Committee turns with feelings of sadness from them to many—*too many* other students whose examination went through all the grades of poor scholarship. In some of the studies they showed the most lamentable ignorance of even the simplest elements."[18]

Harry Burgwyn was not one of them. The students were graded quarterly, in September, December, March, and June. During his two years at Chapel Hill, Harry was invariably rated as "g" (good) or "vg" (very good) in every subject. He was just as proficient in Latin and French as in mathematics and chemistry.[19] He roomed at Professor F. M. Hubbard's house about half a mile from the campus. He evidently relished the following description of his scholarly dedication in the lugubrious setting of a rented room in the Hubbard domicile:

> According to my promise contained in my letter to Maria I seat myself to write you about your promising son, hoping that it will be an adequate theme to you; & if you would like to see the aforesaid individual, just picture to yourself a Chapel Hillian on a shuck chair writing with his desk covered with books & papers & pencils etc., & you will have his ambrotype exactly. Imagine to the North a dilapidated structure, sometimes facetiously called a house, whose nearest side rejoices in having four windows in the form of a cross out of which three pillows, two without & one with a case, protrude & which I suppose are intended to keep out the wind.[20]

Harry's letters do not indicate that he was particularly gregarious, but he was no recluse. He refers to several college friends with whom he enjoyed a close relationship. And he very much enjoyed female company. Not infrequently in letters to his mother, he mentioned certain young ladies and asked to be remembered to them. In anticipation of Christmas vacation, he wrote his mother on 31 October 1857 that he had invited several friends to visit.[21]

Except for his official grades and the record of his graduation in the faculty minutes, there is little available information, other than his letters home, to provide an insight into Harry's life and character while at Chapel Hill. Nor is there much room for speculation. His academic record speaks for itself, and his letters indicate a pattern of consistent sobriety, maturity, and concern—with a humorous twist upon occasions. An autograph album of a student at the university, member of the class of 1859, bears Harry's signature along with the usual date of birth and place of residence. He listed himself as a "Scientific Student of 1858 & 59" and as a member of the Phi Society and the Zeta Psi fraternity with "Engineering" as his future profession.[22] The minutes of the Philanthropic Society do not indicate that he played an active role in its affairs. The Treasurer's Book lists a couple of modest fines for "Sitting on Table on forbidden Ground" ($1.75) and for talking without permission (.30). On 20 April 1859 he was credited with the payment of $1.00 for his diploma.[23]

Harry expressed recurring concern for his mother's health and his father's business affairs. His mother was subject to frequent colds, and Harry repeatedly admonished her to be careful of her health. On one occasion he reasoned with her: "I study Latin hard & do a good many things for you & I hope that [you] will do two things for me—& they are not to go into the pantry before breakfast or after supper. Make Ruthey attend to them before breakfast & Maria after supper."[24]

A few months later, he gave his father sound advice about selling Alveston, one of the plantations whose operation had apparently occasioned considerable concern:

> Now, when your crop falls short of your calculations you are put to a great worry & botheration, but once free of selling Alveston, & little I should think would be the difference whether you made 3,000 or 3,500 barrels of corn; for if you have as much money as suffices to support your family & yourself & your plantation twice as well as at present, I don't think you would mind that loss sufficiently to be worried & pestered about it as much as you are now. . . . Again mother's health requires that she should not stay on the plantation so much as she usually does. The 1st of June she should be at Old Point [Comfort]; the latter part of July & 1st August she should be in the mountains; from the middle of August till the 1st of Oct. she should be in some northern city. This will [be] a considerable expense & yet

it is necessary & no amt. of money should be placed in comparison with her health.[25]

The following year he again voiced concern over his father's affairs. His concern was about Wilkins, the overseer at Thornbury:

I am very sorry indeed to hear from you that father had decided to employ Wilkins again. I suspected he would as soon as I heard that he was remaining at Thornbury from day to day. I despair now of ever seeing him go away. He will stay with father until he loses him some $4 or $5,000 & then for the next three or four years there will be a great hue & cry versus that "miserable scoundrel Wilkins" as there before was against the "villain Reid" & the "treacherous Sterling" or the "drinking Fairgreve" & that "miserable fellow Boyce." I would not be at all surprised if next year Wilkins were head overseer & then there would be no telling where it would stop. My heart sinks within me though I try to hope for the best.[26]

In that same letter, he confided to his mother that "my not getting the appointment to West Point was, as you may imagine, a great disappointment to me. I had hoped that after so many endeavors I would at last get it, but l'homme propose mais Dieu dispose." A few lines later he reported that "there is a young man just here from the Institute of Virginia. I am going to call on him & find out from him something about the place. I think I mentioned to you that I had written Colonel Smith a letter requesting a catalogue & some information as to the requirements for entering certain classes. When I come home I will tell you all about it."[27]

In another letter, shortly thereafter, he again referred to his keen regret in not receiving an appointment to the academy but apparently found some solace in the thought that "I cannot but rejoice that I am now entirely independent of any of the favors of government & need not be bothered to death with waiting on the powers that be." Furthermore, he added, "I am now free to indulge before anyone in invectives against the deceitful Buchanan & his vacilating & contemptable policy in being afraid to put out the members of Congress by summoning them to attend an extra session."[28]

It is understandable that Harry should have been upset over his failure to receive an appointment from the president, but it is not clear why he should have so roundly condemned Buchanan for not calling the Congress into extra session. After all, he may have unwittingly tailored his own fate. Back in February, President Buchanan had accepted Governor Swain's invitation to speak at the university commencement exercises the following June. About the same time, Harry had engaged a room for his sister Maria in the hope that she could be present for his graduation. It was this room that Mrs. Swain sought for Buchanan. Harry described the following episode to his mother on 20 February 1859, when inquiring whether Maria was coming to the next commencement: "I engaged Chunk Bruce's room for her or rather asked Chunck [sic] to let me have for a lady. He promised it to me & came to me the other day & asked me if I wanted it. I told him yes; he then said that Mrs. Swain had wanted to get it for Mr. Buchanan but that old Buck could not get it. So I will cut the President out of his room even if he cuts me out of my cadetship at West Point."[29]

Harry was cut out of his cadetship at West Point—a wry twist of fate perhaps, even the work of retributive justice. In the University of North Carolina student records for the year 1859 there appears on the same page the names of the following:

The Degree of Bachelor of Science is conferred upon
H. K. Burgwyn, Jr.
R. E. Lester
G. W. Gaza
R. C. Martin, Jr.
Wm. Sims
R. N. Sims
"The Honorary Degree of L.L.D. is
Conferred upon His Excellency, James Buchanan,
President of the United States of N.A."[30]

Harry's sister Maria was there to witness the event. She had left home for Chapel Hill on 30 May and had undoubtedly established herself in Chunk Bruce's room.[31]

On 21 July, the family went to Stribling Springs, Virginia, for their summer vacation, and it was from there that Harry left for the Virginia Military Institute on 8 August 1859.[32]

CHAPTER 5

A CADET AT VIRGINIA
MILITARY INSTITUTE

The following letter preceded Harry's arrival at the Virginia Military Institute by about a month:

> Harry has always been a hard [working] student & I trust will continue so. I fear only the first month or two etc., as I well know the effect of association. I will esteem it a favour if you will see that he is made acquainted with some of those *you* esteem most highly. He has always eschewed low & vulgar companions, & being somewhat reserved in his manner is not likely to seek companionship unless he is thrown into it. His college life has bro[ugh]t on indolence of body which has been increased by his rapid growth, being only 17 yrs.; he is about six feet high.[1]

This admonitory note on behalf of his son was addressed to Colonel F. H. Smith, superintendent of the Virginia Military Institute. Harry's father again expressed concern for his son's health in a subsequent letter to the colonel: "This will be handed you by my son Henry K. Burgwyn who joins your Corps of Cadets & will, I trust, avail himself of the many advantages offered by your institution. Being but lately arrived from low country, I dare say the drill will bear heavily on him at first, but I trust to his perseverance to overcome this difficulty. It is only the first few months that I fear."[2]

Harry may have known of his father's concern, but it is unlikely that he was aware of these letters, and he would probably have resented any inference that he was not physically capable. These two letters, though well-intentioned, are almost apologetic in tone and hardly do the young man justice when one considers his subsequent record. In less than a month, however, Harry was forced to apologize for himself. He had gone absent without leave. To Colonel Smith he explained:

> The unfortunate circumstances which have occasioned my un-
> authorized absence have doubtless ere this been explained to

you by Cadet Morrison & by Mr. Walker of Washington City, who brought me the note from mother saying my sister was so ill that it was not thought she could survive twenty four hours. When I mention to you that my father was absent at the White Sulphur Spring & my sister was so low you can readily understand my anxiety to be with her. This must be my excuse for committing so gross a breach of military etiquette as leaving the V.M.I. for a time without the permission of its commanding officer. I will return at the earliest possible moment.[3]

Unfortunately, the above three letters are the only ones extant relating to Harry during his first year at VMI. The order books of the institute, however, provide a chronological background against which to measure his interest and participation in what must have been a challenging first year. He was formally admitted as a cadet on 12 August 1859 along with twenty-six other young men.[4] On 26 August he was assigned to room 60. His roommates were Walden, I. Morrison, Stark, and Hill.[5] On 3 September, Order No. 203 provided that "Cadet Burgwyn has been assigned by the Academic Board to the 2nd Class. He has upon examination been sustained upon all the preceding branches except Math. & Drawing, and he will be required to make up his deficiency in Shades, Shadows and Perspective, and Drawing by the 1st of January next."[6]

On 31 October the superintendent announced that he had accepted on behalf of the institute an invitation from the Seaboard Agricultural Society to attend the annual fair in Norfolk beginning 7 November. The corps of cadets left Lexington on Friday, the fourth.[7] Harry was presumably given permission to visit Thornbury en route, for his mother noted in her diary that "Harry, after passing a short time with us, joined the Cadets in Norfolk, November 7, 1859."[8]

Hardly had the corps returned to Lexington before Colonel Smith, in anticipation of orders from Governor Henry A. Wise, alerted those cadets who had been detailed for special duty at or near Charlestown, Virginia. In mid-October, John Brown had seized the United States Arsenal at Harpers Ferry. Captured by the United States Marines under the command of Colonel Robert E. Lee, he had been tried in the Virginia circuit court at Charlestown, convicted of both treason and murder, and sentenced to be hanged on 2 December 1859. Governor Wise, fearing an attempt to rescue the prisoner and the possibility of violence, was counting upon the cadets and other military forces to preserve order on the day of execution. Harry Burgwyn was one of those selected for this special service. In issuing his alert on 19 November, Colonel Smith made a moving appeal to the young men:

The Superintendent need scarcely say to those detailed for this important service that there never was a time in the history of the State when more prudence, judgment, and fidelity, were demanded than at the moment. He implicitly confides in the Cadets, that they will promptly discharge every duty, and obey every command, that they will abstain from all thoughtless levity and from all forms of indiscretion and immorality, and that they will remember that called into service for duty as men, they will acquit themselves like men, and as *True* sons of a common mother. His own word stands pledged for this. He looks to each and every one to redeem it.[9]

The following day Governor Wise telegraphed the superintendent from Charlestown: "Here an hour ago—you are not needed now—quiet at present—but you will please be ready at a moments warning—will notify."[10]

By 27 November the special detachment of cadets had reached Charlestown and was placed on a war footing, "subject to all the rules and articles of war governing an army in the field."[11] On 1 December, the day before John Brown's execution, General Order No. 4 read in part: "Every Cadet will have his musket in perfect firing order, for inspection this evening at 3-1/2 o'clock, and 12 rounds of ball cartridges in good order in his cartridge box. The Cadets will lie down in their clothes and accoutrements, with their arms loaded by their sides, to be ready at a moments warning for any emergency tonight."[12]

Governor Wise had left nothing to chance. On duty in Charlestown on 2 December were fifteen hundred militiamen of the Fourth Brigade, Virginia Militia, under the command of Brigadier General William B. Taliaferro, four companies of United States troops under the command of Colonel Robert E. Lee, and eighty-five cadets from VMI. Major Thomas Jonathan Jackson commanded the artillery unit consisting of two howitzers supported by twenty-one cadets. The infantry unit of sixty-four cadets, selected from the two upper classes, was commanded by Major William Gilham.[13]

Governor Wise may have overreacted, but John Brown's raid at Harpers Ferry on 16 October, coupled with news of his bloody atrocities in Kansas, had brought home to Virginians the possibility of imminent slave insurrections and violence induced by abolitionists. The execution was carried out as planned. There was no disorder, and, in the words of Major Jackson, John Brown behaved with "unflinching firmness." The cadets were lined up immediately behind the gallows. They were dressed in red flannel shirts and gray trousers. They numbered eighty-five upon arrival at Charlestown. On this day, however, there was one more. Among them stood a man in his middle sixties, also dressed in a red flannel shirt and gray trousers. He was Edmund Ruffin, the renowned agronomist and an extreme secessionist.[14]

Ruffin had arrived in Charlestown on the afternoon of 27 November, having ridden over from Harpers Ferry on the special train assigned to the VMI cadets. From the time of his arrival to the day of the execution, he was busily engaged in visiting and talking with any and all who would listen, both military and civilian. He made the "grand rounds" at night to visit the posted sentinels around the town and used "every suitable occasion to express my disunion sentiments. Sometimes they are approved, but more generally disapproved." On 1 December, with the approval of Colonel Smith, Ruffin received on loan the arms and uniform overcoat of a private and was given permission "to join, for tomorrow, that admirable corps." At two o'clock the following morning, he started out on the grand rounds in company with Major Gilham.[15]

In his brief tour of duty as a cadet, Ruffin appropriately observed that it "required all the constraint of their [the cadets] good manners to hide their merriment. However, I entered into familiar chat with them, & soon made some acquaintance; & before half the duty for the day was over, I think from their manner, that I had gained much on their favor, & perhaps on their respect." There is no record that he did, but young Harry Burgwyn had every reason to make himself known to Edmund Ruffin. His father, a member of the advisory board to the superintendent of agriculture, had visited with Ruffin in Washington on 10 January of that year, and as recently as 2 September the two had met again at White Sulphur Springs.[16] They apparently enjoyed each other's company. They had been drawn together initially through their interest in agriculture, and Ruffin had visited Thornbury in 1856.[17]

It is likely that Harry and his fellow cadets were deeply affected by what they saw and felt while on emergency duty at Charlestown. For all of them, so young and untried, it must have been an exhilarating experience. For some few it may have been a lark, but for most, the exhilaration must have been tempered by sobering reflections as they made their way back to Lexington by way of Richmond. There is no record of Harry Burgwyn's reflections before or after—only a note in his mother's diary, dated 26 November 1859, acknowledging receipt of "a letter from Harry from Lexington saying Col. Smith had been ordered to take the Cadets to Charlestown to be present at the execution of John Brown."[18] This first military experience surely made a profound impression upon Harry Burgwyn. But perhaps more importantly, it brought home to Harry and his fellow cadets the imminent and very real possibility of sectional strife.

Selection for this emergency service at Charlestown had undoubtedly been hailed by the students as welcome relief from the daily tedium of school life. The two-week furlough from the classroom probably impaired the academic standing of some, but not of Harry Burgwyn. On 6 January 1860 the academic board released its order of merit of the cadets in their respective classes. Harry was rated third in mathematics, first in chemistry, and first in Latin.[19] But he received his first demerit for rule infraction on 12 December 1859. In fact, he had two infractions the same day: "no shoulder belts on post at night" and "late going on post." These incidents occurred shortly after his return from Charlestown and perhaps were excusable. He was cited nine more times for rule infractions before the end of the academic year, for talking, tardiness, and loitering where and when he should have been acting otherwise.[20] In this regard he was probably a typical VMI cadet.

Although the hanging of John Brown was a memorable event in the academic year 1859–60, it did not relieve the monotony of barracks life for Harry Burgwyn. Nor did the surrounding mountains, which seemed to bar the way to a more relaxed life in a more congenial setting, afford any relief. This frustration with school life would go unnoticed except that Harry had displayed the same restless desire to be done with schooling while at Chapel Hill. Whether this was a subconscious reaction to his failure to enter West Point it is difficult to say, but his determination to graduate as quickly as possible was always foremost in his mind. He was in a reflective frame of mind when he wrote his mother on 3 June 1860:

> I am very busy now indeed preparing for my June examination; the board meets the 23rd of this month & very probably we will be examined in Nat. Philosophy either that day or the following Monday. So you see we have hardly three weeks more to study & I am precious glad of it. When I endeavor to look back at the time when I first entered, it appears as if I had been here years, but when I recollect that I have only been here 10 months, & try to see if it has appeared long, I am bound to confess that the time has passed very rapidly; but somehow or other I can hardly realize that there is such a thing as a world different from

*Cadet Harry Burgwyn during his first year at Virginia Military Institute
(courtesy Burgwyn family)*

that in which we move or places other than those bounded by the mountains which appear to offer an impassable barrier to any egress. I think this is the natural effect of a monotonous military life. This effect is counterbalanced at West Point by the cars & steamboats passing up & down the river, but here is increased rather than otherwise by the mountains. I am truly glad I will only have one more year to stay. I do not see how I could agree to remain here twenty four more months.[21]

But this unpleasant reaction to his environment did not affect his academic performance. By 17 June he reported to his father the following comparative class standing: "On Latin I will probably be first—on chemistry the same—on Natural Philosophy the same—on mathematics I stand third & I will probably stand as low as 8th, 9th, or 10th on infantry tactics." He then refers to his chief scholastic rival, H. W. Hunter, but says, "I think I have much the best chance of being first in general, which is considerably beyond my first expectations which always were in advance of yours."[22]

On 29 June he modified his expectations somewhat by prophesying that he would stand tenth on infantry tactics. He also conceded that "if I do not stand 1st in general, demerit will throw me." He went on, "I would not give my stand for that of any man in the class. I passed a very good examination on Latin and chemistry & made two tenths above the maximum on Nat. Philosophy. I had by far the hardest subject in the whole course & Col. Smith gave me 3.2, the max, being 3. I had the first mark on that by one whole number which is a greater difference than has been between the first & second men for two or three years. The Prof. on Nat. Phil. [T. J. Jackson] has somehow or other a great tendency to put the man who stands first in Math also first on his course, but as there is so great a difference between my mark & the man next below me I think I can overcome his prejudices & compel him to put me first."[23]

The official report issued by VMI rated him accordingly:

July 10, 1860
Quarterly Report of Cadet Burgwyn of the 2nd Class,
consisting of 17 members

Studies	*Standing in Studies*
Mathematics	3rd
Nat. Philosophy	1st
Latin	1st
Chemistry	1st

Infy. Tactics	10th
General Merit	2nd [class standing]
Conduct	37 Demerit for the year
Health	Good[24]

Harry failed to rank first in his class as he confidently expected. He came out second to Hunter, which he attributed to his thirty-seven demerits, believing that he had received more than his arch rival. In September, referring to the new catalog of the institute, which he was sending home, he appropriately confessed to his mother that "I was mistaken in supposing that I had more demerit than the man who stood above me: he having 44 & I 37."[25]

On 2 July Harry's name was listed among those cadets granted leaves of absence three days later.[26] On that date, upon recommendation of the commandant of cadets, he was named second lieutenant of C Company to go into effect at the relief of the first class.[27] So he must have left on his furlough with a light heart and no little satisfaction. He had done exceptionally well his first year and would enjoy the pleasure and relaxation of a month in Raleigh with his family and friends.

Harry's parents had rented the Lemay house in Raleigh for the summer. Before their return to Thornbury in the fall, the house would be filled with a succession of relatives and guests. These visitors would mean countless hours of work for Anna, an immaculate housekeeper, as Harry was aware and wrote his sister:

> I only wish I was with her to witness her unfeigned joy at having to fix up a whole house without asking help from anyone. How much enjoyment she will take in putting up this & pulling down that, in sweeping a cobweb *out* of one place & *into* another, only to remove them again, for it is too much pleasure to be enjoyed all at once. If I ever become a rich man I intend to import a cargo of spiders & buy mother a couple of hundred brooms of all kinds, long & short handled, just that the spiders may spin their cobwebs & that mother may sweep them away.[28]

He returned to VMI on 10 August and two days later wrote a long letter to his mother. Clearly he missed the company of the young women and sent love to the Misses Cottons and Austin, Miss Ellen Lewis, Miss Seawell, and "by no means least but first, Miss Malvina [Henry] & all others who inquire of me." On returning to school as a first classman he was conscious of his change in status and relished it. "At night," in the same letter to his mother, he said, "I have a good deal of fun in annoying the sentinels; some of them get so confused that they really do not know their right hand from their left. One sentinel last night let me get so close to him that by a sudden jump I pinned his arms & then wrenched his bayonet off his gun, so that he was perfectly defenseless; but another whom I attempted to treat in the same way gave me a tremendous poke in the ribs with his bayonet but did not hurt me much."

In a more reflective mood, comparing the previous year with the start of his senior year, Harry expressed his reaction:

> I recollected as I was going over to the office that one year ago exactly I went over to Col. Smith's office to report myself & to begin attending to my duty as a pleb. If the contrast on the cars was depressing [on the train back to school], I can assure you that the recollection of this was the reverse. Then I knew no one, was uncertain as to the position I might be able to attain in my class & among the cadets; now I was intimate with almost everyone in camp, was to command instead of being commanded, & I was assured of my position and stand. The thought was refreshing.[29]

He was clearly a man of ambition, determined to be a leader. This is not an isolated insight into Harry's motivational drive. It appears time and again and was part of his life's pattern until the final day. And yet, with all of this drive and determination, he was deeply and sentimentally disposed toward the members of his family and his friends. Not the least among these was the family nurse and governess, Madie, for whom everyone held great affection. Upon learning of her illness in late August, he paid a loving tribute to Madie in a letter to his mother: "I declare I do feel very sad when I think of poor Madie's being so low: just to think of the invariable & attentive kindness to us when we were children at Hillside, in Jackson, or on the plantation, always the same disinterested, kind, invaluable & reliable Madie: always acting & working according to the best of her judgement for what she conceived to be our good. It is truly sad."[30]

This letter was written by Harry while in summer encampment. It was addressed from Camp Hardee, and he was having a miserable time. A few days earlier he had written his mother:

> I commenced my usual Sunday letter on yesterday but I was so very much annoyed by men coming in & leaving my tent that I was compelled to give up in despair. Even now there are five men besides myself in my tent which is only ten feet square.

. . . I am more and more tired of camp life; though I do not complain, yet you have no idea of the trouble I have. . . . I made myself go to almost all the squad drills in order to accustom my voice to giving commands & thus improve it. I notice a considerable improvement in it already. I have to read out three or four pages of reports every evening before the batallion & there has been no complaint of indistinctness. . . . Some of the inconveniences of camp are a most undue allowance of filth considering that we have been accustomed to consider ourselves as gentlemen. Last Sunday week we had a tremendous rain & you could not step outside of the tent without getting up to your ankles in mud, the worst kind of clayey mud which sticks to your shoes & dirties your tent, your clothes, your bed & everything. . . . I know you will find this a most miserable apology for a letter, but could you [do any better], writing in a close, dirty tent by the light of a single candle stuck up by being melted & set down in the tallow?[31]

Harry doubtless did not realize that his military training and camping experience would be called upon in the near future; nor, in reading the above letter, would one suppose that he would impetuously embrace the tedium, the drudgery, the physical deprivations, and the dangers of war. In August 1860, when this letter was written, eight months had passed since the hanging of John Brown. Only eight months remained before the firing on Fort Sumter. From this point on, Harry showed increased concern over the possibility of disunion accompanied by sectional strife. Available letters to and from his parents, especially correspondence with his father, provide a reflection of the Southern point of view, at least as seen through the eyes of a well-to-do, politically active family.

But not until 9 December 1860 did Harry express himself about the issues dividing the North and the South. He was writing to his mother, a New Englander. In part, he said:

I am quite impatient to hear from Father in relation to my application for a situation in the N.C. Volunteers. I hope he will present it at once. Really I see no hope for any pacific settlement of the questions now at issue between the North & the South. When I say pacific I use the word in the sense of secession. . . . The Republican members of Congress do not appear to show the slightest spirit of concession. They insist on the Constitution's being interpreted in a strictly republican construction: The Legislature of Vermont obstinately refuse to repeal a law peculiarly repugnant to the sensibilities of a chivalric people. Even if we submit to the domineering rule of those who arrogantly style themselves the interpreters of God's will & expect that they may hereafter forbear, who have never shown that they know what forbearance is, why what reason have we to suppose that there will not be in each successive presidential election the same disastrous excitement which is now so greatly injuring the interest of everyone. . . . All business is at a standstill. I am told that money can hardly be obtained at all in this section of Virginia. The cause of secession is growing rapidly here & I think is likewise increasing in other parts of the State.[32]

A few days later, Harry seemed even more resolute: "The dissolution of the Union certainly appears inevitable & what will become of us I hardly dare think if we have war. My judgment apart from my feelings would make me believe that we could not have war for there is no reason, no cause which would make the North desire to fight us. Yet my feelings would cause me to think that a settlement can not be made until some of our grievances have been settled by the sword. Whatever happens I am ready."[33]

On 22 December, learning that South Carolina had seceded, Harry was prompted to write a long and thoughtful letter to his father:

I take this opportunity of asking your views, not only as to what I myself ought to do at present, & in case my state secedes, but also to get your views on the state of affairs. I am truly impatient of the present position of comparative inaction which I am compelled to assume. . . . What I shall do therefore in the event of N.C.'s seceding is a matter of uncertainty & disquietude. I think it is my bounden duty to go at once, leaving this place, & do what I can to produce an efficient army. Col. Smith coincides with me in this view. . . . He thinks war is imminent unless the whole South secedes: this however he thinks will be the case: his idea then is that a new confederacy should be formed, which would be joined by all the present states except the New England states & those bordering on the Northern Lakes. Part of N.Y. might join it. The remaining states would either form a new confederacy or join themselves to Canada. The New England states, ruled partly by strong minded women, have become so corrupted by infidelity & free love associations, etc., as to be completely rotten & unworthy of any connection.[34]

What is intriguing about this letter is the attitude of Colonel Smith that war was imminent "unless the whole South secedes";

the point being that the North would not challenge the solidarity of a united confederacy, which might even be joined by all the other states except those in New England and those bordering on the northern lakes. Even part of New York might join such a confederacy. Obviously, Colonel Smith was overly optimistic, but there must have been a generally shared feeling in the South at the time that the North might not challenge secession if it meant all-out war and that such a war would be of short duration.

Harry's father was clearly of this opinion. In December 1856 he had written an open letter to the editors of the *Journal of Commerce* in New York in which he described himself as a Southern planter with close family connections in the North. He appealed for a better understanding "of the peculiar situation of our people," decried the work of the abolitionists, and predicted that "this glorious Union . . . is ere long to be shattered to pieces, because a set of stubborn men insist on forcing an abstraction—that 'slavery is a great civil and moral evil'—upon another part of our common country, against their wishes and interest."[35]

Nearly four years later, probably in the early fall of 1860, the elder Burgwyn wrote a lengthy letter to the *North Carolina Standard* in which he ranged from the "muttered vaporings" of a few fanatics in the 1830s, to John Brown's raid in 1859, to the Republican publication of Hinton Helper's book "to create insurrection and treason among us." This letter was not solicitous or an appeal to reason. Rather, it was designed to explore the question whether the people "would be any better off in a Southern Confederacy than in one with such discordant elements in it as the present one with the North, and especially with that puritan people of New England." According to Burgwyn, a confederacy of the slave states "would offer to the friendship and alliances of Europe the 'material interests' of a doubly profitable trade—that of a *supply* of raw products, and a *demand* for manufactures and other goods." He reasoned that the South would thereby realize a substantial trade surplus and that a reduced tariff of 20 percent would provide ample revenues for its domestic requirements. If, on the other hand, there were a disruption of this trade, he quoted Lord Stanley, the son of the premier of England, as saying that "the deprivation of the supplies of cotton, would, in six months, produce almost universal bankruptcy, and in twelve months an insurrection of the working classes."[36] Burgwyn then made the following assumptions:

> Let us suppose that the fifteen Southern States were to "accept the annulment," and call a convention among themselves "to

form a more perfect union" under a new confederation . . . would not the North pause before attempting to "whip in" such a people armed for defence of such a cause? . . . There will be no attack upon us . . . on a calm consideration of the two parties, after separation. . . . And now let us consider what this relation is likely to be. It must either be *civil war,* carried on with all the horrors that ever attended such contests, or it will be a friendly alliance of contiguous and homogeneous people, whose interests, education and general character are in accordance. In short, if it assumes a peaceful nature, it will resemble much the alliance that now exists between England and Scotland. . . . Can there be any doubt as to which course would be adopted by the Northern states upon a withdrawal of the South from the present confederacy? [37]

"When the time of real trial comes," he concluded, "all Southern men will be found bound together, and ready to defend their rights to the last."[38] Henry King Burgwyn, Sr., was clearly rationalizing the probability of a Southern confederacy without the probability of war. His letter is important because it expressed contemporary Southern leadership thought at the time. His misconceptions and false assumptions were shared by many. He and they had long since developed a defensive posture against the so-called aggressions of the North. The tariff had been a problem for years. The hated voice of the abolitionist would not be stilled. In addition, the South had been steadily losing ground politically. Wave on wave of immigrants were swelling the free-labor states of the North and Midwest. Few found their way to the slave South. There were now eighteen free states and fifteen slave states.

The industrial North was pitted against the slave South, and the North was in the majority. The campaign of 1860 was at its height, and slavery was the issue. In all respects, the South was almost a separate nation and, if necessary, could sustain itself as such. There were thoughtful Unionists in the South, but their voices could not be heard above the clamor of an election year. Some were too fearful to speak out. The North contributed its share to national divisiveness. Its aggressions were the verbal and written assaults of extremists. They were answered in kind, and few were the voices of tolerance and understanding on either side. In the highly charged, emotional context of the times, with all hope of compromise seemingly ended, war seemed inevitable. The secessionists would not back down. The time would come when the government of the United States of America could not back down.

It is not the purpose of this study to analyze the events leading up to the Civil War, but it is important to understand the motivational context in which the youthful generation of Harry Burgwyn was called upon to fight it. In a letter to his father on 22 December, he left little doubt as to where he stood: "I am truly impatient of the present position of comparative inaction which I am compelled to assume; & I know of no power which (you agreeing to my course of action) would prevent me from joining the army of the Southern states in general & my own State in particular. . . . I consider that my allegiance is emphatically due to N.C. & please God I will not fail in it."[39]

These were the words of a proud young Southerner. In the event of war, there was no question where Harry's allegiance would lie. He belonged to the aristocracy of the South. He was a part of the "slave oligarchy," the ruling class. Barely turned nineteen, Harry obviously reflected the opinions of his father. North Carolina and the South were the objects of his devotion, and he would defend them at any cost.

But North Carolina was still months away from secession and war. Governor John W. Ellis, although an avowed states-right man, had exercised judicious restraint throughout his first term. In his first inaugural address before the Senate and House of Commons on 1 January 1859, he had regretted that the "same tranquility and repose which have so constantly attended our domestic concerns . . . have not so uniformly characterized our association among the States of the Union." Ellis was alluding, of course, to the sectional discord arising from the "aggressions" of the North. But they were not the words of a fire-eater. "Grievous as are these causes of discontent," he said, "we are not prepared for the acknowledgment that we cannot enjoy all of our constitutional rights in the Union. . . . In the meantime, our bearing in the Confederacy should be in accordance with the consistent and dignified character of the State . . . abstaining from hasty and intemperate threats, as inconsistent with the dignity of a sovereign state, yet not slow to protest, firmly and deliberately, against impending injuries; always deliberating considerately and discreetly, resolving with decision, and executing those resolves with certainty, boldness, vigor and courage."[40]

For Governor Ellis the year 1859 was highlighted by President Buchanan's visit to the state to attend the commencement exercises at Chapel Hill in June. He arrived by train at Weldon on Tuesday morning, 31 May, and was officially welcomed by the governor. They traveled by train to Raleigh the same day. All along the route the president was greeted by large crowds who had assembled at every depot stop. On Wednesday, 1 June, the party continued by train to "Durham's Station," where they transferred to carriages for their trip to Chapel Hill. The president was given a warm reception. During the two-day event he attended all exercises, addressed the senior class, and was awarded the honorary degree of LL.D. The *North Carolina Standard* wrote, "The Union according to the Constitution, seemed to be uppermost in his thoughts."[41] In addressing the graduating class he spoke as one who sensed an approaching crisis:

> I would advise these young men to devote themselves to the preservation of the principles of the Constitution, for without these blessings our liberties are gone. Let this Constitution be torn into atoms; let the members of this Union separate; let thirty Republics rise up against each other, and it would be the most fatal day for the liberties of the human race that ever dawned upon any land. Let us keep together, then, for better or for worse, as man and wife.[42]

During most of that year, however, there is little evidence in his official correspondence that Governor Ellis was unduly concerned with the possibility of approaching sectional strife. It was not until mid-October 1859 that John Brown struck at Harpers Ferry. His capture and subsequent execution only intensified sectional bitterness. On 10 December Governor Ellis placed an order with the secretary of war for two thousand long-range rifles with bayonets, prefacing his letter with the comment: "The Sense of insecurity prevailing among the people of this State, renders it necessary that I should apply to you for arms to place in the hands of the militia."[43] The request was rejected because it would have used up the quotas available to the state for the next six years.

Public concern would increase as the year 1860 progressed. It was an election year. The Democratic National Convention was scheduled to meet in Charleston in April. The "Black Republicans," sensing victory in the air, consciously fanned the flames of sectional discord. The Southern Democrats were equally contentious. Governor Ellis was increasingly importuned to call a special session of the legislature so that more and better arms could be provided the local militia units and volunteer companies. To these entreaties the governor responded, "I deem it important too, to avoid all such action as would tend to increase the excitement now existing among our people, justly as this excitement has been provoked."[44]

But Ellis was less restrained in accepting his nomination by the Democratic State Convention for a second term as governor. Although most of his speech was devoted to domestic matters, he unequivocally asserted that the national presidential contest would be over the issue "whether African slavery shall be abolished here in the states, where it now exists. Let us not be deceived upon this point," he said. "Men may talk about our rights in the territories, but depend upon it they are not the questions now in issue. The abolition of slavery here at home is the design of our opponents." That issue, he said, would be between the Democratic party and the "Free-soilers, black Republicans and Abolitionists, consolidated and combined." He rejected the idea that the Democratic party would differ and become divided in the Charleston Convention.[45]

It was not until October 1860 that the governor's correspondence began to reflect increasing preoccupation with the national election and related matters. On 5 October Governor William H. Gist of South Carolina asked Ellis what would be the reaction of the people of North Carolina if Lincoln were elected to the presidency. Two weeks later, emphasizing the lack of unanimity on any public question, Ellis replied fairly and with candor. "Upon the whole," he said, "I am decidedly of opinion that a majority of our people would not consider the occurrence of the event referred to [election of Lincoln], as sufficient ground for dissolving the Union of the States." He continued: "I could not in any event assent to or give my aid to a practical enforcement of the monstrous doctrine of Co-ercion. I do not for a moment think that North Carolina would become a party to the enforcement of this doctrine and will not, therefore, do her the injustice of placing her in that position even though hypothetically."[46]

A month later Governor Ellis was of a more positive mind. In addressing the opening session of the General Assembly on 20 November, he reacted officially to the "doctrine of Co-ercion." Although the governor may have favored secession all along, this was probably his first public statement about coercion. He was fully aware of the strong Unionist sentiment in the state; John C. Breckinridge had carried North Carolina by only 848 votes in the presidential election on 6 November. But as chief executive, Governor Ellis was justified in alerting the citizens to the probability of federal coercion in the event of secession by any state. Furthermore, he was justified in recommending to the General Assembly that "consultation with other Southern States" should be held, followed by a convention of the people. He also referred to the subject of military defenses, urging "a thorough reorganization of the militia and the enrollment of all persons between the ages of 18 and 45 years." In addition, he proposed that a corps of ten thousand volunteers be organized separate from the militia.[47]

Events moved swiftly thereafter. In his personal journal on 24 November, Ellis noted with satisfaction the general approval of his message throughout the state. But, he said, "The Standard [*North Carolina Standard*] of this City dissents. His comments on the Message are disapproved by the entire party in the Legislature and have in fact placed the Editor [William W. Holden] without the pail of the party."[48] On 6 December Ellis seemed pleased to record that "near twenty-five county meetings have been held. All for Southern rights except a meeting in the City of Raleigh." Four days later Isham W. Garrott of Alabama presented his credentials as commissioner from Alabama to North Carolina, reporting that Mississippi, Alabama, Florida, Georgia, and South Carolina "would secede from the Union before the 1st of Feb. 1861." On 19 December Ellis noted the arrival of Jacob Thompson as commissioner from Mississippi to North Carolina.[49] A few days earlier, Ellis had transmitted to the General Assembly a communication from Governor Sam Houston of Texas, which read in part:

> The present agitation throughout the country, and particularly in the South, arising from the election of a President and Vice President upon a sectional issue, calls, in my opinion, for the calm deliberation of statesmen. The assembling of delegates from sovereign States, in a consultative character, and within the scope of their Constitutional powers, "*to preserve the equal rights of such States in the Union*," may result in the adoption of such measures as will restore harmony between the two sections of the Union.[50]

Throughout the month of December Governor Ellis had been kept closely informed on developments in South Carolina. His correspondent in that state, a prosperous merchant and member of the South Carolina Secession Convention,[51] wrote the governor on 20 December. His message was startling but not unexpected. It read in part: "The Convention is unanimous for secession and before the sun sets this day, South Carolina will have resumed the powers delegated to the federal government and taken her place among the nations as an independent power. God save the state."[52]

The governor's reply was mailed on Christmas Day. His commendation of the action taken by South Carolina was clear and strong: "The Great step taken by your State on that day was duly telegraphed to this place, and though not unexpected, produced a profound Sensation. We felt a personal interest in your proceedings, as the Cause of South Carolina is the Cause of the South. As such it will be maintained and defended though it be at the cost of the blood and treasure of the South." Ellis was right, but it is doubtful that he remotely conceived of the magnitude of the ultimate sacrifice in "blood and treasure." Not only did he welcome the move by South Carolina but clearly established himself as the leader of the secession movement in North Carolina by adding: "The Legislature of North Carolina will most certainly call a Convention. There is a fierce opposition here to Southern rights, growing mainly out of old party divisions, but we will overcome it. The people are fully alive to their interests."[53]

And yet Governor Ellis was neither intemperate nor foolhardy. On 31 December he received a telegram from "the people" of Wilmington requesting permission to seize Fort Caswell. *"Refused by me"* was his laconic diary entry.[54] Governor Ellis acted wisely. In the weeks and months ahead the state's actions would be characterized by moderation and caution. The governor, for his part, would make no moves designed to invite hostilities, but his driving motivation would be aimed at secession and preparation for war.

CHAPTER 6

YOU CAN GET NO TROOPS
FROM NORTH CAROLINA

As Cadet Harry Burgwyn prepared for the winter and spring terms of his final year at the Virginia Military Institute, excitement prevailed on the campus. It had intensified since the election of Lincoln. According to one historian, "a spirit of intense restlessness pervaded Barracks" during the winter of 1860–61. Although never insubordinate, the cadets gave vent to their feelings by provoking disorders almost daily. On 22 February, two fourth classmen hoisted a secession flag on the tower of the barracks. It was immediately hauled down by the guard, which only intensified enthusiasm for secession among the corps of cadets.[1]

The people of Lexington and Rockbridge County, on the other hand, were strongly pro-Union, which almost provoked a bloody confrontation in March between the cadets and the townspeople. It was averted at the last moment by the timely action of an officer.[2] At a meeting following this incident, the cadets were sharply reprimanded by the superintendent and Colonel John T. L. Preston. The cadets implored Major T. J. Jackson, who had witnessed the confrontation, to comment. According to one observer, Jackson was reluctant to speak, but finally he rose and said:

> "Military men make short speeches, and as for myself, I am no hand at speaking, anyhow. The time for war has not yet come, but it will come, and that soon; and when it does come, my advice is to draw the sword and throw away the scabbard."
>
> The personality of the speaker, the force of those simple words thus uttered, elicited a response of approval I never heard surpassed, except for the Confederate yell often heard on the battlefield, a little later on. This simple speech and manner of Jackson established in the minds of his audience the belief that he was a leader upon whose loyalty and courage we could rely.[3]

There is no record of Harry Burgwyn's involvement in any of these incidents. That he was well informed on developments is clear from his letters. He certainly favored secession, once South Carolina and the other cotton states had moved, but the possibility of war never appeared imminent to him. He seemed not to believe that the North would take up arms against the South. Like many others of his day, he believed that a peaceful separation could be effected. Almost up to the firing on Fort Sumter he was apparently more preoccupied with graduation and his future career than anything else. But in a long letter to his father on 11 January 1861, he expressed concern about the threat of coercion and the possibility of conflict and his hope that North Carolina

> may be stirred up into something like vitality. The action of Gen. Scott in advising coercion is I think worthy of the severest condemnation from all, but if you recollect a letter I wrote you some time in October you will not be surprised at it. In that letter I gave you an account of a debate in Society on the question "Should the South secede in the event of Mr. Lincoln's election!" In the course of the debate Col. Smith read a copy of a letter sent to him from Gen. Scott submitting to the Pres[i-dent] his views in relation to the existing apprehensions. His idea even then was to garrison every fort in the Southern country with such a number of U.S. troops as would render any attack on them "simply ridiculous." From this it may very readily [be] conjectured that his idea was to garrison all the seaport forts of the Southern Confederacy & by prohibiting in consequence the levying of duties by such on imports that he might compel them to resort to direct taxation which they could not stand if their exports paid a duty to the Gen[eral] Government. I sincerely hope that his treachery is prevented by the prompt action of the cotton states in seizing beforehand the forts within their own limits.[4]

He concluded by admonishing: "Hoping that our old state may be waked into something like a decided course of conduct," and then asked in a postscript: "Is there any prospect of Gov. Ellis' taking forts Macon & Johnston?"[5]

There is no record of his father's reply, but he must have responded during a break in his travels. Henry King Burgwyn, Sr., had always led a peripatetic life. His professional agricultural interests, his many and long summer visits to New England, and his vacation trips to White Sulphur Springs and other resorts in Virginia and North Carolina all had resulted in a wide circle of friends and acquaintances.

Articulate as well as gregarious by nature, he apparently enjoyed the companionship of men in a convivial setting. He was interested in politics, savored political discussions, but never sought political office. During the winter of 1861, Henry was on the move. In the event of secession and war, his property interests on the Roanoke and those of Anna in New England would surely be threatened. He was obviously concerned and, of necessity, had to be involved. It probably suited his temperament, for he seemed to be exhilarated by the political turmoil of the day. In fact, events were unfolding very much along the lines he had predicted several years earlier. He enjoyed sharing his reflections and opinions with both Anna and their oldest son, and Harry appears to have been strongly influenced by his father.

Henry went to Washington in the latter part of February. Stopping en route for a few days in Richmond, he reported to Anna that "the Convention & Legislature is in session. The Governor took me in to the opening of the former yest[erda]y & I got a seat in front of the President's chair! Nothing has yet been done to indicate the action of the Convention but in conversation with some of the leaders, the idea seems to be that Virg[ini]a will do all she can to mediate, & as long as possible, but finally unless she can get such a settlement as will bring the Cotton States back, she will join them. There is a stronger feeling against So[uth] Car[olina] here than in No[rth] Car[olina]."[6]

While in Washington he interviewed many important people. His observations appear to conform generally to those expressed by his son. A letter to Anna on 18 February 1861 sheds light upon the attitudes and opposing points of view of that day:

> I have been very much delighted Dearest Menie by the receipt & perusal of your letters this morning & hasten to reply. . . . Have had constant interviews with various gent[leme]n, free conversations with members of the Peace Congress here & others from North & South. The former are as impracticable as ever & I am *thoroughly assured that nothing satisfactory will be effected here by either Congress* & that unless Virginia & the other states go out an attempt at coercion by blockading our coasts will be attempted. What that will lead to is Civil War unless England & France intervene. There is but little doubt that both are ready to acknowledge the Southern Confederacy and that the Northern politicians are straining every nerve to prevent this, even to the threat of considering it a declaration of war. . . .

I have had free conversations [with] a number of gent[leme]n from Maryland & Tennessee. They assure me that both will go out if something satisfactory cannot be effected by the Peace Congress & I am assured by members of that body that not even the Crittenden resolutions can be carried through that. Therefore there is no chance whatever of the Border States remaining with the North. The only difficulty is whether they will go out in time to prevent an attempt on the part of the North at coercion; this will bring on Civil War unless, which I think very probable, the Administration should not have money enough to pay either Army or Navy. . . . You have no idea what a picture Wash[ington] presents at this mom[en]t; crowds of anxious faces fill the hotel & streets; men from the South preparing for a contest, & those of the North striving to extract from South-ern[er]s some gleam of hope & adjustment. . . .

The city has about 1100 troops; they surround the Capitol, fill the Treasury & other buildings; a troop are stationed directly opposite this Hotel, Willards, & the streets are spotted with uniforms; a large & full battery of horse artillery move up & down Pennsylvania Avenue & "the car is rattling over the stony streets" daily; & we are daily expecting marshal law to be proclaimed; what a commentary upon a "Free Government." . . . Senator Clingman has written home that the North have [not] offered & will not offer anything in the Peace Congress which is at all satisfactory; & one of the members told me yest[erda]y that so far the North, instead of offering concessions, had made no proposition which was not requiring more from the South.[7]

He concluded by suggesting that "Minnie take this letter, or William, & read the political portion to Gov. Ellis and say I have not time to write him particularly."[8]

Henry was even more despondent in his next letter:

It has been a painful time I have had here & in Rich[mon]d. You cannot tell the pain to men who feel like myself that the rights & liberties of their country run so great a risk of being sold by ignorant or selfish politicians. I have had a long & interesting interview with the French Minister this morning. He says his gov[ernme]nt is fully alive to the importance of a direct trade with the South & is now engaged in the closest inquiry into the resources of the South.

Lincoln arrived in the Hotel this morning at 5 in the morning, no one knowing a word about [it] for hours after. His friends are evidently afraid of his danger! Did you ever know such folly?[9]

But on Monday, 25 February, Henry was more cheerful. After mentioning that he had dined on Saturday with several government officials, he suggested that Anna would "see by the papers how Lincoln crept to bed in the house yest[erda]y morning to avoid Baltimore. It causes much sensation & the gent[leme]n of his party are deeply mortified; his buffoonery is said to be more fit for the Clown's part in a Circus than for President. The house is filled with police, both in plain clothes & in full uniform & crowded to excess with Black Rep[ublicans]."[10]

While Harry's father was preoccupied with the political situation in Washington, events were moving rapidly to a climax in North Carolina. The situation there was no less uncertain, no less confused, but the pro-Union forces, both in Raleigh and throughout the state, were a match for the secessionists. Throughout January the legislature had been engaged in heated debate over a convention bill, which was passed by a two-thirds vote of both houses on 29 January. It provided for the election of delegates on 28 February. At the same time the people were to vote their preference for or against a convention. If a majority favored a convention, the governor could not call it into session earlier than 11 March. The number of delegates (120) would be based on each county's representation in the General Assembly. The contest between the Unionists and secessionists began in earnest as each side campaigned for control of the convention. A majority of the press opposed secession during the campaign.[11] W. W. Holden was the unquestionable leader of the pro-Union press. In the 31 January issue of the *North Carolina Standard* he declared himself in strong and aggressive terms:

We come forward to say, in the very outset, that the issue presented is Union or Disunion! Let the Union men of all parties rally in every neighborhood and County in the State. Let mass meetings be held in every County, and the best, the ablest, and the strongest Union men be nominated. Henceforth there are but two parties in North Carolina. All other parties and all other issues are at once lost sight of in this struggle for the Union according to the Constitution. . . . Nominate no man— vote for no man who will not frankly and emphatically pledge himself to exhaust all honorable efforts to preserve the Union. Let there be no equivocation—no dodging.

The issue to be determined is the most important ever sub-mitted to our people. Let every citizen who prefers peace to war, concord to discord, civil rule to military rule, and re-construction and union to final separation and disunion, bestir himself and put forth all his efforts.

With this clarion call the issue was joined. Class was pitted against class. The conservatives or Unionists warned of civil war; the seces-sionists aroused the latent fear of the people to the possibility of mil-lions of slaves being "set free among us, to stalk abroad in the land . . . committing depredations, rapine, and murder upon the whites." Many people of more moderate views opposed secession yet wanted assurance that the rights of North Carolina and the South would be protected. They were known as conditional Unionists. Popular sen-timent varied according to sections of the state. Unionists were strong in the northeast and particularly strong in the piedmont and western areas. The secessionists were strong in the middle-eastern slaveholding counties and in the cotton counties of the southwest. Politically, the leading secessionists were Democrats. Opposition to disunion was exceptionally strong among the Whigs.[12]

North Carolinians still hoped for compromise and waited expec-tantly for the report of the Peace Conference. But when they went to the polls on 28 February it was not generally known that the confer-ence had adjourned the day before—a failure. The convention was defeated by the narrow margin of 47,323 votes to 46,672. Of the 120 delegates chosen, 50 were unconditional Unionists, 42 were se-cessionists, and 28 conditional Unionists. Clearly, North Carolina leaned strongly in favor of the Union on 28 February 1861—before the threat of coercion became a fact.[13]

There is nothing in his official correspondence to indicate Gover-nor Ellis's reaction to the convention vote. His disappointment and chagrin were undoubtedly magnified by W. W. Holden's account of the Unionist celebration in Raleigh: "We have never witnessed such enthusiasm in Raleigh as that exhibited on Thursday night last by the Unionists. Large crowds of men and boys were on the streets un-til past midnight, singing Union songs, hurrahing for the good cause, calling out the successful candidates, and other Union men, who re-plied in brief speeches which added to the general enthusiasm."[14]

As for the Burgwyns' reaction to the convention vote, history is silent. While in Washington Harry's father had met frequently with Daniel M. Barringer and David S. Reid, members of the Peace Con-ference from North Carolina, but he never alluded to the campaign being fought out in his home state during the month of February. Because he reported to Governor Ellis from time to time, and judging from the tenor of his letters and public statements,[15] he appears to have been a secessionist and to have voted for the convention. Harry's letters are also silent on this point, and there are only five letters extant, which he wrote to his parents between 11 January and 19 April. They contain many revealing passages about Harry himself, his relationship to his family, his reaction to his environment, his ambitions, and what he thought of the future.

To his mother, on 3 March, he wrote:

> As for what I expect to do if there is no war I can not at all say. . . . I have thought that I would accept for one year an assistant Professorship of Mathematics at this place if one were offered me as it probably will be. The objections to this plan is that I am heartily & sincerely tired of this place & am afraid that I would get dissatisfied with my position. If a Southern Mil[itary] Inst[itute] were to be put in operation, I would like to get an assistant professorship there very much indeed; for one year only however. Another idea was to study law somewhere for one year & various other conceptions have occurred. . . . You have promised you know to come & see me graduate & I confidentally [sic] expect father to accompany you. You were not present at Ch[apel] Hill & I think you owe to me as well as to yourself. . . .[16]

On 10 March Harry made the following observation to his mother about the possibility of war: "I have no idea of what will be the result of the action of the Va. Convention. If it passes an ordinance of secession it will still be too late to preserve its honor. Unless it passes such an ordinance I think there will be a conflict between the Southern & Federal troops. I have never thought that the war would be of long duration."[17]

But his comparative academic standing was uppermost on his mind when he wrote his father a few days later:

> I am getting along, as I told you I intended to, much better in my studies though it is utterly impossible to say whether I will graduate 1st or 2nd; the former more probably. How they will act however I know not. Last year I was marked 4 tenths on tactics & they made it count 72 whole ones against me at July. I had 2 whole ones above the man who stood 1st in general on

Nat. Phil. which counts one half more than that on which I was marked. At present my marks show me to be 1st on Moral Phil.; 1st on Nat. Phil.; 1st on Artillery Tactics; 1st on Nat. History, with Hunter 1st on Military History; 1st on Mental Philosophy, with one other man having the same mark; 1st on Engineering, three others having the same mark; 1st on Mineralogy, 1 other having the same mark.

In other words, I have the first mark by myself on 4 of these 8 studies & the 1st on all other 4; some other men however sharing the same mark. My object now is to graduate first on all of these eight & if they can, in face of that, throw anybody above me, why I cannot help it. My time is as you may imagine very thoroughly occupied with learning & recitating 5 lessons a day. I confidently hope that you will come up here the 4th of July & see me graduate. It would be a considerable relaxation to you & a source of much pleasure to me. What shall I do after graduation is the question which is now agitating the mental portion of my constitution "C'est Selon."[18]

Harry was undoubtedly maintaining a rigorous schedule of study. And it was beginning to tell on him. His next letter to his father reflects considerable disconsolation, probably the result of overwork coupled with the uncertainties of the future. It was written on 23 March:

I have intended, for some time, to write you in relation to what I must do after graduating; & as you will probably be in Raleigh & have sufficient time to answer my letter, I defer it no longer. . . . I have reflected lately a good deal on the choice of a profession & am just as far from coming to a conclusion as I was when I commenced. I have seriously reflected on the subject of taking an Asst. Prof. here for one year; but in reality I am so tired of this place, that by doing so I feel I would be imposing a task, which would be so disagreeable as to make me regret my action. . . .

If Va. were to secede by the 4th of July, & make a law by which all the Prof[essors] here should hold a commission in the *regular army* of a Southern Confederacy, the advantages of such a position would overcome my dislike to accepting it. . . . It appears to me, speaking as I shall endeavor to do impartially, that the people of this section is an inferior race to that of any other portion of Va. or of the South. Whether I am right or not is

Cadet Harry Burgwyn (center) with four classmates at Virginia Military Institute (courtesy V.M.I. Alumni Review)

not of much consequence but certain it is that there is no society whatever. . . .

The same objections do not apply to an Asst. Prof. in a Southern State. In all probability a Southern M.A. [Military Academy] will be established in some of the Southern States; perhaps the Alabama or La. Mil. Inst. [Louisiana Military Institute] will be converted into a S.M.I. [Southern Military Institute]. If such be the case & I could get a situation as Inst. of Math, I would probably be glad to accept it. . . .

If however I do not accept a position, either here or elsewhere, what shall I do? I do not wish to loll away the best portion of my life in idleness & become an encumbrance to my friends & a burthen to myself; yet what shall I do? Every prof[ession] is open to me & I can choose any. An Engineer's life would not suit me, I think. A Dr.'s still less, & what shall be said of a lawyer's? If I possessed the requisite energy, & had not the unfortunate laziness which characterizes me, that would be my choice. I would never be content with occupying a subordinate position such as a pettifoging country lawyer, & I will not attempt to conceal from myself the fact that I can only become otherwise by hard study. This is what I am now heartily tired of; whether my weariness of study will wear off after a vacation I do not know, but if I had to run for a stand a year instead of three months I believe I would knock under. . . . The prof[ession] of Law however is the only one by which a man in this country can rise to power.

In the same letter, knowing that his parents were planning to buy a house, Harry suggested to his father: "I would suit myself & mother if I were you & go just where you preferred. I would prefer Norfolk to Richmond myself but I would a great deal rather have you please yourself. I would rather live near the water. What do you think of Montgomery, Ala.? Why not take Mother & Maria on a Southern trip; & look out as you go for a place suited by climate & society. If you could purchase with Northern funds lots in the future capital of the S. Confederacy they would prove a very profitable investment."[19]

But when Easter Sunday, 1 April 1861, arrived, Harry was thinking only of home, graduation day, and a long summer vacation. To his mother he wrote:

This is Easter Sunday & for the 2nd time in my life have I missed the good dinner which a provident regulation provides for a hungry sinner. My dinner today consisted of cold corn beef cold roast ditto steam cooked potatoes & various other similar dishes. My roommates are at this moment discussing a one hour & 15 minute sermon & loud are their exclamations against it. I console myself with the reflection that 3 months will end all my troubles at this place. If ever a poor mortal wished for a period to arrive I wish for the 4th of July 1861. What are your plans for the summer. I am almost perfectly indifferent as to what I do or where I spend the summer. A thousand ideas have flitted across me & been as quickly rejected as conceived. So I think I shall let you choose for me altogether.[20]

By mid-April, everything had changed. Graduation exercises on 4 July 1861 were not to be held. Fort Sumter had fallen. On 15 April Governor Francis W. Pickens of South Carolina telegraphed Governor Ellis: "Fort Sumter surrendered after our troops had made terrible havoc upon it. There is a fleet off our bar, with several thousand troops on board. If they attempt a landing, we are prepared for them. We will do our duty. Fort Pickens has been reinforced. Will North Carolina stand this?"[21]

This was only one of many messages that crackled through the telegraph office in Raleigh on that memorable day. From Wilmington came the demand: "Our people will take the forts. Send us your orders or we go without them and hold against all comers." Back went the reply: "Forts Caswell and Johnston without delay, and hold them communicate orders to military of Wilmington to take until further orders against all comers." From J. S. Wheeler in Washington, D.C.: "This city is in a state of the wildest excitement to-day. President by his proclamation calls on the states for seventy-five thousand troops . . . this city is to be placed immediately under martial law by proclamation . . . the Virginia Commissioners have gone and are hopeless as to any adjustment, they will recommend the immediate secession of that state. It is said the Confederate Congress will reassemble and war declared forthwith." From Governor Ellis to Marshall D. Craton: "You will proceed with your Company to Fort Macon and take possession of the same in the name of the State of North Carolina. This measure being one of self defense and protection merely, you will observe strictly peaceful policy and act only on the defensive."[22]

But the key to war, the inevitability of that "irrepressible conflict" on the fateful day, 15 April 1861, lay in the following telegraphic exchange between Secretary of War Simon Cameron and Governor John Willis Ellis:

Washington
April 15th 1861.

Call made on you by tonights mail for two (2) regiments of military for immediate service.[23]

Raleigh, N.C. Apr 15th 1861.

Your dispatch is recd. and if genuine which its extraordinary character leads me to doubt I have to say in reply that I regard the levy of troops made by the administration for the purpose of subjugating the states of the south is in violation of the constitution and a gross usurpation of power I can be no party to this wicked violation of the laws of the country, and to this war upon the liberties of a free people. You can get no troops from North Carolina. I will reply more in detail when your call is received by mail.[24]

In Virginia, the response to President Lincoln's call for troops was no less positive. Governor John Letcher immediately ordered Colonel Smith, superintendent of VMI, to Richmond for special duty. Before leaving, Colonel Smith issued Order No. 60 on 18 April in which he placed the command of the institute under Major Preston and emphasized the responsibilities of every cadet:

The most particular attention of every cadet is called to his duties. There must be no short comings on the part of any at such a time as this. Every true son of the state of the South must now show his loyalty by the most rigid attention to duty, and respect for authority. Those who have had the privileges of this Institution cannot render a greater service to the State than by making themselves the examples of order, attention and duty. Dismissal now would be disgrace indeed, & it is hoped that the confidence which is reposed in the Corps of Cadets will be met by a generous & manly spirit of emulation in discharging faithfully the duties which the emergency calls forth.[25]

On the following day, Harry wrote his father. It was his last letter from VMI:

I have only time to write you a few lines to say that I expect to receive tomorrow marching orders for Richmond. What will be done with us after we get there I do not know. I suppose we will be kept there some short time & then be sent off to recruiting stations. Then we will be sent off to the theatre of war as fast as the companies can be formed. They will not, I suppose, send us into action as a body for what absolute effect could a body of

200 men do, most of them boys, in comparison with the good they could effect distributed at the various recruiting stations. I shall go to Richmond better prepared than when I went to Charlestown as far as armament & clothing is concerned; though I will be quite deficient. If we go to Richmond & I am deficient I shall endeavor to get some money from Ballard of the exchange; or I may get some from McIlwaine. I will draw very moderately; nor more than I need.

I do not believe we will go; considerable dissatisfaction exists among us that they should expect us to fight as privates through the war; or at all events commence it in that way. We would thus be the only ones in the whole army who would be denied the opportunity of distinguishing ourselves while having more military knowledge than any of the others.[26]

On 21 April Major Preston received a message by special courier ordering the corps of cadets to Richmond together with "all the Ordnance and Ordnance stores with full supply of ammunition." In his Order No. 63, Major Preston delivered a ringing call to arms:

When the muster is held for men who have souls to defend their native soil from violation, insult and subjugation, the heart of every true Virginian responds to the voice as with stern delight he answers, Here! Words are not necessary now to stimulate.

The Corps of Cadets will prove their birth & breeding and exhibit to Virginia the worth of her favorite Institute—the Cadet will not fail to manifest the advantage which the military education gives to him over those not less brave than himself. The Corps will go forth the pride of its friends, the hope of the state and the terror of her foes—may the blessing of the God of Hosts rest upon every one who is battling in this holy cause.

The march will be performed as directed by special order.[27]

CHAPTER 7

IN DEAD EARNEST

From this point on, Harry Burgwyn would dedicate every waking moment to only one objective—preparation for war. Self-discipline, a determination to lead, to excel in battle, to gain recognition, but in a sober, hardworking, unselfish manner, seem to have dominated his every thought and action. He did not object to father or friends speaking on his behalf for a commission or transfer to a better post, apparently because he was satisfied he could justify any confidence expressed in his capacity for leadership.

Harry left Lexington with the cadet corps on 21 April 1861. He carried a letter of recommendation from Major R. E. Colston, professor of military history and strategy, who referred to him as "a distinguished member of the Class now about to graduate." Major Colston continued, "I have not the slightest hesitation in asserting that Mr. Burgwyn will prove a skilful and efficient officer, and that his qualifications are above those of the average of graduates both of this Institution and of the Military Academy at West Point."[1] The corps, two hundred strong, with four six-pounder guns and baggage wagons bringing up the rear, reached Staunton at ten o'clock that night after a long and wearying thirty-eight mile march. The cadets were quartered in hotels overnight and departed by train the next morning. The trip was uneventful except for the derailment of the engine as the train passed through the Blue Ridge tunnel.

They reached Richmond late in the afternoon of 22 April and were reviewed by the governor in front of the state capitol and then marched to the new fairgrounds, about a mile west of the city.[2] According to Harry, the cadets did not reach the fairgrounds until one o'clock the following morning. The same day he wrote his father indicating that they would be used to drill recruits and volunteers and would be made officers as soon as companies could be trained and organized. He was still impatiently waiting for his commission from North Carolina and added, "I would leave here tomorrow if my commission in the N.C. Forces were in my hands. I think I ought to go there in preference to the Va. [Forces]."[3]

There is only one other extant letter from Harry while he was stationed at the Camp of Instruction in Richmond. He had learned from a fellow cadet that his father was in the city. The note was brief and undated. On the back of the single folded sheet was the address:

H. K. Burgwyn Esq.
Exchange Hotel
Polit[e]ness of   Richmond
Major T. J. Jackson   Va.[4]

Earlier, Major Jackson had rendered Harry another favor. He had written for him a letter of recommendation to Leroy P. Walker, secretary of war of the Confederate States of America. Jackson assessed Cadet Burgwyn as follows: "Sir—the object of this letter is to recommend Cadet H. K. Burgwyn, of North Carolina, for a commission in the Artillery of the Southern Confederacy. Mr. B. is not only a high-tone Southern gentleman, but, in consequence of the highly practical as well as scientific character of his mind, he possesses qualities well calculated to make him an ornament, not only to artillery, but to any branch of the military service."[5]

Available records do not indicate how long Harry remained in Richmond, but he must shortly have been transferred to North Carolina, for on 22 May a resolution was mailed to him by the LaFayette Light Infantry expressing unanimous appreciation of "the benefits received by the very excellent lessons in drill given them by Captain H. K. Burgwin, Jr., during their sojourn at Camp Ellis at Raleigh." As further evidence of their respect and esteem, the company resolved to present him with a dress sword suitably inscribed.[6]

Just the day before—on 21 May—Captain Burgwyn had reached the town of Jefferson, in Ashe County, North Carolina, where he had been sent to recruit a company of mountain men from that northwestern section of the state. He had traveled by train to Statesville, going by way of Salisbury, and then by hired buggy to Jefferson. Harry had enjoyed his seventy-mile, two-day drive through the foothills and up into the mountains. The foothill country reminded him of the Occoneechee Neck "except that ours is richer & has the appearance of low bottom lands while this has more the appearance of high table country." He wrote his mother on 21 May, "The people up here appear to be good natured, easy [going] people with not a superfluity of energy & rather disposed to take the world as it is." Harry liked what he saw: "We crossed the Yadkin near Wilkesboro & just before crossing it I saw a very pretty mountain cottage & some very fine level bottom land. It was a very pretty place & the land was very fine. If I had any money to invest & could not think of any better way I believe I would purchase a farm of one or two hundred acres in these mountains somewhere & then raise stock on it." Harry was so impressed with the beauty of northwestern North Carolina that he could not resist this final observation: "After this war is over I intend to get a pair of saddle bags & come to this part of the state, buy a good horse & travel all over it."[7]

But his delight in the beauty of the countryside was tempered by his bitterly frustrating experience in recruiting mountain men. In a letter to his sister Maria, written on 27 May, he indicated that regulars could be recruited only if Governor Ellis refused to receive any more volunteer companies of one-year provisionals. "If he does receive them," Harry added, "then I look upon my chance of getting regulars as so small that I would not be surprised if I came to Raleigh either to recommend a draft—to try to recruit elsewhere—or solicit a staff appointment or go in the artillery & get stationed at Fort Macon. For if the same reluctance exists in other parts of the State to enlisting for the war, I can tell the Gov. that he will not be able to get 10,000 regulars. All will, in preference, go as 12 months volunteers." If he was able to raise his company, he hoped to take it to Raleigh to drill, "it being utterly impossible to do so here."[8]

Harry's patience was wearing thin. Only a month earlier he and his fellow cadets had made the long march to Staunton with enthusiasm and high expectations—thirsting for combat and glory. Now he was completely isolated from the rest of the world, wasting his time and energies in a fruitless cause. If he could not recruit a regular company, he would join one. On 28 May he fired off a letter to his father: "I am trying to get the appointment of Major in Major (now Col.) Munford [Montford] Sidney Stokes' regiment. Dr. Coxe—Mr. Rives—& Mr. George Bower of this place have all written Major Stokes commending me & I think you might do something by seeing him & showing my recommendations."[9]

But the appointment failed to materialize. By 2 June Harry had about given up hope. In a letter to his mother he sadly concluded:

> I have been here now nearly two weeks & have endeavored to see as many persons as possible. I have attended public meetings called together for the express purpose of getting volunteers; at each of these I have made public speeches & private explanations. [The] sum total of my efforts equals the names of 2 men who are from Virginia & are undecided as to finally joining in my Company. I hope I am not easily discouraged & hope that my patriotism is far from being exhausted but a reflecting mind must institute sooner or later the inquiry, if it takes two

weeks time & great trouble to secure 2 uncertain men how long
will it take to get 64. . . . It is the opinion of my friends & Col.
Bower that I can not get my full Company. I wish you would
read this over to father & ask him to write me what to do.
Could he not get a staff appointment for me such as aid to a
Brigadier Genrl or Major Genrl. or such as that. Would it not be
better for me to get changed to the Artillery Corps & get sent to
Fort Macon or do anything in preference to wearing out my
time in useless efforts to induce the lazy mountaineers to enlist for the war.[10]

Harry must have left Ashe County a few days later. His movements
between then and 5 July, the day he was given command of the Camp
of Instruction at Camp Carolina near Raleigh (known as Crabtree),
are not clear. The first entry in his journal, begun on 27 August, tells
of his election as lieutenant colonel of the Twenty-sixth Regiment
"after being disappointed in the organization of the 12th Reg."[11]
How long, if at all, he was attached to the Twelfth is not clear, but
it was organized at Garysburg on 15 May 1861 and mustered into
Confederate service three days later. On 22 May the regiment left
Garysburg by rail for Richmond.[12] Between 18 April and 22 May, nine
companies (mostly from eastern North Carolina) had been organized
and ordered to Garysburg, where they were assigned to the Twelfth
Regiment.[13]

If indeed Harry was involved with the Twelfth, he must have gone
almost directly to Garysburg from Richmond in late April or early
May,[14] from there to Camp Ellis at Raleigh, and then on to Ashe
County. Governor Ellis placed him in command of the Camp of Instruction at Camp Carolina on 5 July 1861.[15] Harry was presumably
promoted to the rank of major at the same time, for on 10 July, following the death of Governor Ellis (7 July), he ordered the Guilford
men to march under arms to the Executive Mansion "to act as guard
to the Gov.'s Remains." He signed this order as "Major Commanding
Camp of Instruction."[16]

The record of Harry's activities, and those of his father, for the remainder of the year 1861 shows the almost insurmountable problems caused by the exigencies of the war. The governmental pro-
cesses of the Confederacy, whose constitutional commitment to the
principle of states rights proved to be anathema to cohesive cen-
tralized authority, were doomed to indecision, confusion, delay, and
constant frustration. The state governments were no less confused.
The division of authority and responsibility between their respective

capitals and Richmond was a source of constant annoyance, which worsened as the war progressed. In the light of these problems, North Carolina's contribution to the war effort was particularly remarkable.

The untimely death of Governor Ellis on 7 July 1861 was probably hastened by his inordinate preoccupation with the war effort. Slowly dying of consumption, the governor worked extremely hard in the early months of 1861.[17] He displayed a rare capacity for executive leadership in time of crisis. Careful not to preempt undelegated authority, he moved with foresight and precision. Even before final passage of the $300,000 appropriation measure by the General Assembly on 8 January, Ellis had contacted Joseph R. Anderson and Company (Tredegar Iron Works) in Richmond for estimates on the cost of an armory and for prices on cannon, shot, and shells.[18] On 27 December the company supplied the requested information in considerable detail.[19] Just as "in dead earnest" characterized Harry Burgwyn's reaction to the possibility of war, so did it apply to Governor Ellis. Even before Lincoln's call for troops on 15 April 1861, his published correspondence is filled with references attesting to his initiatives on behalf of North Carolina.

On 12 January, Major Daniel Harvey Hill and Colonel Charles C. Tew submitted to the governor a list of arms and munitions of war for purchase at an estimated cost of $242,405. The list included a variety of items from breech-loading rifles, rifle muskets, and revolvers to batteries of rifled cannon, balls, shells, grape, friction primers, cartridge boxes, bayonet scabbards, swords, knapsacks, tents, lead, percussion caps, and two powder magazines. Only a little over a year earlier, the governor had reported to a correspondent, "Fifteen hundred flint and steel rifles and some two thousand flint and steel muskets, together with a small number of pistols and cannon, are the only fire arms now to be found in our armories, and these, for all practical purposes, may be considered as almost useless."[20]

Governor Ellis selected Charles C. Lee as his agent and on 19 January instructed him to "proceed North, stopping at Richmond, Va., Baltimore, Wilmington Del. Philadelphia, New York, New Haven, Springfield, Hartford, and such other places as you may think desirable for the purposes herein stated."[21] Out of this trip came many purchase orders matched by an equal number of delays and much correspondence. The sudden and inordinate demand for war materiel from so many different quarters was the real problem. On 22 January, Lee wrote Ellis that "I find it is next to impossible to get anybody to fix a definite time for the delivery of articles the demand being so great." On 28 January Eli Whitney, Jr., of Whitneyville, Connecticut (near New Haven), told Lee that "I can furnish arms up to the time that a State secedes—after that time I could not send arms to such State. I can furnish 400 to 500 of the Mississippi Rifles (model of 1842 like sampel) *now*."[22]

But on 2 February there was good news for the governor. J. R. Anderson and Company (Tredegar) of Richmond agreed to furnish the state with four six-pounder and four twelve-pounder brass guns and four twenty-four pounder howitzer guns with necessary carriages and linking, as well as two ten-inch and two eight-inch Columbiads, all with carriages.[23]

Two days later the Ordnance Office in Washington acknowledged that "334 long range rifles, with swords bayonets and appendages, have been ordered to be forwarded to the State from the U.S. Armory at Harper's Ferry, Va. The whole being equivalent to 453 7/13 Muskets—there remains a balance due to the State, of 9/13ths of a Musket." On 16 March, E. I. DuPont de Nemours Co. acknowledged receipt of a Bank of North Carolina draft on the Merchants Bank of New York for $3,825 covering a shipment of powder. But time was running out. Within a month, in response to Lincoln's call for troops, Ellis would reply, "You can get no troops from North Carolina."[24]

Ellis's accomplishments on behalf of North Carolina are best seen in two letters written to President Jefferson Davis. On 25 April he reported the seizure of Forts Macon, Johnston, and Caswell together with his opinion as to their relative strength and importance. He also reported the seizure of the United States Arsenal at Fayetteville with its thirty-seven thousand stand of arms and arms-making equipment. He concluded this letter, "The people of my State are now thoroughly united and will adopt the speediest method of union with the Confederate States."[25] Two days later he wrote:

> The State is to all intents practically out of the Old Union, and we are deciding the speediest mode of giving legal sanction to this State of facts. Unexampled unanimity prevails and we will be a member of the Confederate States by the 20th May. . . . All the lights have been extinguished on the Coast. Vessels have been sunk in Ocracoche Inlet and a fleet of armed vessels (small) is now being fitted out to protect our grain crops lying on the inland waters of the No. East part of the State. A good Ship Canal connects those waters with the Chesapeake at Norfolk.
>
> Beaufort Harbor, protected by Fort Macon is a most eligible point for privateering &c. Dept[h] of water on the bar is from 17

to 21 ft. We have on these waters some bold and Skilful Seamen who are ready to go out as privateers at once. The forms required in procuring letters of Marque present a great obstacle. Had you an authorized agent here who could deliver letters and receive the bonds &c. the work would be greatly facilitated. The enemy's commerce between N. York and all the West Indies and South American ports could be cut off by privateers on the coast of No. Ca.[26]

On 29 April, he issued an order through John F. Hoke, adjutant general, to Colonel Elwood Morris, engineer, "to proceed to Ocracoke and Hatteras, plan and construct fortifications. To employ hand vessels and use all powers necessary to carry out this enterprise." On 30 April, the Bank of Yanceyville tendered the state of North Carolina "a loan of twenty-five thousand dollars for the use of the state in its present emergency in Equiping and raising Volunteers for the defence of Southern rights." And on 30 April, General William H. C. Whiting, from his coast defense headquarters at Wilmington, reported that "the secretary of war of the Confederate States has directed the transfer to North Carolina of 20 thirteen pds cannonade guns from the Virginia navy yard for flank defences of Forts Macon & Caswell & for defence of the line of the [Neuse] against [land expeditions]."[27]

On 1 May, the governor addressed the opening session of the General Assembly. Declaring that "the right now asserted by the constituted authorities of that government, to use military force for the purpose of coercing a State to remain in the Union against its will, finds no warrant in the Constitution," Ellis proceeded to demonstrate that neither the Declaration of Independence nor the Constitution gave or intended to give such authority to the central government.[28] He was convinced that he did not "mistake the people" in refusing President Lincoln's call for troops.[29] Their indignation, he asserted, was effectively demonstrated by "the alacrity with which they have sprung to arms—outstripping the slow forms of law, and enabling me to assemble an army from the plough and the work shops, in less time than it has required to convene the General Assembly."[30]

But Ellis did not feel that existing laws were adequate for the emergency and urged the raising and organization of ten regiments to serve for the duration of the war. Of the $300,000 appropriation for arming the state made at the last session of the General Assembly, he had expended $35,320.55, but outstanding contracts would add approximately $25,000 more. Because the state was presently provided with arms, primarily gained by the seizure of the United States Arsenal at Fayetteville, he recommended that the balance of the appropriation be used for the preparation and manufacture of arms and munitions of war. Ellis expressed appreciation to the governors of Virginia and South Carolina for their timely assistance in "placing our fortifications on the sea coast in a defencible condition" and added, "I cheerfully reciprocated this favor to the extent of my ability by sending to the Governor of Virginia a [p]ortion of the arms in our possession, and which could conveniently be spared." On the assumption that North Carolina would secede from the Union and join the Confederate States, the governor recommended the calling of a convention, whose action "should be final."[31]

On the same day he wired President Davis: "Convention bill passed also a resolution authorizing me to send troops to Virginia at once without limit. Our mint at Charlotte will coin for the Confederate Government if desired. Ships of war are hovering on our coast near the Cape Fear—Design unknown. I am preparing to manufacture percussion caps, will succeed. More troops are offering than we can provide for."[32]

The act calling the convention authorized the governor to schedule the election of delegates for 13 May. There were to be 120 of them, and they were to convene in Raleigh on Monday, 20 May.[33] The legislature then authorized the governor to enlist and organize fifty thousand volunteers for twelve months' service and ten regiments of state troops for the duration of the war. To meet such heavy organizational expense the state was authorized to issue bonds in an amount not to exceed $5,000,000. These funds were quickly committed, and the governor notified the convention on 27 May, one week after the Ordinance of Secession, that an additional $6,500,000 in bonds would be necessary to finance the first year of the war.[34]

Colonel John F. Hoke, adjutant general of the state, was entrusted with the organization of the volunteers, but the act providing for the ten regiments of state troops stipulated the appointment of a special adjutant general for their organization and training. Governor Ellis selected Colonel James Green Martin for this important assignment. A graduate of West Point, Colonel Martin was serving as quartermaster at Fort Riley when the war began. He had fought in the Mexican War and lost his right arm at Churubusco. On 14 June 1861, he resigned his commission and tendered his services to the state of North Carolina.[35] The following month, Hoke resigned his office to assume command of the Thirteenth Regiment of volunteers, and

Governor Henry Toole Clark appointed General Martin as his successor. The legislature ratified his appointment in September.[36]

Although Ellis was dying in the last months of his administration he was in command until the last. Raw volunteers were pouring by the thousands into inadequately prepared and staffed training camps. Equipment, with the exception of the arms seized at Fayetteville, was virtually nonexistent, and the coastal defenses were of antiquated construction without guns, ammunition, or trained personnel. Communications were flooding into the governor's office from all directions. When Governor John Letcher of Virginia was not calling for help, Jefferson Davis or Robert E. Lee was.

With more exasperation than despair, the governor wired the Confederate secretary of war, Leroy P. Walker, on 17 May: "I have already sent nine thousand five hundred (9500) muskets to Richmond. Can't possibly spare more. Virginia has already more guns than men. North Carolina has not. I must beg of you to accept four (4) regiments twelve (12) months men, they are now in camp. Two (2) regiments are on their way to Richmond. Please answer."[37]

A week later, Henry King Burgwyn, Sr., in Richmond at the time, sent an urgent message to Ellis in support of Governor Letcher's plea for more troops. Virginia was being threatened with invasion from two points:

> I have just seen Govr Letcher, he desires me to say he is much in want of more small arms. Some of the Troops from Georgia & the South have appeared here without arms. He asks for 6 to 7.000 more. Virg[ini]a is threatened with invasion from two points, simultaneously; at one, Alexandria, 5000 are already landed & in possession with demonstrations of advance; at the other, Old Point & Hampton, the enemy are rapidly strength'g themselves. Govr Letcher earnestly desires a concentration of at least 5000 men at Suffolk, to command the junction of both R Roads & to support Norfolk, he will send you drill masters at once to *that* point, some are already there. There should be a still larger force at Weldon & Garys[burg] as a reserve, ready to reinforce either Richmond or Norfolk.[38]

Although North Carolina was reluctant to leave the Union, her people supported the Southern Confederacy with a rare display of unity and enthusiasm. It would not always be so, but in the early months of the war, party differences were forgotten and the governor's office operated in an atmosphere of patriotism. In naming John F. Hoke and J. G. Martin as adjutant generals and Major John Devereux as quartermaster general, Ellis had made excellent appointments. On 21 April 1861 he appointed Major William H. C. Whiting "Inspector General in charge of the defence of the State of N.C."[39] Whiting, a graduate of West Point and a trained engineer, had worked on the Cape Fear River in 1856–57. He was admirably suited to study the state's coastal defenses. Although he was on this assignment hardly a month, Whiting made a prophetic report to Governor Ellis in which he strongly emphasized the necessity for establishing a flotilla defense of Fort Macon and the inland waters against enemy attack and penetration.

The month of June 1861 was to be the governor's last. He had lived to see the organization of fifteen regiments with at least fifteen more being actively recruited.[40] He had also witnessed the launching of the state's little gunboat squadron, often referred to as the "mosquito fleet." On 20 June 1861, in a letter to Christopher G. Memminger, treasurer of the Confederacy, the governor confided: "I shall leave here tomorrow for the Red Sulphur Springs Va. My labors have broken down my health and I am forced to leave business for a few weeks. . . . Business will go on as usual till my return."[41] He must have started on his last journey with a sense of satisfaction and accomplishment, for, under trying circumstances, he had done well.

Events of the summer of 1861 proved to be both ill-timed and ill-planned. North Carolina was not ready for war. Following the death of Governor Ellis on 7 July, Henry Toole Clark had to assume his new administrative reponsibilities in a time of crisis and deal with a central government yet untried and without clear direction. On 28–29 August, the blow fell. Forts Clark and Hatteras, guarding Hatteras Inlet, were forced to surrender, almost without a fight, to a combined army and navy assault under the joint command of Major General Benjamin F. Butler and Commodore S. H. Stringham.[42] This loss was a severe blow to the safety of North Carolina and to the ultimate security of Richmond, for the inlet was the key to the Pamlico and Albemarle sounds. Roanoke Island, Fort Macon, and the defenses of New Bern were opened to direct naval attack and naval support for assault troops. The fall of Hatteras would prove to be a major disaster, for the loss of Roanoke Island on 8 February 1862 opened the way to the Norfolk defenses, "unlocking two sounds, eight rivers, four canals and two railroads."[43] Elizabeth City fell two days later, and within a week the drive to New Bern was begun.

The fall of Hatteras was hailed as a "glorious victory" for the North, which had not yet recovered from the rout of General Irvin McDowell at the First Battle of Bull Run in Virginia on 21 July.

Admiral David D. Porter later wrote, "This was our first naval victory, indeed our first victory of any kind, and should not be forgotten. The Union cause was then in a depressed condition, owing to the reverses it had experienced. The moral effect of this affair was very great, as it gave us a foothold on Southern soil and possession of the Sounds of North Carolina if we choose to occupy them. It was a deathblow to blockade running in that vicinity, and ultimately proved one of the most important events of the war."[44]

Although North Carolina and the South never overcame the loss of these strategic waters, it was not a mortal blow. But it did place Richmond and its rail connections to the South in constant jeopardy, thereby requiring the protective presence of Confederate troops at all times in southside Virginia and northeastern North Carolina. It was in this area, between Kinston, North Carolina, and Petersburg, Virginia, that Harry Burgwyn would spend most of his active service.

During the months of July and August 1861, the Twenty-sixth North Carolina Regiment was mobilized and trained at Camp Carolina, the Camp of Instruction, which was located at Crabtree about three miles north of Raleigh. This regiment consisted of ten companies from central and western North Carolina. The companies had been organized in their home counties and reported to the Camp of Instruction as follows:

1. [Co. A]—Jeff Davis Mountaineers, Ashe County;
     Captain Andrew N. McMillan.

2. [Co. B]—Waxhaw Jackson Guards, Union County;
     Captain J. J. C. Steele.

3. [Co. C]—Wilkes Volunteers, Wilkes County;
     Captain Abner R. Carmichael.

4. [Co. D]—Wake Guards, Wake County;
     Captain Oscar R. Rand.

5. [Co. E]—Independent Guards, Chatham County;
     Captain W. S. Webster.

6. [Co. F]—Hibriten Guards, Caldwell County;
     Captain Nathaniel P. Rankin.

7. [Co. G]—Chatham Boys, Chatham County;
     Captain William S. McLean.

8. [Co. H]—Moore Independents, Moore County;
     Captain William P. Martin.

9. [Co. I]—Caldwell Guards, Caldwell County;
   Captain Wilson S. White.

10. [Co. K]—Pee Dee Wild Cats, Anson County;
    Captain James C. Carraway.[45]

Major Harry Burgwyn was in command of the Camp of Instruction, having been appointed to that position by Governor Ellis on 5 July. This young commander, a strict disciplinarian, was undoubtedly viewed with apprehension by the raw recruits. One in particular, Corporal John R. Lane,[46] Company G, from Chatham County, was struck by the manner and bearing of the colonel. Lane's first impressions were lasting, and later he recalled:

We took the train at Company Shops (now Burlington) for Raleigh; arriving at this place, the company marched out to Camp Crab Tree, a Camp of Instruction, and were assigned our position in camp a little after dark. On the next morning when we awoke, we saw the sentinels at their posts and realized that we were indeed in the war. Immediately after roll call—but there was no roll call in our company—Major H. K. Burgwyn, Commander of the Camp of Instruction, sent down to Captain W. S. McLean, demanding the reason for his failure to report his company.

Before the excitement occasioned by his message had subsided among the commissioned officers, an order came for a corporal and two men to report at once at headquarters. Captain McLean selected Corporal Lane, his lowest subaltern officer, and two of the most soldierly-looking men, S. S. Carter and W. G. Carter, to report to Major Burgwyn.

Accordingly, these three worthies appeared before the commandant, wondering whether they were going to be promoted, hanged or shot. This was our first sight of the commanding officer, who appeared though young, to be a youth of authority, beautiful and handsome; the flash of his eye and the quickness of his movements betokened his bravery. At first sight I both feared and admired him. He gave us the following order: "Corporal, take these men and thoroughly police this Camp; don't leave a watermelon rind or anything filthy in Camp."

This cheering order completely knocked the starch out of our shirts and helped greatly to settle us down to a soldier's life. The cleanliness of the camp was reported by the officer of the day as being perfect. You may be sure our officers reported the company promptly after that.[47]

The Twenty-sixth North Carolina was formally organized on 27 August. The ten companies were ranked alphabetically from "A" through "I," with the tenth company, the Pee Dee Wild Cats, being assigned the letter "K." To complete the regimental organization, the company officers elected Zebulon Baird Vance, colonel and commanding officer; Harry K. Burgwyn, Jr., lieutenant colonel; and Abner B. Carmichael, major.[48]

On that same day Harry Burgwyn commenced his war journal. The first page bore the caption:

> Journal of Events from Aug 27th 1861 to
> *Strictly Private*
> H. K. Burgwyn, Jr.
> Lt. Col. 26th Regmt N.C.V.[49]

The second page, to emphasize the confidentiality of the journal, was blank except for the words "Strictly Private." Harry's first entry bore the date of 27 August 1861. It was brief, to the point, and meaningful: "I was to day elected Lt. Col. of the 26th Regmt. N. C. Troops. I am now 19 years 9 months & 27 days old & probably the youngest Lt. Col. in the Confederate or U. S. service. The command of the Camp of Instruction was given me on the 5th July & after being disappointed in the organization of the 12th Reg. I have been elected to a position in this. May Almighty God lend me his aid in discharging my duty to him & to my country."[50]

He did not have long to wait. The Twenty-sixth received orders the following day "to get ready to leave as soon as possible—the taking of Hatteras has changed our destination from Virginia to the eastern part of our state." On 1 September Harry recorded: "All ready to start & anxious for a brush with the enemy. I am myself very desirous for the Colonel [Vance] to take charge & relieve me of what is truly a very [great] responsibility. Took leave of all at home. Father is in New Bern where he was sent by the Gov. to take possession of some arms which are supposed to be on board of an English vessel now laying off Beaufort."[51]

The regiment was ordered to Bogue Banks in support of Fort Macon, which commanded the harbor entrance to Beaufort. Traveling by way of New Bern, the Twenty-sixth reached the coast and was busily engaged in preparing its encampment by 6 September. It was there that Harry had his first "brush with the enemy." He reported, "I must not forget to say that of all the nights I ever spent in the neighborhood of musketoes last night was the worst. No sleep visited my weary eyes until very late & oh the musketoes how they did trouble me." His complaint concluded with the obviously satisfying comment: "The camp is named after father—Camp Burgwyn."[52]

On the same day, Harry's father, on board the British ship *Alliance,* then at anchor off Beaufort, sent an urgent message to Governor Clark on the inadequate defenses of Fort Macon:

> I learn from *undoubted authority* that it is *known* on board the *Rinaldo* that it is the intention of [the] U.S. Squadron to attack Fort Macon with a very large force & that, too, in the course of a very few days; & further that the unanimous opinion on board *that ship* is that the fort in its present condition will be wholly unable to withstand an attack made by such a force as will probably be bro[ugh]t against it (this I get confidentially). Such *is* & has been my opinion from the first. There is not a single experienced gunner in the Fort, not a rifled cannon, nor mortar, only one ten inch & one eight inch Columbiad & these in the hands of raw troops. I feel deeply for our friend Bridgers who is perfectly competent to direct & maintain the defence if he is properly supplied; as it is, it is a sacrifice. There should be another regiment ordered to the Bogue Banks at once or to Carolina City—not Morehead. The 2 Columbiads from Beacon Isl[and] should be sent to Fort Macon. I have written to Pres[iden]t Davis the state of things here, & asked for 50–100 experienced gunners, for 2 or more rifled guns, for ordnance officers. There is not one at the Fort (of experience I mean). . . .
>
> Col[onel] Bridgers' plan of defence is admirable & I would entrust him with the command of the Fort in this emergency as soon as anyone. I should like to see a Carolinian in command. A locomotive should be kept here *all the time* to supply the telegraph. There is wire at Goldsboro (bro[ugh]t by this ship) to lay a telegraph hence to Raleigh.[53]

The early months of Governor Clark's administration must have been extremely frustrating. Even in normal times, several months would have been required for the smooth functioning of any new administration; but to have been thrust into an executive role in a state just committed to war, in a nation newly formed, untried, poorly organized and financed, was an impossible situation. The governor had the support of the convention and the General Assembly, as well as of the Military and Naval Board under the chairmanship of Warren Winslow.[54] In the early months of the war, Clark enjoyed the enthusiastic and patriotic support of the people, which served as a sustaining force until military requirements and operations could be organized on a more professional basis.

The governor did not want for advice. It poured in from all sides, modestly at first but in torrents after the fall of Hatteras. Much of it was good, and all of it was urgent. The problems with respect to the coastal defenses were obvious to many, but the resources necessary to their solution—supplies, ordnance, trained manpower, and competent leaders—were not available. The division of responsibility between the state and the Confederate governments relative to military expenditures further complicated the situation. In early September the House and Senate passed resolutions requesting Governor Clark to submit to them a full account of the fortifications and arms of the state, as well as pertinent correspondence of several of the army and naval officers concerned with the defense of eastern North Carolina. The General Assembly was obviously alarmed, but the governor was unable to supply certain information because of the divided authority between the Confederate and state governments.[55]

Although the General Assembly had appropriated a substantial sum for the conduct of the war, finances were a matter of constant concern, especially before the responsibility for expenditures was clearly delineated between the Confederate government and the state governments. It was early determined that North Carolina must assume direct responsibility for clothing her own troops. During the transitional period between state and Confederate authority, on 14 October 1861, the Bank of Wilmington declined to lend the state any more funds. The bank had loaned $200,000 to the state and $40,000 to the town of Wilmington against an advance of "50 thousand dollars placed by the Confederate Govt in the hands of the Gov-[ernor] of this state for the purpose of placing the southern part of our Coast in a state of defence and [on] which 50 dollars has not been yet applied to that object and as a consequence the work must have ere this have stopped but for the advances made by the Banks here to the town."[56]

Although expenditures for ordnance and supplies were heavy,[57] payments to the soldiers and laborers constituted the gravest problem in the early months of the war. Captain Dimmock, in charge of the engineering department on Roanoke Island, for example, appealed on behalf of the free Negro laborers:

Not knowing under whose immediate jurisdiction the payment
& clothing of the Negro laborers upon the coast defenses of

North Carolina may come I address you[r] Exc[ellenc]y directly, hoping it is in your power to correct a condition of affairs, among the needy & ragged Negroes, that demands prompt action.

Many of the Negro laborers engaged upon the defensive works at this point—all I believe of whom are free—were secured many months since and have worked at Beacon Island, Oregon Inlet & now here without having received either salary or clothing. A miserable squalid set, they traverse the leads, with their wheelbarrows, without a sufficient amount of dirty rags upon their persons to prevent indecent exposure. With scarcely an extra shirt &, I believe, entirely without blankets, these hands were taken during & before May last & led to believe their days of occupation, upon the coast defenses, would be but few—hence nearly all came unprepared for so long a term & entirely unprovided, even if they had been able to have rendered themselves comfortable. The alacrity with which these poor creatures work, & the sadness of their appearance, has weighed upon me like a nightmare, since I took charge of the defenses of this place, & now induces me to urge your Exc[ellenc]y to have them clothed at once & their wages paid, if only in part. Many of them I would have sent home, despite of the pressing necessity for their aid, but for their nakedness and want of money.[58]

Hardly less depressing but equally urgent was a letter from Colonel Zebulon Vance, of the Twenty-sixth North Carolina, stationed at Camp Burgwyn on Bogue Banks:

I am sorry to say that a portion of my regiment are almost in a state of mutiny on account of the non-reception of their pay—most of them are suffering for the most ordinary articles of everyday use which they are unable to purchase, whilst many others left behind them destitute and dependant families who are daily appealing to them for aid. Even such articles as fresh fish tho' both plentiful & cheap here they are unable to buy—this state of things cannot be endured much longer by men who have nearly four months pay due them. If not relieved soon I fear I shall not be able to maintain discipline.[59]

Lieutenant Colonel Harry Burgwyn was obviously aware of this situation, but it is doubtful that he fully comprehended the long-range impact of the loss of Hatteras upon North Carolina and the South. He was primarily concerned with the condition of the camp and with the training and care of his men. Nevertheless, he was concerned about an overall strategy of defense for that part of the coast commanded by Fort Macon. To the privacy of his journal he confided a perceptive analysis on 17 September:

> I will here detail at some little length the plan which I have formed with myself to defend the Coast. There are two points which in my opinion are the key points of these coasts. One is at Capt. Pender's battery where both regiments are now stationed & the other is a position similar to this but about 2 miles or possibly not so much nearer to Fort [Macon]. . . . My plan is to place the 7th Regmt. at that position allowing us to retain our position here. Then place each company of the 26th & 7th Regmts. 300 yards apart varying the distance slightly so as to place each company behind high sand banks. The two regiments would thus occupy a line of 6000 yds. or about 3 1/2 miles. The entire distance between us & the Fort is about 6 miles thus leaving only two and a half miles unguarded which is in range of the heaviest columbiads & rifled cannon of the Fort. . . .
>
> The advantages of thus scattering our forces so that by making each company at night guard the 300 paces it has to defend, we would have a chain of sentinels for 6 miles whereas now we have them for only 2000 yds. 2ndly, by making each company construct bomb proof shelters & a fine road for itself behind the sand banks; the danger from the enemy's shells is absolutely null & that great desideratum, a military road to secure our connection, is obtained. . . . I am field officer of the day with only 25 men under me. An unnecessary waste of rank it appears to me. I greatly lament that I have been unable to excite more attention to the necessity of aiding nature by art & rendering our security perfect.[60]

While Harry was concerned with the defense of his limited sphere of responsibility on Bogue Banks, General Richard C. Gatlin was preoccupied with the defense of three hundred miles of North Carolina coastline. Gatlin had hardly been notified of his appointment as brigadier general by the War Department and assigned to the command of the Department of North Carolina and its coast defenses on 19 August before he was confronted with the loss of Hatteras, the key to the defense of the Pamlico area north. Until he was relieved from duty seven months later because of ill health, Gatlin's report on "Affairs, generally, in North Carolina, August 20, 1861–January 11, 1862," appears as a document of despair, a monument to frustration, an indictment of the War Department in Richmond, or a combination of all three. The net result was too little and too late for the defense of eastern North Carolina.

General Gatlin did all in his power to secure assistance from the War Department but to little avail. Threatened from the north and the east, Richmond, the seat of government, had to take precedence. One could hardly fault Gatlin for his basic strategy, namely, "to place a sufficient number of troops at the exposed points, to hold the enemy in check should he land on the coast, and to establish a reserve of four or six regiments at Goldsborough, to be sent to the coast only upon the landing of the enemy." He recognized the need for placing obstructions in the rivers and for constructing gunboats for use in Pamlico Sound. On 7 September Brigadier General J. R. Anderson was sent to North Carolina to take charge of the coast defenses of the state. Recognizing that one man could not properly oversee the entire coast, Gatlin requested that two additional brigadier generals be sent down so that the coastal defenses could be divided into three commands, conforming to the broken character of the tidewater country. Brigadier General D. H. Hill was then assigned to the command of all that part of the coast lying north of the White Oak River. It was not until 21 December that General Henry A. Wise was placed in command of the District of the Albemarle; General Hill, the District of Pamlico; and General Anderson, the District of Cape Fear. General Hill, however, was relieved by Brigadier General Lawrence O'B. Branch the latter part of November.[61]

The assignment of General Wise to the Albemarle District, following closely upon the appointment of General Branch to succeed Hill, must have occasioned bitter disappointment for Henry King Burgwyn, Sr., military aide to Governor Clark. He, too, aspired to a brigadier generalship and desired "to be appointed to command the defenses from the north line of Gen Anderson to Ocracoke Inlet. The other position ought to be again divided—I have refrained from pressing my claims heretofore because I had hoped for more scientific military men but after the app[ointmen]t of Mr. Branch I can no longer hope for this." Henry Burgwyn expressed his feelings in a long letter to his representative in the Confederate Congress, William N. H. Smith, on 16 December 1861. He asked the congressman to intervene with President Davis on his behalf, claiming that "I have been actively engaged as a volunteer at various times since August last in aiding Commodore Lynch—Col. Vance & others in the defense of Fort Macon, Bogue Banks, New Berne, etc." He felt that the command was "now entrusted to the youngest & probably the most inexperienced Brigdr in the service." He concluded:

> What we require *immediately* which certainly is in the power of the Presdt to afford us, is first to divide Gen. Branch's command into *at least* two sections of the coast & waters; three would be far better & place them under the command of proper officers. Next to send to the aid of each Brig. at least one experienced engineer, one ordnance & two or more artillery officers. It is impossible to make the defenses necessary without an engineer competent to this duty. And the artillery is of little use without experienced ordnance officers to prepare & attend to the munitions. Nor can the men be properly drilled to the great guns without artillery officers. Witness the consequence of a neglect of these things at Port Royal.[62]

On Christmas day, young Harry Burgwyn returned to duty near Morehead City after a severe case of typhoid fever. The following day, in a letter to his father, he reported that "Gen Gatlin told me that Gen Wise has command of Roanoke Island & a portion of our coast relieving Gen. Branch of that command. He supposed that they therefore regard the coast defenses of N.C. as divided in three parts—Gen. Anderson, Branch & Wise. I am much afraid that that will interfere with your prospects. Roanoke Island from what I hear will be taken without difficulty if the enemy attack it. I sincerely hope you may succeed for Branch is not competent."[63]

The Burgwyns were not alone in their disappointment with the turn of events as the year 1861 came to a close. Governor Clark had encountered considerable disappointment from the day he assumed office. Within days following the fall of Hatteras, news reached the mainland that the citizens of Hatteras Island had pledged their allegiance to Lincoln's government.[64] But worst of all, the governor was having problems with Richmond. Virginia was being favored to the detriment of North Carolina. He earnestly besought equitable treatment in a letter to Judah P. Benjamin, acting secretary of war, on 27 September 1861:

> Besides the arms sent to Virginia in the hands of our volunteers, we have sent to Virginia 13,500 stands of arms, and now we are out of arms, and our soil is invaded, and you refuse our request to send us back some of our own armed regiments to defend us, and we are left to chances of buying a few odd arms

which may be gathered up. We have disarmed ourselves to arm you, and now the additional grievance is added that our volunteers in Virginia are paid from the first step in the service, while volunteers who remained in this State are not to be paid thus.

The recent invasion compels us again to buy a Navy for our protection, not receiving it from the Confederate States. We are denied powder, on the ground that we have received more than any other state, without advertising to the fact that the powder has been made into cartridges and sent back to Virginia with every regiment, and now we are driven to the expense of our powder mill.[65]

Obviously stung by the criticisms leveled at his department, Secretary Benjamin replied to Governor Clark on 29 September. He was candid in both explaining and refuting the charges, not omitting criticism of the governor for his own failure to issue appropriate orders. In summary, the secretary made a masterful plea for a better understanding of the magnitude and complexity of the Confederacy's plight:

Pray consider that the war has recently assumed such formidable dimensions as to make it impossible that human beings can satisfy all the exigencies of all the people at every point that may be exposed or threatened with attack—In Missouri, in Kentucky, in Western Virginia, on the Potomac, in the peninsula below the city, on the whole Southern sea-board, in Western Texas, every where, ceaseless efforts and vigilance are required. I feel sure that in view of this extended field of labor you will rather be disposed to aid in patriotic effort to defend your own coast by hearty cooperation than to complain of neglect or injustice, which may possibly occur from the causes, but never from the absence of an earnest desire to do everything in our power in defence of your State.[66]

The problems affecting the relationship of North Carolina with the Confederate States of America were only beginning. The year 1862 would bring Zebulon Baird Vance to the fore in state government, and Harry Burgwyn would emerge as a highly competent regimental commander.

CHAPTER 8

THE DESCENT UPON NEW BERN

A curious languor seemed to hang over a divided America as the new year dawned. Both sides were making feverish preparations for continued warfare, but nothing seemed to happen. Still smarting from McDowell's ignominious rout at Bull Run, the people of the North clamored for a major victory in the field and an early termination of the war. The South, too, was impatient as her people expectantly awaited intervention by England and France.

But for Lieutenant Colonel Harry Burgwyn there was nothing but unremitting labor. Having just returned to active duty after a prolonged illness, Harry found "a great many deaths in my regiment, much sickness still & the discipline—wretched."[1] He immediately set to work and, from the headquarters of the Twenty-sixth at Camp Vance near Carolina City, wrote his mother on 3 January 1862 how busy he was: "What with being in command, drilling four hours a day—hearing recitations on tactics—attending to the building of the winters quarters & whatever else might come up my time has been very well occupied." His health was much improved, and "I attended a party on New Year's eve at Beaufort & there saw all the beauties of the burg. Alas poor Yorick, to the eye of so accomplished a judge, all exhibited failings & out of some 60 or 70 there was not one really pretty."[2]

During his illness Harry had failed to keep up the "Journal of Events," which he had commenced on 27 August 1861, the day he was elected lieutenant colonel of the Twenty-sixth. On 23 January 1862, he resumed, explaining:

> Since the events narrated in the previous pages I have been very
> sick with typhoid fever. I left Camp Wilkes[3] on the 24th of Oct.
> & remaining for a few days at Carolina City Hospital where
> I was continually dosed with Calomel by a drunken doctor
> whom I myself had recommended as surgeon to the Regm't., fa-
> ther came down & removed me to New Bern where under the
> care of Dr. Hughes I gradually grew better until the fever left
> me. During this time the great Federal Armada which was com-
> manded by Gen'l Sherman & Com. Dupont passed South & was

exposed to a very severe gale & the crew some 80 odd of the steamer *Union* which went ashore off Bogue Banks were captured by my regiment & sent to Raleigh. After remaining in Raleigh a week or ten days I went to Thornbury & stayed there another week, but on my return from there commenced having chills which so reduced me & weakened my strength as to detain me till the 23rd of December. I arrived here on the next day & on Christmas Day reported for duty. Hereafter I will be I hope more punctual in attending to the journal.[4]

Harry probably found considerable time for reading and reflection during his absence from camp. But during the early days of his illness it is doubtful that he was aware of certain changes in high command that would have a profound influence upon the future course of the war.

On 31 October, the aging General Winfield Scott, after a long and illustrious career in the United States Army, tendered his resignation to Secretary of War Cameron. He was succeeded by Major General George Brinton McClellan—thirty-four years old, ambitious, and "supposedly aggressive."[5] On the afternoon of the same day, General Robert E. Lee returned to Richmond from a disastrous campaign in western Virginia.[6] On 22 October, General Order No. 15, from the Adjutant and Inspector General's Office in Richmond, had established the Department of Northern Virginia consisting of three districts. Stonewall Jackson was named to command the Shenandoah Valley District, P. G. T. Beauregard the Potomac District, and Major General Theophilus H. Holmes the Aquia District. Jackson assumed command on 4 November.[7]

On 6 November Lee left Richmond for Charleston, South Carolina. He had been placed in command of the new Department of South Carolina, Georgia, and East Florida—and not a moment too soon, for the Federal fleet was on its way to Port Royal Sound.[8] Before long Lee would return to Virginia to command the Army of Northern Virginia. It would be under Lee that Harry Burgwyn would distinguish himself at Malvern Hill and Gettysburg.

One wonders if Harry saw the editorial in the 21 December 1861 issue of *Harper's Weekly*. It was captioned "The End and the Way" and read in part:

In order to convince the South that the struggle is hopeless on their part, that we must succeed in the end, and that their best interests will be promoted by a surrender, we must do two things—we must beat them in the field, and we must render the inconveniences of the war intolerable to the Southern people. . . . The measures which are being taken by Government to teach the South the cost of rebellion are of various kinds. The blockade is the first. . . . The sinking of stone-laden ships at the mouth of Southern harbors. . . . A necessary part of the blockade is the descent and occupation of the Mississippi River—from Cairo to New Orleans. If two hundred thousand men under General McClellan are needed for the operation, they will be forthcoming. We must hold Columbus, Memphis, Natchez, and New Orleans. We may hold simultaneously Hatteras, Port Royal, Savannah, Brunswick, Fernandina, and Pensacola. Thus encircled, the rebel-section will be within our grasp, and we can make the rebels feel what it is to be at war. . . . This, we take it, is the programme of the Government, as planned by Generals Scott and McClellan, and approved by Mr. Lincoln.[9]

In the same issue appeared another editorial on finances. It referred to the report of Salmon P. Chase, secretary of the treasury, who estimated that the war was costing $400 million a year, exclusive of the new war taxes. This estimate, the editor concluded, was "based on the hypothesis that the war will last another year. Mr. Chase hopes and believes that it will be over by mid-summer."[10] The reports of the War and Navy departments also appeared in the 21 December issue of *Harper's Weekly*. They were both arresting and foreboding. The secretary of war reported the strength of the army at 660,971 men, including 20,334 regulars. More than 640,000 men had volunteered for service within the year. The report of the secretary of navy was no less impressive: "When the vessels now building and purchased by every class are armed, equipped, and ready for service," the navy would consist of 212 vessels mounting 2,301 guns.[11]

On 25 December 1861, the day Harry returned to camp, the state convention, meeting in Raleigh, pledged, "No measure of loss, no sacrifice of life or property, no privation or want, or suffering, shall cause us to shrink from the performance of our whole duty in the achievement of our independence."[12] One wonders if the editor of *Harper's Weekly* read this resolution and comprehended the relative importance of will as opposed to might.

A few weeks earlier, an editorial opinion somewhat similar to that of *Harper's Weekly* appeared in the 30 November issue of the *Illustrated London News*. Alluding to the battle of Port Royal Sound on 7 November, in which a powerful Federal naval armada under Flag Officer Samuel F. DuPont had quickly overcome the defending forces, the editorial raised some perceptive questions about matters of strategic military significance facing the Confederates:

> It has been the fate of the border Slave States to act as a sort of breakwater to the fury of the Northern storm behind which the revolutionary Gulf States dwelt in safety and comparative repose. On the Northern frontier of Secessia was the "Shell" with which the South incased its softer and more vital parts. All attempts to break through that shell by a front attack have hitherto failed. But the fleet has accomplished what the unaided army could not. . . . The Confederates have to make head against a force of, say, 350,000 Federals pressing upon them on a line of 1500 miles, stretching from the Atlantic to the Missouri. Up to the present time they have done so with a fair amount of success. But can the Confederate Generals create new armies to watch every body of men whom the Federal fleet throw upon their almost undefended coast: Or can they detach a sufficient number of men from the frontier without leaving the road to Richmond, Nashville, and Memphis open to their foes? . . . If the South still preserves the advantage of great earnestness and singleness of purpose, the superior financial strength of the North begins to tell.[13]

In the late autumn of 1861, it is doubtful that Harry had so thorough a grasp of the overall situation. Had he read this editorial, he would have readily comprehended its significance, for he was well aware of North Carolina's inadequate coastal defenses. They had been penetrated in late August, when Hatteras fell, and were destined soon to be penetrated again.

The concluding statement of the editorial would have surely arrested Harry's attention. He could not speak for the South, but he was well aware of the "great earnestness and singleness of purpose" that had motivated his fellow North Carolinians since Lincoln's call for troops. The state had come far in a few short months. By January 1862, when Harry returned to his regiment, the state had armed, equipped, and transferred to the Confederate States Army forty-one regiments—twenty-eight for twelve months service, twelve for the duration of the war, and one for six months. In addition, several battalions and independent companies had been formed.[14]

Newspapers throughout the state regularly ran advertisements of the Quartermaster's Department, signed by John Devereux, assistant quartermaster, directing the sheriffs of the different counties to send blankets and clothing directly to the troops and inviting contract proposals for the manufacture of clothing and hats.[15] Relief societies for the soldiers were formed in many counties and towns. In the 15 January 1862 issue of the *North Carolina Standard,* quoting from the *Richmond Examiner,* North Carolina was ranked first among the eleven Confederate states in the amount of voluntary contributions made to the army by citizens of the several states. Out of a total of $1,515,898, North Carolina citizens had contributed $325,417; Alabama ranked second, with $317,600; Mississippi third, with $272,670; Virginia eighth, with $48,070; and finally Arkansas, with $950.

But Harry was primarily concerned about North Carolina's inadequate coastal defenses. In one letter to his mother in early January, he mentioned that "the people are much alarmed about Burnside. I shall look at the fortifications tomorrow." In another, he said: "We received tonight the news or rather received it as news that 24 Federal steamers were at Hatteras in addition to the usual numbers. It appears to be authentic coming as it does from more than one source. Whether it is for New Berne or Roanoke Island or some point on the S.C. or Georgia coast merely rendezvousing at Hatteras first I do not know. I am sorry to say that without having as yet seen the batteries I share in the general opinion that they can be taken or passed. It is possible that my opinion may be modified after seeing them."[16]

All of eastern North Carolina, indeed the South, had reason for grave apprehension, for Burnside's expedition was proceeding with almost flawless precision. In view of North Carolina's sad state of unpreparedness, the wintry gales off Cape Hatteras appeared to have been her most effective ally. Burnside was delayed a few days by stormy weather and the problem of getting his vessels over the swashes inside the inlet, but he was not stopped. It is interesting to follow his correspondence with the headquarters of the army in Washington from the time he was placed in command of the Department of North Carolina on 7 January 1862.

On that day, Major General George B. McClellan confirmed his verbal instructions to General Ambrose E. Burnside:

> Under the accompanying general order, constituting the Department of North Carolina, you will assume the command of the garrison at Hatteras Inlet. . . . Your first point of attack will be Roanoke Island and its dependencies. It is presumed that the Navy can reduce the batteries on the marshes and cover the landing of your troops on the main island. . . . Having occupied the

island and its dependencies you will at once proceed to the erection of batteries and defenses necessary to hold the position with a small force. . . .

The commodore [Flag-Officer Louis M. Goldsborough] and yourself having completed your arrangements in regard to Roanoke Island and the waters north of it you will please at once make a descent upon New Berne, having gained possession of which and the railroad passing through it you will at once throw a sufficient force upon Beaufort, and take the steps necessary to reduce Fort Macon and open that port. . . . When you seize New Berne you will endeavor to seize the railroad as far west as Goldsborough, should circumstances favor such a movement. . . . A great point would be gained in any event by the effectual destruction of the Wilmington and Weldon Railroad. . . . I would advise great caution in moving so far into the interior as upon Raleigh.[17]

On 13 January, from his base at Hatteras Inlet, Burnside advised McClellan that he had assumed command of the Department of North Carolina. On 26 January he reported that, in spite of severe weather, he had succeeded in getting most of his vessels over the bar by noon on the thirteenth. He confessed, however, that the water was shallower than he had expected so that "it has taken every vessel that has gone over from one to two days to cross, and some it will be entirely impossible to get over. It is positively necessary that we have sent us at once powerful tug-boats, drawing not over 6 or 6½ feet." He did not wish to meet the enemy until he had six to seven thousand men "in full position for battle." He complained about the difficulty of his assignment: "The utter barrenness of the shore, there being only a sand spit, which the high tides often cover, prevent any permanent landing. There is no timber to be had even for fuel, and the great difficulty in transporting men and baggage to and from the shore causes great delay."[18]

On 29 January Burnside assured McClellan of his readiness to advance on Roanoke Island although "we have been incessantly engaged in getting our vessels over the bar into the sound. . . . We have, however, at anchor in the sound this morning transportation for twelve regiments." This was no small feat, for he had been contending with the worst possible weather and had little if any help from the local pilots "either from unwillingness or incompetency."[19]

The abstract from the returns of the Department of North Carolina for the month of January 1862, Brigadier General Ambrose E. Burnside commanding, showed 12,829 officers and men present for duty in the following brigades: First (Foster's) Brigade, 4,363; Second (Reno's) Brigade, 3,697; Third (Parke's) Brigade, 2,867; Williams's Brigade, 1,902. On 3 February Burnside listed ten transports and eight gunboats as being at anchor in Pamlico Sound and capable of transporting approximately 9,000 men. He was ready to go. On the same day he issued General Order No. 5, admonishing the "soldiers to remember that they are here to support the Constitution and the laws, to put down rebellion, and to protect the persons and property of the loyal and peaceable citizens of the State." He concluded by expressing "fullest confidence in the valor and character of his troops" and added, "the commanding general looks forward to a speedy and successful termination of the campaign."[20]

He was not to be disappointed. Roanoke Island capitulated in a single day, on 8 February. Two days later General McClellan, not knowing of the victory, sent off a dispatch beginning: "My Dear Old Burn, I feel for you in your troubles, but you have borne yourself nobly in difficulties more trying than any that remain to you to encounter, and the same energy and pluck that has carried you through up to the present will take you through to the end."[21] But on 12 February McClellan was more enthusiastic: "We are all rejoiced to hear, through rebel sources, of the gallant capture of Roanoke Island and the rebel gunboats. . . . I hope that the effect has been produced of drawing the attention of the rebels toward Norfolk, etc., so that, after having fully secured what you have gained, you will, by rapid counter-movement be enabled to make the second attack [on New Bern] with every chance of success." Then he added the following comments:

> You will have heard of our marked success in Tennessee—the capture of Fort Henry—and the trip of our gunboats into Alabama.
>
> Everything goes well with us, but your success seems to be the most brilliant yet. I expect still more from you. While in the sound, please gain all possible information as to the possibility of attacking Norfolk from the south; that *may* prove to be the best blow to be struck. Although, as I am not yet quite prepared to secure it as it should be, it may be our best policy to defer that until you have accomplished all the original objects of the expedition, when with suitable reenforcements you may attack Norfolk to great advantage.[22]

On 20 February, in great spirits and with only enough time for "a few hasty words," McClellan disclosed that "everything from the west is thus far satisfactory, and your victory has created a profound impression." But with his usual caution, he added, "I still hope that you will be able to seize Goldsborough, though, in the uncertainty that exists in regard to the force of the enemy in front of you, I do not feel able to give you definite instructions. I feel sure that you will gain Beaufort."[23]

The Union forces were now on the move everywhere, and for good reason. On 27 January, to force immediate action on all fronts, Lincoln had issued the President's General War Order No. 1, declaring that "the 22d day of Feb., 1862, be the day for a general movement of the land and naval forces of the United States against the insurgent forces." A month later, Assistant Secretary of War John Tucker was authorized by the president "to procure at once the necessary steamers and sailing craft to transport the Army of the Potomac to its new field of operations." Within thirty-seven days from the date of this order, Tucker would charter 113 steamers and 188 schooners and 88 barges and would transport "to Fort Monroe 121,500 men, 14,592 animals, 1150 wagons, 44 batteries, 74 ambulances, besides pontoon bridges, telegraph materials, and the enormous quantity of equipage, etc., required for an army of such magnitude."[24] At long last, McClellan was on his way. Unhappily for him, the movement of his army from Washington to Fort Monroe would prove to be the only expeditious part of his campaign to capture Richmond.

But 22 February 1862 was a gloomy day in Richmond. That was the day set for the inauguration of the permanent government of the Confederate States. The provisional government had been terminated, and this day had been selected for the second inauguration of President Jefferson Davis. A large crowd was in attendance, and, in the words of Edward A. Pollard, the day was "memorable for its gloom in Richmond. Rain fell in torrents, and the heavens seemed to be hung with sable. Yet a dense crowd collected, braving the rainstorm in their eager interest to hear the president's speech from the steps of the capitol. It was then that all eyes were turned to our chief; that we hung upon his lips, hushing the beating of our heavy hearts that we might catch the word of fire we longed to hear—that syllable of sympathy of which a nation in distress stands so in need. One sentence then of defiance and of cheer—something bold, and warm, and human. . . . That sentence never came. The people were left to themselves."[25]

For Harry Burgwyn, the winter of 1862 was dedicated to honing the morale, discipline, and efficiency of his regiment to a fine edge. Having found its condition "wretched" upon his return, he must have redoubled his efforts, for years later one of his men remembered that "the winter of 1861–1862 was passed in unremitting drill and under strict measure of discipline, which got the regiment into fine condition for the opening campaign; and here they acquired a reputation for efficiency in drill and obedience to orders which they retained with increasing credit until the final surrender."[26] Colonel Vance, too, was concerned for the morale and welfare of his men, but lacking any formal military training himself, he wisely left matters of discipline and training to Harry. Their relationship was affected to some degree—not openly, but in the privacy of his letters Harry complained bitterly.

In one letter to his father, in which he dwelt at length on the fortifications and regiments defending New Bern, he said,

> None of our Regiments are so efficient as they should be. My own is the best & if it had a good Colonel would be a most capital reg[iment]. Col Vance is however a man without any system or regularity whatever & has so little of an engineering mind as to say that the Croatan intrenchments are worthless unless the enemy land & attack us there. His abilities appear to me to be more overated than those of any other person I know of. As an instance of his procrastinating habits: We have been in the service as an organized Reg. since the 27 of Aug. & until today we have not had a color bearer of general guides appointed. To day he appointed him. If I have mentioned the matter to him once I have done so 20 times. Some of his officers are exceedingly inefficient in tactics & could they only be got rid of the Reg. would be much improved.[27]

On 4 February Harry recorded in his journal that "on Sunday Jan. 26th a dispatch was received from Gen. Branch ordering my Regm't. to New Berne. This was in consequence of reliable information that a large portion of Gen Burnside's expedition had succeeded in getting over the swashes & were safely anchored in Pamlico Sound."[28] Colonel Vance had left with six companies that afternoon, and Harry followed the next morning with the remaining four companies. Colonel Vance, it later developed, had located his new camp (Camp Branch, about three miles below New Bern) on clay soil with little or no drainage. Harry again complained, saying that although he had suggested that Vance relocate the camp, "'the men have built chimneys to their tents & dont want to move,' is his reply. He himself is now quite unwell from the unhealthiness of the location."[29]

The very next day, disconsolate, wet, and still smarting from Vance's refusal to move the camp to a better location, Harry unburdened himself. Learning that President Davis had called for twenty-three thousand more men from North Carolina, he inquired of his father:

> I wonder if I could not get the command of a Regmt. I am exceedingly disgusted with my present position. Vance is totally unsuitable in my opinion & I am heartily tired of being under his command. As for discipline not the faintest idea of it has ever entered his head. One or two things of late occurrence I will mention. I reported 27 officers absent from a Reveille & he did not even ask them *all* why they did not go. I reported two or three absent from drill. Not a syllable did he say to them concerning it to my knowledge. . . . If I could get a colonelcy then the objection to leaving this Reg. which I mentioned to you would be to all justified.[30]

A few days later, again to his father and with no little justification, Harry wrote: "I laid by this letter & went to bed about 9 o'clock last night & about eleven there came up the most furious storm which we have ever had I think. . . . My large tent, if you recollect it, had been pretty nearly destroyed, & last night's wind completed the destruction. . . . We are still in the same mud hole. I have remonstrated with Vance time & again & yesterday Col Sinclair (whose regiment together with ours is to form the vanguard) told him if he remained here all his men would be sick. Vance knows nothing about the manége [sic] of a Regmt."[31]

The battle of New Bern was only two weeks off. With the Yankees so close at hand it is doubtful that the Twenty-sixth moved its base camp before the battle. Harry does not allude to the matter again, but Vance's easygoing attitude was a sore point with him and a source of considerable vexation. Yet the two men got along well together, at least on the surface, and certainly Vance held Burgwyn in high esteem. As one historian has observed, "Peculiar as was the companionship of the mountain politician Vance and the martinet young drillmaster Burgwyn, it was for a period the closest of Zeb's life and the memory of it never left him."[32] Harry's penchant for perfection probably encouraged Vance to play a more relaxed role for the sake of balance. Both were born leaders, and each possessed the virtues of the other in their respective fields. They made a good team in spite of their personality differences.

The condition of his men was not Harry's only concern upon returning to camp. Although stationed at Carolina City, he lost no time in examining the defenses of New Bern. This was not necessarily his responsibility, but his father's duties as military aide to the governor to inspect the camps and fortifications in the Pamlico area perhaps inspired Harry to reconnoiter on his own. The two corresponded frequently, and Harry probably felt that his ideas would be passed on to higher authorities. As early as 11 January he wrote a lengthy letter to his father outlining his suggestions on how best to improve the New Bern defenses, which consisted of three forts located on the bluffs of the Neuse River just below New Bern, against an attack by water. About five miles downstream was Fort Thompson, the largest and strongest of the forts, mounting ten guns. Nearest the town was Fort Lane, mounting four guns, and between the two lay Fort Ellis, mounting nine guns. Harry's concern about the two smaller forts was that all the guns bore downriver, were not casemated, and could be easily enfiladed by any vessel after passing the fort "without the possibility of reply from a single gun." Observing that these forts were situated on a high ridge with precipitous slopes on both the river and land sides, Harry recommended that an embrasure be cut through the top of the crest, the gun be planted under a brick arch three feet thick as a counterbattery to enfilading fire, and the whole be covered with ten feet of earth.[33]

As late as 1 February, Harry was still unable to report anything positive on Burnside's movements. In referring to a story in the *New Bern Progress*, purporting to be an extract from a Philadelphia paper, he told his father that Burnside had "lost from 40 to 50 vessels in the late storm." When Burnside was urged by his men to rest during the height of the storm, the latter exclaimed, "I am in the hands of God"; Harry appended: "A few more storms & if he dont mind he will be in the hands of the Devil." Harry was able to report, however, that the new four-gun masked battery, about half a mile below Fort Thompson, was nearly complete and that a couple of guns were to be placed between Fort Thompson and Fort Ellis "to scatter the fire of the enemy & a few charred logs are to be added to addle their brains."[34]

On Friday night, 8 February, not knowing that Roanoke Island had fallen, Harry advised his mother that his father was "still in New Berne & will probably go to Fort Macon tomorrow return Monday & then be governed by the news from Burnside. If Roanoke Island falls he will go to Norfolk to see Gen Huger about the defense of Weldon & the Roanoke & Seaboard R.R. but I forgot I ought not to have said that."[35]

The loss of Roanoke Island was all the proof needed to demonstrate to Harry that an inferior force, outgunned and outmanned, could not withstand the assault of a vastly superior force. At Roanoke Island only 400 men, with but 1,050 in reserve, manned the breastworks along the most strategic line of defense. Against an attacking force of 10,000 men, supported by long-range naval guns, the little Confederate force and its "mosquito" fleet were hardly sufficient for a delaying action. On 15 February, Harry advised his mother that the enemy had occupied Elizabeth City, Edenton, and Plymouth. As to other movements of Burnside the news was uncertain, but there were rumors that his army was sailing to Washington, North Carolina.[36]

On 12 February, W. W. Holden, editor of the *North Carolina Standard*, commented that he had warned for months that Roanoke Island would be captured "if the most effective measures were not taken for its complete defence. From the day Gen. Hill was removed from the charge of our coast, and a political general appointed in his stead, wholly unacquainted with military affairs, we have had but little hope of protection to the northern department of our seacoast."

Holden was unfair in his implied criticism of General Lawrence O'Bryan Branch and other officers. In September 1861, General Daniel Harvey Hill had been relieved at Yorktown and directed to assume command of the defenses between Albemarle Sound and the Neuse River and Pamlico Sound. General Hill was in North Carolina only a matter of weeks before he was recalled to Virginia by General Joseph E. Johnston. Although Hill's stay was brief, and against almost insurmountable odds, he did succeed in improving the defenses of New Bern, Washington, Hyde, and Roanoke Island. But on 18 October, after his first tour of the area, he wrote: "Roanoke Island is the key to one-third of North Carolina . . . four additional regiments are absolutely indispensable to the protection of this island . . . the batteries also need four rifled cannon of heavy caliber." Two weeks later, he reported, "I fear for Roanoke Island." Had Hill been permitted to stay in North Carolina, he surely would have proved more effective than an untrained, inexperienced officer. But the inadequate defenses of eastern North Carolina were more the result of the inattention of the Confederate government than the inadequacies of any one officer.[37]

The reason for Holden's criticism of General Branch, other than political animosity, is not clear. Branch, a nephew of John Branch, a former governor of North Carolina, was a Democrat and a secessionist and had served three terms in Congress. At the outbreak of the war, he served from May to September as quartermaster and paymaster general and then briefly as colonel of the Thirty-third North Carolina Regiment. In January 1862, President Davis appointed him a brigadier general.[38] Harry's father had unsuccessfully sought a brigadier generalship and particularly desired command of the Pamlico defenses. Serving as military aide to Governor Clark, and having made extensive examinations of the coastal defenses in that area, he naturally believed himself qualified and was hopeful of appointment. This expectation was shared by his son, so it is not surprising that Harry was quick to criticize any apparent faults or weaknesses in the man who was given precedence over his father.

But in mid-February, defensive strategy was Harry's principal preoccupation. He was deeply concerned over the battle of Mill Springs, Kentucky, at which a Confederate force was defeated, the loss of Roanoke Island, and the capture in rapid succession of Fort Henry on the Tennessee River and Fort Donelson on the Cumberland, all within a matter of days. These Union successes would enable the enemy to penetrate eastern North Carolina and the mid-South almost at will—and with naval support. On 19 February, he wrote his father at Thornbury:

> We may expect disaster & defeat however just so long as we expose small detachments, unsupported by any convenient troops, to attacks by the enemy. The conviction which I expressed to you that we had better withdraw our troops from Washington & Hyde & concentrate them at the most important point has gained strength with me every day. We have say 2500 men at the two points last mentioned. Now they can be reinforced by no troops that I am aware of except those now here which can not get there under 36 hours: probably in the condition of the roads 48 hours must elapse before they can be reinforced. If New Berne is the most important point concentrate them there if Weldon or Blackwater or a position intermediate from those let them be concentrated there. As for exposing however 3 or 4,000 men to the attack of some 12 or 15,000 & expecting the minority to conquer is the extreme of bad judgment.

He concluded with the urgent appeal: "Get your cotton away even if you have to *haul* it."[39]

A few days later he learned that his father was removing the Negroes from the plantation. "It strikes me," Harry said, "that if the line of videttes which you recommended were established & the Roanoke thoroughly blocked up there would be no immediate necessity for their removal. I should have everything in readiness however to leave at once & send off my cotton even if I had to haul it. Why would not

Gaston be a good place to send it for the present." He then asked his father if he could provide him with a different bodyservant, for "my boy George does not give me satisfaction at all & yet it is impossible to get another. If you could hire me a cook in Weldon I would be very much obliged to you." Referring again to the Confederate defeat at Donelson, Harry suggested that "a military commission should be appointed to investigate thoroughly every surrender which our generals may make & hold them to a most rigid account. A commission should also be appointed to examine officers & reject all who are not sufficiently qualified; the bare fact that such a commission was established would do an immense amount of good."[40]

Two days later, on 26 February, Harry wrote to both his parents. To his mother he said: "We had a rumor last night that he [Burnside] had returned to Hatteras & would attack us here shortly. My candid opinion is that when he does New Berne will fall just as Roanoke did saving that we will not be taken prisoners. It is a very great mistake it appears to me to divide our troops so as to expose the detachments to a certain defeat just whensoever they may be attacked."[41]

To his father, Harry wrote a long and detailed letter with the prefatory comment, "Though you are probably as well aware as I of the almost (& in fact considering the disparity of forces) the absolutely defenceless condition of new Berne I wish to make a few suggestions concerning our condition which have occurred to me from time to time as I ride over the country." He continued:

> We have received orders to continue the breastwork of Col Singletary's as far as a swamp which connects with Brice's creek & is supposed to be impassable. This will extend the intrenchment already some 1700 yds. long 600 more making 2,300 yds. in all which we have to defend. Placing the men one yd apart & forming in two ranks as slender a formation as we could make with any prospects of success & we must have 4600 men. For contingencies we must of course have a reserve of one third the amount (1530) & it will make 6130 men which we should have. . . . Suppose they mass 15,000 men in front & send two flanking columns one of which goes by the road to New Berne & thus gets completely in our rear & the other outflanks our right. It will require as I said 6130 men to man our works. . . . It appears to me therefore to be plain that whenever New Berne is attacked by the force which Burnside will have it will fall. . . . Do not understand me as giving up. My spirits like

yours rise with our disasters not a particle of yielding is in me but I do wish to see better generalship & that a fair show be given to our men.[42]

Harry was never far off the mark in his strategy for defending eastern North Carolina and southside Virginia. The Blackwater River and Weldon were vital to the security of Norfolk and the Petersburg-Richmond area; and, should Burnside establish a base in eastern North Carolina, Goldsboro would be the key point of defense against any westward movement of the enemy. On 4 March he wrote his father that "all the troops in Washington have been ordered by the Presdt. to Suffolk Va. which order reached here Monday evening & was forwarded to Washtg. the same night. Hyde County has been evacuated also. They are now casemating along the bluffs some of the guns which were in the Forts Lane & Ellis. . . . We are engaged in extending the right flank of Singletary's Breastwork which must be a mile longer to reach anything like an impractible [sic] swamp."[43]

On 12 March, two days before the battle of New Bern, Harry again wrote his father. Having learned of the battle of the *Monitor* and the *Virginia* [*Merrimac*], he came up with still more ideas on defensive strategy. He believed the defense of New Bern was hopeless and should be abandoned: "I think it very probable that the Merrimac has played the mischief to such an extent at Newport News that Burnside's attack may be deferred if not entirely abandoned upon Norfolk. That being the case the troops at Suffolk & Weldon ought to be so notified that the troops at Suffolk can replace at a moments notice the troops at Weldon which, if New Berne is to be defended, ought to be thrown here as soon as Burnsides fleet appears in the mouth of the river. Great care must be taken however to ascertain whether it is or is not a feint to distract attention. My opinion is & has been from the start that New Berne ought to be abandoned."[44]

For months, first as aide to Governor Ellis and then to Governor Clark, Henry had been constantly shuttling back and forth between Raleigh, Richmond, Petersburg, Garysburg, New Bern, and the coastal defenses, seemingly to no avail. In spite of everyone's protestations, most of the North Carolina troops were being shipped off to Virginia for the defense of Richmond as fast as they could be organized and trained. Until it was too late, the importance of eastern North Carolina to Northern strategy was neither understood nor acknowledged by the Confederate leadership. North Carolina was neglected and left virtually defenseless; and neither generalship nor strategy seemed calculated to lend any real protection to the inhabitants of the coastal country. Both Burgwyns shared this conviction. But the abandonment of the little town of Winton without a fight to a small flotilla of gunboats from Goldsborough's fleet was the last straw.

From Garysburg on 22 February Henry was in a despondent mood when he wrote to Governor Clark that he feared the government had given up his part of the state to the enemy. He had asked the Richmond government that he be made brigadier of the area between the Roanoke and the Chowan, and he requested Clark's assistance in urging his appointment.[45] Henry King Burgwyn was probably facing his greatest disappointment. He wanted desperately to be a brigadier general. To his great chagrin he had been passed over for a political general who had neither military training nor experience. Now, with the enemy fleet high up the Chowan, not many miles from Thornbury, he was again seeking a brigadier generalship, this time for the area between the Roanoke and the Chowan. Again he would be denied.

But it was too late for a change of command to save eastern North Carolina from the invader, for the master plan to capture Richmond was rapidly taking shape. The conquest of coastal North Carolina was a necessary part of that plan, and Burnside was playing his role to perfection. On 10 March he was advised by Adjutant General Lorenzo Thomas that the "enemy is abandoning his position at Centreville and toward Manassas, and that he has retreated from his batteries near Aquia Creek; a forward movement of the Army of the Potomac has been ordered this day, to seize upon any advantage that may offer. You can make your arrangements accordingly."[46]

On 13 March Secretary of War Edwin M. Stanton wrote Burnside that it might "be important for you to co-operate with contemplated movements of Major-General McClellan, and, if so, you will place your command under his direction and obey his instructions."[47] On the same day, from Fairfax Court House, McClellan indicated to Thomas that it would be difficult to give Burnside precise orders. But, he said, "I think it would be well that he should not engage himself farther inland than at New Berne, and should at once reduce Beaufort, leaving there a sufficient garrison in Fort Macon. He should at once return to Roanoke Island, ready to cooperate with all his available force either by way of Winton or by way of Fort Monroe, as circumstances may render necessary. I advise this on the supposition that Captain Fox is correct in his opinion that Burnside will have New Berne this week."[48]

From his headquarters at Camp Branch, on 12 March, Harry wrote his mother. It was on the eve of the battle of New Bern, and his letter reflected his courage and moral resolve:

Intelligence deemed to be very reliable & in fact undoubtedly so has been received to the effect that the enemy are close at hand & preparing to attack us. 15 steamers are only 7 miles below us & probably they will attack us sometime during to morrow or certainly the next day so look out for squalls. The news was received by our men with no cheering no undue exultation no efforts to keep their courage up by noisy demonstrations but every eye brightened every arm grew nervous & the most deadly determination is on all. You may rely upon a hard fight; but God's Providence is over us all. Though having his omnipotence constantly before me lately, I am much more impressed with it now & I am sure he will order all for the best. I am in the best spirits imaginable. I used to think the night before a battle I would be anxious for my own fate & that of the day. Now if I had my wish exclusive of the fact that our defences may be improved by delay I would not postpone a day. I will let you have intelligence at the earliest opportunity. But be not too anxious. I know well your Christian spirit & reliance upon God[.] O may he take us all into his safe keeping is the prayer of Y[ou]r most affect[ionate] son, H. K. Burgwyn, Jr.[49]

CHAPTER 9

MY COMMAND WAS THE LAST

TO RETREAT

The battle of New Bern on 14 March, was in many respects similar to that of Roanoke Island. Although the Confederate position below New Bern was better fortified and better defended, it yielded to the superior forces of the enemy about as quickly as did the defenders of Roanoke Island. Routed in both instances, the Confederates suffered for want of trained men, experienced officers, adequate arms, and sufficient artillery. Furthermore, there were weaknesses in the defensive works of each place that were quickly exploited by the enemy.

From a military standpoint the battle of New Bern was a comparatively minor engagement. It was essential to the success of the Burnside expedition, however, for the capture of New Bern ensured the fall of Fort Macon and possession of Beaufort, an excellent harbor near the open sea. Although Fort Macon was not formally surrendered until 26 April, Burnside accomplished his mission in about six weeks. It was a brilliant success and was flawlessly executed, hindered only by the intemperate weather. With the exception of the Wilmington area to the southeast, all of tidewater North Carolina would henceforth be under Federal domination until the end of the war.

For the Confederacy, it was a clear signal that the North, too, was in "dead earnest" and had the might as well as the will—with a navy capable of blockading all Southern ports and penetrating most navigable inland waters in support of its armies. North Carolina's feeble defenses, as late as March 1862, were an equally clear indication that its leadership did not yet fully comprehend the magnitude and gathering strength of the opposing forces. In this sense, the battle of New Bern was important to North Carolina, for her next governor fought there. He was Colonel Zebulon B. Vance, commanding officer of the Twenty-sixth North Carolina Regiment. He witnessed firsthand the sacrifices resulting from inadequate training, leadership, and support. This battle, according to one writer, emphasized to Vance that "North Carolina was standing virtually alone in defending her own coastline; and it contributed to his election as governor five months later." The battle of New Bern was also important to Lieutenant Colonel Harry Burgwyn, Vance's subordinate in command of the Twenty-sixth. Although not directly engaged in the fighting, Harry demonstrated his capacity for courageous leadership by his safe withdrawal of his command from the field following the debacle.[1]

Although Burnside was delayed in moving against New Bern, once under way the expedition proceeded with dispatch. And for the first time in weeks the weather was cooperative. Leaving Roanoke Island on the morning of Tuesday, 11 March, the fleet rendezvoused at Hatteras late that afternoon under clear skies. By 2:00 P.M. the following day the advance division of gunboats entered the mouth of the Neuse River. Here the fleet concentrated before moving upstream to its anchorage in three columns off Slocum's Creek—and again under clear skies.[2] With thirteen gunboats and a large number of transports and auxiliary vessels following his flagship, Commander Stephen C. Rowan's armada must have made an imposing sight as it steamed into position for the assault upon New Bern.

News of the fleet's presence in the river reached Confederate headquarters at 4:00 P.M. on Wednesday, 12 March. At dark, learning that "twelve vessels had anchored below the mouth of Otter creek [actually off the mouth of Slocum's Creek] and about forty-five were ascending the river in the rear," General Branch moved swiftly. He ordered the Thirty-fifth Regiment, under Colonel James Sinclair, to proceed immediately to Fisher's Landing, just above the mouth of Otter Creek, to resist any enemy attempt to land. Colonels Reuben P. Campbell and Charles C. Lee were directed to guard the river shore below and above Fort Thompson. By three o'clock Thursday morning, according to Branch, all directions and assignments had been made. He soon learned that the enemy's troops were landing well below Otter Creek (at Slocum's) and would, therefore, encounter the strong Croatan works as they moved up the county road to New Bern. Vance's regiment, under Lieutenant Colonel Harry Burgwyn, together with Captain T. H. Brem's battery, was then instructed to occupy the Croatan works.[3] They could readily do so because the Atlantic and North Carolina Railroad passed directly between Fort Thompson and the Croatan works, a distance of more than six miles.

Colonel Sinclair, with his command, left New Bern by train on the evening of 12 March and arrived at Fisher's Landing, about nine miles below the town, at 8:00 P.M. It was a clear, moonlit night. Band music and singing could be heard in the distance. Preparing for the worst, Sinclair concentrated his men in the rifle pits and breastworks protecting the landing and posted pickets on each side extending three miles from the center. But on the morning of the thirteenth no enemy troops appeared. Instead, they were landing in heavy force three miles below. By 10:00 A.M., however, the Federal gunboats approached Fisher's Landing, throwing shell and canister as they steamed in close to shore. Shortly afterward, Colonel Campbell of the Seventh Regiment, in command below Fort Thompson, ordered Sinclair to fall back into the woods near the railroad and then withdraw to the Fort Thompson entrenchments.[4]

About this time Harry Burgwyn was ordered to occupy the Croatan works. He described the sequence of events:

The morning of the 13th (Thursday) my regmt formed & had previous to this received no orders & were at that time perfectly ignorant where to go or what to do. Early in the morning Col Lee (of Bethel memory) rode to our camp & said that he likewise had received no orders which told him what to do or that his orders were so indefinite that he could not understand them. On Thursday morning the enemy commenced shelling Col Sinclair's Regmt & in a short time they were ordered to retreat by Col Campbell to the Fort Thompson breastworks. Col Campbell the commander of our brigade not being present where it was supposed his headquarters would be Col Vance the next oldest Col. was ordered to take command of the brigade & I was given the comm[an]d of the 26th & ordered to go to the Croatan works.

This was about 10 o'clock. Gen Branch did not appear on the field until after 9. I went to the Croatan works & on my way down found Sinclair's men retreating from their position but kept on & took position at the Croatan works where Brem's battery soon arrived. The enemy were landing during this time & had landed a portion of their force between New Berne & myself before I took position. Soon after I had taken position Col Campbell came up & informed us of that fact & ordered us to retreat to the Fort Thompson works. Very soon after the train passed the Yankees I am told came rushing after us. Upon arriving at the Fort Thompson works we were ordered to occupy from the brickyard to the right of the railroad so far as we could. Subsequently we were ordered to extend our lines so as to occupy from the railroad to Weathersby's house. In this position we remained during the rest of Thursday & that night.[5]

Thursday, 13 March, was a day of feverish activity for General Branch. But it was evident that he did not have enough troops to man a two-mile line of defense. The entrenchments covered a distance of about one mile running westward from Fort Thompson to the railroad. From the railroad to Weathersby's road, a distance of well over a mile, the terrain was intersected by a swamp, and the land between the railroad and swamp was very rough and uneven. To protect this area and at the same time shorten his line, Branch had moved back about 150 yards on the railroad and constructed a series of redoubts and rifle pits running toward the swamp, thus conforming his line to the broken terrain in the rear of Bullen's Creek. The gap of 150 yards, in which was located an old brick kiln known as Wood's brickyard, adjacent to the railroad, was a major flaw in the defensive works that would prove to be fatal.[6]

No more than four thousand Confederate troops were available for duty on the day of the battle. They constituted six regiments of infantry and one of cavalry, a battalion of North Carolina militia under Colonel H. J. B. Clark, and a few independent companies. The regiments were not up to full strength. All but the Thirty-third North Carolina and the Nineteenth North Carolina (Second Cavalry), organized as war regiments for the duration,[7] had been formed as twelve-month volunteer regiments. They were now reorganizing for three years, and a number of men were on furlough prior to reenlistment. In addition, there was much sickness in the ranks, and some companies had almost a third of their men in the hospitals.[8]

All day Thursday the regiments were brought on the field and placed in line. The Twenty-seventh North Carolina (Colonel John Sloan), which had been encamped at Fort Lane below New Bern since early winter, was posted on the extreme left of the Thompson works with its left flank resting on the river. To its right was the Thirty-seventh North Carolina (Colonel Charles C. Lee). This regiment, after completion of its organization in late 1861, had been moved to New Bern, where it remained until the battle. Both regiments occupied the works between Fort Thompson and the old Beaufort road (county road). The Seventh North Carolina (initially held in reserve with the Thirty-third North Carolina) was brought up and placed on the line to the right of the Thirty-seventh, with one company on the left and the other nine companies on the right of the Beaufort road. The Seventh (Colonel Reuben P. Campbell) had been stationed on Bogue Island and later at Carolina City before being taken by rail to New Bern on 5 March 1862. It was encamped at the fairgrounds until early Thursday morning, 13 March, when it crossed the Trent River and was placed in reserve at a point where the public road from Beaufort crossed the Atlantic and North Carolina Railroad—a distance of about two miles from the entrenchments. Later in the day it was moved up to the line.[9]

After withdrawing from Fisher's Landing, the Thirty-fifth North Carolina (Colonel [Reverend] James Sinclair) was posted to the right of the Seventh. And on the right of the Thirty-fifth was posted the battalion of militia under Colonel H. J. B. Clark. On the morning of the fourteenth, before the engagement commenced, however, Sinclair's command, according to his later report, "was divided by a section of Brem's battery and Captain Whitehurst's independent company separating my right wing from my center and left wing." About forty yards between the militia and the railroad was left vacant, as was a sixty-to-eighty-yard trench parallel to the railroad.[10] The militia, only two weeks in service and armed "mainly with hunting rifles and shotguns," was unfortunately selected to occupy the weakest point in the defenses—the 150-yard gap between the entrenchments on the left and the series of redoubts on the right of the railroad.[11]

The Twenty-sixth North Carolina was posted to the right and west of the railroad. Vance was given command of all the defenses from the railroad to Weathersby's road, a distance of a mile and a quarter. He was in temporary command of the post at New Bern on Thursday, when he learned that Burgwyn had been ordered to the Croatan works. Before he could rejoin his regiment, however, it had been withdrawn from Croatan and posted in the redoubts. The night before, Vance, with a detail of men, had thrown up a small entrenchment on the Weathersby road to protect two field pieces of Brem's battery.[12]

According to Harry Burgwyn: "On Wednesday about 5 o'clock we received information that the enemy were coming up the river & made preparations to fight the next day. That night about 10 o'clock I rode down to Brem's Battery . . . & returning at 1 o'clock rested until daybreak." For the first time, Harry comprehended the potential exposure to which his command would be subjected should the enemy elect to attack the extreme right of the Confederate line. His defenses would consist of two guns, three companies of infantry from his own regiment, two companies of dismounted cavalry, and one independent company—which would have to occupy and hold "some 700 yds. & a good road down which the enemy could come in any numbers & bring any amount of Art[illery]. Nor was I stationed behind intrenchments except that the two guns were behind some earthworks which themselves were completely commanded by a hill some two hundred yds. in front."[13]

The Thirty-third North Carolina had been organized in Raleigh in September 1861. The men had enlisted for the duration of the war, and the regiment's commanding officers were initially Colonel Lawrence O'B. Branch, Lieutenant Colonel Clark M. Avery, and Major Robert F. Hoke. After Branch's appointment as a brigadier general, the regimental command devolved upon Colonel Avery, Lieutenant Colonel Hoke, and Major William Gaston Lewis. The regiment was ordered to New Bern in the winter of 1861–62 and was encamped at the fairgrounds with the Seventh North Carolina. Both regiments crossed the Trent early on the morning of 13 March and took up reserve positions about two miles behind the line of entrenchments. Later, the Seventh was moved into the line and the Thirty-third brought up to a reserve position astride the railroad about four hundred yards behind the line and two hundred yards behind Branch's headquarters.[14] The Nineteenth North Carolina (Second Cavalry), commanded by Colonel S. B. Spruill and Lieutenant Colonel W. G. Robinson, had six companies available for duty on the day of the battle. They did not fight as a regimental unit but were given special company assignments. Around 2:00 P.M. on the thirteenth, Colonel Spruill was ordered to dismount two of his best-armed companies and have them report to Colonel Vance. Shortly afterward, two mounted companies were ordered to act as vedettes for the night. At two o'clock the following morning, Company C of Spruill's command reported for duty after a forced march of forty miles from Washington.[15]

General Branch's artillery support consisted of Latham's and Brem's batteries—twelve fieldpieces in all—which were concentrated between the county road and the railroad. Late on the night of the thirteenth, one section of Brem's battery (two pieces) was posted on the Weathersby road to cover the extreme right of the Confederate line. Belatedly, two twenty-four-pounders were ordered up to anchor the entrenchment at the railroad but were not mounted in time for the battle. There was not a single heavy gun directly protecting the railroad and county road approaches of the enemy.[16]

River fortifications consisted of seven forts either laid off or finished. Of these, two were effectively unfinished, and Fort Dixie was abandoned on the thirteenth. Therefore, New Bern was protected from naval penetration by Fort Lane, three miles below the city (mounting three guns), Fort Ellis, one mile farther south (mounting eight guns), the two casemated guns (Fort Allen) just below Ellis and served by men of Company B of the First Maryland Regiment (the only non–North Carolinians on the Confederate side), and Fort

Thompson. The latter was the key to the river defenses. Fort Thompson mounted thirteen guns with ten bearing on the river and only three on the land approaches, reflecting "the belief of the engineers that any attack on New Bern would be mainly or solely by water."[17]

After making his final troop dispositions on the eve of battle, it is no wonder that Branch later reported that it was "painfully apparent" that his force was not sufficient to man the finished works "even with a thin line." Nor was he satisfied with the condition of his works. For weeks he had looked in vain for tools and outside labor but with virtually no success. One small party of free Negroes without implements did show up, but only one slave for hire was tendered. "During all this time," Branch reported, "I continued the troops at work, and when the enemy came into the river 500 per day were being detailed to construct breastworks, with less than half that number of worn and broken shovels and axes, without picks or grubbing-hoes. If the fate of New Berne shall prevent a similar supineness on the part of citizens, and especially slave owners, elsewhere, it will be fortunate for the country."[18]

How prophetic was Harry Burgwyn when, only two weeks before the battle, he wrote his father: *"But what a terrible & unmilitary a mistake it is* to divide our forces by 40 miles which forces when concentrated amount to only a third or 4th of the enemy. If then it be determined 'Deo volente' to defend New Berne I am greatly in favor of concentrating every available man & gun here." Otherwise, he concluded, "We can count ourselves lucky if escaping the bullet in the first place we escape capture or a demoralized retreat in the second."[19]

Under the circumstances, General Branch had probably done the best he could in preparation for the Federal assault. To assist him in the command of troops on the day of battle, he assigned Colonel Charles C. Lee to the left wing of the Thompson works lying between Fort Thompson and the county road. Lee's command embraced his own Thirty-seventh Regiment and the Twenty-seventh North Carolina. To the right wing, lying between the county road and the railroad, Branch assigned Colonel Reuben P. Campbell, commanding his own Seventh Regiment, the Thirty-fifth North Carolina, Captain C. C. Whitehurst's independent company, the two sections of Brem's and all of Captain A. C. Latham's field artillery, and the battalion of militia. Colonel Vance was placed in command of all the defenses to the right of the railroad covering a distance of about one mile. At his limited disposal were his own regiment, two companies of the Nineteenth North Carolina (Second Cavalry), one independent company, and two guns of Brem's battery, totaling not more than one thousand men. Because of his extended line, Vance placed Major Carmichael in command of his immediate left near the railroad and Lieutenant Colonel Burgwyn in command of his right wing resting on Weathersby's road.[20]

On Thursday the thirteenth the Federals, too, had been busily engaged, but perhaps with greater confidence and certainly with greater professional competence. Their day was not easy, however. Approximately eleven thousand troops, with their equipage, had to be disembarked and marched twelve miles under trying conditions. The troops started landing about 7:00 A.M. Although supported by the gunboats, they were unopposed. Using light-draft steamers, with surfboats in tow, the troops were landed on the north bank of Slocum's Creek in rapid order. By 2:00 P.M. the entire force was on shore. The distance from this point to the Croatan works was variously estimated at four to six miles. The lead regiments of Jesse L. Reno's (Second Brigade) and John G. Foster's (First Brigade) commands reached the works about two o'clock to find them deserted. About this time, General Burnside arrived at Croatan and ordered General Foster to proceed with his brigade up the county road and General Reno to proceed up the railroad. General John G. Parke (Third Brigade) was ordered to move behind Foster along the road. After a brief rest, the men were on the march by three o'clock. The advance continued until about eight o'clock, when the men were allowed to bivouac for the night. Some companies did not come up until midnight.[21]

It had been a long, grueling day with intermittent rain. The one county road had been churned into a sea of mud, and the railroad track offered little better footing. The six naval howitzers, under Lieutenant Roderick S. McCook, together with the two guns landed from the *Cossack* and *Highlander*, did not reach Burnside's headquarters until four o'clock the following morning. The naval vessels, along with the armed vessels of Burnside's force, had assisted the men on the march by shelling the road in advance.[22] Fort Dixie was engaged by the *Perry*, which maintained an effective fire until dark.[23] During the afternoon a heavy fog had set in and persisted until well after daybreak. It was a cold, wet, cheerless night for the men in both camps, but the men of the North got the worst of the bargain. They had slogged their way for twelve long hours through the mire and mud of the piney woods country of eastern North Carolina, and they were bone tired when they bivouacked about a mile and a half below the Thompson works, the main line of the Confederate defenses. But

New
Bern

D

C

X

Otter Cr.

B

Neuse

River

⚓

A

Slocum's
Cr.

Carolina City

Morehead City

Beaufort

Ft. Macon

Bogue   Banks

-- Route to New Bern—the Burnside Expedition, 13–14 March 1862
⚓ Anchorage on Night of 12 March 1862
A Landing Place of Troops 13 March 1862
B Deserted Intrenchments-Croatan
X Battlefield 14 March 1862
C Line of Obstructions
D Line of Yankee Catchers

N

0   10
Miles

Naval and land assault on New Bern, North Carolina, 13–14 March 1862
(Atlas to Accompany the Official Records of the Union and Confederate
Armies *[Washington, D.C.: Government Printing Office, 1891–95],
Plate XL3, C Sketch)*

they were ready for battle. Every other engagement of the Burnside expedition had resulted in a quick, decisive victory. They did not expect this one to be different.

At daylight on the fourteenth, General Foster advanced his brigade until he came upon the enemy's position, presumably the cleared space at the edge of the woods. The Confederates had earlier felled trees all along their front, to a depth of about 350 yards, to provide a clearer field of fire. Foster's brigade was posted opposite the Thompson works, with his right wing resting on the river and his left near the railroad. His line of battle crossed the county road about midway. Just to the left of the road were placed the naval howitzers, which were supported by the Twenty-seventh Massachusetts.[24]

General Reno did not get his brigade into line before the battle commenced. Although ordered to advance at daylight and attack the Confederate right, he was delayed by the need for his men to reload their muskets with dry powder because of the heavy rain during the night. About 7:45 A.M., as he was proceeding up the railroad, Reno heard Foster's brigade hotly engaged and soon "saw a large number of the enemy apparently engaged in getting a gun to bear on the railroad." He ordered the skirmishers to open fire upon them and the Twenty-first Massachusetts forward into line. "The enemy now opened a brisk fire upon us from near the railroad, the skirmishers in advance replying briskly, and as soon as the right wing of the Twenty-first Massachusetts got into line I ordered Lieutenant-Colonel Clark to charge and take the brick-kiln, which was gallantly executed." In the meantime, Reno's other regiments were brought up and formed in line to the left of the railroad.[25] Brigadier General Parke's brigade followed General Foster's up the county road. He was directly in the rear of the naval howitzers. He was ordered to support either Reno or Foster if necessary.[26]

The precise time that the actual battle began is not clear. Estimates range from 7:30 to 8:00 A.M. on 14 March. According to George C. Underwood, assistant surgeon of the Twenty-sixth North Carolina: "About 7:30 A.M. the battle was opened by a shot from a Parrott gun from Latham's battery under Lieutenant Woodbury Wheeler. This shot dispersed a squad of horsemen who seemed to be reconnoitering under cover of the woods. Immediately after this, the firing became general. General Foster's attacks on the main works in his front made but little, if any, impression; they were easily repulsed. Doubtless the enemy knew the weak points in the Confederate line of defense."[27] General Branch certainly had suspicions as to how the enemy seemed to have knowledge of his defenses and referred to the matter in his report on the battle.[28]

Whether there were traitorous informers at work in the area has never been documented, but the lead regiment in Reno's brigade advanced immediately up the railroad to Wood's brickyard at the beginning of the battle. And Lieutenant Colonel W. S. Clark of the Twenty-first Massachusetts stated that "it was known that the defenses of the enemy were thrown across the highway to the right of the railroad." Obviously, unaware of the redoubts thrown up by the Confederates to the left of the railroad, the Federals believed they were in an excellent position to flank the Confederate right. It could have been coincidental that the weakest point in the Confederate line was where the entrenchments met the railroad. Once this fact was established, Federal battle strategy for the next three hours was concentrated in that area in an effort to drive a wedge through the center of the Confederate defenses.

When General Reno was forced to divide his attention between the brickyard to his right and the enemy's redoubts in his front, he left Lieutenant Colonel Clark, with his four companies of about two hundred men, in a decidedly unenviable position. With no reinforcements evidently at hand, "and finding it impossible to remain there without being cut to pieces," Clark felt "compelled either to charge upon Captain Brem's battery of flying artillery or to retreat without having accomplished anything to compensate for the terrible loss sustained in reaching this point." He immediately gave the command "charge bayonets" and later reported that he "had the pleasure of mounting upon the first of the New Berne guns surrendered to the 'Yankees.'" He was proceeding to the second gun about three hundred paces from the brickyard when the enemy, seeing that Clark and his men were so few in number and without support, rallied and advanced.[29]

At this juncture, Clark had but one choice. He commanded his men to retreat to the railroad. There he found the Fourth Rhode Island and urged its officer, Colonel I. P. Rodman, to advance at once and charge the enemy's flank. Satisfied that he could turn the rebel flank, Rodman immediately prepared to charge and so informed Brigadier General John G. Parke, commanding the Third Brigade. Parke approved and ordered the Eighth Connecticut and Fifth Rhode Island regiments to his support.[30]

The charge of these three regiments of the Third Brigade was successful in crushing the center of the enemy's works and forcing his entire line, from the railroad to Fort Thompson, to give way. This action occurred in concert with a charge by Foster's First Brigade. The battle had been in progress for about three hours, and only the

Twenty-sixth and Thirty-third North Carolina regiments were still stubbornly holding the line of redoubts running west of the railroad to the swamp. They lay immediately in front of General Reno's Second Brigade. Here, too, incessant fire had been maintained for about three hours. When the rebel center was broken, General Parke ordered the Fourth Rhode Island to attack the left flank of the Twenty-sixth North Carolina. Despite heavy fire, which killed and wounded many officers and men, a simultaneous charge by Parke and Reno drove the Confederates from their last stronghold.[31]

If the Confederates had any basic defensive strategy on the day of the battle, the enemy breakthrough at the brickyard made it immediately inoperative. The Federals had intended attacking at this point, believing it to be the extreme right of the Confederate line, not realizing that a line of redoubts, set back some 150 yards, extended from the railroad to the swamp. But they had not counted on finding the brickyard defended by untrained and poorly armed militiamen with no field guns in place and immediately altered their offensive strategy to take advantage of this fortuitous circumstance. The Confederates had no alternative but to respond by shoring up their threatened center by every available means—which were practically nonexistent. That deficiency was the reason the battle of New Bern was lost almost before it started. There were no reserves immediately available except the Thirty-third North Carolina and part of the Nineteenth (Second Cavalry) Regiment.

As soon as General Branch learned that enemy skirmishers had appeared on the flank of the militia, he ordered Colonel Avery (Thirty-third North Carolina) to dispatch five companies to dislodge them. But before these men, under Lieutenant Colonel Hoke, could get into position, Branch received a message from Colonel Clark, of the militia, informing him that "the enemy were in line of battle in great force on his right." He ordered up the remaining five companies of Colonel Avery's regiment and began a heavy fire. The militia, however, had abandoned their positions, and he was unable to rally them. Colonel Sinclair's Thirty-fifth North Carolina "very quickly followed their example, retreating in the utmost disorder." Branch found a large portion of the breastwork left vacant. He was unable to reoccupy it and watched as the enemy came up to attack what remained of Campbell's command. Although "the brave Seventh met them with the bayonet and drove them headlong over the parapet, inflicting heavy loss upon them as they fled," that regiment was forced to yield. Branch saw no choice but to retreat.[32]

Meanwhile, the left flank of the Twenty-sixth North Carolina under Major Abner Carmichael, together with the Thirty-third North Carolina under Colonel Avery, had been slugging it out with Reno's right and center. Firing from the protection of rifle pits and redoubts, they poured volley after volley into the advancing columns of the enemy as they attempted to expand the salient referred to as the "brickyard" or the "gap." Captain Oscar R. Rand, Company D, Twenty-sixth North Carolina, provided a detailed account of the actions in this sector in a report to Colonel Vance, written shortly after his capture. He confirmed significant facts in other related reports, both Federal and Confederate:

> About 7:30 A.M. the battle commenced on the left and for a time, extending from Fort Thompson along the whole line of the breastworks to the railroad, the roar of cannon and musketry was incessant. . . . Within a few minutes after the battle had commenced, the enemy made his appearance on the right of the railroad directly in front of us. . . . When the advance of the enemy had reached nearly opposite Major Carmichael's position, he gave the order to fire and sent a volley full into the head of the advancing column. The enemy replied immediately and from this time to the close of the action, the firing never ceased. . . . Just at this time, about half an hour after the battle had commenced, Colonel Avery, who had been held in reserve, arrived with the Thirty-third regiment. He with four companies entered the rifle pits occupied by us, while four other companies under Major Gaston Lewis, were ordered to occupy an advanced rifle pit nearest to the brickyard. This movement was attended with great danger, and was gallantly executed. . . . No troops were at any time stationed along the line from the extreme left of the Twenty-sixth Regiment to the brick kilns, a distance of over 200 yards, until Colonel Avery ordered Major Lewis with four companies of the Thirty-third Regiment to occupy it. There were also no troops defending the line from the brick kiln to where the main breastworks touched the railroad, a distance of 200 yards or more.[33]

Colonel Vance reported to General Branch following the battle that the attack "began on my left wing about 7:50 o'clock, extending toward my right by degrees until about 8:30 o'clock, when all the troops in my command were engaged so far as the swamp referred to. The severest fighting was on my extreme left, the enemy advancing under shelter of the woods to within easy range of our lines." The battle continued until noon, when he was informed that the enemy "in great force had turned my left by the railroad track at Wood's brick-yard, had pillaged my camp, were firing in reverse on my left wing, and were several hundred yards up the railroad between me and New Berne; also that all the troops on the field were in full retreat, except my command." He felt his only choice was "to order an immediate retreat or to be completely surrounded by an overwhelming force." He reported that "Lieutenant Colonel Burgwyn arrived with the forces of the right wing in excellent condition, and assisted me with the greatest coolness and efficiency in getting the troops across [Bryce's Creek], which after four hours of hard labor and the greatest anxiety we succeeded in doing. Lieutenant-Colonel Burgwyn saw the last man over before he entered the boat."[34]

It would serve no useful purpose to reconstruct the battle of New Bern on a conjectural basis; for, irrespective of tactical blunders and basic weaknesses in the line of defense, the outcome would have been no different—delayed perhaps, but no different. On 14 March 1862, there was no way the Confederate defenders of New Bern could have long withstood a sustained attack by eleven thousand well-trained, well-armed Federal troops supported by a strong naval fleet. Had there been no "gap" or weakness in the Confederate works, the advance of the enemy might have been checked longer than four hours—but not halted. The firepower of the Federal gunboats was simply too much for the weak battery emplacements along the river. And certainly, outnumbered by better than three to one, the fewer than four thousand Confederates, manning a line over two miles in length, with practically no reserves available, could not have concentrated sufficiently at any given point without creating a corresponding weakness elsewhere in the line. Even before the battle, this problem had concerned Harry Burgwyn and others, but its roots lay deeper. Responsibility for adequate defense lay not with those in the field but with the authorities in Raleigh and Richmond.

On balance, the defenders of New Bern fought well. Had there been no raw, untrained militia defending the most crucial point in the line, had the Thirty-fifth North Carolina been under stronger command,[35] and had the Twenty-eighth North Carolina arrived on the field before and not after the battle,[36] the contest might have reflected great credit upon the fighting spirit of the North Carolina soldier. As it was, general discredit was his reward. On 8 February, he had been routed after a four-hour fight at Roanoke Island. At New Bern, he was again routed after a four-hour battle. But in the latter engagement, several regiments distinguished themselves and gave promise of better days to come. Without question, the Twenty-sixth,

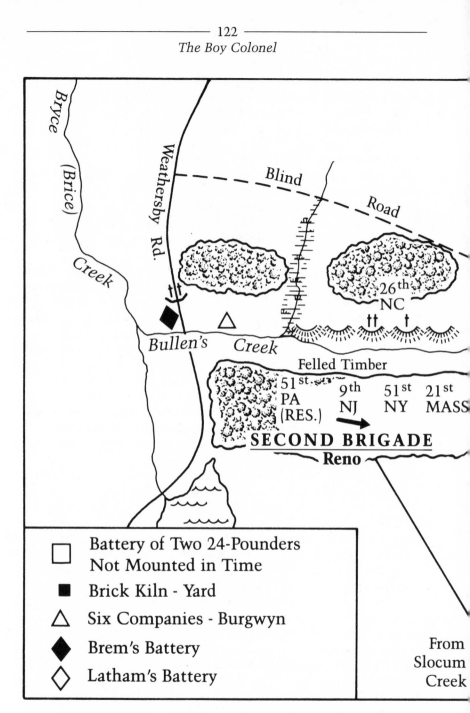

*The battlefield of New Bern, North Carolina, 14 March 1862 (*The War of
Rebellion: A Compilation of the Official Records of the Union and

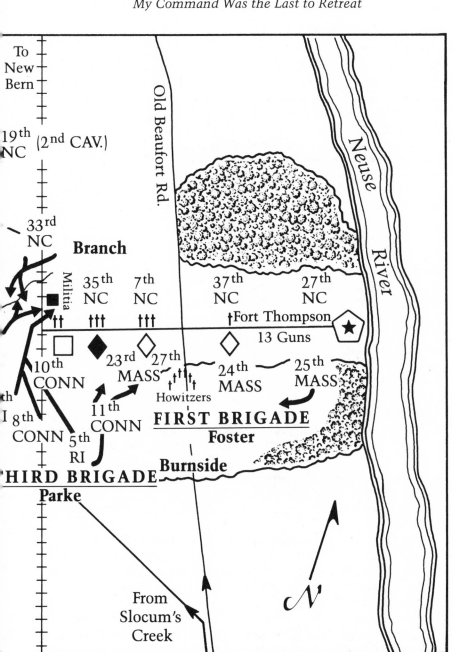

Thirty-third, and Seventh regiments fought exceptionally well. Only when threatened to be taken in the rear, after their flanks had given way, did they withdraw—and in good order. The Twenty-seventh and Thirty-seventh regiments, on the extreme left of the Confederate line, were only slightly engaged by the enemy, but they held their positions until their right flank lay completely exposed all the way to the railroad.[37]

Before the battle, Harry Burgwyn had been greatly concerned about the condition of the river fortifications. Some were not adequately casemated, most of the guns were inadequate, and too few bore on the land side. Forts Lane and Ellis could be taken in reverse if the enemy's vessels were successful in passing the forts and river obstructions. The Federal naval vessels did make safe passage, and with little interference, for the forts had already been taken in reverse by the Federal troops who had quickly penetrated their rear after breaching the Confederate entrenchments—but not before the defenders had succeeded in spiking the guns and blowing up most of the magazines.[38]

Only three Federal vessels were slightly damaged, and at about noon Commander Rowan later reported, "I ran the *Delaware* alongside the wharf and informed the inhabitants that we intended no injury to the town. At this time fires broke out in several portions of the city, it apparently being the intention on the part of the enemy to destroy it." A floating raft in Trent River was set on fire, and it drifted against the railroad bridge, setting fire to and destroying it. "At 2 P.M., our victorious troops appearing on the opposite side of the Trent, the work of transportation commenced, and at sundown the army was in full occupancy of the city."[39]

Presumably, by that time most of the fleeing Confederates had escaped across the Trent and were well on their way to Kinston. They had been ordered by General Branch to rendezvous at Tuscarora Station, eight miles from New Bern, where they entrained for Kinston, arriving there near midnight. They were unencumbered with baggage and camp equipage, for, as Branch later reported, everything had been left on the field because they "had not the field transportation with which to haul it to the railroad." In addition, ten pieces of field artillery were lost.[40]

The men of the Twenty-sixth and Thirty-third regiments, who did not escape through New Bern, never got the message to retreat. Before leaving the field, General Branch had dispatched two couriers to Colonel Avery and two to Colonel Vance with orders to fall back to the bridges, but the couriers never got through. Thirty-six hours later the men of these two regiments, who had borne the brunt of battle, made their way into Kinston. They had fought and marched fifty miles between Friday morning and Sunday morning.[41]

Marching day and night, they had stopped only once for food and rest, at Trenton, in Jones County. From there, Harry dispatched a hurried note to his mother. It read: "The enemy have full possession of our intrenchments. Yesterday we commenced to retreat & I reached here this morning. I am safe & unhurt expect to go to Kinston. My command was the last to retreat."[42]

On Sunday morning, 16 March, Harry's mother, then in Raleigh, received a telegram from his father asking her to meet him at the depot that afternoon. Shortly thereafter, Harry's father received a telegram from Brigadier General R. C. Gatlin saying, "Have not heard of your son. Will go to Kinston & telegraph you as soon as I get any news of him." At 4:15 that afternoon, the general again telegraphed: "Just seen your son. He is quite well." At 1:20 the following afternoon, 17 March, Anna received a telegram from Harry saying: "I arrived here safe & unhurt this morning [16 March] with greatest part of my regiment."[43]

On Monday, he wrote two letters to his mother. The first was brief. The second was much longer and more detailed. In the first, he said that he had saved nearly all in his immediate command. "I retreated from the battlefield not until every other portion had given way & I saved the 2 pieces of artillery which were under my command which was the only artillery saved. I am now trying to get our regiment well organized. . . . The battle was lost by bad arrangement of the troops & the running off of the militia which exposed our centre completely." He expressed concern for his trunks, which contained everything he owned.[44] In the second letter, he described his activities in detail from late Wednesday afternoon, 12 March, until his arrival in Kinston on Sunday morning, 16 March. He had much to say about the battle although he was not directly involved. His description of the retreat of the Twenty-sixth North Carolina is perhaps one of the best accounts extant:

My command was the last to leave & though I say it myself retreated in better order than any other. We were not directly engaged on our right but our left was very hotly engaged. I retreated along the Road marked "Road of County" & sent an officer ahead to find out where the enemy were, who reported them as coming down the Rail Road. I then ordered the Artillery to dash ahead & knowing that the infantry could not get there in time struck off to the right through the woods & upon arriving in sight of the 2nd Bridge found that it was in flames. I then went still farther to the right & crossed Brice's creek where I found Col. Vance & crossed it about 3 hours after I first arrived & then retreated by way of Trenton & Pollocksville to this place.

Of his march to Kinston, he wrote:

The people on the way were exceedingly kind & assisted us all they could. When I arrived at Brice's creek my heart sank within me. An impassible creek was behind me & the enemy not far from us on our right. We however completely fooled the enemy as to our retreat so that he did not see us until I had ferried over the last man & then a few Yankees made their appearance only a few hundred yards from us.

When I arrived at Brice's creek the only means of passing over was one blunt headed skiff which could only carry over 3 men at a time & took about 10 minutes each trip. We heard however that three boats were below & we wandered up & down for one hour & a half to find them[.] At length we found one of them which could carry 10 men & did carry over half of our men across[.] Presently the other two came up & in a little over an hour all of us were safely ferried over. When the boats first came everybody wanted to get in first but I stood down there myself & would only suffer such as I mentioned to go over & told them that any body who pushed forward or asked me to let him go I would not let go over. I actually ordered out one or two who pushed in without permission & had to partly draw my sword out to get one man out. I was the last man to go over myself & William my serv[an]t & I then swam both of my horses across.[45]

CHAPTER 10

AFTER NEW BERN

On the day following his capture of New Bern, General Burnside wrote to his commanding general with undisguised satisfaction: "My dear Mac, We've got New Berne, and I hope to have Fort Macon before long. I've followed your instructions to the letter, and have succeeded. You'll come out all right. You know my faith in you. Hope you'll soon wipe them out. . . . If I had 40,000 men like these I could do almost anything."[1]

But in North Carolina, during the days immediately following the battle, rumor and innuendo were rife and were accorded about as much validity as fact. Time and reflection were essential to a fair interpretation of the battle. Having lost the first three battles fought on their soil, North Carolinians were left with hurt pride and no little shame. Charges of cowardice and incompetency quickly gained currency—so much so that the *North Carolina Standard*, whose editor had been outspoken in his criticism of Generals Gatlin and Branch, was prompted to defend those who fought at New Bern. He singled out the regiments of Colonels Vance, Campbell, and Avery for praise, noting that "our small force compared with the enemy, the indefensible character of the breastworks, the gap left open in them at the railroad, and the blunder of placing raw militia to defend the most exposed position, may well account, without calling in question any man's courage, for the early rout of a good portion of our forces."[2]

In the 26 March issue of the *Weekly Raleigh Register* appeared a letter to the editor signed "Fair Play." Written in defense of General L. O'B. Branch, it roundly condemned the editor of the *Standard* for his "misrepresentations" and "unfounded insinuations." After demonstrating that the outcome of the battle of New Bern was a "mathematical certainty," Fair Play commented: "For three years the *Standard* has been the bitter and relentless assailant of Gen. Branch. Every mode of attack, fair and unfair, has been resorted to,—the cowardly innuendo—the sly insinuation—and even, as in the present instance, bare-faced misrepresentation, all of which has been answered by *silent contempt*."

Between the *Register* and the *Standard* there appeared to be little common ground for agreement on much of anything. Whom one condemned the other praised. On 1 October 1862, General Gatlin submitted his own report on the conduct of affairs from the time of his appointment as a brigadier general on 19 August 1861 until he was relieved from duty on 19 March 1862 because of ill health. Although this report was largely self-defensive, Gatlin did admit that "we failed to furnish General Branch with a reasonable force, and thus lost the important town of New Berne."[3]

Harry Burgwyn leveled his criticism primarily at General Branch. On 18 March he wrote his father that the loss was principally owing to Branch's "bad posting of his troops. He posted the militia at the brickyard & had two large guns brought there too late to be mounted. Had these guns been mounted there is no computing the loss which the enemy must have sustained."[4]

Two days later, in another letter to his father, Harry's mood was more optimistic as he contemplated the future. He remarked that the troops were not discouraged though they had lost confidence in their leader. He had determined that if he ever had "any command unless prohibited by orders I intend to charge the enemy with the bayonet as early as possible in the fight & let the relative bravery of the troops be tested. We should now go to work & have the most thorough drills & discipline possible." Referring to New Bern, he observed: "You will see a great many accounts of the battle but they are all exaggerated. Such expressions as a Col's rising in his stirrups & saying we can die but never surrender are like Wellington's 'La garde se recule.' It is the easiest thing in the world to get up a reputation on that battle field: at least it appears to me from what I can hear. I wish very much indeed I could be elected Col[onel] of one of the new Regiments. I would then have a regiment as was a regiment. Col. V[ance] you know is no sort of a commander. I constructed or laid out almost all of the intrenchments which we occupied & had a great deal more to do with it than he."[5]

On the same day, Major William Gaston Lewis, of the Thirty-third North Carolina Regiment, wrote to his cousin William Battle. He attributed the Confederate defeat at New Bern to several causes, but the main one, he believed, was the lack of sufficient troops to man the works. He blamed the authorities at Richmond for this inadequacy. He also complained that the defensive works were poorly constructed and that the enemy's victory was so easily accomplished because of "the running of the Militia, followed by Col. Sinclair's regiment, before three rounds had been fired by the enemy." Major

Lewis gave a detailed and accurate account of the battle, especially of that part in which his regiment was directly engaged, noting the circumstances that led to his retreat: "The last time they charged me with three or four regiments by front & flank. I ordered my men to meet the charge with the last volley & retreat following me. All of my command behaved well. I lost more men than all the rest of Gen. Branches command together. . . . Our regiment fought an hour after all except Col. Vance's regiment had retreated. Col. Vance was on our right, & only two or three of his companies were engaged. Gen. Branch ordered a retreat. We did not get the order & were thrown on our own resources. If we had given way when the other regiments did the whole command would have been captured as the enemy were nearer to the bridges than our men."[6]

A few days later, undoubtedly prompted by conflicting statements in the press, Lewis wrote his cousin Kemp Battle. He emphasized that "Col. Avery's regiment *was ordered by Gen Branch* into the action about fifteen minutes after the engagement opened, & was under fire the *whole* of it, during the entire fight. Col. Vance had only three companies under command of Maj. Carmichael in the fight, as the action did not extend as far down to the right as he was posted. There is no doubt this regiment would have done gallant fighting if it had had a chance. Maj. Carmichael fought bravely & has not by any means received due praise." Lewis reproved his cousin for giving too much credit to Vance and admonished, "Never put any reliance in newspaper reports of a battle." Major Lewis had another reason for being upset with the press. He had probably seen the resolution from Rutherford County, which had appeared in the 26 March issue of the *Weekly Raleigh Register,* in which Colonel Vance was recommended "to the good people of North Carolina to fill the office of Governor of said State at the next election." This move undoubtedly bore the support of the *North Carolina Standard,* for, in the same letter to his cousin, Lewis added: "The Standard is trying to run Col. Vance for Governor, on the strength of the late fight. Col. Vance has too much sense & high toned honor to attempt to run for any office under false colors. Col. Vance is a brave & high toned gentleman, but he had no [illegible] at the Newbern battle & he knows & confesses it."[7]

The men of the Thirty-third were obviously troubled by the eulogies being accorded Colonel Vance and the Twenty-sixth. Dr. J. F. Shaffner, assistant surgeon of the Thirty-third, joined the fray, and, in a long letter home to "My dear Friend" in Salem, expressed himself in no uncertain terms:

It is pitiable to see the endeavors of some partisan presses to bolster up the name of *Vance*, on what was to us a humiliating defeat. If Col. V. is foolish enough to allow Holden & Co. to run him for Governor for deeds of heroism performed at New Berne, I will freely confess I have been deceived in the man.—Col. Vance himself was not in the fight.—His Regiment occupied the extreme right wing.—Col. V. commanded the centre of his Regiment.—Col. Burgwin the right wing.—Major Carmichael the left wing. . . . We retreated by Col. Vance's command, and he had already gone ahead with larger portions of his force.—I am willing to assert, that the Col. himself did not see an enemy, near enough to hit him. . . . Holden & Co. want to make Vance a Governor, not for Vance's sake, or by reason of his abilities, but to gratify a disgraceful partisan pride.[8]

It was natural that animosities should flare following the collapse of the Confederate defenses at New Bern. Those who had retreated ignominiously did not want to be reminded of the fact, and those who had stood their ground were not averse to public acclaim. The press compounded the problem by printing some stories of the battle which were characterized by exaggeration and inaccuracy, if not willful misrepresentation. For instance, on 22 March the "War News" column of the *North Carolina Standard* erroneously claimed: "It is also said that at a very critical period Col. Vance ordered Maj. Burgwyn to charge the enemy, which was done very handsomely and effectively."

Such a clear misrepresentation of fact was bound to have offended those who knew better. Colonel Burgwyn had never engaged the enemy in the battle. He and his men were posted beyond the swamp on the extreme right of the line and were never attacked. He distinguished himself by his effective conduct of the retreat but had no opportunity to do battle. Understandably such men as Major Lewis and Dr. Shaffner resented the implication that the Twenty-sixth had outfought the Thirty-third, especially if they thought that the commanding officer of the former, Colonel Vance, was trying to make political capital out of clearly erroneous material.

Whether Vance was initially aware of this hostility or jealousy is not known. Neither his actions nor his letters at that time indicate any concern on his part. He was concerned about his men, however, for on reaching Kinston on Sunday morning, 16 March, he immediately wrote a letter to the editor of the *Standard*, which appeared in the 22 March issue. His regiment was "in a most destitute condition" and would welcome contributions of clothing.

That he derived considerable pride and satisfaction from the behavior of his regiment at the battle of New Bern is beyond question. That he attributed this behavior largely to his personal leadership is also beyond question. In a long letter to his wife on 20 March, Vance suggested that he was in the thick of the fight and, when all hope was abandoned, was the only one capable of leading his men to safety under exceedingly trying circumstances. "I believe they would every one follow me into the jaws of certain death if I lead the way," he proudly concluded.[9]

One of the governor's great admirers was Julius A. Lineback, a bandsman from Salem, North Carolina. The band, under the direction of Captain Samuel Timothy Mickey, was originally recruited for Wheeler's Battalion, subsequently captured at Roanoke Island. Seeking assignment for his band with some other regiment, Mickey was in New Bern in early March. The Twenty-sixth was encamped four miles below the town. By chance he met Colonel Vance, and on 7 March, a week before the battle of New Bern, the band became attached to Vance's regiment. Captain Mickey recorded the circumstances of this first meeting:

> I was sitting in the lobby of the Gaston House, New Bern, when a man wearing a Colonel's uniform came in with a loaf of bread under each arm. This was Zeb Vance. I spoke to him and told him my errand. Colonel Vance replied: "You are the very man I am looking for. You represent the Salem band. Come to my regiment at Wood's brick yard, four miles below New Bern." Next morning (March 1862), I went down to the camp, was met by Captain Horton, of Company C, and as the result of my visit, the band was engaged and at first it was paid by the officers.[10]

Julius Lineback faithfully recorded "the incidents and experiences of army life that came to the band boys as we were familiarly called in those days." The first few days in service made an indelible impression upon him. When he and his fellow bandsmen left Salem on 5 March, little did they expect to witness a battle the following week. As he later noted: "We had hardly gotten ourselves fixed in our novel quarters when, about dark March 13, news reached camp that the enemy was advancing up the river. We spent an anxious night. We had not expected to so soon run up against the serious side of army life, and heartily wished that the disturbing element had kept quiet sometime longer."[11]

The young, peace-loving, Moravian boys who made up the band

became the "musical heart and soul" of the Twenty-sixth. None appreciated them more than Zeb Vance, and the affection was mutual. These young men came from an area of the state that had been recently accused of being disloyal to the Confederacy. The accuser, writing under the pen name of "Traveler" in the *Richmond Examiner*, had singled out Forsyth County as the "hotbed of Toryism" and the editorial policy of the *People's Press*, published in Salem, as the "spirit of disloyalty to the South." The "Traveler" article appeared in the 11 January 1862 issue of the *Examiner* and was reprinted a week later in the *People's Press*. It accused the people of Salem of being politically "rotten to the core" and favoring restoration of the Union.[12] Although there may have been elements of disloyalty and disaffection in Forsyth County, a number of her young citizens were volunteering and dying. Shortly after the battle of New Bern, Dr. J. F. Shaffner furnished the *People's Press* in Salem with a list of casualties among troops from the area.[13]

That there were Union sympathizers in North Carolina in the winter of 1862 should not be surprising. Hardly a year had elapsed since the defeat of the convention by a vote of the people. Such distinguished citizens as Zeb Vance, John M. Morehead, John A. Gilmer, Jonathan Worth, and William A. Graham had strongly opposed the convention. Although the call for the convention had been narrowly defeated, of the 120 delegates chosen, 78 were conditional or unconditional Unionists and only 42 were secessionists. All of the counties in northwestern North Carolina, including Forsyth, Davie, Iredell, Rowan, Davidson, Randolph, and Guilford, had supported unconditional Union delegates. Stokes, Rockingham, and Caswell had supported conditional Union delegates. Even six counties in the northeastern part of the state had voted for unconditional Union delegates, as had Hyde County. In the less than a year of North Carolina's allegiance to the Confederacy, the continued presence of Union sentiment in some parts of the state was to be expected.[14]

Following the battle of New Bern some Confederates began to feel that they had been victimized by traitors. General Branch reported that the accuracy with which shells were "thrown over a thick, intervening woodland" convinced him "of the necessity of driving traitors and enemies in disguise from all towns and neighborhoods of which we desire to hold military possession."[15] In a letter to his cousin, Kemp Battle, Major Lewis wrote that "Gen[eral] Burnside told the bearer of a flag of truce, he knew our exact number & how they were posted, & that the result would have been the same; it made no difference where the militia had been posted, as he would have attacked them anyhow. They made no attack on our water batteries, but as soon as the infantry retreated, they ran their gunboats up to Newbern without hindrance, as our batteries were evacuated of course."[16]

Perhaps the most blatant display of Union sentiment occurred at the Beaufort County seat of Washington, when that town was attacked and captured by a small Federal expeditionary force on 21 March. Reporting that the mayor had come down to meet the troops, one commanding officer noted with evident satisfaction that he noticed "considerable Union sentiment expressed by the inhabitants." He said that "from quite a number of houses we were saluted by waving handkerchiefs, and from one the national flag, with the motto, 'The Union and the Constitution,' was displayed. A large number of the inhabitants expressed a wish that sufficient force could be sent there to protect them against the rebels."[17]

In spite of North Carolina's great war record, however, she would never rid herself of accusations of disloyalty. She led all of her sister states in the commitment of troops to the confederacy and in casualties, but she also led in the number of desertions. The problem of desertion began in the winter and spring of 1862 and persisted throughout the war. It undoubtedly gave credence to the belief in the North that there were a sufficient number of loyalists and disgruntled inhabitants in the state to establish a civil government.[18] Lincoln thought so and would shortly have a former North Carolinian appointed military governor of the state.

But on Sunday morning, 16 March, there was no evidence of despair or disloyalty when the men of the Twenty-sixth and Thirty-third regiments marched into Kinston. They were bereft and defeated but not for long. They were escorted into town by the regimental band of the Twenty-sixth. On the day of the battle the band had been sent to New Bern, but when the Confederates retreated across the Trent and burned the bridges behind them, few waited for further instructions. The bandsmen took the first available flatcar for Kinston. They did not learn that their regiment had escaped relatively unharmed until Sunday morning. "With glad hearts," wrote Julius Lineback, "we went out to meet and escort it into town, to the courthouse square where the men were soon supplied with food by citizens, and enjoyed the rest and sleep they so badly needed after their severe and fatiguing march."[19] The *People's Press* in Salem had reported that the band had reached Kinston the day before. Learning of Vance's approach, the bandsmen went out to meet him and led the march into Kinston to the tune of "Dixie."[20]

The condition of the men was indeed destitute. J. J. Young, acting quartermaster of the Twenty-sixth, reported later that "the whole reg[imen]t lost their overcoats & all the clothing they had except what they had on." Specifically, he reported the loss of 230 tents, 495 guns, 879 knapsacks, 806 haversacks, 524 canteens, 569 cartridge boxes, 84 camp kettles, 1 wagon, 1 ambulance, 1 team and 2 sets of harness, as well as a great number of axes, spades, picks and hatchets.[21] Colonel Vance appealed immediately for public support. P. F. Pescud, a Raleigh druggist, joined in the appeal, advertising in the *State Journal:* "Col. Z. B. Vance's brave and gallant men are entirely destitute of socks, or a change of underclothing. The undersigned calls upon the ladies of Raleigh and the surrounding country to aid him in making them comfortable. I wish to send them a box of socks, shirts, drawers, etc., on Saturday of this week or early next week. Who will be the first to send a contribution?"[22]

In mid-March 1862, imminent peril had become a reality to North Carolinians. All of tidewater North Carolina, with the exception of the Wilmington area, was clearly under the domination of the Federal forces. The Burnside expedition had been in progress since early January, and many had predicted the outcome. The fall of New Bern, therefore, was not surprising, but it undoubtedly served to galvanize North Carolina's determination to resist to the bitter end. It also underscored the absolute necessity of furnishing the state with greater protection in both men and arms. These had been generated in substantial numbers only to be siphoned off by the Confederate authorities, principally for the defense of Richmond, despite repeated protests from Governor Clark. But on 29 March, the *North Carolina Standard* confidently reported: "In North Carolina there is no lack of men for the war. Our people are coming up to the rescue from every quarter. Their alacrity in filling up the ranks and multiplying volunteers for the war, recently, exceeds all former manifestations of enthusiasm."

There was genuine concern for the security of property east of the Wilmington and Weldon Railroad. On 15 March, Brigadier General Gatlin published an order from the secretary of war that "all Cotton, Tobacco and Naval Stores within this Department, must be removed West of the Wilmington and Weldon Railroad; or if distant from any railroad or navigable stream, put in such places of security that they cannot be reached by the enemy." In the same issue of the *State Journal* Harry Burgwyn's father advertised for a plantation on or near a railroad line that had accommodations for fifty to seventy-five Negroes.[23]

In such fashion did North Carolina greet the early spring of 1862.

Her efforts on behalf of the Confederacy had yielded practically nothing to aid her own defense. But her will to fight was unimpaired. If anything, her people were more determined—and undoubtedly more objective. Henceforth they would have to look to themselves and to their own resources, for they were in trouble and fighting at a disadvantage. Like the Confederacy, they were in a period of transition, militarily and politically. Both had suffered severely during the winter, and the North was on the march. Southerners were beginning to realize that they were in for a long, bitter struggle. The illusion of a short war and an easy victory had certainly been shattered. It would soon express itself politically with the election of Colonel Vance to succeed Governor Henry Toole Clark.

Clark's position had been unenviable, but under the circumstances he had performed well. History has neglected Clark's contribution to North Carolina's war effort because he has been overshadowed by Ellis and Vance. The *Western Sentinel* came to his defense in an editorial display of fairness and even-handed justice: "Gov. Clark, in North Carolina, has done all for the defense of the State that an enlightened, patriotic and faithful citizen could do. Thrown unexpectedly into the executive chair, burdened with at least ten-fold its ordinary duties, without experience or preparation, he has organized, equipped and sent into the field in a less time than twelve months, not less than fifty or sixty thousand men." Because the coastal defenses were the charge of the Confederate government, Clark could not be held responsible for any losses.[24]

But at this time the brightest hope for the South lay in the leadership that General Robert E. Lee would shortly bring to the Army of Northern Virginia. In early March, he was recalled from his command of the Confederate Department of South Carolina, Georgia, and East Florida and, on 14 March, was appointed military adviser to President Davis and charged "with the conduct of military operations in the armies of the Confederacy under the direction of the President."[25]

It was none too soon, for on the same day General McClellan issued his famous Order of the Day from Fairfax Court House: "Soldiers of the Army of the Potomac! For a long time I have kept you inactive, but not without a purpose. You were to be disciplined, armed, and instructed. The formidable artillery you now have had to be created. Other armies were to move and accomplish certain results. . . . The period of inaction has passed. I will bring you now face to face with the rebels, and only pray that God may defend the right!"[26]

About the same time, the Shenandoah Valley campaign was opened, in which Stonewall Jackson would demonstrate his rare capacity for outwitting and outmaneuvering the enemy. His diversionary operations in the valley would play a key role in preventing a larger concentration of McClellan's troops as they converged upon the Confederate capital. In June, Jackson would be summoned to join Lee in the defense of Richmond. Together they would usher in a new day of hope for the South, though fleeting, and to their Army of Northern Virginia would be drawn many troops from the state of North Carolina. The Twenty-sixth North Carolina, under Colonel Harry Burgwyn, would be among them.

It was fortunate for the Confederates that General Burnside did not follow up his victory at New Bern by moving immediately upon Kinston and Goldsboro, for the troops were disorganized, poorly equipped, and totally incapable of any sustained defense. But Burnside needed to consolidate his own position by bringing up sufficient reinforcements. His lines were attenuated. Garrisons had to be maintained at all strategic points in the wake of his conquest. Fort Macon had to be placed under siege. Burnside had suffered heavily in crossing over the bar at Hatteras. Additional horses and wagons, as well as railroad equipment, would be needed for transport if he were to conduct an offensive either in the direction of Norfolk or of Kinston and Goldsboro. And entrenchments to the rear of New Bern between the Trent and Neuse rivers were essential to any significant movement away from his base of operations.

Burnside had missed a golden opportunity, but if his reaction to the battle of New Bern was one of prudent caution, that of the Confederacy was one of alarm and immediate response. Within days, the high command in North Carolina was completely reorganized.

On 15 March General Gatlin was relieved of command "on account of ill health" and was succeeded by Major General Theophilus H. Holmes. Brigadier General Samuel G. French was ordered to Wilmington to replace Brigadier General Joseph R. Anderson, who was assigned a brigade command under Holmes. And Brigadier General Robert Ransom was ordered to proceed to Goldsboro without delay.[27]

Simultaneously, orders were issued to rush reinforcements in from Virginia. On 23 March Robert E. Lee advised General Holmes "to ascertain whether the enemy will advance upon Goldsborough or Wilmington, and to use your whole force to repel them and to protect the railroad," adding that "the troops from the Department of Northern Virginia will be forwarded to you as soon as possible." By 31 March General Holmes was able to report 20,372 officers and men "present for duty" in the Department of North Carolina.[28]

But no sooner were the reinforcements in place before it began to appear that they would shortly be needed again in Virginia. On 28 March General Holmes advised Lee that Burnside showed no sign of advancing toward Goldsboro; rather, he seemed to be planning to occupy the counties along the coast and Fort Macon. Lee responded that he expected Burnside to join McClellan in a two-pronged attack on Norfolk. He therefore urged Holmes "to watch the movements of the enemy vigilantly, and at the same time so to post your troops that while restraining his operations you may readily re-enforce any point attacked. If Wilmington should be the point, you must concentrate there. If Norfolk, it will be necessary to move all your disposable force there. With this view it might be well to hold a portion of your troops at Weldon."[29]

This latter point raised a serious question with General Holmes. In two successive messages in early April, he emphasized to Lee that the confidence of the people had only recently been partially restored by the concentration of troops under his command. Declaring that his "efficient force (12,000)," including the troops defeated at New Bern, was barely sufficient to resist a Burnside advance, Holmes flatly stated that "a serious panic will result if it be materially diminished, and as there is a general feeling that North Carolina has been neglected by the Government, the steps I have taken to reassure the people and restore confidence would be to a great extent nullified and hence it is that I shall wait until I am certain that a blow will be struck at another point, or until, in your superior wisdom and better information, you shall direct me otherwise."[30]

Holmes lacked sufficient arms for his men although every effort was being made to collect them from private sources. As the general called for more arms and men, Governor Clark found himself in confrontation with both Holmes and the authorities in Richmond. In compliance with a directive from Richmond, Clark had made a call upon the state for her quota of five regiments, which had been "handsomely responded to by the tender of more than a hundred companies—besides filling up ten war Regiments with new enlistments." These new companies were pouring into the Camp of Instruction at Raleigh but could not be clothed, equipped or armed.[31]

On 23 April, learning that "a shipment from England on board of the 'Southwick' of a lot of Enfield Rifles for the State of North Carolina bought by her agent" had been made, the governor advised Secretary of War George W. Randolph that he did not know when the ship would arrive and desired information. He noted that she also carried arms and munitions for the Confederate government.[32] Clark wanted it clearly understood that part of the cargo on the *Southwick* was destined solely for North Carolina.

There is little wonder that anxiety and despondency pervaded eastern North Carolina. Yet the people of the state had responded to every call for troops; on 21 April Clark reported that the state's quota, thirty-eight thousand (one-sixth of the eligible white population), was then in the field, that "12 Regiments of troops originally for the War service have been fully recruited," and that "the 12 months Regiments have very generally re-enlisted." In addition to these troops, he reported, "within the past two months I have recruited for the war about 10,000 Troops who are mostly now in our Camp of Instruction (Camp Mangum) near this place and some companies are still recruiting." On 29 April Governor Clark reported to Weldon N. Edwards, president of the State Convention, that "the operations of the Conscription Act, retains in the Field all our present force, and there is now in Camp an excess ('ten organized Regiments, and two others nearly ready to organize') of the quota required from this State."[33]

CHAPTER 11

WE LITERALLY HEAR NOTHING OR
KNOW NOTHING

General Holmes was no sooner in command of operations in North Carolina than he began to exhibit signs of disenchantment and lack of confidence. In mid-April he entreated General Lee to be relieved of command, pleading his own inability. Eventually he asked Lee for the services of General James Johnston Pettigrew, saying, "I need his strength to discipline new recruits rapidly."[1]

To say the least, Holmes was a frustrated commanding general. Indeed, frustration was the lot of both Holmes and Burnside, the latter for want of transportation, the former for want of men and arms. Both were forced into a protective holding pattern pending developments before Richmond. And combat between their opposing forces was necessarily limited to occasional skirmishes between reconnaissance units. This situation gave the Confederate troops in eastern North Carolina invaluable time for reorganization and training. It is doubtful that the men shared the frustration of their commanding general, for they were too busily engaged in the daily routine of camp life to have much concern for the broader implications of the war effort.

The expiration dates for the twelve-months volunteers were rapidly approaching. Colonel Vance, considered the "best stump speaker in the army," was repeatedly called upon to address the regiments, urging their reenlistment for the duration of the war. According to one biographer, "He reinforced his appeals with the stirring martial refrains which the Moravian musicians seemed best able to produce." One of these bandsmen, Julius Lineback, considered Vance a "fluent and eloquent speaker" and wrote that the band "felt flattered and consented to blow as much war spirit into the men as we could." In later years, Dr. Thomas J. Boykin, regimental surgeon of the Twenty-sixth North Carolina, said that when the address ended and the call for reenlistment was made, "*every man* in the regiment marched up and re-enlisted for the war."[2]

Vance was beloved by the members of his regimental band. He had arranged to have them paid by private subscriptions from the officers of the regiment. During the many weeks that the Twenty-sixth was encamped in and near Kinston, the band gained the affection of the troops as well as of the townspeople. Julius Lineback later recalled that residents of Kinston visited the camp in the evenings, and the bandsmen "were vain enough to imagine that our music was a large part of the attraction for them." Their popularity led to the idea of giving concerts in Kinston. With the consent of Colonel Vance and General Ransom, the first concert was held in the Methodist church to a capacity crowd so that a repeat performance was required. "Those concerts," according to Lineback, "netted $420.65 which sum was equally divided between the six regimental and the brigade hospitals." The professional capability of this little Moravian band was fully matched by the patriotic generosity of its members.[3]

If frustration was not the lot of most of the men, boredom was. Julius Lineback wrote in his diary that "the men became restive and anxious for more active and exciting occupation than the double daily drill and dress parade afforded, and often expressed the wish that they had something more to do."[4] Harry Burgwyn's greatest concern, however, was not boredom but the uncertainties of his situation. His letters written during this period show no break in consistency. He was concerned for his future, as always, and the desire to command a regiment was ever on his mind. With him, concern for overall strategy was a self-imposed duty, to which he frequently alluded. He was reelected lieutenant colonel of the Twenty-sixth by a narrow margin, reflecting the negative reaction of his men to a stern disciplinarian. Of the two, Colonel Vance was more popular, but Vance wisely left the management of the regiment in Burgwyn's capable hands. Some of his letters during this period reveal the man who would shortly come to be known as the "Boy Colonel of the Confederacy."

Only six days after the battle of New Bern there was little doubt in Harry's mind that Burnside could be stopped if he should elect to march on Goldsboro. In a letter to his father on 20 March, from his encampment about six miles above Kinston, Harry wrote that his troops were destitute. They were "not a particle discouraged but have lost a great deal of confidence in their leader & some time must elapse before they can know their new generals. Gen. Ransom has been sent here & Gen. French I hear is to go to Wilmington." Three days later he gave his father detailed information on the composition of the First and Second Brigades following their reorganization, the new location of his regiment, a minute description of his "perfectly destitute" condition, and further reflections on the battle of New

Bern. By 30 March the regiment was on the march but moving so slowly that Harry doubted that action was imminent; earlier he had conjectured that it might make a raid on New Bern.[5] On 1 April he wrote:

> I think that the enemy can be very effectually met if the proper generalship is shown. I am preparing as well as I can a map of the roads around here & shall collect as much information concerning the topography of the country as possible. We learn that the enemy are completing a line of entrenchments around the rear of New Berne from Neuse to Trent River exactly what Branch ought to have done as soon as he thought the town was in danger. Our infantry pickets extend some two or three miles below here & the cavalry go down to sometimes 6 or seven miles of New Berne & have had one or two little skirmishes with the enemy.[6]

Burnside was convinced that the Confederates were "concentrating in large numbers at and near Kinston." On 3 April he advised Secretary Stanton that he would move against them "as soon as sufficient re-enforcements and transportation arrive . . . unless I receive instructions from you to make the attack on Weldon and Gaston instead of Goldsborough and Raleigh." On 17 April Burnside reported to McClellan that he was "building just in rear of the town [New Bern] an inclosed bastioned field work capable of holding 1,000 men and mounting thirty guns, which will be finished in a few days." His command consisted of about fifteen thousand men, distributed as follows: "Three regiments at Roanoke [Island], one-half of a regiment at Hatteras Inlet, three regiments and a battalion with General Parke and on the [rail]road, and thirteen and one-half regiments with the battery at this place [New Bern]."[7]

Frustrated for want of news, Harry urged his father to "bring or send some papers as we get none. We hear that they are taking the troops around Goldsboro to Va. Write me what is expected for we literally hear nothing or know nothing. On 7 April he unburdened himself about reenlistment problems and declared that he was "heartily tired of taking all the blame upon myself & getting the least part of the credit":

> I do not think my regiment will reenlist for the war—unless the Government changes its policy. If the furloughs to reenlisted men are to be stopped they will not get many more men to revolunteer. It seems to me that our government has acted

with about as little foresight as was possible. When this war is ended & history records its events it will be universally acknowledged that this was emphatically a movement of the people & not of the government. If short furloughs were to be granted our men would reenlist without any difficulty & if they do not I am afraid they will not.

This makes me doubly anxious to secure a position before my commission expires for there is a great difference between a man's seeking a commission with one already in his pocket & a man's trying his luck with nothing to fall back upon or to boast of. . . . If Vance were to leave I could get the command of this regiment. . . . I do not care about being out of the service for a single day & am willing to take a raw regiment & trust to chances for getting it well disciplined before carrying it into battle.[8]

Harry's frustration was undoubtedly deepened by the feeling that he did not have Vance's undivided attention and support as he strove to train and discipline the troops under their command. Not only was the colonel being touted for governor, but, apparently elated by his success at New Bern, Vance quickly initiated an abortive effort to raise a legion for the war. On 3 April he wrote the secretary of war, George Wythe Randolph, requesting authority to recruit two regiments of infantry, two companies of cavalry, and one of artillery. He guaranteed to have "the requisite number of men within thirty days." On 18 April, he dispatched a notice to several North Carolina newspapers, which began "I AM AUTHORIZED BY THE SECT'Y OF WAR TO raise a LEGION for the war" and ended "Turn out, and let's make short work with Abe." Although Vance failed for want of support from both state and Confederate authorities, he apparently devoted considerable effort to the cause.[9]

On 20–21 April the election of field and company officers of the Twenty-sixth North Carolina was held. The following day Harry reported to his father that "by order of Genl. [Robert] Ransom an election for field & company officers of my regiment was held on yesterday & the day before which resulted in Col. Vance's reelection, my own, & the election of our former Adjt. as Major; so I am secure of my position for the war. A large number of Co[mpany] officers were turned out & some of the best we had were thrown aside. There was a great deal of trickery & electioneering & at one time my election was more than doubtful."[10]

By the end of April Harry was involved with court-martial duties in Kinston, which afforded him some relief from camp routine and an occasional trip to Raleigh. Feeling *"exceedingly* shabby in my external appearance," he wrote his mother to order him a pair of shoes and other items of clothing. Shortly afterward Harry learned of the fall of New Orleans. Although he tended not to believe it, he wrote his father:

> The fall of N.O. if it is true that it has fallen is not without the consoling reflection that the Yankees will have to encounter "Bronze John" or "Yaller Jack." This I believe is the year for a yellow fever feast & a dainty meal I hope he'll have. The acclimated Louisianians proved a tough morsel but if he does not relish a tender batch of psalm singing Yankees I am much mistaken. If you go to Richmond I shall rely upon your writing me a full account of the "situation." We can never have an idea of what is going on behind the scenes from mere newspaper accounts. Burnside has evidently sent off the larger portion of his force somewhere: we do not exactly know where. I do not think he has more than 5,000 men with him at New Berne. . . . The impression I believe seems to gain ground that there is to be no fight at Yorktown.[11]

A few days earlier Burnside had attempted a foray above Elizabeth City in an effort to destroy the locks of the Dismal Swamp and Currituck Sound canals, but it proved abortive. On 19 April General Reno, with two full regiments and parts of three others, had encountered the Confederates within about a mile and a half of South Mills. A sharp engagement ensued. The Confederates withdrew in good order after inflicting heavy casualties. Reno did not pursue because his men were exhausted. The locks were not destroyed, and the battle of South Mills was considered a Southern victory.

Back in camp, Harry had little news to report in early May, but in writing his parents he always reflected on "the situation," as he termed it. When the fall of Norfolk seemed imminent, Harry wrote to his father on the subject of "despondent, chicken hearted men who seem to think that we are ruined simply because we evacuate politically important places. To Iron Clad gunboats the Va. [*Merrimac*] has been the only obstacle to the advance of these Yankees on Norfolk for six or seven weeks. When the enemy get a few more boats they can attack Norfolk with some of them & while the Va. is busy with these they can run by the batteries at Yorktown with the others. It is necessary therefore to keep the Va. & all other means to defend Richmond." To Harry, "even the evacuation of Norfolk though to unthinking men a most disastrous thing for us is in reality under the present circumstances not only a necessity but a capital move." In the final analysis, he observed, "Our country may suffer & a great deal of our property lost but the success of our cause is not even endangered until the immense armies we have in the field are destroyed."[12]

On 11 May, seizing upon the leisure of a Sunday afternoon, Harry wrote his mother a long letter about the importance of having a full complement of men in his regiment and explained why he would not want his brother Willie to serve in his regiment:

> My own regiment numbers now nearly 1100 men after we discharged a great many inefficient dilapidated individuals & in a few days more we hope to get the other 150 so as to complete our numbers to the required maximum. . . . We have just received news which I published before the head of my regiment that Jackson had gained a complete victory over Banks & that Beauregard had attacked the enemy at Corinth & driven him several miles from his position. For some time past I have seen evidencies of superior generalship on our part which foreshadows more successful efforts upon decisive points. I look upon the evacuation of Norfolk as both wise & necessary. Norfolk is a salient liable after the Fall of Roanoke to be taken at any moment. Had Burnside marched upon Suffolk immediately after the Fall of Roanoke Island I know of no reason why he should not have possessed it. . . . You have seen in the papers that Vance has been made a Brigadier General. He has received no official announcement to that effect; he received a leave of absence for 15 days & is now absent from his regiment. . . . If Vance is made a Brigadier it is barely possible that he may appoint Jordan as his Ast. Adj. Gen. & if so the Adjt^cy. of my reg[i]m[en]t will be vacant. Willie will want me to appoint him but I know we will not get along well together & am really too afraid of his disposition to appoint him. I feel certain that it will be as it was at Crabtree & that under the circumstances in which we would be placed there would be difficulties & disagreements which would make us both unhappy, & then in a fight were I to see him fall I could not attend properly to my regiment. . . . I shall be very unhappy if the convictions I entertain should compel me to refuse him.[13]

Harry's reference to Jackson's victory over General Banks and to the evacuation of Norfolk provides the clue to Northern strategy as the spring campaign opened in Virginia. It also explains why Harry had been so anxious to discuss the "situation" with his father. Except for perhaps one trip to Raleigh in mid-April on court-martial duties, it is doubtful that they had had any opportunity to share opinions about the course of the war, and particularly about the threatening developments in Virginia and North Carolina.

Certainly the winter of 1862 had been disastrous for the Confederacy. Key defensive positions, not only in eastern North Carolina but along the coast, in western Virginia, and in the western theater of operations, had, one by one, yielded to the superior strength of the aggressor. These Union victories would mean the permanent occupation of Kentucky and Missouri and the partial occupation of Tennessee.

The North was elated. "At last events are moving with breathless rapidity," editorialized *Harper's Weekly* in late March, chronicling the victories—Leesburg, Winchester, Brunswick, Fernandina, Columbus, Manassas—so that "one by one every rebel strong-hold is forced or turned. . . . There is not a point in the line of three thousand miles at which the rebels can make a stand."[14] Within weeks New Orleans and Norfolk would also fall to the enemy. Would the capital of the Confederacy be next?

Since early spring the gravest threat to Richmond had been posed by the presence of McClellan before Yorktown and McDowell before Fredericksburg, with General Nathaniel P. Banks, heavily reinforced, threatening Winchester and the lower valley of the Shenandoah. General Frémont, moving from the west, menaced Staunton in the southern or upper part of the valley. McClellan's superior forces enjoyed strong naval support, which would soon be penetrating far up the James and York rivers. And McDowell was so situated above Richmond that Banks could move swiftly to his support from the valley. If a junction between McClellan and McDowell could then be effected, the fate of Richmond would be sealed. This was the general situation on 12 April, when the authority of General Joseph E. Johnston was enlarged to include the departments of Norfolk and the Peninsula. By 17 April the main body of his army had joined General John B. Magruder's small force defending the Yorktown line, bringing their total strength to about fifty-three thousand men. Benjamin Huger's force of nine thousand was stationed at Norfolk on the south side of the James River. In their front lay a formidable array of military and naval might.[15]

Johnston did not believe that his defenses along the Warwick River, roughly spanning the Peninsula between Yorktown and Gloucester Point on his left and Mulberry Point on his right, could do more than delay McClellan's advance against Richmond. In addition, the smoothbore batteries protecting Johnston's left flank at Yorktown lay dangerously exposed to the long-range, rifled cannon of the Federal fleet. If these could be silenced, the enemy could move up the York River and threaten him from the rear. All of this he had earlier reported to the president, urging that the Federal army, instead of being delayed in its approach, "should be encountered in front of Richmond by one quite as numerous, formed by uniting there all the available forces of the Confederacy in North Carolina, South Carolina, and Georgia, with those at Norfolk, on the Peninsula, and then near Richmond, including Smith's and Longstreet's divisions, which had arrived." This recommendation drew little support from Davis and his advisers. General Lee, on the other hand, was disposed to keep the Federals occupied on the lower Peninsula as long as possible and then to prevent a Federal concentration before Richmond by making a bold counterstroke in northern Virginia. Johnston later wrote: "The belief that events on the Peninsula would soon compel the Confederate Government to adopt my method of opposing the Federal army, reconciled me somewhat to the necessity of obeying the President's order." [16]

On the night of 3–4 May, Johnston suddenly withdrew from the Yorktown line. On Monday, 5 May, the Confederates fought a bloody, rear-guard action in abandoning the Williamsburg entrenchments. By 9 May Johnston's army had withdrawn to a point only fifteen miles from the Chickahominy and less than thirty miles from Richmond. A fleet of Federal ironclads and transports lay at West Point, on the York River, only thirty-five miles from Richmond. On 10 May the Federal forces occupied Norfolk. The next day, the *Virginia* [*Merrimac*] was blown up, and General Huger began retreating up the south side of the James River in the direction of Petersburg. On 15 May five Federal gunboats attacked Drewry's Bluff, only seven miles from Richmond, but were driven off after a three-hour bombardment. [17]

By 22 May Johnston's line of defense was drawn up practically on the outskirts of Richmond, with his right flank across the Charles City Road, five miles southeast of Richmond, and his left resting at the Fairfield Race Course, almost on the northeastern edge of the city. At Mechanicsville, just north of the Chickahominy and east of the Virginia Central Railroad, and only five miles above Richmond, the Confederates maintained part of one division for guarding the railroads connecting with Fredericksburg (the Richmond, Fredericksburg, and Potomac) and the Shenandoah Valley (the Virginia Central). At the same time, McClellan had two corps stationed eight miles northeast of Richmond at Cold Harbor. The rest of his forces were crossing the Chickahominy at Bottom's Bridge as they advanced up the Williamsburg road and parallel to the York River Railroad. They were then within fifteen miles of Richmond.[18]

And just sixty miles to the north, at Fredericksburg, lay McDowell within easy marching distance of McClellan's right flank. If the two could be united, Johnston would be faced with the overpowering might of 150,000 Federal troops. On 24 May advance units of McClellan's forces occupied Mechanicsville. Since Lawrence O'B. Branch's brigade had already been pulled back from Gordonsville and stationed at Hanover Courthouse, and Joseph R. Anderson's brigade ordered back from the line of the Rappahannock, McDowell could move almost unopposed to the outskirts of Richmond.[19]

But a remarkable drama was unfolding in the valley west of the Blue Ridge mountains. Stonewall Jackson, Harry Burgwyn's old mentor at VMI, was on the warpath, and Banks was in great difficulty. When the spring campaign opened, Jackson had at his immediate disposal thirty-six hundred infantry, six hundred cavalry and six batteries of twenty-seven guns. Banks had crossed the Potomac and was approaching Winchester with thirty-six thousand infantry, two thousand cavalry, and eighty pieces of artillery. After twice offering battle to the enemy's advanced guard to no avail, Jackson reluctantly abandoned Winchester to Banks's lead division on the morning of 12 March. He then fell back to Strasburg, eighteen miles to the south. When General James Shields's division of eleven thousand men and twenty-seven guns followed on the eighteenth, Jackson, hoping to draw Banks up the valley, had already moved to Mount Jackson, twenty-five miles farther south. McClellan could not see the point of chasing Jackson's insignificant force. By 20 March he had detached two of Banks's divisions for the protection of Washington east of the Blue Ridge and had ordered Shields back to Winchester to cover Harpers Ferry, the Baltimore and Ohio Railroad, and the Chesapeake canal.[20]

When Turner Ashby, Jackson's cavalry leader, reported that Shields was retreating toward Winchester, Jackson followed quickly in pursuit. His instructions were to hold the enemy in the valley. Marching thirty-six miles in a day and a half, his men reached the outskirts of Kernstown, three miles below Winchester, shortly after noon on 23 March. Led to believe that only four regiments of infantry, a few batteries, and some cavalry barred his way to Winchester, Jackson attacked immediately. It soon became evident that he had taken on Shields's entire division. What Jackson thought would be a minor engagement flared into a major battle. After three hours of intensive fighting his center gave way, and only darkness saved his men from being completely routed.[21]

Outnumbered almost three to one, Jackson had fought a good fight, nonetheless, and, though defeated, felt that he had been justified in the assault. The following day he reported to General Johnston: "As the enemy had been sending off troops from the district and from what I could learn were still doing so, and knowing your great desire to prevent it, and having a prospect of success, I engaged him yesterday about 3 p.m. near Winchester and fought until dusk, but his forces were so superior to mine that he repulsed me with the loss of valuable officers and men killed and wounded."[22]

But McClellan was not deterred in his determination to bring Banks's forces over the mountains to Manassas for the greater protection of Washington. On 24 March, the day after Kernstown, McClellan wired Banks, to resume his movement on Manassas, leaving Shields's command at or near Strasburg and Winchester. Banks promptly replied, "The enemy is in full retreat. Our men are exhausted, but will overtake them. I think they fly rapidly."[23]

By mid-April Jackson was still in retreat, but he was neither overtaken nor did he "fly rapidly." Maintaining almost daily contact with General Richard S. Ewell, who was stationed just east of the Blue Ridge below the Rappahannock, he was withdrawing up the valley in calculated stages. On 14 April he advised Ewell, "My desire is, as far as practicable, to hold the valley, and if I fall back from New Market toward Madison Court House I hope that Banks will be deterred from advancing much farther toward Staunton by the apprehension of my returning to New Market and thus getting in his rear." Three days later Jackson sent a cryptic message: "The enemy have advanced in force to Mount Jackson. I am falling back via Harrisonburg to Swift Run Gap. Please move early tomorrow morning to Swift Run Gap. . . . I hope that you will not make a forced march, as it is desirable that your command should come up in the best possible condition." By 20 April Jackson had swung eastward from Harrisonburg to Conrad's Store in Elk Run Valley, at the base of Swift Run Gap. The same day he advised Ewell to halt his command near Gordonsville and await further instructions.[24]

Jackson had finally reached a protected position that offered considerable maneuverability. With Swift Run Gap to his rear he could be quickly reinforced by Ewell from the east or, if necessity demanded, he could move behind the protective screen of the Blue Ridge. To his front lay the South Fork of the Shenandoah River. Should Banks attempt the capture of Staunton, Jackson could threaten his rear at several points. He could also move northward down the Luray Valley, along the eastern slope of the Massanuttens, to Front Royal and Winchester. But, at the moment, the authorities in Richmond were more concerned about McDowell's pressure on Fredericksburg. On 21 April Lee wrote Jackson, "If you can use General Ewell's division in an attack on General Banks, and to drive him back, it will prove a great relief to the pressure on Fredericksburg; but if you should find General Banks too strong to be approached, and your object is to hold General Ewell in supporting distance to your column, he may be of more importance at this time between Fredericksburg and Richmond." Jackson replied, "My object has been to get in his [Banks] rear at New Market or Harrisonburg if he gives me an opportunity, and this should be the case if he should advance on Staunton with his main body."[25]

Banks was now in force at both places. General Frémont occupied the strategic communities of Romney, Moorefield, Franklin, and Monterey to the west of the Shenandoah mountains, and General Louis Blenker was bringing up reinforcements by way of Winchester.[26] General Robert H. Milroy, part of Frémont's command, was threatening Staunton from the direction of Monterey. Only a small Confederate force of three thousand men under General Edward Johnson stood in his way. The combined forces of Milroy and Banks could easily handle Johnson, occupy Staunton, and then move on Jackson.

To these dire possibilities Jackson had three alternative solutions, no one of which suggested a retreat or a concentration of forces in a defensive position. Jackson advised Lee that of the three plans, he preferred attacking the force west of Staunton, which would leave him only Banks to contend with. With reinforcements, he could defeat Banks, "and if he should be routed and his command destroyed, nearly all our own forces here could, if necessary, cross the Blue Ridge to Warrenton, Fredericksburg, or any other threatened point."[27]

Lee was unable to send any reinforcements to Jackson because "the force of the enemy opposite Fredericksburg is too large to admit of a reduction of our army in that quarter." The same day, in a dejected frame of mind, General Ewell reported to Lee that he had no force between his position and that of General Field below Fredericksburg, except three cavalry companies left on the line of the Rappahannock. He noted that "the enemy seem to be living on the

country, paying for nothing and wantonly destroying the resources."
After seeing Jackson, Ewell added: "I have just returned from my interview with General Jackson. He moves toward Staunton and I take
his position."[28]

On 1 May Lee instructed Ewell to occupy Jackson's position until
his return, admonishing him to keep his command "in readiness to
move toward Fredericksburg or to co-operate with General Jackson
in any movement he may make against the enemy at the White
Plains or Salem, as occasion may require." To Jackson, Lee wrote
that after considering the three plans of operation Jackson had proposed, he believed that "you must use your judgment and discretion
in these matters, and be careful to husband the strength of your command as much as possible."[29]

This was the beginning of Jackson's remarkable forward thrust to
rid the valley of the enemy. His repulse by Shields had forced him to
withdraw steadily up the valley until it was overrun by bluecoats
from Harrisonburg all the way to the Potomac. Now, a month later,
operating from a position of comparative weakness, Jackson decided
to leave the protection of Swift Run Gap and move in a long sweep
around Banks's front to join forces with General Johnson west of
Staunton. One of his staff officers wrote in a private letter, "As sure
as you and I live, Jackson is a cracked man, and the sequel will show
it." To Jackson, this move was a carefully calculated gamble. Henceforth, the unexpected, the forced march, and the skillful maneuver
would be characteristic of the man who, within thirty days, would
become a living legend. The famed Shenandoah Valley campaign was
under way. By 6 May Jackson had joined Johnson and was marching
west to confront Milroy. Two days later his forward units met Milroy
at the village of McDowell and forced him to withdraw westward,
through Monterey, seeking the protection of Frémont's forces at
Franklin. Jackson dogged his heels all the way but, on 12 May, decided to return to the valley, his principal objective being the destruction of Banks's army. By 17 May Jackson was out of the mountains and had reached Mount Solon, a few miles below Harrisonburg
and the southern terminus of the Massanutten mountains. In just
eighteen days his men had covered two hundred miles. With Frémont neutralized for the time being, Banks was isolated and exposed
to the combined attack of Jackson, Ewell, and Johnson.[30]

When they moved out on the turnpike at dawn on 21 May, the
Confederates believed they were moving down the valley to attack
Banks at Strasburg until suddenly the head of their column was
turned eastward on the road cutting through the Massanuttens to

Luray, where they camped for the night. The next morning, Jackson turned north and, with Ewell in the lead, moved swiftly down Luray Valley. He bivouacked on the night of the twenty-second about ten miles from Front Royal. In four days the troops had marched sixty miles. Neither General Banks nor Secretary Stanton believed that the Confederates had even passed Harrisonburg; yet Jackson was now in position to strike a devastating blow on the morrow. According to one observer, "Washington seemed so perfectly secure that the recruiting offices had been closed, and the President and Secretary, anticipating the immediate fall of Richmond, left for Fredericksburg the next day. McDowell was to march on the 26th, and the departure of his fine army was to be preceded by a grand review."[31]

But by 2:00 P.M. on the twenty-third, the Federal pickets before Front Royal were driven in, and, in the words of Jackson, "the Federals retreated across both Forks of the Shenandoah, attempting in their retreat to burn the bridge over the North Fork; but before they could fully accomplish their purpose our troops were upon them, and extinguished the flames, crossed the river, the enemy in full retreat toward Winchester, and our artillery and infantry in pursuit."[32] From this moment until Banks's demoralized forces were driven across the Potomac, Jackson never relented in his pursuit. On Sunday, 26 May, he rested his men and held divine service "for the purpose of rendering thanks to God for the success with which He had blessed our arms and to implore His continued favor."[33]

To Harry Burgwyn and his fellow Confederates stationed in and around Kinston, it is little wonder that perplexity and uncertainty characterized each day as the month of May unfolded. Although McClellan's advance on Richmond was apparently progressing according to plan, it was not clear whether Burnside would support McClellan by making a bold thrust into Virginia from his base at New Bern. McDowell, from his position at Fredericksburg, was poised to join McClellan in the capture of Richmond provided Banks could relieve him of the responsibility for protecting Washington. But the position of Banks in the valley depended upon the whereabouts of Stonewall Jackson—and where was he? Only Jackson seemed to be master of his own destiny.

So, on 20 May, "expecting every moment for the cars to come and carry us off" because it was "well ascertained that Burnside is with McClellan," Harry was obviously expecting, and eagerly awaiting, an early opportunity to go into battle when he advised his father that he was sending one of his soldiers on Waverly to be exchanged at Thornbury for another horse. This note was written from his headquarters eight miles above Kinston and was his last, at least extant, during the critical month of May: "What our destination may be I know not. Petersburg first & there we will find out I suppose." In a postscript he said that Ransom had told him that he would have his brother William elected to a lieutenancy in a few days.[34]

It is clear that Harry expected to entrain for Virginia at any moment. But the order to the Twenty-sixth apparently never came. Nor can it be determined that the Twenty-fifth and Thirty-fifth regiments of his brigade actually reached Virginia. They may have gone to Weldon or Petersburg and were later recalled. The regimental histories are silent on this point, and there are no known letters from Harry covering the period from 20 May to 17 June 1862. The battle of Seven Pines was fought on 31 May–1 June, and none of the regiments of General Ransom's First Brigade participated. Governor Clark had long been fearful of the inadequate protection afforded eastern North Carolina and had made this concern clear to President Davis and General Holmes.

Even then, three of the five brigades under Holmes's command were stationed in Virginia sometime during the month of May: the Second Brigade (Brig. Gen. L. O'B. Branch), the Third Brigade (Brig. Gen. J. R. Anderson), and the Fourth Brigade (Brig. Gen. J. G. Walker). Only Ransom's First Brigade, protecting the Kinston area, and French's Brigade, protecting the District of the Cape Fear, remained in North Carolina.[35]

But on the eve of the battle of Seven Pines, Richmond was urgently calling for still more troops from North Carolina. On 30 May G. W. Randolph, secretary of war, wired General Holmes, who was in Petersburg at the time, "Bring your command here as rapidly as possible and report by letter. Send on in advance to General Johnston. He will instruct you."[36] On the same day Governor Clark telegraphed Holmes: "Justice to the defence of North Carolina and to me require that a portion of the best should be retained. You must leave two of the three regiments, Hall, Hill or Ramseur. Please to issue the order immediately before they leave Goldsboro. If they have already left, I must ask their return."[37] The governor's insistent plea for protection undoubtedly accounted for the few troops that did remain in the state during McClellan's presence before Richmond.

CHAPTER 12

IN DEFENSE OF RICHMOND

As late as 25 May, General Joseph E. Johnston had not made known his specific plans for the defense of Richmond either to General Lee or to President Davis. Only after Lee had made a special point of visiting with him on 26 May did Johnston reveal his intention of attacking McClellan's forces north of the Chickahominy on 29 May. It would be a last-ditch effort in an almost hopeless situation.[1]

Each day added to the fear of impending disaster. On 27 May, Johnston was advised that McDowell had started his march on Richmond. The same day a strong Federal force struck Branch's brigade at Hanover Courthouse, only twenty-five miles from McClellan's right flank. All the while, urgent calls were going out to the authorities in North and South Carolina to speed reinforcements to Richmond's rescue. Even if Holmes's and General Roswell Ripley's troops from the Carolinas made it in time, together with Huger's forces, Johnston could not possibly muster more than eighty-odd thousand men against almost twice that number. Then, on 29 May, the day of Johnston's planned attack on McClellan north of the Chickahominy, came news of a "miracle." The previous day McDowell had suddenly halted his advancing columns, turned them around, and headed back to Fredericksburg.[2]

Behind this miracle of deliverance lay the effective cooperation and mutual understanding of two brilliant military leaders—Robert E. Lee and Stonewall Jackson. From the time he assumed the role of adviser to President Davis, Lee had recognized the great importance of Jackson's position in the Shenandoah Valley, particularly in northern Virginia, where Washington's rail and water connections to the west were vulnerable to attack. The strategic value of this area was generally recognized, and the passage of the Potomac by either side was cause for alarm to the other. Since the rout of the Federals at First Bull Run or Manassas on 21 July 1861, the authorities in Washington were never without concern for their safety. As for the defense of Richmond, the senior generals in the Virginia army early recognized that defensive strategy alone could not save the Confederacy from the overpowering might of the Union forces and that bold counterstrokes must be delivered if the South hoped to save Richmond and preserve its independence.[3] None understood this situation better than Lee and Jackson.

As he withdrew up the valley it is doubtful that Jackson fully comprehended the magnitude of his victory over Banks. Nor was he aware that on 31 May–1 June, one hundred miles to the east, the battle of Seven Pines was being fought. Now assured that Richmond would not be assailed by the combined forces of McDowell and McClellan, General Johnston had abandoned his plan for attacking the enemy north of the Chickahominy. Armed reconnaissances on the morning of the thirtieth indicated the presence of Federal outposts in strength two miles west of Seven Pines, practically on the outskirts of Richmond. It was here, along the Williamsburg road, on the south and west side of the Chickahominy, that Johnston planned to attack the following day.[4]

The battle proved to be bloody and indecisive. Both sides fought doggedly, and both stood their ground. From the standpoint of the Confederacy it was a "frightfully mismanaged battle," characterized by confusion and misunderstanding.[5] According to an observer, "It was a splendid feat of arms; but it accomplished no important results, and the ground which it gained was unimportant, and was speedily abandoned."[6] Johnston considered Seven Pines to be the least appreciated action of the war because it was unfinished and the Federal commanders claimed victory.[7]

Johnston had been wounded late on the afternoon of 31 May. He was borne from the field in great pain. That night President Davis advised General Lee that he would be assigned immediately to the command of the Army of Northern Virginia—a fateful decision that would have a profound impact upon the course of the war in the months and years ahead. There was another significant casualty at Seven Pines that same day. It was the near fatal wounding and capture of Brigadier General James Johnston Pettigrew, a brilliant young North Carolinian whose future service in the army would be closely linked with that of Lieutenant Colonel Henry King Burgwyn, Jr. Pettigrew was left for dead on the battlefield. Shot through the throat, and believing that he was about to die, he had refused to be taken to the rear. Later, during a counterattack, he was shot in the arm and bayoneted in the leg. He lay on the field all that night and was picked up the next morning by men of the Twentieth Massachusetts Regiment. He was subsequently taken to the house of Doctor William F. Gaines behind the Federal lines. During the ten days that he remained there Pettigrew was given good treatment and improved rapidly. During this time, he was under the special care of a captured Confederate surgeon, Dr. J. F. Shaffner of the Thirty-third North Carolina Regiment.[8]

Following the battle of Seven Pines, General Lee moved swiftly to improve the army's discipline and organization. On 1 June, the day he assumed command, his first official order was to deplore the loss of Johnston and to express his assurance that "every man has resolved to maintain the ancient fame of the Army of Northern Virginia and the reputation of its general and conquer or die in the approaching contest." The announcement of Lee's selection as commander was received with little enthusiasm. Many of Johnston's lieutenants resented the idea of a staff officer leading them. Some questioned his aggressiveness and capability for field service. Johnston, however, understood what Lee might accomplish when he said, "I possess in no degree the confidence of our government, and now have in my place one who does possess it, and who can accomplish what I never could have done—the concentration of our armies for the defence of the capital of the Confederacy."[9]

Lee's concern was not with his critics but with the defense of Richmond. And in the days immediately following Seven Pines, circumstances worked in his favor. A cautious McClellan was unwilling to attack until his losses could be replaced. His army still lay astride the swollen Chickahominy. Most of the bridges then under construction had been washed away, and the rains continued to pour throughout the first week in June. Lee properly concluded that McClellan must be held on the Chickahominy while the Confederates moved swiftly to strengthen the defenses of Richmond. But Lee also concluded that McClellan's superior strength could not be fended off indefinitely and that he must be attacked and driven away. To accomplish this, the earthworks protecting the city would have to be so constructed that they could be held by a relatively small force while the main body of the army maneuvered for attack. And, in all probability, Jackson would have to unite with Lee to mount a successful drive.[10]

But Jackson was retreating up the valley. On 1 June he had barely escaped the converging columns of Frémont and Shields near Strasburg. As Jackson moved rapidly south, Frémont clung to his heels. Only constant rear-guard action and the burning of bridges finally put a day's march between the two. Shields, on the other hand, was directed to move up Luray Valley, to the east of the Massanuttens, with the objective of flanking Jackson, capturing the bridges over the South Fork of the Shenandoah, occupying Port Republic, and cutting off his escape route through the passes of the Blue Ridge. This was Jackson's strategy in reverse, but the wily Confederate commander anticipated Shields. He, too, realized his exposure to a flanking movement; so he beat Shields to the bridges and burned them and by 6 June was at Port Republic, where he could maneuver against Frémont and Shields as they converged against him.[11]

Shields was certain that he could defeat Jackson, but he was not properly informed as to Jackson's whereabouts. Rather than being at Staunton on the morning of 8 June, as Shields believed, Jackson's command had taken position in Port Republic, a small community at the junction of the North and South rivers, where they joined to form the South Fork of the Shenandoah. It was here that Jackson planned to deal separately with Frémont and Shields before their forces could unite; for between them they mustered almost twenty-five thousand men. Frémont had reached Harrisonburg, but Shields, in his haste to head off Jackson, had moved impetuously. His command was strung out for twenty-five miles up the valley of the South Fork of the Shenandoah. The location of Port Republic between the two rivers afforded Jackson a perfect setting for his strategy. The South River was passable only by two deep fords. The North River was spanned by a bridge connecting the Harrisonburg road with Port Republic.

Jackson reasoned that if Frémont followed him farther south, he could be intercepted near the village of Cross Keys, only four miles northwest of Port Republic. At this point the road from Harrisonburg crossed Mill Creek, offering a strong defensive position. If Frémont could be held in check there, Jackson, by returning swiftly across the bridge into Port Republic, could attack and destroy Shields's advanced units before they could be concentrated. Holding the bridge was obviously indispensable to Jackson's strategy. He had chosen his ground well, but he was concerned about the high bluffs rising above the west bank of the Shenandoah just below Port Republic. They commanded the open valley on the east bank through which Shields would be marching. If the bluffs were occupied by Frémont, his guns could pour a deadly, enfilading fire into Jackson's ranks should he become involved with Shields. Frémont must, therefore, be held back from the bluffs until Jackson could dispose of Shields. It would require split-second timing, and his plans almost went awry.[12]

On the morning of 8 June, Jackson was ready. Ewell's division of three brigades occupied a narrow ridge overlooking the valley of Mill Creek. His total strength numbered no more than six thousand infantry and probably five hundred cavalry. Frémont had ten thousand infantry, two thousand cavalry, and twelve batteries. The main body of Jackson's army was near Port Republic, four miles in the rear. The battle of Cross Keys opened about 10:00 A.M., when the Federal batteries began firing heavily on the Confederate position. Jackson himself had not yet come up. Earlier that morning he had almost been captured by a cavalry unit of Shields's command, which had unexpectedly forded the South River, dashed into Port Republic, and captured or dispersed most of Jackson's staff. The raiders were quickly repulsed and driven out of town, but had their assault been strongly supported the outcome could have been disastrous.[13]

The battle of Cross Keys, according to one observer, was won by the Confederates more because of Frémont's timidity than through a fair test of arms. Of twenty-four regiments on the field of battle, only five were used in the initial attack, directed against the Confederate right, which lay concealed on the wooded ridge. When the Federals blundered into close range, the Confederates under Isaac Trimble greeted them with a sheet of fire. Stunned by this deadly reception, the Federals soon fell back across the clearing and rallied on their reserves. After a brief pause, General Trimble decided to follow up his initial success by combining a flanking movement with a frontal assault. Reinforced by six regiments from Ewell, the Confederates succeeded in throwing back the entire left wing of the Federal army to the protection of its line of guns. At this juncture, Jackson hesitated to bring on a general engagement. Shields was in his rear and moving rapidly on Port Republic. Only a portion of Frémont's army had been involved, and his superior strength would be difficult to overcome. But night was falling, and Frémont, "cowering on the defensive," was not likely to be too enterprising the next morning.[14]

While Ewell's division bivouacked on the field within sight of the enemy, Jackson was busy throughout the night making dispositions for the morrow. With the exception of one brigade under Colonel John Patton, who was instructed to cover the rear and "to make a great show," Ewell's men were ordered to rejoin Jackson's main column at Port Republic in preparation for an attack upon Shields. When asked by Patton how long he might have to hold the enemy in check, Jackson replied, "By the blessing of Providence, I hope to be back by ten o'clock."[15]

He was not back by ten o'clock, but shortly after that hour, on 9 June, General Trimble, with the last of Jackson's men, had crossed the North River into Port Republic and destroyed the bridge. Before five that morning, however, General Charles S. Winder's brigade had passed through Port Republic, crossed the South Fork, and was moving down the river road to attack the forces of General Shields. After advancing about a mile and a half, it encountered and drove back the Federal pickets. But the enemy had selected an excellent defensive position. Six guns had been planted on high ground, commanding the valley road from Port Republic and the foothills on the Confederate right. A bold effort was made to capture the guns, but Winder's men were driven back in disorder. A flanking movement through the woods against the Federal left met a similar fate. At this critical juncture, the advanced units of Ewell's division came into sight. Realizing that the Stonewall Brigade would be routed if the guns were not silenced, Jackson directed a young staff officer, Major Jedediah (Jed) Hotchkiss, to lead the head of Ewell's approaching column "around and take that battery." Some thirty minutes later, as the Confederate line was breaking in disorder, General Richard Taylor and his Louisianians suddenly emerged from the thick underbrush and swarmed up to the guns. Almost abruptly, the Federal advance was halted as the men turned their attention to the threat in their rear. Twice the Louisianians were driven back, but on the third assault the battery was carried. By this time, the remainder of Ewell's division had reached the field, and shortly the Federal command was in full retreat. It was now 10:30 A.M.[16]

For almost five hours Jackson had been too long and too heavily engaged below Port Republic to attempt to do battle with Frémont the same day. Fortunately, Frémont's advance from Cross Keys had been exceedingly cautious. Having been on the march since dawn, his men did not reach the bluffs of the Shenandoah, a distance of only seven miles, until noon.[17] "While the forces of Shields were in full retreat," reported Jackson, "and our troops in pursuit Frémont appeared on the opposite bank of the South Fork of the Shenandoah with his army, and opened his artillery upon our ambulances and parties engaged in the humane labors of attending to our dead and wounded and the dead and wounded of the enemy."[18]

The following day Frémont began withdrawing his forces and retreated down the valley. On the morning of the twelfth, Colonel Thomas T. Munford, of Jackson's command, occupied Harrisonburg. At the same time Jackson's other troops recrossed South River and encamped near Weyer's Cave, where they rested until the seventeenth before moving toward Richmond. Jackson concluded his final report on the memorable valley campaign as follows: "For the purpose of rendering thanks to God for having crowned our arms with success, and to implore his continued favor, divine service was held in the army on the 14th."[19]

On 18 June Harry Burgwyn wrote his mother from near Kinston. Orders had just been received that morning from General Holmes "to be ready to leave at a moments notice; where to go we know not but presume it to be for Richmond Va. or for Stonewall." He urged his mother "to send Pollok to Hutchins at once for my saddle & spurs & to let him bring them down to me immediately. Also let him bring me a bottle of brandy & one of whiskey. Somebody went into my tent the other day & my key being in the trunk drank up almost all my liquor."[20] The next day Harry sent a brief note to his father begging his assistance in finding a replacement for his horse Waverly. He also asked his father to send down "the small liquor case, i.e., the box with decanters and glasses all arranged," for "we may go to Stonewall & then on long fatiguing marches it would be invaluable."[21] His frequent allusions to "Stonewall" clearly indicate that Harry hoped his regiment might be assigned to the general's command. Having recently served as a student under Jackson, he undoubtedly followed his exploits with more than normal interest and certainly with pride and enthusiasm. Harry was not destined to fight under Jackson, but one may assume that his military acumen and high sense of discipline would have quickly caught the approving eye of his old professor. The Twenty-sixth North Carolina left for Petersburg on Friday, 20 June.

In the meantime, plans and dispositions for the defense of Richmond were rapidly taking shape. As early as 10 June, Major General D. H. Hill had written Secretary Randolph, "It is now plain to my mind that Richmond can only be saved by a wide sweep entirely to the rear of the enemy. Without Beauregard this cannot be done. Let us give up the South for the time to capture McClellan. A wide detour to the rear by 50,000 men would accomplish the object. The enemy has now ditched himself up to the very gates of Richmond. In a week or two weeks at furthest he will open his siege batteries and the capital must fall." General Lee was contemplating a similar move, but not with Beauregard. On 11 June, he ordered Jackson to "leave your enfeebled troops to watch the country and guard the passes covered by your cavalry and artillery, and with your main body, including Ewell's division and Lawton's and Whiting's commands, move rapidly to Ashland by rail or otherwise, as you may find most advantageous, and sweep down between the Chickahominy and Pamunkey, cutting up the enemy communications, etc., while this army attacks General McClellan in front."[22]

Lee lost no time in implementing this basic strategy. He admonished Secretary Randolph to keep news of Jackson's movements secret from the press. He then sent a dispatch to Brigadier General J. E. B. Stuart, commanding cavalry, requesting him "to make a secret movement to the rear of the enemy, now posted on Chickahominy, with a view of gaining intelligence of his operations, communications, etc." The next day, 12 June, with twelve hundred picked men from his cavalry regiments, Stuart started on his daring reconnaissance mission around McClellan's right flank. Two days later, word was received that he "had ridden to McClellan's rear, had destroyed a wagon-train, had captured some 165 men and more than that number of horses, with only one casualty, and had circled entirely around the rear of the Federal army."[23] On 16 June Lee acknowledged the receipt of dispatches from Jackson renewing his earlier suggestion that his command be increased to forty thousand men so he might drive the enemy down the valley and invade the North. Lee instead ordered him to join the main army.[24]

On 18 June Lee advised Major General T. H. Holmes, commanding the North Carolina Department, that Burnside's force of fourteen thousand men had joined McClellan's army. Should Burnside ascend the James River, Holmes was "to oppose him with your whole force, and it was with this view that I desired you to concentrate at or near Petersburg, so as to have your command available to move speedily to the threatened point." Lee feared the possibility of Burnside seizing the batteries at Drewry's Bluff by moving up the James, landing, and taking them from the rear.[25] On 21 June Lee further advised Holmes that he was "very anxious to get the assistance of Ransom's brigade in the operations of next week." Two days later, he ordered General Ransom's brigade to Richmond.[26]

The Twenty-sixth North Carolina had a slow, tedious trip to Petersburg. By the time the regiment reached camp, one-half mile from Petersburg, the men were physically worn and thoroughly exasperated. In a letter to his father, written on Sunday, 22 June, Harry Burgwyn referred to it as a "most fatiguing journey of about 30 hours. . . . We are much to my regret in Genrl. Ransom's brigade which now consists of the 24th—25th—26th—35th & 49th reg[i]m[en]ts N.C.T. & the 1st N. C. Cav[alry]." Optimistically he reported: "Ransom says the army at Richmond is in the finest spirits & that Lee was in very fine spirits. If they attack now as soon as Stonewall gets into position (& it will not take him long to do it) we will derange McClellan's plans entirely. Let us begin with Stonewall's tried troops (he has been recently reinforced with 18,000 troops from here) & before McClellan knows what is happening his whole line may be turned."[27]

The Twenty-sixth did not leave Petersburg until Tuesday, 24 June, and then not on schedule. Orders were received to leave for Richmond at one in the afternoon, but it was nine that evening before the last of Ransom's brigade entrained. Harry's regiment "reached Richmond at 1 o'clock [on the morning of 25 June] & bivouacked, for almost the first time, with mother earth for a couch & the broad canopy of Heaven for a coverlet. With a commendable prudence & with a forethought worthy of all praise I went to the Exchange Hotel & secured a bed smiling grimly at the thought that it would be my last for many a day."[28]

Almost in sight of Richmond were massed four Federal corps of the Army of the Potomac. Their line of seventy-five thousand men extended from the Chickahominy on the north to White Oak Swamp Creek on the south. The Sixth Army Corps (Brigadier General William B. Franklin) occupied the right flank resting on the south bank of the Chickahominy. To its left was stationed the Second Corps (Brigadier General Edwin V. Sumner), followed by the Third (Brigadier General S. P. Heintzelman) and Fourth Army Corps (Brigadier General Erasmus C. Keyes). The extreme right of this extended line was anchored on the north side of the Chickahominy by the Fifth Army Corps, about twenty-five thousand strong, under the command of Brigadier General Fitz John Porter. Porter's left rested on New Bridge near Gaines' Mill. His right was so aligned as to intercept enemy movements on the roads leading from Mechanicsville down the north side of the Chickahominy in the direction of McClellan's supply base at the White House (West Point) on the Pamunkey.[29]

As early as 24 June, McClellan learned that Jackson was at Fredericks Hall and preparing to attack his right flank and rear in order to cut off his communications with the White House and throw the right wing of the army into the Chickahominy. "Fortunately," McClellan later reported, "I had a few days before provided against this contingency, by ordering a number of transports to the James River, loaded with commissary, quartermaster, and ordnance supplies. I therefore felt free to watch the enemy closely, wait events, and act according to circumstances, feeling sure that if cut off from the Pamunkey I could gain the James River for a new base."[30]

General Lee was certainly in no position to "wait events." Against superior forces he had no choice but to strike, and a flanking movement against McClellan's right was clearly preferable. Only the day before, 23 June, he had conferred with four of his divisional commanders, Jackson, James Longstreet, D. H. Hill (Jackson's brother-in-law), and A. P. Hill. Jackson had arrived at Lee's headquarters about 3:00 P.M. Having left Fredericks Hall at 1:00 A.M., he had covered the distance of fifty-two miles in fourteen hours by riding relays of commandeered horses. Lee's first council of war lasted into the late afternoon. Thursday, 26 June, was agreed upon for the combined attack on Porter, requiring the junction of all four divisions north of the Chickahominy. Their number would exceed fifty thousand men. But an effective junction with Jackson on the day of the battle would demand the utmost in detailed planning, reconnaissance, and competent staff work.[31]

The afternoon of 23 June was spent in detailed discussion of precisely when and where each of Lee's three divisions would cross the Chickahominy in concert with Jackson's movement from the northwest. Appropriate orders would be issued the following day. It was agreed that Jackson would move his division to Ashland, sixteen miles north of Richmond, by the night of the twenty-fourth. The following day he was to march southeast, with Stuart's cavalry covering his left, and encamp at some convenient point west of the (Virginia) Central Railroad. At the same time, General Lawrence O'B. Branch's brigade of A. P. Hill's division was directed to cross the Chickahominy and take the road leading to Mechanicsville. When these movements were "discovered," A. P. Hill would cross the Chickahominy near Meadow Bridge with the rest of his division and move directly upon Mechanicsville.[32]

Presuming that the Federals could be driven from their position at Mechanicsville, the divisions of Generals D. H. Hill and Longstreet would then cross the bridge over the Chickahominy near that point. D. H. Hill would move to support Jackson with Longstreet supporting A. P. Hill. The four Confederate divisions would thus be poised "to sweep down the Chickahominy and endeavor to drive the enemy from his position above New Bridge, General Jackson bearing well to his left, turning Beaver Dam Creek and taking the direction toward Cold Harbor." The advancing Confederates would then move toward the York River Railroad, close upon McClellan's rear, and force him down the Chickahominy. "Any advance of the enemy toward Richmond," Lee's order read, "will be prevented by vigorously following his rear and crippling and arresting his progress."[33]

Lee's greatest risk, however, was in leaving only the two divisions of Generals John B. Magruder and Benjamin Huger to defend the Confederate capital should McClellan elect to make a powerful counterstroke directly upon Richmond with the main body of his army. These two divisions were stationed some five to seven miles east and northeast of the city and could hardly muster more than twenty-two thousand men. They were ordered to "hold their positions in front of the enemy against attack, and make such demonstrations Thursday [26 June] as to discover his operations. Should opportunity offer, the feint will be converted into a real attack, and should an abandonment of his intrenchments by the enemy be discovered, he will be closely pursued." To bolster their strength, Ransom's brigade was temporarily detached from the command of Major General T. H. Holmes and placed in reserve on the Williamsburg road under the Command of General Huger.[34]

As commanding general, Lee was undertaking his first major assignment of the Civil War. For his battle strategy to succeed, his division commanders would have to perform according to plan. As a team they were yet untried. The greatest stress would fall on Jackson. On the night of the twenty-third he made the long, sleepless ride back to Fredericks Hall to join his command. From then until Malvern Hill, Jackson would practically live in the saddle. Future operations would depend heavily on his movements, and Lee's orders left much to his judgment. Jackson was directed to reach Ashland by the night of the twenty-fourth. The following night he was to halt near Slash Church just west of the Virginia Central. At three o'clock on the morning of the twenty-sixth, he was to advance on the road to Pole Green Church, advising General Branch of his movement. That would signal the beginning of the attack on Mechanicsville.[35]

But Jackson failed to meet this schedule. His army was still at Ashland at three o'clock on the morning of the twenty-sixth and did not cross the railroad until nine. The problem was that he was operating in unmapped country, lately occupied by the enemy. Bridges were down, roads were obstructed, and federal pickets constantly harassed his line of march.[36]

Having heard nothing from Jackson by early afternoon of the twenty-sixth, General A. P. Hill felt compelled to cross the Chickahominy and engage the enemy's outposts above Mechanicsville, although his orders were to wait until assured that Branch and Jackson were in communication and moving against the enemy's strong position on Beaver Dam Creek. Hill attacked at 3:00 P.M. and was repulsed with heavy losses. It was not until around five o'clock that Jackson reached Hundley's Corner, three miles north of the Federal position. Between them lay a dense forest. Jackson heard the cannonading but ordered his troops into bivouac.[37] Unfortunately, he had no reason to assume that Hill had attacked in contravention of orders or had been repulsed. His own orders directed him to "bear well to his left, turning Beaver Dam Creek, and taking the direction towards Cold Harbor." Jackson could have reasonably assumed that his own position at Hundley's Corner made the Federal position on Beaver Dam Creek untenable.

The initial contact between Lee and McClellan, however, occurred just east of Richmond on Wednesday, the twenty-fifth, south of the Chickahominy. On that day McClellan ordered General Heintzelman "to drive in the enemy's [Huger's] pickets from the woods in his front, in order to give us command of the cleared fields still farther in advance." As McClellan later reported, "This was gallantly and handsomely done under a stubborn resistance."[38] And it was here, for the first time, that Harry Burgwyn was actually involved in combat. From then until the last of the seven days he and the men of the Twenty-sixth North Carolina would be constantly exposed but not heavily engaged until the battle of Malvern Hill on 1 July.

This prolonged experience in the field would make a profound impression upon young Harry. Two weeks after the battle, from his headquarters near Drewry's Bluff, he wrote his mother a long account of his actions and of the events in which he participated. It is not the purpose of this study to provide a detailed account of the Seven Days' battle, but because the first two days were crucial to Lee's strategy, it is appropriate to report on Harry's actions and reflections as related to the engagements taking place on both sides of the Chickahominy, for the Confederates would succeed in turning McClellan's right flank and forcing General Porter south of the Chickahominy:

> *Wednesday, the 25th of June.* After an early breakfast at which recollecting I would not have another such for a considerable time, I was unusually particular. I walked up to the Capital Square & shortly after received orders to report to Genl. Huger on the Williamsburg road, some 5 miles from town & immediately opposite the field of "Seven Pines" on which you recollect one of the bloodiest battles of this revolution was fought. We had scarcely got to our position when quite a heavy cannonnading, & a very sharp rattling fire of musketry warned us that fight had commenced & was getting to be pretty warm. We halted some mile & a half from our advance forces & waited until 2 o'clock when our regmt. the 24 & 35 was ordered forward. We could now see the ambulances & infirmary men pass by with the wounded soldiers on board, & occasionally a suppressed groan would give us assurances that war was no pas-

time. The 24 & 35 regmts. were ordered to the trenches, & ours was moving down when Genl Huger met us & said he had troops enough & wanted us to be kept as a reserve. . . .

For some two hours we lay behind a short strip of timber, with the shells falling all around us, until one of our batteries was ordered up to reply & in a very few discharges silenced the guns that were annoying us. Towards sunset Genrl. Lee came upon the field & ordered up all our brigade to recover the ground which our pickets had lost in the morning, & for half an hour the musketry was as rapid as I could desire. The enemy then fell back & we prepared for the night.

My regmt., & Col Ransom's [35th], was detailed for picket & just as it was getting dark we were notified to go on picket. Perfectly ignorant of the locality, having never been in the woods before, & ignorant of the position of both friends & foes, I was ordered, when it was so dark we could not see 10 paces, to go in a certain direction until I met a Georgia regiment. The woods were full of bogs, swamps & bamboo briars, & Col Vance started with 5 companies to see the Georgians & I was to post the balance as well as I could in the direction indicated. I had not gone I suppose 200 yds before I found myself completely lost in a swamp which threatened to mire us all at every step, & which I could not get through possibly. I tried one avenue & then another until about 11 o'clock at night I gave it up & started to find Col Vance & commence again. During my various perambulations it is not surprising that I missed the designated position & posted some of my men entirely within the enemies lines.

Scarcely therefore had I reached Col Vance's left & was trying to find him, when a straggling shot or two warned me to go back & see what our men were firing at. Just as I was moving back a terrific fire was opened upon us along our whole line. A portion of my men were fired at front & rear & at distances not exceeding 10 yds. Some of Col Vance's men were on one side of a fence & the Yankees poked their guns through the cracks to fire at them, he likewise having lost his way & posted his men in the wrong position.

The consequence was that our men were driven completely in & not knowing where they were became considerably scattered in falling back. I collected them however some distance in rear of their former position & sent to Genl. Ransom for orders stating that we had been driven in. Now what do you think his orders were[?] He who ought to have superintended, either personally or through an aid[e], the posting of his troops on picket, from a convenient position in the rear orders us to retake our former position, a position which in the first place I could not have found to save myself from the gallows, & in hunting which I was liable at any moment to run upon a concealed foe.

I started my men some 100 in number ahead however & moving cautiously on became in a very short time exposed to a hot fire from a foe I could not see, & whose position I could only judge of by the direction of his balls, & at the same time unable to fire for fear of injuring friends who, better posted than myself, were replying to his fire with effect. I remained there until I received orders to unite with Col. Vance & take up a convenient position & be ready at daylight to advance to the picket line. As soon as daylight broke we advanced & found that the enemy had likewise fallen back & we took our proper position for the first time. When I came to look upon the ground over which I had wandered the night previous in vain attempts to stumble upon a position I could not know to be right even though I held it, my only wonder was that I did not fall right into the enemy's hands.

Thursday, the 26th of June. As I stated above on this morning we retook our picket line, & about 9 o'clock received orders to extend it & to advance some 300 yds. This we did & our regmt. as thus extended occupied a distance of about 3/4 of a mile. During the day nothing of any moment occurred except the killing of 2 Yankees who advanced a little too near our position. . . . During the day our men who you will see had had no sleep for 2 nights became excessively fatigued & sleepy. I myself would fall asleep while one end of the line would be firing occasionally, & if I awoke it would only be to see if there was any general fire, & if not to turn over & sleep again.

About 5 o'clock P.M. we were relieved & on going to camp I heard that the order had been issued by Genrl. Lee for the attack to commence that afternoon, & that Genrls. D. H. Hill's of N.C. & Longstreet's divisions had been moved to our left so as to bring a preponderating force upon the point of attack. Scarcely had I reached camp when there broke upon the stillness of a beautiful summer's evening a most terrific cannonading. I can liken nothing to it. It seemed as if the discharges of artillery were like an angry surf beating upon the beach, except that the intervals between the discharges were much shorter than between the beating of the waves. We were too far to hear the musketry. All listened to the terrific fire in calm confidence that an all just God would lend his aid to the right side, & many a prayer was that night offered up that our side might be victorious. The firing was kept up with no intermission until after 9 o'clock & after recommending our cause & myself to God for his protection, I laid myself down to a much needed rest.[39]

This had been a bad day for the Confederates north of the Chickahominy. A. P. Hill's division had borne the brunt of the attack on Porter's well-fortified position on Beaver Dam Creek. During the night of 26 June, the Federals withdrew southeastward and took up a strong position at Gaines' Mill, their left covering two bridges over the Chickahominy, Alexander's and Grapevine, connecting with McClellan's right flank. Here the battle of Gaines' Mill was fought the following day. Porter's reinforced command occupied a strong position on a wooded plateau facing north and west. To attack, the Confederates had to advance through open country, cross Powhite Creek, and ascend the slopes in the face of galling fire. At 2:30 on the afternoon of the twenty-seventh, A. P. Hill opened the attack and fought for an hour without support.[40]

According to plan, Longstreet was not to move in support until it was ascertained that Jackson's appearance on Porter's right would force the enemy to weaken his left. Here again, the Confederate attack "failed in combination." Jackson had been delayed. He had taken the longer road to Old Cold Harbor to avoid the enemy sharpshooters and arrived in the rear of D. H. Hill's command. But Jackson made no effort to join the battle. Both he and Lee believed that once Porter realized that Jackson was practically in his rear, he would quickly extend his front to cover his line of retreat to the White House. But there was no such response from the enemy because McClellan, fearing such a flanking movement, had already begun moving his base of operations from the York to the James River.[41]

When Lee saw that A. P. Hill was in trouble, he ordered Longstreet in support. When the sound and direction of the firing indicated to Jackson that the original plan of operation had failed, he quickly made his dispositions for attack. D. H. Hill was to lead. The remaining troops were "to advance instantly en échelon from the left." These orders were given verbally and communicated to the brigadiers by a young staff officer. But, mistakenly, the subordinate had inferred that they were to await further orders before engaging the enemy.[42]

This mistake occurred around 4:00 P.M. and without Jackson's knowledge. The attack by D. H. Hill and Ewell met with heavy resistance. A counterstroke drove Ewell's men back across the swamp, but there was no reserve support forthcoming. Jackson was deeply agitated and momentarily thought all of his troops were engaged and about to lose the day. Fortunately, his chief of staff had detected the error of the aide-de-camp, and the "Valley army was coming up." Even then, the supporting columns did not come into battle according to plan, causing much confusion within the ranks. But their presence made the difference. Lee and Jackson ordered a general advance almost simultaneously. As the sun set, the Confederates carried the day, and Porter's men streamed across the Chickahominy.[43]

For Harry and his men 27 June was also a long and arduous day, but they were not as intensively engaged as were the Confederates north of the Chickahominy. By maintaining steady pressure on the enemy, however, Huger's forces were successful in advancing their forward position along the Williamsburg road to within a half mile of the enemy's entrenchments at Seven Pines. Harry vividly described that decisive day:

> *Friday, the 27th of June:* At daybreak the same terrible cannonading was resumed, & at intervals we could catch musketry. We then surmised the truth, that our forces, who used the musket much more than the enemy, were driving the enemy from his strongholds & gaining the day. Our balloon was seen early in the morning hovering over our positions, & doubtless affording valuable intelligence. Not for an instant did the firing cease; but terrible distinct & awfully fast it seemed if possible to increase. None of our men were doubtful of the result. They knew the character of their comrades too well & the feat of bringing Stonewall Jackson upon the enemy's rear was so conclusive of Genrl. Lee's superior generalship that none doubted the issue.
>
> About 9 o'clock our regiment was ordered out as a support to a Georgia regiment which was ordered forward to feel the enemy in our front; & as we moved on we heard the glorious intelligence that Stonewall had as usual done his part & that our troops had possession of Mechanicsville completely defeating the enemy who had vaunted so long & so highly over our badly

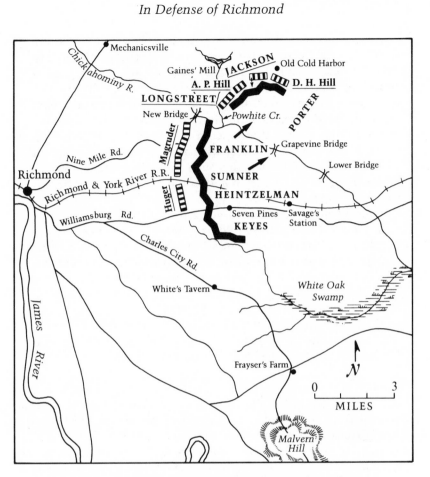

Battle of Gaines' Mill, 27 June 1862 (Civil War Atlas, adaptation, courtesy Department of History, U.S. Military Academy)

equipped but courageous soldiers. As we advanced in support of the Georgians I saw many instances of the battle on Wednesday. Trees struck by balls & cut off by shells & solid shot, guns & equipments & bits of clothing, & finally unburied ghastly bodies of dead Yankees met our gaze at every step. The sight was one calculated to excite reflections of the most serious character, & I often wished that Lincoln & his cabinet could behold some of the scenes to be met with at every step we took. Not that I believe it would have any such effect upon them as would make them stop the war, but it could but influence them if they were men.

After advancing some 400 yds a few scattering shots & finally two or three volleys told us pretty plainly where the enemy were. We then threw out skirmishers & reported results. 12 pieces of artillery were then ordered up on our right 4 in battery & 8 in reserve & the officer in charge of the battery came up to see our position. I pointed it out to him & suggested to him the position of the enemy & where I thought his shells could be thrown to the best advantage. . . . This seemed to take the enemy quite by surprise for he made no further advance until after we were relieved & it was quite late at night.[44]

The battle of Gaines' Mill was a Confederate victory, but at a cost of eight thousand killed and wounded.[45] Darkness and the tangled undergrowth of the Chickahominy swamp prevented effective pursuit of Porter's Fifth Army Corps. From then until the battle of Malvern Hill on 1 July, there were three days of confusion and uncertainty. On the morning of 28 June, Lee learned for the first time that the enemy was abandoning its base at the White House on the Pamunkey. But it was not until evening that a general movement behind the enemy's lines around Seven Pines was detected. Lee concluded that McClellan was retreating to the James and ordered pursuit the following day.

McClellan had in his command ninety-five thousand men, more than five thousand wagons, and more than fifty field batteries. To reach the protective cover of his gunboats on the James, McClellan had only fourteen miles to march; but across his front lay White Oak Swamp, and coming up on his flank and rear were Lee and Jackson.[46]

Early on 29 June, Magruder and Huger were ordered to advance along the Williamsburg and Charles City roads and strike the enemy's flank. A. P. Hill and Longstreet were to recross the Chickahominy, pass around to the right of White Oak Swamp, and threaten the Federal rear. Jackson was ordered to cross the Chickahominy at Grapevine Bridge and follow McClellan through White Oak Swamp. Magruder attacked the enemy's rear guard near Savage's Station late in the afternoon but was repulsed. Huger was prevented from supporting Magruder by "an urgent message from Lee." Jackson was delayed in crossing the Chickahominy because of the necessity of rebuilding Grapevine Bridge. And Jeb Stuart had gone off to destroy the Federal supplies at the White House. During the night McClellan's forces succeeded in negotiating White Oak Swamp and burned the bridge behind them.[47]

On Monday, 30 June, the battle of Frayser's Farm was fought. The two divisions of Longstreet and A. P. Hill challenged the Third Army Corps, which was reinforced by three divisions from the Second, Fifth, and Sixth. The Confederates fought without support. Huger was delayed coming up by obstructions on the Charles City road. Magruder did not arrive until the fight was over. By nightfall Jackson was still north of White Oak Swamp. His troops had reached the bridge over White Oak about noon but were met by determined resistance. Longstreet and Hill were, therefore, hard put to stand up to the counterstrokes of the enemy. During the night the entire Federal force fell back on Malvern Hill. Again, as at Beaver Dam Creek and Gaines' Mill, the Confederate attack "failed in combination."[48]

For the men of the Twenty-sixth North Carolina, the last two days of June were characterized by constant alert, confusion, and delay. They doggedly followed McClellan all the way to Malvern Hill but did not engage him until late in the afternoon of Tuesday, 1 July. Harry wrote of those days:

Sunday, the 29th of June. You recollect we were on picket last night in support of Col. Jones Va. rgt. Early this morning we received orders to advance & feel the enemy & ascertain his exact position. I neglected to state that during the night we had heard rumblings of wagons & apparently a great commotion in the enemy's camps. Large fires were seen to burn brightly, & all were confident that he had retreated. Soon after daybreak we pushed forward vigorously & when within some quarter of a mile from the enemy's intrenchments, I sent a couple of men up a tree to reconnoitre, who reported the enemy's camp apparently vacated, but a large quantity of tents standing. We pushed ahead & some 20 minutes from that time I had the satisfaction of standing upon the enemy's intrenchments & surveying "wide o'er the fields a waste of ruin laid." The enemy's tents were standing, & in them was undoubtedly a large quantity of plunder. I formed my men in good order however & would not allow a man to leave the ranks.

Upon this field of "Seven Pines" the devastation & traces of war were marked. Here lay the putrid remains of an artillery horse; here the ghastly skull of some poor fellow who had found, if any grave, certainly an untimely one. Again we would see a wagon fast in the mud & nearby cannister, grape & rifled cannon shot all in confusion [illegible]. Not a step could you go through the trees without seeing somewhere the marks of musketry & artillery. Canteens, axes, spades, shovels, & tools of various descriptions were found in promiscuous & indiscriminate heaps. We were not permitted however to enjoy the contemplations of such a sight, but were ordered to get to camp as quickly as possible, get breakfast & start to head off the enemy along the Charles City Road. It was expected he would concentrate & make an attempt to reach the City by the Charles City Road.

We started about 10 o'clock & were just well started, & in proper order when down came a messenger from Magruder to Huger saying the enemy were in large force in his front, & he wanted Huger to protect his right. This was the first of Magruder's blunders. He here by wrong information detained Genrl. Huger for some 3 hours. Huger disliked to delay but could not help himself. At length an order came from Genrl. Lee ordering Huger to follow the Charles City road & then we marched on, but in the meantime the enemy had got an important start. We bivouacked that night as usual & remained at our bivouac until Monday, June 30th. About 1 o'clock today we received orders to march, & we arrived about 4 at the White Oak Swamp where our advance forces were engaged in vigorously shelling & fighting the enemy some mile from our position. The cannonading continued till dark & as soon as that fairly set in the enemy commenced his retreat, throwing away his india rubber coats, knapsacks, & everything which could in any way impede his progress, leaving also many of his killed & wounded to be cared for by our men & not even a surgeon to remain with them.

Tuesday, the 1st of July: We bivouacked last night at White Oak Swamp & moved early this morning following up the enemy as before. About midday we came upon the battleground where

Genrl. Longstreet's division had fought the day before, & where several batteries of the enemy were charged & taken. Here the carnage exceeded anything I had yet beheld. In places the Yankees were lying almost in heaps. Their wounded had not even been moved & groans & lamentations filled the putrid air. Jackson's troops had come up to the enemy & soon his shells were shrieking through the air making hideous noises, the whole conspiring to impress the scene strongly upon my memory. We soon moved on & about 4 o'clock were put in position to prevent a flank movement by the enemy while Magruder was preparing to commit his huge blunder of attacking 32 pieces of cannon & the larger part of McClellan's army with his division alone & without waiting for Jackson to get in the enemy's rear as Lee had intended.

Sure enough about 5 o'clock Magruder commenced by ordering a charge upon the batteries. Father can give you a good description of the field as he rode over it. The enemy's artillery, the very best they had, was posted upon the crest of a gentle slope of cleared land [Malvern Hill] laid out in clover & corn which extended nearly a mile. On both his right & left were two valleys of low grounds from which gentle ravines led up to the enemy's artillery. Instead of moving up these[,] Magruder ordered the attack to be made in front & whole ranks were swept away by discharges which drove Magruder's men back with very heavy and useless slaughter.

About 7 o'clock our brigade was ordered up to the charge & on we went. Upon passing Ransom who was not *yet* in he halted us & made us form in close order. The shells were then raining around us. Ransom told us very soon to go ahead & off we went without as usual a soul to show us the way; the roads forked & we took the wrong one as was afterwards found out. We had not proceeded far when we met skulkers from all states & regmts. going back to the rear telling everywhere their regmts. had been cut to pieces etc. One of these I gathered hold of & drawing my sword threatened to kill him unless he led me into the battle. He was one of our brigade & carried us on, thinking it would be better to risk death from the enemy than to get it from his friends. All this time the shells were bursting over our heads & cutting down trees & lopping off huge limbs. We moved forward & took advantage of a little swell in the ground to re-form our line. Then for the charge. Over a fence & up the slope we commenced to move.

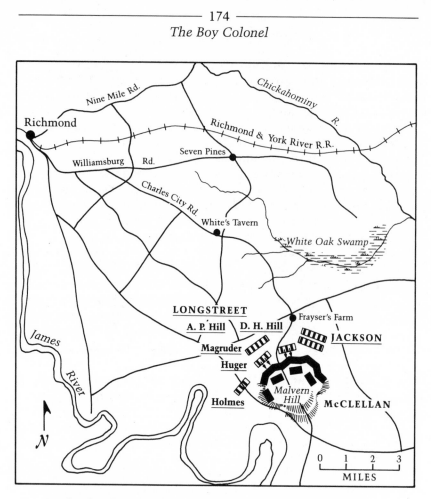

Battle of Malvern Hill, 1 July 1862 (Civil War Atlas, adaptation, courtesy Department of History, U.S. Military Academy)

It was now quite dark & we could not distinguish friend from foe & judged of the enemy's position solely by the flashes of his cannons & they were fast enough to leave very little doubt. On we went until within some 4–500 yds from the battery when we were falsely told that our friends were in front & ordered to lie down and then we lay at that distance from the enemy's cannon which were playing upon us all the time & not being able to fire a gun. One of our companies, not hearing the orders, got separated from the rest & charged almost up to the guns: one of their men being found next day within 15 yds. of the guns. Presently this company likewise received orders not to fire, & we all lay till 10 o'clock receiving the enemy's fire in silence & steadiness.

They ceased firing about this time or perhaps a little earlier, & I sent to Genrl. Ransom for orders, which were to move quietly off the field. This I did & left it in admirable order. . . . Before leaving the field I detached 30–40 men to bear off our wounded & had the satisfaction of seeing them all as well cared [for] as could be under the circumstances. The night air was rendered horrible by their cries. I could distinctly hear their cries: "3rd Alabama come & take me off; 2nd Louisiana give me some water." etc. etc. The enemy commenced retreating as soon [as] the firing stopped, & then ended the last great battle of the series. When the war of artillery was at its height, I took out my watch & timed the discharges. They were 48 one minute & 40 the next.[49]

CHAPTER 13

THE BOY BECOMES A COLONEL

The Seven Days' battle was a signal victory for the Confederate cause. Not only was Richmond saved but the mood of the South was suddenly transformed from one of gradual withdrawal and ultimate defeat to one of hope and possible victory. The South would no longer be on the defensive. And for a time, the Army of Northern Virginia would challenge the enemy on its home ground. The combination of Lee and Jackson would be a force to be reckoned with, and their victories had only begun. This was the essential result of the seven-day confrontation before Richmond, and its reality was not lost on President Lincoln.[1]

Nor was the significance of North Carolina's participation lost on the people of that state. Her troops had played a major role in the defense of Richmond. Of the ninety-two Confederate regiments engaged, forty-six were from North Carolina.[2] Official returns, however, reveal that only twenty-eight North Carolina regiments sustained battle casualties. Out of a total of 16,782 Confederate casualties, North Carolina troops suffered about 23 percent or 3,810 in killed and wounded. This number was 35 percent greater than the losses suffered by Georgia, the next highest in casualties (2,814), and about 60 percent greater than those (2,392) of Virginia. North Carolina and Georgia accounted for approximately 40 percent of the total killed and wounded before Richmond.[3] Not only did North Carolina suffer grievously during the Seven Days' battle but she had been left virtually defenseless. By the seventh day only two North Carolina infantry regiments, the Fiftieth and Fifty-first, were left in the state.[4]

For Governor Henry Toole Clark the months of May and June had been painfully frustrating. The closer McClellan came to Richmond, the more insistent were the calls for troops from North Carolina. As week followed week North Carolina became increasingly exposed to further Federal penetration. Burnside, from his base at New Bern, was prepared to strike at any moment. Lee recognized the problem and feared the possibility of simultaneous attacks upon both Richmond and Raleigh. In fact, during the Seven Days' battle, it is said that he telegraphed General James G. Martin at Kinston every night to determine whether Burnside had moved on Goldsboro.[5] Lee had every reason to be apprehensive, for on 25 June McClellan had urged Burnside by telegraph to "advance on Goldsborough with all your available forces at the earliest practicable moment" and if possible, "destroy some of the bridges on the Raleigh and Gaston Railroad and threaten Raleigh."[6]

Burnside had earlier assured McClellan that he could "put 7,000 infantry in Norfolk in five days, but no artillery, cavalry, or wagons. . . . We can move on Goldsborough at sixty hours' notice with 10,000 infantry, twenty pieces of artillery, five companies cavalry." But Burnside did not move. By 28 June, with McClellan's situation worsening, both President Lincoln and Secretary Stanton urged Burnside to send all the reinforcements he could spare to the James River without abandoning his own position. But Burnside still clung to his base at New Bern. On 4 July McClellan reported to Lincoln that he had ordered the general to send him such reinforcements as he could afford. The following day, Secretary Stanton advised Burnside that his department had no further orders to give "but hopes you will with all speed reach General McClellan with as large a force as possible." It was not until 7 July that General Burnside finally arrived at Fort Monroe with "near 8,000 good men."[7] During the Seven Days' battle he had missed a golden opportunity in North Carolina.

But the mere presence of Federal troops in eastern North Carolina, heavily fortified at New Bern and with rail and water access to the Atlantic, would be a continuing menace to Richmond as well as to the Army of Northern Virginia. Lee's every move must necessarily take into account this constant threat to his rear. Burnside's failure to capitalize on his advantage during the Seven Days should not minimize the magnitude of his successful campaign in eastern North Carolina during the spring of 1862. He had not only deprived the Confederacy of one of its richest farming areas but had also eliminated the coastal waters north of Wilmington as a haven for blockade runners.[8]

But Governor Clark's principal source of frustration still lay with the Confederate government. Clark hoped and believed that the troops sent to Virginia would soon be returned for the defense of the state. All the while a sizable Federal army lay entrenched at New Bern, ready to advance on Goldsboro at any time. And the Federal navy continued to patrol the inland waters. Clark's frustration was further compounded by the workings of the Conscript and Partisan acts. Time and again he appealed for clarification and relief because there seemed no way to alleviate the situation in North Carolina.

On 12 July Clark advised General Holmes that if he had two more regiments the Yankees could be driven from the state. Two days later, the governor again wrote General Holmes, decrying the number of conscripts that were flocking to the Partisan Rangers (detached cavalry units operating locally) rather than be enrolled. He questioned the policy of having such independent companies, especially inasmuch as they were mounted, which made them quite expensive. Before the month was out, Clark directed his appeal to the secretary of war. The ranger service was a popular way for men to avoid being conscripted, and he feared that "if they are entitled to the same clothing and equipment, with our other State Troops already in service, that it will about absorb the provisions for our Regular Troops."[9]

A few days earlier, almost in despair, Governor Clark had written President Davis a lengthy letter about "the situation of Camp of Enrolled Conscripts for this State." Explaining that he had heard much complaint and dissatisfaction and that it was not within his province to investigate, he felt it was his duty to call the matter to the president's attention: "The conscripts were ordered to report all on the same day, where accommodations had only been provided for 6 or 700. Not being able to get accommodations and neither received or attended to and unnoticed many left in disgust for their homes, determined to come no more without force. After getting into camp discontent and complaints increased almost to mutiny and desertions are constant and numerous. I have heard of more than 100 of a night and a successful desertion leaves discontent and mutiny behind and carries it with them to their homes."[10]

On 3 August, declaring that "we have yielded up our Seaports and rivers and have sustained immense losses thereby—losses, which in the item of provisions and army-supplies, the Confederacy is yet to feel and which we cannot now estimate," Governor Clark appealed to General Lee to mount an expedition against the Yankees in New Bern, Washington, and Plymouth. The governor may have been overly optimistic as to the probable success of such a venture, but he had every reason to make the suggestion because his generals had been removed from the state, "leaving but a few undrilled, unreliable troops and lenient officers, who will never exact the discipline necessary to make soldiers."[11]

Lee's reply was both thoughtful and understanding. He explained that General Holmes and part of his command had been brought to Virginia to participate in "the late battles" and that it was Holmes who later brought the brigades of Generals Martin and French "because the enemy being in and upon James River it was thought proper to provide against any attempt he might make to penetrate North Carolina and cut the Railroad from the North which might have been among his designs." Lee was careful to emphasize that he too had been "an eyewitness of the outrages and depredations upon private property committed by the enemy in this State, and can fully appreciate what you say of the injuries sustained by the people of North Carolina. Nor am I unmindful of the importance of protecting the line of RailRoad, and as far as practicable, the valuable private interests in the section of the Country to which you refer." Lee also mentioned that Major General D. H. Hill had replaced Holmes in command of the North Carolina district and added that he had referred Clark's letter to Hill.[12]

Desperate as he may have felt in the summer of 1862, Governor Clark was doing all in his power to support the cause. But desertions had become a serious problem, as he notified the secretary of war. He proposed issuing a notice "offering a restoration to ranks *without* punishment to all in this State who will report themselves to me or to a Confederate Officer by the 20th or 25th August, if not by then to be captured at all hazards and punished rigorously to the limits of law."[13]

Two days later Clark issued a proclamation declaring the election of Zebulon B. Vance as governor. He must have felt a sense of great relief. Seemingly every problem associated with war had fallen heavily upon the shoulders of Governor Clark, and, if his letters bear faithful witness, he strove manfully to discharge his responsibilities under exceedingly trying circumstances. Certainly, most of the problems that Vance would face had already appeared during Clark's administration.

The gubernatorial election of 1862 was unusual in that neither candidate campaigned actively. Colonel Vance, supported by the Conservatives, remained with the Twenty-sixth North Carolina in Virginia, and William J. Johnston, supported by the Confederates, stayed at his post as a railroad official in Charlotte. The party newspapers were about evenly divided between the candidates, with eleven supporting Johnston and ten backing Vance.[14] The newspaper campaign was characterized by considerable vilification and slander, especially in the state capital and between the *North Carolina Standard* and the *State Journal*.

The lead editorial of the 4 June issue of the *Standard* began: "In obedience to what we believe to be the wish of a large majority of the people of the State, we hoist to-day the name of the patriot, soldier, and statesman, Col. Z. B. Vance, for Governor." Declaring that Vance had not sought the office and preferred to remain in the field, W. W. Holden stated his belief that Vance "will not refuse to serve the people, if it should be their wish to make him Governor, and at the same time Commander-in-Chief in this State." On 16 June, in a letter to the editors of the *Fayetteville Observer*, Vance indicated his willingness to serve if elected. Professing to be above party strife in its support of Johnston, and apparently stung by Holden's outspoken support of Vance, the *State Journal* struck back in a bitter editorial on 9 July, accusing Holden of promoting party strife in denouncing President Davis as "politically and morally corrupt" and in characterizing the state government as a "military despotism." A week later it accused the *Standard* of "base flattery, cruel injustice, and wanton hypocrisy" in heaping "fulsome eulogy" upon Vance and slandering an entire brigade (Ransom's), adding, "Now we undertake to say that such a piece of putrid, flimsey, flabby flattery never before was penned or spoken, by arrogant demagogue, abject menial, or specious imposter." On 19 July Holden replied to the *State Journal*'s accusation by addressing himself to the *Richmond Enquirer*'s account of the dispute. "The Enquirer," he said, "and those for whom it speaks, are opposed to Col. Vance because he was an old Whig and refused to go for secession until Lincoln's proclamation. That paper is still laboring under the delusion that there is a Democratic party. . . . The Democratic party was destroyed at Charleston and Baltimore, and the *Enquirer* aided in destroying it."

In an open letter to candidate Johnston, Holden predicted his defeat by a large majority because "*the verdict of the army is against you.*"[15] Holden's prediction turned out to be conservative. Vance won by a vote of 54,423 to 20,448; Johnston carried only twelve of the state's eighty counties.[16] The army vote was four to one in favor of Vance; Johnston received only 3,691 of the 15,374 soldier ballots cast. In his own regiment, only 7 out of 700 ballots were marked against Colonel Vance. Because Vance had neither sought the office nor campaigned for it,[17] his overwhelming victory bespoke broad public confidence in his ability and integrity. His support was bipartisan. The Conservatives recognized his prewar nationalistic sympathies and the Confederates his willingness to fight for the cause.

Harry Burgwyn must have been keenly interested in Colonel Vance's gubernatorial aspirations, but in no available source does he say or even intimate that Vance was a candidate for governor. Because Harry was always candid and outspoken in correspondence with his parents, one would expect him to have had some reaction to the forthcoming election, especially in view of his own commanding officer's candidacy. A possible explanation could be that the Twenty-sixth North Carolina was plunged into the Seven Days' conflict very shortly after Vance indicated his willingness to serve. Following the battle, the regiment was bruised and tired, and Harry was considerably the worse for wear. He was badly fatigued and suffering from diarrhea, and he and his men were undoubtedly more concerned with military than with political preoccupations.

On 11 July Harry wrote to his mother that he was now "comfortably (comparatively) situated" and expressed satisfaction with the fortifications at Drewry's Bluff: "They exhibit the only good engineering I have seen in the Southern Confederacy & this is capital. . . . The fortifications around Richmond I regard as being exceedingly imperfect: so much so as to be absolutely worthless, bearing no kind of comparison with those of the enemy." A few days later, in a letter to his father, Harry said that the fortifications in the vicinity of Drewry's Bluff were being strengthened "to prevent a land attack or perhaps to render the position so strong that a few troops can defend it against a great many." He also expressed the hope that "we may be able to invade the enemy's country. It would exhaust us far less & him far more."[18]

On 26 July Harry reported to his father that he had applied for a leave of absence on medical grounds but that it had to be approved by General Lee. The following day, in a brief note to his mother, Harry expressed doubt that he would get sick leave although there was no prospect of an immediate engagement. As in almost every other letter, however, he could not resist commenting upon the military situation. Much work was being done on entrenchments, which led him to believe that "Lee's intention is to make these intrenchments so strong that he can leave comparatively a small force in front of McClellan & then move the bulk of his forces on to Washington or through the Valley into Maryland." Large numbers of troops were passing through, "which are said to be going on to Stonewall Jackson."[19]

His furlough was granted shortly thereafter, and he departed for home in need of rest and medical attention. He would be absent from camp for about a month. In the meantime, the fulfillment of his hope that Lee would move the bulk of his forces on to Washington or through the valley into Maryland was soon set in motion. Harry Burgwyn's hope, however, was Lincoln's greatest fear. Jackson's valley campaign and his subsequent movements had created the desired effect. The government in Washington was justifiably apprehensive about its safety, and none more so than President Lincoln. On 26 June, the day the Seven Days' battle opened, Lincoln brought together the forces of Banks, Frémont, and McDowell into one unified command, the Army of Virginia, under Major General John Pope. On 11 July Lincoln called upon the states for three hundred thousand additional men to serve for three years. The same day he appointed Henry W. Halleck general-in-chief of the Union armies, giving him control of all the land forces. And before the month was out, Lincoln signed the Second Confiscation Act, a modified version of the first, which was the prelude to his later Emancipation Proclamation. Out of McClellan's failure before Richmond had come the realization of a long war and the need for stern measures and a committed nation.

Elated as the Southerners may have been following the Seven Days' battle, the plight of Richmond was still far from relieved. McClellan was reorganizing and recruiting as he rested some ninety thousand troops at Westover and Berkeley. Major General Burnside was at Fort Monroe with a ten-thousand-man force, and before the end of July, Pope would have fifty-six thousand men concentrated under his command. Lee, too, was faced with the necessity of reorganization and recruitment, but his most pressing concern was to determine the next move of his adversaries, whether in concert or singly, and on what line. He would not have long to wait, and, fortunately, the overbearing, swaggering Pope would provide the cue. McClellan, characteristically, would be slow to move, but the impetuous Pope came charging out of the Washington-Manassas area. Lee learned on 12 July that he had occupied Culpeper. The next day, Jackson was ordered to move in the direction of Louisa and Gordonsville.[20]

At about this time, and seemingly with a great sense of pride, Harry Burgwyn informed his mother: "This is kept very quiet & but little is positively known, except that 'Stonewall is a moving' & will surprise the Yankees as much again as he did before. The 'great Western Genrl. Pope' will meet the wrong customer when he gets afoul of Jackson. We will not hear from Jackson any more until he returns thanks for another victory & forces some Yankee Genrl. to make another brilliant & successfully disastrous retreat."[21] Harry surely would have considered it a privilege to serve under Jackson, but it was not to be. His destiny lay elsewhere.

The next six weeks would provide ample evidence of the Lee-Jackson combination functioning at its best, with Stuart's cavalry ever on the move, probing and fighting. At Cedar Run (Slaughter's Mountain), on 9 August, Jackson met Pope's advance units under Banks and, after an intensive fight that lasted into the night, finally drove him back on Culpeper. Both sides suffered, but Pope's thrust southward was arrested. About this time Lee learned that Burnside had been ordered to Fredericksburg by way of Aquia on the Potomac and that McClellan had been ordered to follow Burnside. If McClellan and Burnside could be joined with Pope, an army of 150,000 men would be marshaled against the Confederate defenders of Richmond, who represented less than half that number. On 13 August Lee moved swiftly to concentrate his forces at Gordonsville in support of Jackson. Two days later, he left Richmond to take personal command in the field. The second battle of Manassas was imminent, and Jackson's campaign, which had begun at Cedar Run, was about to make history.

Second Manassas would prove a mortal blow to the Army of Virginia under General Pope, but it was not a rout comparable to that of First Manassas. The men could still regroup and fight. But the campaign to capture Richmond had begun with great expectations in early spring, and now, five months later, the Federal forces were back where they had started, "discouraged, cynical and resentful." First under McClellan and then under Pope, they had fought well and suffered much, but the fruits of victory had consistently eluded them. The Army of Northern Virginia under Lee had outfought and outmaneuvered them, but the Union forces had come to suspect that they were also the victims of the incompetency and competitive jealousies of their leaders. The nation now faced a grave crisis. The victorious Confederates were poised on the threshold of Washington and would shortly invade Maryland. Lincoln desperately needed a general skilled in defense. Against all advice, and declaring that he "must use the tools we have," the president chose McClellan.[22]

For Harry Burgwyn the month of August was one of much needed rest and recuperation. He was fortunate to spend it with his family in Raleigh. As for his thoughts and actions during this period one can only conjecture. The intimate relationship he enjoyed with his parents surely led to countless hours of discussion about the war, its consequences, his future, and that of the family. News from the several battle fronts was considerably delayed in transmission; nonetheless, the three Raleigh papers undoubtedly provided a broad base for contemplative discussion.

News from Virginia was good. Harry must have derived immense satisfaction from reading the published account of Jackson's official report on his victory at Cedar Run on 9 August. Harry had earlier predicted that "we will not hear from Jackson any more until he returns thanks for another victory." The first sentence in Jackson's report read, "On the evening of the 9th instant, God blessed our arms with another victory."[23] And a story about Stonewall's passion for secrecy, which appeared in the *North Carolina Standard* on 13 August, must have elicited a smile of understanding from one who had served as a student under Jackson at VMI:

> We have heard a good story on Stonewall Jackson. It has come to be commonly said in camp that nobody knows Stonewall's secrets except his old negro body servant. Some one talking to the old negro, asked him how he came to be so much in the confidence of his master. "Lord Sir," said he, "massa never tells me nothing, but the way I knows is this—Massa says his prayers twice a day, morning and night—but if he gets out of bed two or three times in the night to pray, you see I just commences packing my haversacks, for I knows there will *be the devil to pay next day.*"

War news from other fronts was also encouraging. From Richmond, Kentucky, under date of 25 July, came news that Colonel John Hunt Morgan "had taken eleven cities and towns, with very heavy army stores, and has a force sufficient to hold all the country outside of Lexington and Frankfort. . . . The bridges between Lexington and Cincinnati have been destroyed."[24] The 13 August issue of the *North Carolina Standard* carried an article about General Nathan Bedford Forrest and his late "dashing exploits" about Chattanooga, especially his brilliant achievement at Murfreesboro and the capture of Lebanon. But in eastern North Carolina there was cause for continued concern bordering on alarm. Harry undoubtedly read the news report that "four Yankee gunboats went up Chowan river on the 8th inst., as far as Winton, and shelled the Village, burning two of the dwellings. They then steamed up the river—where, it is not known."[25] A week later he would probably have seen the editorial addressed to "Our People of the Eastern Counties," which stated that "our northeast Counties beyond the Chowan are literally *overrun* by the Yankees. Every day they are becoming more aggressive, tyrannical and oppressive." Ten to fifteen thousand slaves had been lost to their owners, and confiscation of food "will soon rob our people of all their means." The editor warned that a similar fate awaited other areas of the state unless the enemy was driven back.[26]

Harry could not have read this admonition without fully comprehending its significance. His family's plantation and possessions were concentrated on the east bank of the Roanoke just below Weldon. This area was a prime target for the enemy because Weldon served as a junction for the Wilmington and Weldon, the Seaboard and Roanoke, the Petersburg, and the Raleigh and Gaston railroads.[27] Its strategic importance and its vulnerability to attack were fully appreciated by both North and South. Should Weldon fall to the enemy, the lifeline to the Army of Northern Virginia would be broken, for the Wilmington and Weldon provided the only rail link to a major seaport still operating in the Southeast.

These considerations influenced a subtle change in Harry's outlook with respect to the war and his future role in it. During the hectic days preceding the confrontation with McClellan before Richmond, his letters had clearly revealed the normal reaction of a youthful leader impatient with the dull routine of camp life in North Carolina and eagerly anticipating combat and an opportunity to prove himself. He had been disillusioned by the poor generalship exhibited at the battle of New Bern but had been deeply impressed by Jackson's valley exploits and gave every indication of wanting to serve in his command. But now, in August 1862, the tide had turned. The Yankees were on the run and the Confederates in hot pursuit. The Army of Northern Virginia would shortly invade Maryland. Perhaps Harry's services might be better used in defense of his native state, for his own home was virtually under siege. Circumstances, in combination with his own desires, would soon move him in this direction.

The election of Colonel Zeb Vance as governor of North Carolina on 7 August elevated Harry Burgwyn to the command of the Twenty-sixth North Carolina, but not without considerable frustration and emotional discomfort. On 11 August, at their camp near Petersburg, a meeting of the officers of the Twenty-sixth was called for the purpose of planning "a complimentary farewell to our Colonel, Z. B. Vance, Governor-elect of North Carolina." On the fifteenth, at night in the open air, "not less than two thousand soldiers crowded around" to hear read a resolution expressing pride and gratification, mingled with regret, for one "who, after twelve months in the difficult relationship of commander and commanded, leaves without a foe, honored and respected by all." A sword was presented to Colonel Vance by Sergeant Major L. L. Polk, "with an exceedingly neat and appropriate address." If Harry had been in camp at the time, he would have undoubtedly participated in the program.[28]

It is likely that he first learned of the ceremony from the following letter, written from camp near Petersburg on 11 August, which contained some very disquieting information:

Col. Vance will leave here in a day or two or at least this week and as a friend I would advise you if your health will permit to return to the regiment. I heard from Col V this evening that Gen Ransom said that he should not recommend you for Colonel on account of your age. He said he did not intend to have any more boys to command regiments in his Brigade. I have spoken to several of our officers & they will not submit to have any one else. They swear that they will not stay under an officer appointed over them. Ransom may have said this in one of his frets without meaning anything. As it was told me confidentially you will of course say nothing about it. The Reg' will stick up to you without a doubt.[29]

Remembering that he had been reelected lieutenant colonel of his regiment the previous April by a very narrow margin, Harry must have been deeply gratified by this manifestation of loyalty expressed by Captain John Thomas Jones, Company I, and his fellow officers. But this support could hardly compensate for General Ransom's refusal to observe "the rule of promotion as governed by the Army Regulations." Jones had enjoined Harry to confidentiality, but apparently he discussed the matter with his father, who lost no time in acting on behalf of his son. The following letter reflects the relationship between the two. Each was ambitious, and, if the occasion demanded, neither was timid in asserting his rights or expectations:

My Son Lt. Col. Burgwyn has received information from several friends, officers of the army, that Genrl Ransom has intimated an intention of interfering with his promotion to the vacant Colonelcy of his regmt. consequent upon Col. Vance's resignation.

Of course this has occasioned me no small vexation as independent of other considerations it must appear to the public as a want of confidence in Lt. Col. B. & that too immediately after his having been engaged in the recent affairs about Richmond. In short in [it] can only appear as a decided slur upon him & of course I shall not submit quietly to it. But further than this it is a matter that specially & imperatively demands the attention of every commissioned officer in the Brigade; for if the rule of promotion as governed by the Army Regulations is allow[ed] to be contravened by Genrl. R. upon no other cause than that now alleged viz youth *after competency* to command & lead successfully both into action & in retreat (as was the case at New Berne) has been shown by the officers then no officer can feel himself secure in his rights let his services be what they may.

Should Lt. Col. B. have been proved incompetent from any cause to the fulfillment of his duties, I should be the last person to take any objection for I desire too strongly the success of our arms to be willing to aid in the promotion of any such person. But the statements & reports of his superior officers do not show this, and he has a letter of *very* high recommendation from Stonewall Jackson to the Sectry. of War which amply contradicts any such supposition. As does his letters from all his professors at the Mil. Academy.[30]

Colonel Clarke responded almost immediately. "Having not heard even a whisper of the matter," he wrote, "I am slow to believe that Gen'l Ransom would attempt to interfere to prevent the promotion of Lieut. Col. B; but I have seen so much lately that was unexpected that I have almost adopted the motto 'nil admirari.'" He was confident that such a move would meet with "little sympathy or encouragement in the Brigade, for I have heard Lt. Col. B. spoken of frequently as an excellent officer, and one who would make the Reg't. far more efficient than it has been under the present command." Furthermore, "I cannot believe that Gen'l R. will attempt to have him superseded; and if he does I doubt his success in an undertaking so unjust." He suggested that Burgwyn consider "the propriety of inquiring of Gen'l. R. if he has any such intentions. I repeat, I cannot believe the report—."[31]

But Harry's friend and fellow officer, Captain Jones, was filled with anxiety. From Richmond, on 21 August, he dispatched a hurried note: "Your letter I only rec'd just before I left Petersburg. I am this far on my way to Stonewall. Have not had time to tend to the matter you spoke of. I believe now there will be no difficulty in your way. For God's sake come to us as soon as you can."[32] The following day, Captain J. J. Young provided Harry with detailed information on what was being done in his behalf to thwart General Ransom's objective: "A committee waited on Gen Ransom yesterday to know if the regt recommended officers to fill the vacancies if he would approve them. He emphatically denied to approve you[r] recommendation consequently the committee recommended no one for Col. . . . Please come to us as soon as you can. I wish for you to resist to the last this usurpation of power. I am too angry to act." Captain Young and other officers threatened to resign if Harry was not elected.[33]

In the meantime, Harry and his father had not been idle. Recognizing the need to become directly involved, Harry returned to Peters-

burg on 22 August and reached Richmond the next day. That his father accompanied him is indicated in a letter Harry wrote to his
mother:

> I learn from Willie who is in town today that our brigade has
> been transferred from D. H. Hill's Division to Gen. G. W. Smith's
> Division. Gen Smith is to be left I understand here with 3 bri-
> gades to defend Richmond in case of an attack. My brigade is to
> be stationed as far as I can judge for some time near Chapin's
> Bluff, close to the point where the pontoon bridge crosses the
> James. I am in town today but will probably go out this after-
> noon. I am here trying to get transferred to Pettigrew's brigade.
> Gen Ransom wrote a letter recommending Col Ruffin for the
> command of my regmt. Willie tells me however that Gen. R.
> confessed he had tried his best to get Ruffin but that he could
> not succeed. I have no fear of his success. Father is to see the
> Secretary of War today.[34]

The next day Harry Burgwyn became colonel of the Twenty-sixth.
From his camp "4 miles on the River road below Richmond," Harry
confided to his mother:

> I had a long conversation with Ransom to day; in which after
> speaking of some regimental business, he opened the subject of
> field officers for my regiment. He said he had recommended
> Col. Ruffin, & not myself, & had gone to see the President
> upon the subject. The Presdt. replied by showing him the Con-
> script Act & saying it was impossible to prevent my promotion
> & that the utmost which could be done would be to get some
> Capt. who by good & meritorious conduct was deserving of it
> to be promoted as Maj. So, said Gen Ransom you are Colonel of
> the 26th Rgt. After considerable conversation upon this sub-
> ject, & the subject of the promotion of the other officers, I
> asked him if Gen Hill had told him anything about sending us
> to N.C. He said he had not, but that he Gen R. would facilitate
> it as much as possible, & actually made an appointment to
> meet me at 12 o'clock to morrow to go to see Gen Smith (G. W.)
> to prevail upon him to transfer us, & said he had no doubt he
> could get Gen S. to make the order. Gen R. added that he would
> not be willing to weaken his brigade by giving us up without an
> equivalent in the shape of some other Regmt. I then told him
> what Genrl. Martin had said & that Gen. M. had promised to
> send a regiment here if he could get mine back to N.C. This he
> said would satisfy him.

Father is still in Richmond, & I go in to town early to morrow morning to see him & the Sect. of War as well as Gen Smith. I hope this transfer can be effected & am inclined to think it can. I shall try to make an active campaign of it in N.C. if I can.[35]

It was a very exuberant young man who, three days later, assured his mother that his objectives had been fully achieved. "Having defeated the machinations of Gen. Ransom upon all points," he happily reported, "I take very great pleasure in telling you to day that, when our Brigade received orders to move to Jacksonville [Jeffersonville] in Culpepper County, I received orders that I was transferred to Gen. Johnston Pettigrew's Brigade at Petersburg; for which place my regiment leaves this afternoon. So soon as the Colonelcy was settled, I set myself hard at work to get transferred. When I saw Ransom, he almost palavered me, & I got him to approve my application for a transfer." The rest of Ransom's brigade had left for Jeffersonville, but Harry did not expect "any hard fighting for some time to come. The campaign appears to have degenerated into a flight & a pursuit." Harry added that his brother William "left us this afternoon in good spirits & properly provided with whisky & instructed in its use. We shall not be able to write him until we learn where he is stationed. He was provided with canteens, haversack, something in it, & a good dinner in his stom—. Thus armed & accoutered, & with a stout heart & a trust in Providence, I believe he will succeed."[36]

CHAPTER 14

I AM PROUD OF MY COMMAND

Harry probably made his decision to be transferred to Pettigrew's brigade while he was convalescing in Raleigh. He had undoubtedly talked with General Martin while in Raleigh, and it is probable that the idea of going with Pettigrew was sparked by a brief announcement that appeared in the 20 August issue of the *North Carolina Standard* stating that General Pettigrew was recovering well from his wounds and had reported for service.

James Johnston Pettigrew, who had been severely wounded and captured at Seven Pines, spent his thirty-fourth birthday as a prisoner of war at Fort Delaware. Born of a distinguished family in Tyrrell County, North Carolina, on 4 July 1828, Pettigrew early established himself as a brilliant scholar. Graduating from the University of North Carolina in 1847 with highest honors, he soon selected law as his profession and was admitted to the South Carolina bar in 1849. He was profoundly influenced by his father's first cousin, James Louis Petigru, a distinguished member of the Charleston bar, and by James Cathcart Johnston, a wealthy bachelor and close friend of the Pettigrew family in North Carolina. In the 1850s he was privileged to study and travel extensively in western Europe. During this time he earned a degree in civil law at the University of Berlin, mastered the writing and speaking of German, French, Spanish, and Italian (he was later to learn Arabic and Hebrew), and developed a sound knowledge of the theory of music.[1]

It was in Spain that Johnston Pettigrew found his greatest inspiration. To one of his chivalric bent, it was indeed a land of enchantment. The moorish kingdoms of the south were profoundly appealing to his romantic sensitivity, and he found Andalusia and Valencia a paradise. Both his genius and his idealistic nature had drawn deeply from his experience, and the remainder of his life would be spent in restless pursuit of excellence, glory, and even death.[2]

The intensity of the secession movement in South Carolina galvanized his attention, and he came to feel that the hostility of the federal government was growing intolerable. The more the idea of secession was discussed, the more preoccupied he became with military training and preparation. Before long he was working closely with Governor William Henry Gist and his successor, Francis Wilkinson Pickens. In late November of 1860, he was unanimously elected colonel of the First Regiment of Rifles of South Carolina. On 20 December, during the first parade of his regimental command in Charleston, Pettigrew received and read aloud South Carolina's ordinance of secession.[3]

On 27 December he and his men occupied Fort Moultrie, which had been abandoned by Major Robert Anderson's Federal troops the night before. That same afternoon, under orders from Governor Pickens, they occupied Castle Pinckney, another Federal fort located near the city. In Pettigrew's mind South Carolina was now virtually at war, and he gave unstintingly of himself. But by the time Fort Sumter was fired upon, the Confederate government had taken over the responsibility for defending Charleston, and Johnston Pettigrew found himself "a secondary officer doing secondary duty in a secondary army."[4]

Disappointed in his effort to organize an elite regiment of volunteers for the army in Virginia, he offered his services to the governor of North Carolina. It was not until 11 July that he was notified of his election as colonel of the Twenty-second North Carolina Regiment, which was being organized at Raleigh. He accepted with alacrity, for his first allegiance was to his native state. The regiment soon departed for Virginia.[5]

During the fall and winter of 1861–62, Pettigrew was stationed at Evansport on the Potomac. His enterprising skill and energy quickly attracted the attention and commendation of his immediate superiors. In February, much to his surprise, Pettigrew was commissioned brigadier general in the Provisional Army of the Confederate States. He declined primarily because he believed no one should be commissioned general who had never led troops in combat. He was summoned to Richmond by President Davis to explain his refusal but again respectfully declined the appointment. Under pressure from General Holmes and others, and assured that the Twenty-second would be included in his brigade, Pettigrew finally accepted. His commission was returned by the War Department on 22 March.[6]

His reluctance to accept promotion was no pretense. Conscious of his inexperience, Johnston Pettigrew wanted no favors deriving from political influence or station in life. He was zealous in the pursuit of excellence, and his promotion was the result of recognized merit. Although he was not a professional soldier, his study of military science and rare intellectual capacity, coupled with an innate and fearless sense of duty, marked him as a leader. Prudence would be no impediment to his courage. He was convinced that the South was fighting for a just cause and that no sacrifice in her behalf could be too great.

Pettigrew assumed the command of his brigade about mid-March 1862. About the same time, General McClellan started moving the powerful Army of the Potomac to the York and James rivers in preparation for the Peninsula campaign.[7] Undoubtedly the promise of early action persuaded Pettigrew to accept a brigadier generalship. Until now he had been keenly disappointed in his expectations of distinction on the field of combat. His new brigade was soon headed for the Peninsula, where it was to join the Confederate forces facing McClellan at Yorktown. The Confederates slowly fell back on Richmond during the month of May, and it was not until the last day of the month that Pettigrew's brigade was given an opportunity to see action. And it was at Seven Pines that Johnston Pettigrew was left for dead on the battlefield.[8]

Early the following morning, 1 June, he was picked up within the Federal lines by men of the Twentieth Massachusetts Regiment. After being treated at two field hospitals, he was taken to the home of Doctor William F. Gaines, where he remained for ten days. His wounds were not as serious as first believed. His neck would soon heal, but his right arm was permanently disabled, and it would be some time before he would regain full use of his injured leg. After leaving Dr. Gaines, Pettigrew was taken to Baltimore by way of Fortress Monroe. The six days spent in Baltimore provided a pleasant interlude before he was taken to Fort Delaware. While receiving medical treatment in Baltimore, he was permitted to stay at Guy's Monument House hotel, where he received the solicitous attention of friends and relatives living in the area. This generous treatment by his captors was permitted on the condition that he not attempt to escape.[9]

His six weeks at Fort Delaware were not unpleasant. Mail and gifts were allowed, and offers of personal assistance were tendered by acquaintances living in Pennsylvania and New York. The paralysis of his right arm continued to be a source of great concern, but he was refused permission to go to Baltimore for special treatment. In early August Pettigrew was exchanged for a Federal brigadier and immediately reported for duty in Richmond.[10] On 11 August he was temporarily assigned to the command of Colonel Junius Daniel's brigade. A week later Brigadier General J. G. Martin was assigned to the District of North Carolina, extending from the right banks of the Roanoke to the South Carolina line, and Pettigrew was ordered to relieve him of the charge of his brigade.[11] According to his biographer, Pettigrew was disappointed not to rejoin his old brigade but instead to be given "a new command in a backwater away from the glorious fields of the war." Nevertheless, he accepted the command "and prepared to do his duty."[12]

It was in this manner that the lives and military fortunes of Johnston Pettigrew and Harry Burgwyn were brought together. They had much in common. Of aristocratic heritage, both were gentlemen born. Each was highly educated and early displayed a mature sense of responsibility to his family and to his privileged station in life. Both were strongly provincial in their patriotic devotion, and there would never be any question as to their absolute dedication to the cause of the Confederacy. Johnston Pettigrew was thirteen years older than Harry Burgwyn. In experience, breadth of study, and travel, he was superior to Harry. And he was undoubtedly more idealistic. A romanticist by nature, Pettigrew was imbued with a sense of the heroic and melodramatic, and his courage and fearlessness in the face of danger were equal to the best among his legendary heroes.

Harry's letters do not reveal so idealistic a nature. They portray him as no less dedicated and determined but perhaps more pragmatic in his judgments and outlook on life. For instance, military preferment through political intercession, in satisfying his own ambition, presented no problem to Harry, whereas promotion through political persuasion would have been offensive to Pettigrew. On the other hand, what Harry may have lacked in idealistic motivation was more than compensated for by a sense of self-confidence that was anything but misplaced. Both had natural leadership capabilities, and both aspired to leadership. But Harry Burgwyn was more of a martinet. Johnston's manner was perhaps better calculated to inspire; yet Harry's insistence upon strict military discipline and training would, in the end, earn for him the unstinted devotion of his men.

Both men had undergone their baptism of fire, Pettigrew at Seven Pines and Burgwyn during the Seven Days' battle. Neither was found wanting. Pettigrew later attributed his refusal to be taken to the rear after being wounded to his belief that his wound would be fatal. "It was useless," he reported, "to take men from the field, under any circumstances for that purpose." He was mortified to have been captured, for it would appear that he might have surrendered. While recuperating at Dr. Gaines's house, Pettigrew sent a note to General Whiting under a flag of truce in which he said, "I never would have surrendered, under any circumstances, to save my own life, or anybody else's." He was concerned about his reputation, and surrender was not an acceptable option. He was determined to distinguish himself in battle regardless of sacrifice. Indeed, if there had been no Civil War, it is not unlikely that Johnston Pettigrew would have sought out and found some other cause from which to realize a sense of "glorious" fulfillment.[13]

Harry Burgwyn was motivated more by a sense of duty than a desire for personal glory. He was ambitious almost to a fault. He yearned to achieve, but not necessarily on the field of battle. But once he became committed to the war effort, his desire for distinction as a successful leader was no less persuasive of courageous sacrifice than that of Johnston Pettigrew. In January 1862, reflecting upon the magnitude of Burnside's expedition, Harry had confided to his journal: "Though not desirous of being killed I am very anxious to be in at least one fight before I go out of service & my reputation will greatly depend upon my conduct on that occasion."[14] Again, in late February, in a long letter to his father outlining the vulnerability of the New Bern defenses, Harry was constrained to add: "Do not understand me as giving up. My spirits like yours rise with our disasters. Not a particle of yielding is in me, but I do wish to see better generalship & that a fair show be given to our men."[15] Two days before the battle of New Bern, he wrote his mother, "I used to think the night before a battle I would be anxious for my own fate & that of the day. Now if I had my wish exclusive of the fact that our defences may be improved by delay I would not postpone a day."[16]

In a note to his mother following the battle of New Bern, Harry was careful to add, "My command was the last to retreat."[17] Later, in further reflecting upon the poor Confederate leadership exhibited during the battle, he wrote his father: "If I have any command unless prohibited by orders I intend to charge the enemy with the bayonet as early as possible in the fight & let the relative bravery of the troops be tested."[18] But Harry's sense of bravery on the battlefield was not oblivious to the horrors of war. He was deeply affected by what he had witnessed during the Seven Days' battle. To his father he sadly acknowledged: "I have seen enough of the horrors of war to ardently desire that this 7 days battle with its terrible carnage & suffering may pave the way for a permanent & speedy peace & that we may all be speedily reunited again. May God grant it be so."[19]

On 27 August 1861, Harry Burgwyn had been elected lieutenant colonel of the newly organized Twenty-sixth North Carolina. Almost a year later, 24 August 1862, he was named colonel of the Twenty-sixth. And on 27 August 1862, his regiment was transferred to General Johnston Pettigrew's Brigade at Petersburg. It was then, probably for the first time, that the two met. Pettigrew was still ailing, but his determination to be in active service was so great that he had "walked to R[ichmond] all the way from Varina, the landing place on the James, a distance of 12 miles, under a hot sun. Louis Young who rode to meet him urged his taking his horse—No, he replied, I wish to test my capability for active service."[20]

That mutual admiration and respect would characterize the relationship between Pettigrew and Burgwyn is self-evident, but to one privileged to observe them in camp and in action, "it seemed as if Pettigrew and Burgwyn were made for each other. Alike in bravery, alike in action, alike in their military bearing, alike in readiness for battle and in skillful horsemanship, they were beloved alike by the soldiers of the Twenty-sixth. Each served as a pattern for the other, and in imitating each other they reached the highest excellence possible of attainment in every trait which distinguishes the ideal soldier."[21]

The Pettigrew Brigade was originally organized by Adjutant General James G. Martin of North Carolina. It consisted of the Eleventh, Seventeenth, Forty-fourth, Forty-seventh, and Fifty-second North Carolina Volunteers. As a brigadier general in the Provisional Army of the Confederate States, Martin had led his brigade to Virginia during the Seven Days' battle but arrived too late to participate. He was then ordered into camp near Proctor's Station midway between Petersburg and Richmond and near Drewry's Bluff. In late July, Martin resigned as brigadier general so he might resume his duties as adjutant general of North Carolina. President Davis accepted Martin's resignation but subsequently rescinded his action upon the urgent remonstrance of General Lee. On 18 August General Martin was assigned to the District of North Carolina under the command of Major General D. H. Hill. Upon his return to the state he took with him the Seventeenth North Carolina, commanded by his brother, Colonel William F. Martin. It was this regiment that was replaced by the Twenty-sixth North Carolina, much to the satisfaction of Colonel Harry Burgwyn.[22]

The Twenty-sixth North Carolina was the only battle-tried regiment in the brigade. During its year of service it had been exposed to the usual problems and privations of active military life. In battle it had acquitted itself with distinction, if not glory, and was recognized for its able leadership. In commenting upon his brother's new brigade, William S. Pettigrew wrote that "Col. Burgwin's Regiment is said to be one of the best in the service."[23] Although Harry would have appreciated this assessment, he was dissatisfied with the condition in which he found his regiment upon his return from furlough. To his mother, he wrote, "I found my regiment greatly disorganized by the indulgences given it by the Senior Captain in whose charge it had been. . . . There is I am glad to say a strong disposition to assist me in my efforts, & after a few days I think everything will go along smoothly & with order."[24]

Harry's major concern, however, was with recruitment and reorganization. He had no sooner returned to his command than he wrote one of his officers, then recruiting conscripts in North Carolina, urging him to hasten their arrival. "We are discharging a great many men," Harry emphasized, "& it is absolutely necessary for our ranks to be filled up."[25] Later in the month he reported to his father that "Capt. Lane brought in about 110 conscripts so that my regiment now numbers in all some 1150 men, perhaps the largest regiment in the C.S.A."[26]

The problem of filling two field officer vacancies troubled him greatly. These vacancies were occasioned by his own promotion to the colonelcy and the recent death of Major James S. Kendall. "The scheme by which I hoped to get the ones I thought most highly of," he wrote his mother, "has failed (viz election) on account of the jealousy of the different officers & I must now try to get the Presdt. to appoint. Gen. Pettigrew will aid me all he can I know & I have no doubt but that with the exercise of a little judicious firmness I can succeed."[27] Harry much preferred a Captain Rand as his successor, but, according to the secretary of war, Rand lacked the appropriate seniority. Even Governor Vance intervened in his behalf, but to no avail, and Harry regretfully concluded that "I shall have to put up with 'such as the law allows.'"[28]

By mid-October, however, time and "a little judicious firmness" had relieved the situation. It was a very pleased and confident young colonel who wrote his mother on 14 October that his complement of officers was complete. He was expecting a shipment of conscripts, and believed that if given another month his regiment would be at full strength and "as well drilled as any in the Confederacy. I am proud of my Command I assure you & when occasion offers shall try to make them proud of me."[29]

If nothing else, the first six weeks of Harry's new command afforded him considerable opportunity for playing a positive and responsible leadership role. Before he could resolve his organizational and recruitment problems, however, he had to prepare for an abortive expedition against Suffolk. On 13 September, Harry advised his father that he had just received orders to move the following morning to Ivor Station on the Norfolk and Petersburg Railroad, either to "attack the Yanks at Suffolk or keep them closely confined. Our Force is 5 Rgts of inft. & 6 pieces of Artillery numbering from 2300 to 2600 men I suppose. Whether we are to have any cavalry I know not. I suppose so however." In a separate letter to his mother the same day, he expressed great confidence in "Gen. Pettigrew's able leadership" and urged her not to be "uneasy at all for I would not be much surprised if our going down there was merely to hasten the reported evacuation of Suffolk."[30]

The Twenty-sixth probably moved at dawn on the nineteenth, but it did not proceed far. From Camp French, near Petersburg, four days later, Harry reported that they had marched to near Blackwater Station, then received orders to backtrack and were back at Petersburg.[31] On the same day Johnston Pettigrew wrote his brother: "We have just returned from our rather badly conceived expedition, which occupied a week. The Yankees outnumbered us, but they were green and we were green and I think we could have caught them." A few days later Pettigrew was more explicit. "Our expedition against Suffolk and Norfolk fell through. Instead of striking like the lightning of the tropics," he told his brother, "we spent a whole week in rolling up our little thunder cloud, right before their faces, so that any fool would have raised his umbrella. It really seems to me that we might have concocted a plan to drive them out of the whole country south of the James River."[32]

Similar fruitless expeditions would be undertaken during the coming months. In southside Virginia and eastern North Carolina the Federals had come to stay. At Norfolk and Yorktown they controlled the mouths of the James and York rivers. Their possession of Hampton Roads provided them with the finest harbor in the Southeast for the concentration of naval forces and supply services and would pose a constant threat to the safety of Richmond. In eastern North Carolina, with the exception of the Cape Fear River below Wilmington, the Federals controlled (or could quickly do so) every waterway into the Atlantic. Having captured Fort Macon at Beaufort, they controlled the harbor at Morehead City, from which naval expeditions could penetrate as far inland as New Bern, Washington, Plymouth, Elizabeth City, Edenton, and Winton. This naval support made possible the permanent and heavily fortified Federal garrison at New Bern. The same was true of Washington, although it was not as strongly garrisoned. Only very small Federal detachments were posted in other areas.

This strong Federal presence in eastern Virginia and North Carolina obviously influenced every move of the Army of Northern Virginia. By the same token, the moves and countermoves of the Federal garrisons were largely conditioned by General Lee's actual or probable moves. And his offensive strategy, in turn, was developed with a weather eye on his defenses at Richmond and the strength of the Confederate forces in southside Virginia and eastern North Carolina. These forces were supposed to protect the food resources of the area as well as the major supply lines between Wilmington, Goldsboro, Weldon, Petersburg, and Richmond. As a consequence, the inhabitants of both regions lived in a stalemated environment in which neither side seemed disposed to mount a major offensive.

Raids, demonstrations, and reconnaissances would, for months to come, constitute the basic strategy of each. It is in this context that one can best understand the friction that existed between the civil and military authorities in North Carolina and Virginia. It was a matter of relative importance and relative strength. North Carolinians felt that they were playing a far greater role in the defense of Richmond than was reasonable in the light of their own meager defenses. The authorities recognized this dilemma but could do little to ameliorate it. Available manpower and equipment were simply not sufficient to support the movements of the Army of Northern Virginia and, at the same time, provide adequate protection for an area subject to Federal penetration almost at will. Following the Seven Days' battle, however, it was determined that the military command structure for this exposed region must be strengthened.

On 17 July, by order of the secretary of war, Major General D. H. Hill replaced Major General Theophilus H. Holmes in command of the Department of North Carolina. On 28 July, General Lee urged J. G. Martin not to resign his brigadier generalship, but rather to accept immediate command of the forces in North Carolina so that General Hill might concentrate his time and attention on the troops in Virginia, especially those along James River.[33]

While General Hill was busily engaged in fortifying strategic points in southside Virginia, the Federals were similarly employed in eastern North Carolina. General Burnside, who had left New Bern belatedly to join McClellan in Virginia, was succeeded by Brigadier General John G. Foster on 6 July, as commander of the Department of North Carolina. His force at that time comprised the First Division, consisting of seven regiments and one battalion of infantry, one regiment of cavalry, one of artillery, and the marine artillery. All were stationed in New Bern except for a few detachments on guard duty along the railroad line to Beaufort and on Roanoke Island. In his first report on 8 July, Foster emphasized, "I am at present engaged in strengthening and fortifying the place at every possible point of attack, and consider myself abundantly able to hold the position against almost any force that may be brought against it."[34]

Subsequent reports during the next several weeks indicate that General Foster was diligent in completing necessary fortifications and reconnoitering the area under his command. On 21 July he reported to Secretary Stanton that work on the defenses of New Bern was "progressing very favorably, and before long I expect the town to be sufficiently fortified to be held by a small force." In addition, the construction of works for the defense of Washington was rapidly nearing completion, and "the work on block-houses on the line of the Atlantic and North Carolina Railroad is going on with proper dispatch." By the end of the month Foster was able to report that the fort at Washington was ready to receive its guns and that all other construction work was proceeding satisfactorily. Most important, during a two-day intensive reconnaissance effort, detachments were sent out to Trenton, Pollocksville, Young's Cross-Roads, and "up the railroad to break up the picket headquarters on the Neuse Road." Only light resistance was encountered in any direction, and only small, scattered units of the enemy were in evidence.[35]

On 7 August, additional reconnaissance efforts were reported, and, on the tenth, General Foster assured Secretary Stanton that such reconnaissances, both by land and water, "have had the effect of causing the enemy to withdraw their pickets to within 5 miles of Kinston, thereby putting an end to the harassing practice of picket firing." By the seventeenth, Foster's military strength in New Bern had increased to seven and one-half regiments of infantry, one of artillery, one of marine artillery, and one of cavalry. The artillery consisted of seven field batteries (two of six pieces each, three of four pieces each, and two of three pieces each). These forces added measurably to Foster's confidence and led him to conclude: "In any case of an advance I shall not expect to occupy the places that I capture up the country, but rather to have for an object to destroy the railroad bridges, etc., so as to cut off the communication of the army at Richmond with the South."[36]

It was in this "backwater away from the glorious fields of the war" that Pettigrew yearned for action and Burgwyn became deeply troubled by the growing realization that only devastation and ruin lay ahead for those trapped in eastern North Carolina under Federal domination. But even then, in Harry's view, peace could not be far off. His letters home during the fall months of 1862 provide an insight into his personal concerns, opinions, and reactions. They reflect the attributes of a strong-willed, knowledgeable, intelligent young man—achievement-oriented but of a compassionate nature with a firm trust in Providence.

On 9 September, in regard to the Maryland campaign, he surmised:

> There appears to be no doubt that Jackson with a powerful army has crossed the Potomac & is now in Maryland. . . . It is pleasant though idle to speculate on the result of these battles. The Northern people must see that they are to day farther from subjugating the South than they have ever been before. 300,000 men, slain by the sword, or perished by disease, must be a strong peace argument. It seems to me that if we gain Maryland, that Davis should at once issue a proclamation to the world that all we desire is separation upon terms that the Federals give up every foot of Southern soil & allow Maryland, Ky. & Missouri a chance to vote one way or the other.[37]

Believing that his regiment was about to become engaged in the abortive Suffolk expedition, Harry admonished his mother not to be anxious: "With a firm trust in Providence & a resolve to be as prudent as my duty will allow I have no doubt of our success & my own safety."[38]

Later on, rumors that a Yankee force of twenty to forty thousand men was being concentrated at Suffolk occasioned grave concern in Confederate ranks. Harry immediately alerted his father: "I think I should keep a close look out for Thornbury & prepare *at once* a place in the West for my Negroes. The authorities do not intend to care how much the Yankees injure us provided Richmond is safe & the force in N.C. is so ridiculously weak that it amounts to absolutely nothing. You may depend upon it so soon as the River [Roanoke] is at all navigable gunboat raids may take place at any moment. If the Weldon bridge is not burnt this winter then I will be greatly mistaken. As an investment it may not cost you much."[39]

In October Harry learned of the death of his cousin, General George Burgwyn Anderson, who had been wounded at the battle of Sharpsburg (Antietam). It was the first battle death in his family. Harry was in a reflective mood when he wrote his parents on 3 October 1862, his twenty-first birthday. At this milestone in his life, Harry's sense of filial gratitude and responsibility must have been heartwarming to his mother and father. "Reviewing at this point in my life the causes & promptings of my actions," he wrote,

I am most sensibly aware of the benefits which your good teach-
ings & instructions have conferred upon me. Indebted to you
alone have I been for the education & opportunities for improvement, which, at the very outset of my life, place me where
others are only beginning. I can well acknowledge that my
judgment was often at fault. Disinclination to earn my portion
with the sweat of my brow would upon one occasion have
changed the whole character of my pursuits, & at this moment
made me a subaltern. A firm & judicious insisting sent me to a
Military Institute & made me a Colonel.

It would then ill become me ever to forget what your influence
has done for me hitherto & to show ingratitude & inappreciation
by not hereafter, as before, seeking advice & instruction. Too
sensible of my own liability to err am I not to do so, & I shall
always repair in doubt or in error to you who have always resolved the one & corrected the other.[40]

In the same letter Harry expressed delight in learning of his
younger brother William's "maiden battle [Sharpsburg] in which he
won his spurs. I was perfectly certain he would behave well, but it is
most gratifying to hear that he extorted an encomium from Ransom
himself." And in a touching reference to his still younger brother,
Pollok, he added, "nor do I know when I have been more affected
than I was by Pollok's 'Deed of law' & gift of his horse, the short &
simple annal of his affection. Please give him my best love, & tell
him that to morrow morning I will write him & thank him."[41]

Two days later he did write to Pollok. In thanking him for the gift
of the horse Harry took the occasion to give his fifteen-year-old
brother some thoughtful and timely advice. One wonders if, even
then, Harry had a premonition that he might not live to witness his
twenty-second birthday:

The affection I have for you also prompts me to make use of
this occasion to talk to you upon some points, which you are
now well able to understand, & may perhaps soon be called to
act upon. As at my age of 21, I have certain responsibilities &
duties, so do you at 15 have analogous & similar ones. At your
age, you are most especially called upon by study—diligence—
sobriety & attention to fit yourself for the position to which
you may be called.

In the first place, William & myself are in the army, & though
perhaps exposed to no immediate danger, are both liable to be

cut off at any time, & then you would be the oldest son: the great reliance of your father & mother. The short space of 24 hours might call upon you to console & comfort both father & mother for our loss. . . . That you will appreciate it, I do not doubt, but what I want to impress upon you is that now—*now*—*now*—is the time to do all this.[42]

CHAPTER 15

SKILL UNDER FIRE

In early October, General Pettigrew issued a circular indicating that the brigade might be ordered off at any moment, "& that an hour or two at most would be our notice." Harry conjectured that an attack was anticipated upon Richmond or the bluffs on the James. He doubted that it would be upon Weldon.[1] The attack from Suffolk never came, but by mid-October Harry was confident that his regiment was ready for action. He was anxious to spend a few days with his family and was encouraged to do so by General Pettigrew. On the nineteenth, Harry suggested that his father "send a horse or buggy for me to Garysburg on Wednesday."[2]

Harry must have spent a couple of days at Thornbury, for, on Saturday, the twenty-fifth, he wrote his father: "Imagine my surprise when just as I entered Petersburg I saw my Rgt on the cars for Weldon. I saw Gen. French & received his instructions & left the town in an hour after I entered it. We reached this point (Tarboro) this morning at 2 o'clock, & will probably leave here this afternoon. The expedition consists as well as I know of the 17th 26th & 59th Rgts. & probably some cavalry. I think I shall be absent from Petersburg only temporarily." He expected to be back in Petersburg within a week and thought he might again be able to spend a night with his family.[3]

Two days later, from Williamston on the Roanoke River, Harry could give his father more pertinent information about the expedition. He left Tarboro Saturday afternoon and marched approximately eight miles before bivouacking. On Sunday he marched to within six miles of Williamston and the following day passed through that place en route *"towards* Washington." His precise destination was a secret, but Harry urged his father not to be anxious. He was under the command of Col. J. D. Radcliffe.[4] On Saturday, 1 November, Harry again wrote his father. Poised within six miles of Washington, with only five companies of his regiment immediately available to him, and no artillery, he gave full rein to his frustration. With Harry, inaction invariably bred impatience, and he spared neither prejudice nor opinion:

When I left Gen. French he told me he had ordered Col. Radcliffe to attack Plymouth, & that my Rgt was temporarily detached from my Brigade to make a feint towards Washington & to prevent the enemy from cutting Col. Radcliff off at WmSton after he had attacked Plymouth. I reached this point on Tuesday the 28th ult. & Col Radcliffe in command of 3 companies of Cavalry, one Battery of Artillery & 2 Rgts of Inft. reached the vicinity of Plymouth about the same time & there he is still & as far as I know has done nothing but arrest some few "Buffalo Yankees." Had I been in his place Plymouth, which never has had according to the best of my information more than 300 men, would have been mine long ago.

When I reached this point, Washington . . . if I had had artillery I would not have hesitated to attack the place, but I had not a piece, & could not hope to take it fortified as it was by Block Houses & one fort mounting 8 guns. Two days after my arrival I received orders to send 5 Co's to WmSton & now have here only 5 Companies of my Rgt & some 13 or 14 troopers. I advanced my pickets & reconnoitering parties to within a mile of town on one road & ½ on another, & so directed their attention to me that the Yankee Colonel sent immediately for reinforcements, & on yesterday 12 steamers & transports arrived off Washington provided with troops & disembarked them. I presume they landed from 2 to 3000 men. They have not yet advanced, however, & I believe as they are mostly raw troops I can give them some mighty big scares if they do. . . . When I go back to Petersburg I intend to make Gen. French an offer to take the town of Washington if he will give me 2 field 32 pdrs & 6 field pieces—2 companies of cavalry & my Rg't of Inf. or to keep the Yanks closely confined in Washington & Plymouth if he will give me one battery of Artillery & 3 Co's of Cavalry, or to confine them right to their strongholds if he will give me that number of troops & send me on the North side of the Roanoke. As I am doing nothing here but play 2nd fiddle I do not care how soon they let me return. Give me the command & I'll whip the Yanks & get distinction for myself.[5]

Harry did not have long to wait. The very next day the enemy advanced in force from Washington and drove in his pickets. Following a skirmish, he drove them back.[6] Three days later he gave considerably more detail. His letter provides perhaps the best account extant of the engagement at Rawls' Mill and complements the official report of Major General John G. Foster. After learning that the enemy was strongly reinforced at Washington, he sent a courier to Colonel Radcliffe but knew help could not reach him for at least a day.

I was fully aware of the defects of this situation & made all my dispositions for extricating myself. I had a correct map made of the roads & made every supposition that were I in the enemy's place what would I do etc. When they advanced I gave instructions for the picket guard to retire before the enemy skirmishing with him as he advanced & for that purpose detailed 12 picked men to keep behind & feel the enemy. As soon as the enemy drove in our pickets he ceased advancing on my position directly but turned off to another road so as to cut me off from Williamston at a place called Rawl's Mill 5 miles from Williamston. They tried to conceal their intentions by massing their cavalry in front. I thought something strange of their not following up at once & as soon as I discovered their object I joined all my troops & retreated to Rawl's Mill to which point I had ordered the Lt. Col. [Lane] to advance by Special Courier at Daybreak. I reached there some hour before sunset & immediately reconnoitered the ground.

I had scarcely passed a fork on the road when a courier overtook me almost breathless with haste & informed me that the enemy were close at hand. I galloped back & passed the fork only two minutes before the enemy came up to it. They pushed me so closely that I saw at once I must check their advance in order to retire at all. To this I was the more impelled because I could not hear one word from Radcliffe & I knew that unless I checked the enemy he would be inevitably cut off & captured. My position was a very strong one.

The enemy were advancing from A to cut me off at B as I was retreating from C to WmSton. The road crossed a creek & the ford was some 2 feet deep & sixty or 100 feet [wide]. As I afterwards learned they started a column from Washington which was delayed by my burning up a bridge or two & cutting down some trees. There was considerable water & briers on both sides of the road as it crossed the creek & they could not flank me without going some distance to the right. Their cavalry without suspecting anything came gallantly down the ford & when within 15 yds a full company turned loose on them & as well as I can learn but 7 men[?] were left of the enemy.

We held them in check some two hours & they ceased firing

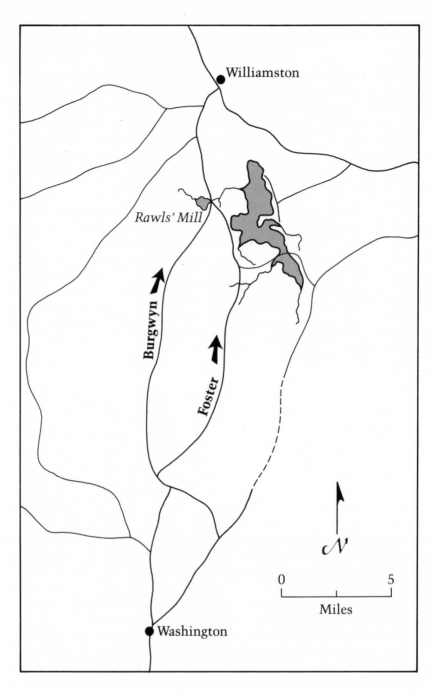

Colonel Burgwyn's engagement with General Foster at Rawls' Mill,
2 November 1862

altogether when we retired in pursuance of orders. Two pieces of Moore's Battery came up just as we ceased firing & I gave the enemy a few shells simply for the moral effect. When Radcliffe came up & took command the fighting was all over & I was on the WmSton side of the mill pond. After that you never saw such confusion & disorganization. Not a rout or anything like that for the troops were all right but there was no plan no order & no management nor has there been much since.[7]

At the time this letter was written Harry's regiment was quartered a mile and a half below Tarboro. Two days later the regiment was apparently still there, for on the tenth, with reinforcements coming up, Harry wrote his father that General Pettigrew was expected the following day. "Our force," he reported, "now consists of 7 Rgts Inf. & 16 pieces of Art. & I suppose 500 Cav." In the belief that Nathan G. Evans's Brigade would shortly arrive, Harry added, "I think the government is determined to make some effort to save our section."[8]

All the while, General Foster was moving away, first to Hamilton and then to Williamston, but not in the direction of Weldon or Washington. His command reached Plymouth on the night of the tenth, and on the following day the troops were reembarked for New Bern. Although his only encounter was with the Twenty-sixth North Carolina, Foster considered his expedition successful because it was "instrumental in saving the town and forces at Plymouth from destruction and capture." Considering the relative strength of his command, Foster should probably have had more to show for his efforts.[9]

For his part, Harry was not successful in whipping the Yanks, but he had handled his command with presence and skill. Although under orders of Colonel Radcliffe, Harry exercised independent command when "left in front of a very greatly superior force with not a man to support me within 11 miles & without a possibility of any additional support until a whole day should elapse." He had been ordered "to make a feint towards Washington & to prevent the enemy from cutting Col. Radcliffe off at WmSton after he had attacked Plymouth." Harry's regiment was within six miles of Washington on 28 October. Two days later he was ordered by Radcliffe to send five companies back to Williamston under Lieutenant Colonel John Lane.

With only five companies (approximately five hundred men) under his immediate command, without benefit of cavalry or artillery, he had no choice but to await the enemy's first move. Two roads led out of Washington to Williamston, and, again, Harry was left no alternative but to divide his meager force so as to watch both roads. That he used this waiting period to study and devise his defensive strategy there can be no doubt. Facing an enemy ten times his immediate strength, as General Foster's report later attested, Harry succeeded in checking its advance by forcing engagements at both Little Creek and Rawls' Mill, thereby gaining time for Radcliffe's command to re-group below Williamston.[10]

Without artillery or cavalry support, there was no way Harry could have stood and fought. Even though his strikes were comparatively feeble, in his hit-and-run, tactical withdrawal, Harry did force his adversary to unlimber on two separate occasions and succeeded in further impeding his movement by felling timber and burning bridges—all the while eluding capture and suffering only minor casualties. Whether General John G. Foster knew that Colonel Harry Burgwyn was blocking his way as he moved out of Washington on that Sunday afternoon, 2 November, has never been revealed. But had he known, it is likely that the general would have given his young friend, whom he had tutored at West Point in 1856, high marks for steady nerves and skill under fire.

Although General Foster's expedition was abortive, the Federal threat was clear to the people of eastern North Carolina, for large numbers of slaves had been freed and considerable private property destroyed.[11] The response of the Raleigh press was immediate: "We have constantly warned our people, for months, of the impending danger to our Eastern Counties, and urged them to remove their slaves. . . . But the storm so long gathering is now upon them, and we fear that not only great suffering will ensue, but that millions of property will be destroyed." The same article reported that three companies of the Twenty-sixth had been sent below Hamilton or Williamston to help the residents remove their Negroes and other movable property from beyond the enemy's lines. "The Yankees, hearing of this, determined to prevent it, if possible, and hence moved a force in the direction of Hamilton or Williamston. Colonel Burgwyn, with his small force, determined to arrest their progress, and hence attacked them, keeping in check a very superior force of the enemy until re-inforced, when he determined to fall back to a better position." Another article in the same issue reported: "We learn that Col. Burgwyn displayed much promptness, skill, and courage in holding the enemy in check on the occasion, and that his regiment, the 26th, covered themselves with new honors by their firmness and daring."[12]

Shortly after the engagement at Rawls' Mill Harry made a brief visit to Thornbury before returning to his headquarters near Petersburg.

On 19 November, he advised his father that the Federals had made a demonstration from Suffolk. He might be ordered to leave at any moment and expected enemy action within three to four weeks.

Harry was right about the timing of the enemy's next movement, as well as its cooperation with Federal forces in North Carolina, but Weldon would not be the point of attack, as he had surmised. More immediate was Harry's concern for his father's plantation at Thornbury. He warned him to remove as much produce as possible, especially cotton.[13]

James Johnston Pettigrew was equally concerned. Only a few days earlier he had written his brother William urging him to assist their friend and benefactor, James Cathcart Johnston, in the removal of slaves from the latter's plantation at Caledonia. He emphasized that the war "will be this winter, somewhere between Petersburg & Wilmington, and everyone should prepare for it. The people in that region have evidently not dreamed of what war is; the reality will be a terrible awakening, and the vast preponderance of the enemy will make it possible for them to send their marauding columns in half a dozen different directions at once."[14]

Governor Vance thoroughly understood the plight of the people in eastern North Carolina, where his service as colonel of the Twenty-sixth during the first year of the war had brought him into contact with the depredations of the Yankees. He had also been exposed to the privations suffered by the Confederate soldiers during that first year. An avowed champion of the people, he would never deviate, in word or deed, from his concern for both soldier and citizen. In his inaugural address at Raleigh on 8 September, Vance strongly supported the Conscript Act, enacted by the Confederate Congress the previous April, saying that "within five weeks of its passage one hundred and forty-seven of our best trained and victorious regiments would have been disbanded and scattered to their homes. And this during the very darkest days in the history of the war. . . . The Confederate Government having failed to provide in time for this terrible emergency, utter ruin was at the door and must be averted; the law was passed, and the country was saved." Vance was also deeply concerned about the physical well-being of his former comrades in arms. In mid-October, he made an "eloquent and soul-stirring appeal" to the people for shoes, clothing, and blankets.[15] But at the heart of his involvement with problems of extortion, conscription, civil liberties, Yankee depredations, and marauding "buffaloes" (a term applied to whites and slaves known to be Unionist sympathizers) was the governor's genuine concern for the welfare of the soldiers in the field and of the suffering poor at home. Perhaps the most disquieting letter he ever received was from the surgeon general of North Carolina, Edward Warren, whom the governor had dispatched to Virginia, with supplies and money, to bring some measure of relief to the suffering North Carolinians in Confederate hospitals. Written from Staunton, it read in part:

> There are at least 3000 soldiers in the Hospitals here & of the number at least 1/4 are North Carolinians. I had supposed the condition of the sick & wounded at Charlottesville bad enough, but it is infinitely better than that of the poor creatures in these Hospitals. Dirty, naked, without shoes, hats or socks, wounded in every possible manner, utterly dispirited & entirely indifferent to everything they present a picture of wretchedness & misery which no tongue or pen can describe. They are arriving at the rate of one thousand a day from the Army in trains which consume a whole week in making the journey, and in this way hunger is added to their other sufferings. Taking all things together, the condition of these poor unfortunates is enough to wring tears from hearts of stone, and to stamp the authorities of the Confederacy with a brand of unutterable disgrace.[16]

When on 17 November Governor Vance presented his first message to the General Assembly of North Carolina, he left little doubt as to the monumental problems facing the state: "The long continuance of the contest, the slaughter of our soldiers, the occupation of our territory by the enemy, the destruction of our homes, and the blockaded condition of our coast, have reduced us to straits, and given rise to a class of evils, in the presence of which ephemeral patriotism must perish, and the tinsel enthusiasm of novelty give place to that stern and determined devotion to our cause, which alone can sustain a revolution." Emphasizing that "the subject of first importance is the prosecution of the war, and the means of defending our State against the invasion of the enemy," the governor recommended the raising of "at least ten regiments of reserves" for the protection of the state and requested authority to employ slave labor on state defenses. He also recommended the purchase of a large quantity of corn and pork to be stored in the interior and used to feed the citizens of the state.[17]

In discussing the difficulties faced by the quartermaster's department in providing the troops with clothing, shoes, and blankets, he observed that the administration of his predecessor (Clark) had contracted with the Confederate government to receive the "Commutation clothing money" for her troops with which to provide her own shoes and clothing. This arrangement, he declared, was predicated upon the agreement that North Carolina would sell her surplus supplies to the Confederacy provided the latter would withdraw her purchasing agents from the competitive field in North Carolina. In this manner the state could comfortably clothe and shoe her own troops and supply the Confederacy at reasonable rates. But such had not been the case. "The country was soon, and still is, swarming with agents of the Confederate Government, stripping bare our markets and putting enormous prices upon our agents. This is especially the case in regard to shoes and leather. The consequence has been our troops could get only half supplies from home, and nothing at all from the Confederate Government, because of our agreement to furnish them ourselves."[18]

Considerable progress had been made, however, in the production of powder. Although the first mills, constructed during Governor Clark's administration, had been accidentally destroyed, their replacements would soon begin operations. With the Confederate government supplying about three thousand pounds of niter per week, it appeared that the new mills could meet a weekly production schedule of four thousand pounds of powder. In addition, the quartermaster department had contracted with manufacturers in the state for the production of three hundred new rifles per month and for the repair of three hundred old muskets and rifles on a similar basis, so that the department could keep on hand a sufficient number to supply five thousand men.[19]

But all of this activity required money, and the governor dwelt in considerable detail upon the state's debt position and the means of financing an expanding war effort. Declaring the state debt to be "very heavy" ($20,983,361.01 on 30 September 1862), but recognizing that the Confederacy owed the state "between five and six millions," Vance believed that interest on the state debt should be paid punctually, that "the debt ought not to be allowed to grow any larger, if practicable to prevent it," and that the payment of monies owed by the Confederate government to the state should be "applied forthwith to the extinguishment of the debt of the State, as far as it will go." He recommended a tax increase of 25 percent and that "a tax of twenty-five per cent, be laid upon the net profits of all persons who have, during the present year, speculated in the necessaries of life, such as corn, flour, bacon, pork, shoes, leather, cotton cloth and yarn and woolen goods, and to be continued during the next year or longer, if necessary." Vance was clearly opposed to profiteering in time of war.[20]

In other wide-ranging references to problems of state occasioned by the war, the governor revealed that he had decided to employ the militia to collect delinquent conscripts, deserters, and absentees rather than have the citizens witness "the disagreeable spectacle of Confederate soldiers traversing the country" for that purpose. Because the crime of desertion was apparently not an offense against the common law, he recommended the passage of legislation to allow punishment of anyone who might aid and assist or prevent the capture of deserters.[21]

In concluding this first message to the General Assembly, Governor Vance made it plain that, war or no war, state support of public education must continue. It was unthinkable that the Literary Board would be deprived of the funds necessary to make the usual semiannual distributions of the common school fund. To use this fund for war purposes would be "an absolute robbery of the poor children of the State." As for Chapel Hill, "Our time-honored old University, though thinned, as have been our male schools everywhere by the patriotism of the boys who have rushed to fill up our armies, is still in full operation, the President and Faculty having bravely resolved to hold their position as long as they have a squad to muster."[22]

The governor's entire speech left no doubt about his position. It was exceptional for its clarity and for its reliance upon the fundamental principles of moral and constitutional law. That this was his platform of personal commitment, as governor of the state of North Carolina, would soon be apparent to the Confederate States of America as well as to the enemy. Regarding "our intercourse with the authorities of our young Confederacy," he said, "having demanded firmly the rights which are due our State, let us yield them no grudging support, but in all things pertaining to the general weal, sustain and strengthen them with our whole hearts." As for the enemy, he reminded the legislature, "Men enough to protect and drive back the invader, we can always get, if we can properly clothe and feed them. Let us do this and preserve our paper from depreciation and all will be well."[23]

CHAPTER 16

GOLDSBORO UNDER ATTACK

While Governor Vance, the former colonel of the Twenty-sixth North Carolina, was preoccupied with legislative problems, his successor, Colonel Harry Burgwyn, was busily engaged in preparing winter quarters for his regiment and in conducting the operations of a "valorous" court-martial. Writing to his mother on 8 December, Harry described the huts, which were

> made of logs, chinked and daubed & have a chimney to each of two huts. I allow 6 huts or 12 rooms to the enlisted men of every company, so that from 8 to 10 men will occupy every room. Each room is 16 feet square. The huts are arranged on the three sides of a large square & on the fourth side will be the huts for the officers my own will be in rear of the fourth side, its important position will be duly designated by the flag of the Rg't & by its exhibiting rather an elaborate style of architecture in comparison with the others. Perhaps too the dignity of its occupant will be necessarily exhibited in the quiet yet imposing appearance which will undoubtedly pervade its exterior.[1]

Other than noting that part of his brigade (Pettigrew's) was posted on the Blackwater and that "Moore's Batallion of Artillery numbering 10 pieces left Petersburg this morning for Wilmington, N.C.," it is significant that Harry made no mention of any imminent troop movement or possible engagement.[2] Rumors of impending enemy moves were rife. Indeed, the Army of the Potomac, under Major General Ambrose Burnside, was threatening Fredericksburg from Stafford Heights on the north side of the Rappahannock. And across the river, on the hills behind the town, lay the Army of Northern Virginia, ready to oppose any move by Burnside in the direction of Richmond. And yet, on 8 December 1862, no one seemed certain when or precisely where Burnside might strike, or whether there would be a concert of moves against Richmond involving Federal troops based at Suffolk and New Bern.

This uncertainty was clearly revealed in General Lee's confidential letter to President Davis on that date. This memorandum was largely based upon information received from a scout who had just returned from a mission of several weeks behind enemy lines between Washington and New York. According to Lee, the scout reported "vast preparations for our suppression, and the expression of great confidence on the part of the North." Reinforcements were still coming to General Burnside's army, and a large naval expedition was being outfitted at New York.[3]

Although this information was far from comforting, Lee's reasoned response was characteristically reserved and to the point: "It is difficult to say, from this statement, what is the actual plan of the enemy; but I think that Burnside's army is much magnified, and that Banks' expedition is probably designed for some point south of James River. The Monitor and four other iron-clad boats are now in Hampton Roads, and they are probably intended to operate in those waters. If the troops in North Carolina and around Richmond can keep back attacks directed from south of the river, this army, if not able to resist General Burnside's advance, can retire upon the capital, and then operate as circumstances may dictate; but if the operations of the enemy south of James River cannot be resisted, it [the army] had better at once approach nearer Richmond. In this latter event I would leave a covering force here to embarrass General Burnside's advance."[4]

Federal plans were also developing in North Carolina, and Major General John G. Foster, commanding the Department of North Carolina, was on the alert. He advised General Halleck on 1 December that he had just arrived at Fortress Monroe, Virginia, to confer with General John A. Dix, commanding the Department of Virginia. The following day, Major General John J. Peck, commanding at Suffolk, wrote Dix that his interview with Foster was "all that could be desired" and that "I proposed to demonstrate strongly on a given day, which he did not expect, and which pleased him very much." On 7 December, Halleck approved the temporary detachment of a brigade from Dix to assist General Foster. Dix was to have the remainder of his troops ready to be transported by water by the time the brigade returned. Commander William A. Parker, of the United States Steamer *Cambridge* lying at Beaufort, N.C., wrote Foster on 8 December that the time was right to attack Wilmington and the adjacent forts.[5]

These reports clearly indicate that General Foster was planning offensive action in North Carolina to coincide with Burnside's attack on Fredericksburg. Union forces were also threatening the Confederates south of the James River with the intention of giving the impression that a serious attack on the Blackwater was contemplated rather than being a diversionary demonstration. So intent was General Foster upon having this cooperative movement clearly understood that he signed a joint "memorandum of understanding" with Lieutenant Commander C. W. Flusser to the effect that the demonstration on the Blackwater would last for a week, "unless Captain Flusser hears from General Foster to the contrary, and even then the strong show of force is to continue for a few days longer, and even until General Foster sends to inform him that the main attack is completed. The force then is to make some hostile demonstration on the 11th, to keep it up until the 19th, and then to maintain a hostile attitude until he hears from General Foster."[6]

By 10 December it was becoming increasingly clear to the Confederate authorities that the Federals were preparing a concerted drive on Richmond from the north and south, with Burnside initiating the major thrust by attacking Lee at Fredericksburg. In a message to one of his generals posted in the Shenandoah Valley, Secretary of War James A. Seddon, advised that "General Lee communicates his opinion that the enemy are preparing with a very large force to move from the Rappahannock line for the attack on Richmond, and it is from various sources of information apprehended that, just before or concurrently with such movement, large forces, either for combined attack or to cut off railroad connections, will be advanced on the south side of Weldon and toward Petersburg."[7]

That same day, in a communication to General Halleck, General Foster outlined his reasons for an immediate movement against the enemy:

The information that I have received is to the effect that the enemy's Government is turning its attention to the importance of guarding the lines of communication to the south, and, if possible, of recovering some portion of the eastern portion of this State, the rich products of which would at this time be very valuable as supplies to their commissariat. Two brigades have already arrived to re-enforce the troops already in the State for this purpose. I think by timely action I may disappoint their expectation, and shall therefore move on Kinston to-morrow morning at daybreak. I hope to defeat two brigades that are known to be there before assistance can arrive from Wilmington or Weldon or Tarborough. Succeeding in this, I shall push on to Goldsborough, destroy its railroad bridge, and another bridge across a swamp 10 miles south of Goldsborough, and then return to New Berne to prepare for an immediate attack on Wilmington.[8]

Each side was somewhat aware of the moves of the other in the early days of December, but their intentions were obscured from each other either by design or by miscalculation. Lee was uncertain of Burnside's precise movement until the very last. And the Confederate defenders on the Blackwater, at Kinston, Goldsboro, and Wilmington were unsure as to where and when the Union forces at Suffolk and New Bern would strike.

It is understandable why Harry Burgwyn could have been engrossed with preparing winter quarters on 8 December and then, three days later, could have written to his father that orders had been received to march to the Blackwater. "It was rumored last night that Banks was coming up the Peninsula. The result before Fredericksburg is most anxiously waited for. Everybody is confident that Lee will whip Burnside to pieces; but it ought to be done very soon for Foster is today reported advancing on Kinston & Gen. Evans has telegraphed for all the reinforcements which can be spared to be sent to him."[9]

Harry's wish was almost immediately fulfilled. Two days later, on 13 December, Burnside was nearly whipped "to pieces." The battle of Fredericksburg was a slaughter because Burnside determined to attack the strongly defended right and left wings of Lee's army in simultaneous but virtually separate battles. Burnside's strategy of dividing his army and separately attacking the enemy at its strongest points, rather than concentrating upon its weakest position, clearly was not calculated to carry the day at Fredericksburg. Burnside's casualties of 12,653 were almost exactly comparable to those of McClellan at Sharpsburg. Lee's were considerably less than half, 5,309, which included a number of only slightly wounded.[10]

Burnside's imprudent aggressiveness at Fredericksburg was in sharp contrast to his failure to cooperate with McClellan during the Seven Days' battle by mounting diversionary operations in North Carolina. Ironically, the attack on Kinston by his successor in command of the Department of North Carolina, General Foster, coincided with Burnside's crossing of the Rappahannock on 11 December. Foster had long anticipated cooperating with the Army of the Potomac. As early as 24 September, he had requested additional troops on the premise that, "seeing the turn affairs are taking in Virginia and Maryland, the occupation in force of this department may be most advantageous to the campaign."[11]

Foster apparently shared Harry Burgwyn's belief that cutting the Wilmington and Weldon rail link in North Carolina would do immeasurable harm to the Confederate cause. He was convinced that the enemy was determined to stand its ground in the eastern counties and, if possible, to drive him out. On this basis, he requested ten thousand additional troops in hope of cutting the Weldon and Wilmington rail line and taking Wilmington, the works at Fort Fisher, and the mouth of Cape Fear River. By 10 December, however, General Foster's plans had been altered. Instead of advancing upon Weldon, he reported to Halleck that he was about to move against the enemy at Goldsboro.[12]

If Foster's intent was to play a diversionary role, it had its desired effect; for on 14 December, Harry advised his father that the Fortyseventh and Forty-fourth regiments had left for Kinston, leaving only his own and the Fifty-fifth. Two days later he wrote to his mother, "I have only time to write in the hurry of a move that I leave here in a few minutes for Kinston N.C. . . . Gen G. W. Smith is in command of our troops & is one of the very best officers we have. Gen. Pettigrew & Gen. French both go down with us. I hear that 6 Rgts. are coming to Goldsboro from Richmond. The Yankees have as usual chosen the very worst point for attack."[13]

By the night of the sixteenth the Yankees were bivouacked within eight miles of Goldsboro. General Foster's command, consisting of four brigades of infantry (10,000 men), six artillery batteries (40 guns), and a cavalry unit of 640 men, had performed well. Leaving New Bern on Thursday morning, the eleventh, the Federals had encountered little more than road obstructions and burned-out bridges before reaching Southwest Creek, only a short distance from Kinston, on Saturday night. The following day, Foster encountered the enemy in force, holding a strong position in the woods on the south bank of the Neuse River about a mile from Kinston. Advancing under effective artillery support, the Federals made a concerted drive down both sides of the road and, after heavy fighting, forced the Confederate defenders into precipitate retreat. The bridge over the Neuse was fired as they crossed, but the fire was extinguished before much damage could be done.[14]

According to Brigadier General N. G. Evans, commanding the Kinston defenses, the engagement lasted three hours before he was forced back across the bridge and through town under heavy cannonading. He reformed his line in the rear of the town. About 3:00 P.M., Foster sent a flag of truce to inquire whether Evans proposed to surrender. Upon being declined, Foster waited for his artillery to cross before renewing the attack. By the time he was ready, however, the enemy had retired and, with night falling, he was unable to pursue. His troops bivouacked in a field on the outskirts of town.[15]

Foster was determined to waste no time in getting to the vicinity of Goldsboro. The following morning, Monday the fifteenth, he recrossed the river and took the river road north. Leaving a strong detachment of cavalry in Kinston to make a demonstration on that side of the river—and a small force to destroy military stores and burn the bridge—Foster marched his command to within approximately three miles of White Hall before halting for the night. Upon learning that Foster was moving rapidly toward Goldsboro on the opposite side of the river, Evans immediately dispatched the Eleventh North Carolina (Collett Leventhorpe) and six hundred dismounted cavalrymen under Brigadier General Beverly H. Robertson to dispute the Federals' crossing at White Hall. With the remainder of his force he intended to pass through Kinston and attack Foster's rear, but finding the enemy gone and the bridge burned, Evans ordered his entire command to Mosely Hall to give Robertson direct support.[16]

News of Foster's rapid advance was greatly disturbing to the authorities in Richmond. Secretary Seddon telegraphed General Lee at Fredericksburg that the enemy was pressing Evans at Kinston and he feared loss of the railroad connection and Raleigh. The Confederate commander, General Gustavus W. Smith, wanted reinforcements from Richmond and the Blackwater, trusting Lee to sustain Richmond if necessary. General Smith's wire to Lee the same day was even more disquieting: "I arrived here (Goldsborough, N.C.) at 3 p.m. [15 December]. The telegraph with General Evans is cut off. By latest information he was at Falling Creek, 6 miles this side of Kinston. Enemy now estimated at 30,000, and scouts report re-enforcements constantly arriving from New Berne. Governor Vance is here. All accounts agree that our troops behaved admirably in the engagement yesterday."[17]

In the meantime, Major General S. G. French had assumed command of the Confederate forces at Mosely Hall. On the evening of 16 December, General Smith sent a dispatch to French saying that no reinforcements had arrived. He added: "I think if it is practicable that General Pettigrew had better come up in the first train with Burgwyn's regiment, and that his troops should follow." That same evening

Foster had moved to within eight miles of Goldsboro, where he bivouacked for the night. That morning, from his position below White Hall, General Foster had ordered five companies of cavalry and one section of artillery to proceed to Mount Olive, a station on the Wilmington and Weldon Railroad, fourteen miles below Goldsboro. Upon arriving, the men tore up the track for about a mile and then destroyed the bridge over Goshen Swamp.[18]

On the morning of the seventeenth, the Federals advanced on Goldsboro, the object being to destroy the railroad bridge over the Neuse. In their way stood Brigadier General Thomas L. Clingman, commanding the Eighth, Fifty-first, and Fifty-second North Carolina regiments. Clingman had reached Goldsboro only the day before, accompanied by the Eighth North Carolina. He was immediately ordered to cross to the south side of the river and take position on the railroad between Goldsboro and Dudley's Depot. "I selected a point," reported the general, "where the railroad is crossed by the road from White Hall, along which the enemy were expected to approach, and which is about 1½ miles south of the railroad bridge." Clingman was later reinforced by the Fifty-first and Fifty-second regiments.[19]

Early on the seventeenth, he rode a locomotive into town and reported in person to General Smith, who instructed him to report to Brigadier General Evans and, with his brigade, to accompany Evans on a reconnaissance mission to determine the Federal position and strength. While these officers were meeting, an alarming dispatch was received. The enemy was reported to be rapidly approaching the railroad bridge. General Evans peremptorily ordered Clingman "to go on and fight the enemy."

Although braced to the best of his ability, Clingman's meager forces could not withstand the concentrated artillery and musketry fire of the enemy. His two regiments defending the railroad bridge broke and fell back twice before being reformed "and carried back in good order to the county bridge." They rejoined the Eighth Regiment stationed there, recrossed the bridge, and, with the two-gun battery under the command of Lieutenant Thomas C. Fuller, took up a defensive position on the north bank of the Neuse. Colonel Stephen D. Pool's battalion of artillery was placed in position on the north side of the river to protect the railroad. About an hour after these dispositions were made, Clingman was summoned to General Evans's headquarters. "On my going back to the field where he was posted," reported General Clingman, he was ordered to hold the county bridge. Later, General Evans again sent for Clingman and ordered him to advance across the county bridge and attack the enemy. By this time, the Sixty-first North Carolina had joined Clingman's command. With these four regiments, and the two guns, he crossed the river. Skirmishers soon discovered that the enemy was posted in line of battle from the river for a mile and a half along the railroad. Clingman then divided his force, leading two regiments down the riverbank to within three hundred yards of the enemy's right. The two remaining regiments, with the guns, he led down the county road, taking the crossroad through the open field that carried him to the enemy's left. He then formed in line of battle and advanced on the railroad, as did the two regiments stationed near the river.[20]

Before the Confederates could reach the railroad, however, the enemy had abandoned his position and moved back to higher ground. For the rest of the day, Clingman's command, separated from the enemy by four hundred yards on his right and by more than a half mile on his left, was subjected to a heavy bombardment, which lasted until dark. But it was a disheartened General Clingman who reported on the battle, commending the courage of his men despite their failure to repulse the enemy.[21]

Harry Burgwyn had arrived with his regiment at Goldsboro on Tuesday morning, the sixteenth. They were immediately ordered to Mosely Hall, and from there to White Hall, and, at two-thirty the next morning, back to Goldsboro. He wrote of the battle to his mother:

> Yesterday quite a sanguinary engagement took place a mile or two from my present position. Gen N. G. Evans it appears was ordered to make a reconnaisance after the Yankees burnt the bridge across the Neuse River. . . . The bridge was burnt before Gen Pettigrew got on the field. Gen. Evans instead of making a reconnaisance simply made a fight & got himself involved & had to be extricated. Entre nous Gen. E. was drunk according to the best of my information. . . . The consequence was the Rgts which charged lost a good many men (the 52nd about 75 or 100) & when within some 1/2 mile of the batteries they broke: not being supported the break became a run. They were rallied however by two Rgts of Pettigrew's Brigade mine was one which came up & assumed position—along the RailRoad & remained there until about 10 o'clock P.M., when in consequence of the terrible cold they were ordered off.[22]

Two days later, from his headquarters in Goldsboro, Harry advised his father that reliable information indicated the Yankees had passed

Kinston the previous day on their way back to New Bern. But Weldon, as always, was uppermost on his mind:

> There is not in my mind a shadow of a doubt that they will make an attack on Weldon either immediately or in the course of a month. I am positively *certain* now that the Government will concentrate its troops for the defence of Weldon at Garysburg if the attack is from the North & at Weldon itself if the attack is from the South. . . . Let me urge again upon you to prepare to remove without a moments delay all your valuables from Thornbury. I have seen again the terrible delay, confusion, & trouble when troops are suddenly poured in at any point. I would almost as soon (as far as destruction to property is concerned) have a force of the enemy as of our own troops on your plantation. One fortnight of energetic action now is worth probably $200,000 to you. So do not delay. . . .
>
> We have I think the finest Brigade in the C.S.A. The inspector general reported to Gen Smith that I had the finest Regt. he ever saw. Everybody says the same thing. . . . We have enough men here to whip the Yankees & we will do it I am confident if we can ever get our generals to come out of their d—— houses & stay in the field.[23]

General G. W. Smith's report to Secretary Seddon on 18 December, the day after the fight, did not radiate the same confidence. Although the enemy had succeeded only in burning the railroad bridge before turning back to New Bern, it was clear that the organized resistance of the Confederates had been "too little and too late." Explaining his failure to pursue or even harass the enemy's rear, Smith declared: "The enemy were in very large numbers, their second position was a very strong one; night was at hand; only a portion of the troops from Richmond had arrived; none of the artillery and none of the cavalry from either Richmond or Petersburg. I did not consider it advisable to attack them again. The enemy retired during the night."[24]

On the other hand, General Foster, who had retreated "with such celerity," was delighted with the outcome of his expedition. From Fort Monroe, on 23 December, he advised General Halleck that the expedition was "a perfect success." He realized, however, that the Confederate forces had been increased so he doubted that he could continue with his plan of movement unless he received reinforcements.[25] The following day Harry wrote his father, regretting that he could not come to Raleigh for Christmas. His request for a leave of absence had not been viewed with favor, so he had decided not to press the matter. But he was concerned about General Foster's future movements. He expected Foster to move against the Weldon bridge.[26]

The last known letter that Harry wrote in the year 1862 was on 28 December. Again, it was to his father. In the light of recent events, the tone of that letter should have undoubtedly reflected more enthusiasm, for the Confederates had won a signal victory at Fredericksburg, and General Foster had not lingered long in the vicinity of Goldsboro after having burned the railroad bridge. The *North Carolina Standard* claimed that the Northern newspapers admitted the battle of Fredericksburg "to be the most disastrous flogging they have yet had," and "that the best appointed army in the world has been defeated by an army of raggamuffins." The paper continued, "Late Northern rumors state that Greeley of the New York *Tribune* says that the Confederate States must be recognized, as there is no chance to whip them, and peace is the only panacea for the present difficulties. If true, it is important, and shows that even Greeley is coming to his senses." Foster's campaign, was "a flash in the pan," declared the *Standard*, but "the failure of Foster must not lull our people to rest. We may look for advances of the enemy at sundry points during the winter."[27]

CHAPTER 17

A WINTER OF TEDIOUS MONOTONY

However General Lee may have reacted to the course of events during 1862, he certainly was gratified that the Yankees did not spend Christmas in Richmond. Lee might have expected that the North, after repeated reverses in the field, and tiring of the conflict, would sue for peace, or that Great Britain, her textile industry virtually destroyed for want of cotton, would have no choice but to intervene. Surely the Confederacy could not sustain herself for another two years against an adversary with seemingly unlimited resources.

And yet Lee's hopes, and those of the Confederacy, must have been buoyed by the recent successes of the Army of Northern Virginia. During the seven months under Lee's command, that army had participated in thirteen battles and, with the exception of Boonsboro and Sharpsburg, had "remained masters of the field." Although the Confederates had suffered 48,171 casualties, they had inflicted better than 70,000 on the enemy. During the same period, their firepower was substantially increased by the capture of 75,000 small arms and 155 cannon against the loss of approximately 6,000 small arms and only 8 cannon.[1] Had not the combination of Lee and Jackson wrought miracles as they maneuvered their forces on both sides of the Blue Ridge? And where, now, were their adversaries?

By late 1862, a foreign observer and special correspondent for the *Illustrated London News* was convinced of the South's invincibility. From Richmond, on 20 September, he dispatched a long report remarkable for its almost blind faith in the Southern cause and its future:

> The more I see of the Southern army the more I am lost in admiration at its splendid patriotism, at its wonderful endurance, at its utter disregard of hardships which, probably, no modern army has been called upon to bear up against. Wretchedly equipped, the soldiers of the Confederacy advance to meet their foes, the light of battle shining on their countenances, determined to be victorious or die. . . .
>
> How long England and France will submit to be bamboozled by the hollow representations of the Federal Government re-

mains to be seen; as it is they have held aloof long enough, and precedents which they have followed in other cases demand that the two powers at the head of civilization should interfere to stop the butchery which disgraces the century we live in. . . . Surrounded as I am by the Southern people, living in their midst, associating with their soldiers, I emphatically assert the South can never be subjugated.[2]

Another contemporary observer, expressing the Northern point of view in *Harper's Weekly*, provided a more reasonable perspective as he traced the progress of events during the first two years of the conflict. Recognizing that "we began the war with a pretty general contempt for our adversary, and a complacent self-assurance of early and easy triumph," the writer admitted that this "delusion was dispelled on 21st July on the field of Bull Run." He then outlined the key events in this unfolding drama. This observer may have erred somewhat in detail as well as in interpretation, but for a contemporary assessment of the general trend of the war it was remarkable for its realistic evaluation. Especially perceptive were his concluding remarks:

Though they [the Confederates] seemed to win every battle, and we seemed to hear of nothing but reverses, we continued to hold Nashville, Memphis, New Orleans, Corinth, Norfolk, Beaufort, Fort Pulaski, Pensacola, San Augustine, and to control the Mississippi River, with the exception of a few miles above and below Vicksburg. The difference between them and us appears to be that their triumphs are barren of practical results, while ours have almost invariably secured for us substantial advantages in point of territory, strategic points, or influential towns.[3]

Jefferson Davis was fully aware of this situation. Years later his widow recalled that "the year 1863 opened drearily for the President, but the Confederates generally seemed to have, for some unexplained cause, renewed hope of recognition by England and France, and with this they felt sure of a successful termination of the struggle. Mr. Davis was oppressed by the fall of Donelson, Nashville, Corinth, Roanoke Island, New Orleans, Yorktown, Norfolk, Fort Pillow, Island No. 10, Memphis, General Bragg's defeat at Murfreesboro, the burning of the *Virginia*, and the ram *Mississippi*, the sinking of the *Arkansas*, and other minor disasters. The victory at Fredericksburg was the one bright spot in all this dark picture."[4]

To one of Lincoln's cabinet members, Gideon Welles, the year 1862 closed "less favorably than I had hoped and expected, yet some progress has been made. It is not to be denied, however, that the national ailment seems more chronic. The disease is deep-seated. . . . We have had some misfortunes, and a lurking malevolence exists towards us among nations that could not have been anticipated. Worse than this, the envenomed, relentless, and unpatriotic spirit of party paralyzes and weakens the hand of the Government and country."[5]

From these observations it is evident that attitudes had changed markedly during the bitter fighting of 1862. At the beginning of the year the South had labored under the illusion that England could not tolerate the loss of cotton for her mills and would be compelled to intervene on the side of the Confederacy. Hundreds of thousands of men, women, and children had been thrown out of work. "The catastrophe is as complete, for the time being, and will be, in all likelihood, for months to come," reported the *Illustrated London News*, "as if an earthquake had swallowed up the mills in which they were wont to win their bread."[6] But Britain still maintained her neutrality, in spite of strained relations occasioned by the cotton famine, the *Trent* affair, and the depredations of the CSS *Alabama* against American shipping on the high seas—the *Alabama* having been built and outfitted in a British yard. Even France, also a neutral, had been rebuffed by both England and Russia in her effort to promote mediation. Yet hope of intervention still lingered in the mind of the South and, indeed, was nurtured by some of the more favorably disposed members of the British press. Barring the unrealistic possibility that the North, tiring of the conflict, might sue for peace, the South now faced the increasingly grim reality of a protracted war of attrition, which her comparatively limited resources could not long sustain. In the words of Zeb Vance, the South had reached the point at which "ephemeral patriotism" and the "tinsel enthusiasm of novelty" must "give place to that stern and determined devotion to our cause, which alone can sustain a revolution."[7]

The North, too, had suffered from illusions, ranging from the probability of a speedy conquest of the South to an early reconciliation of their differences over the slavery issue. And both governments had suffered from internal political dissension. The very nature of the Southern Confederacy, having been founded upon the principle of states' rights, had already proven the key to its governmental ineffectiveness. In the North, the policy differences between the Republicans and Democrats, complicated by the politicians of the border slave states, had undermined public confidence in President Lincoln.

The slavery issue would not go away. As the war progressed, antislavery sentiment in the North had grown in intensity. It was this issue that would sustain the North and ultimately provide the moral justification for a fight to the finish.

On 22 July 1862 Lincoln had surprised the members of his cabinet by reading the text of his first draft of the Emancipation Proclamation, in which he declared "that on the first day of January, in the year of our Lord one thousand eight hundred and sixty-three, all persons held as slaves within any State or States wherein the constitutional authority of the United States shall not then be practically recognized, submitted to, and maintained, shall then, thenceforward, and forever be free." After a full cabinet discussion it was decided to postpone the issuance of the proclamation until a more favorable time. In the judgment of the president, that time came immediately after the battle of Antietam. The proclamation was issued on 22 September and appeared in the press the following day. Although the Democratic minority in the House and the proslavery conservatives from the border slave states opposed emancipation, the House sustained him by a substantial majority. The governors of seventeen states presented a written address to the president "reiterating devotion to the Union, loyalty to the Constitution and laws, and earnest support to the President in suppressing rebellion." Lincoln would not have "to wait long for the full tide of approval, for which he looked with confidence and which came to him from that time onward with steadiness and ever-growing volume, from both the armies in the field and the people in their homes throughout the loyal North."[8]

And this sentiment would apply as well to the British. "Later, and in the long run," a distinguished historian of that period has observed, "the British decision against intervention was taken by massive middle-class and working class opinion, swayed by two forces, one moral and one material. . . . The Emancipation Proclamation dispelled the first ground of British doubt. The news of Antietam and the immense Northern preparations for the campaign of 1863 ended the second doubt." Thus the Emancipation Proclamation persuaded both Britain and many Northerners to stand firm.[9]

If the year 1863 "opened drearily" for President Davis, it could not have been much less so for General Lee. He had reason to be proud of the past performance of the Army of Northern Virginia and confident of its future fighting capability; yet, given the circumstances of the past seven months, simply defending Richmond must have weighed heavily upon him and provoked grave apprehensions. Although thwarted in their Peninsula campaign to capture Richmond in early summer, and then summarily ejected from northern Virginia by early September, were not the Federals back before the year was out, trying vainly to reach Richmond by Christmas? Stopped on the heights before Fredericksburg, there they still remained, preparing for yet another campaign against Richmond in the spring. Lee had earlier followed them into Maryland only to be repulsed at Antietam. Both sides had suffered severe losses. A more aggressive commander than McClellan, however, might conceivably have destroyed the Army of Northern Virginia had he thrown his reserves against Lee the following day. Reluctant in pursuit, McClellan had permitted Lee weeks in which to collect his scattered forces and restore their organizational strength.

But even by early November, when it first became apparent that the enemy was quitting his base on the Potomac and moving east of the Blue Ridge, the Army of Northern Virginia was seemingly ill-prepared to take on another major engagement. General Lee was deeply concerned about the condition of his cavalry. He reported to Secretary Randolph that three-fourths of General Stuart's horses were afflicted with sore tongue and that "a more alarming disease has broken out among them, which attacks the foot, producing lameness, and in some cases loosening the hoof and causing it to slough off." On 14 November, replying to Randolph's request for the "number of shoes required in this army," Lee reported that 6,648 men in Longstreet's Corps alone were without shoes, which did not include General Ransom's division of two brigades, the reserve artillery, or the cavalry.[10]

By the time of the battle of Fredericksburg, rest and reorganization had restored the Army of Northern Virginia to fighting trim, but even then it would suffer increasingly for want of supplies, equipment, and adequate transportation. Granted that Lee would continue to pose a formidable threat to the safety of Washington, his ability to operate in a relatively stable military environment, in terms of logistics and maneuverability, had steadily diminished as the enveloping strength and staying power of the Federal forces increased. What they had captured, they tended to hold. If thwarted initially in some strategic thrust, they would be back again, stronger and more persistent than ever. And their permanent presence in eastern North Carolina had become a matter of grave concern to the Confederacy. The productivity of that rich agricultural region was placed in serious jeopardy, for raids, and the threat of raids, were profoundly demoralizing to both owners and slaves—impelling the one to move to a safer clime and the other to escape to an unknown destiny. Furthermore, the Wilmington and Weldon Railroad, connecting Richmond with its only effective port of entry on the Atlantic seaboard, was in constant danger of being severed.

The battle of Fredericksburg had hardly been won (13 December 1862) and General Foster's raid on Goldsboro turned back (17 December 1862), before the authorities in Richmond were alerted to the possibility of another major thrust by the enemy, probably aimed at Wilmington. On 3 January 1863, Secretary Seddon confirmed this movement in a long letter to General Lee, apprising him also of reliable intelligence indicating a large concentration of vessels at Old Point and the strengthening of Federal forces at Suffolk. Seddon added an even more ominous note: "There is said to be between political parties in North Carolina at this time much bitterness and that no little disaffection to the Confederacy exists, and that adverse military events just now in the State might eventuate in very grave efforts to separate from the Confederacy and arrange with the Federal Government."[11]

Thus did Lee address the new year. It was a far cry from the beginning of 1862, when both the North and the South waited impatiently for McClellan's strategy to unfold. Now, a year later, in spite of the successful combination of Lee and Jackson, the overall momentum of war was clearly running in favor of the North. And, above all else, support for the war effort by the Northern people would shortly be galvanized into a unity of purpose sadly lacking in the past. The Emancipation Proclamation would provide the moral justification so necessary to sustain the spirit of a people facing the fratricidal carnage that lay ahead. The Army of Northern Virginia could protect Richmond only by watching both sides of the James River. To this end, General Lee would soon dispatch Longstreet to the south side of the James, and, a few weeks later, both Longstreet and General D. H. Hill would be given direct responsibility for the protection of North Carolina.[12]

Colonel Harry Burgwyn, observing that enemy troop movements had been going on since the battle of Fredericksburg, and convinced that General Foster was "preparing an expedition of from 30 to 40,000 men aimed at Weldon," wrote his father, earnestly imploring him to "procure *at once at once at once* a plantation whatever be its price." Obviously irritated by his father's continued procrastination, Harry remonstrated, "You may write 1,000,000 letters & I can tell you that the good will be nothing. Now for your own sake do be up & doing. Discard afternoon naps & morning smokes & keep constantly before your eyes the maxim of Caesar, 'We willingly, readily believe what we wish to believe.' My sole object is to urge to action." The next morning Harry again wrote his father, advising him that the authorities believed "the enemy was aiming for Wilmington" and that General Pettigrew's brigade, he understood, would be "ordered from Blackwater to concentrate at Goldsboro." He added, "I think it exceedingly likely that the enemy are going to feint upon Wilmington & strike in the rear."[13]

Later that same day Harry wrote his father another and much longer letter, marked "Private & Confidential" and filled with a sense of urgency:

> Yours of the 1st came to hand as I was riding to town with Gen. Pettigrew; both of us expected to get off on the morning train & go to reconnoitre the country at Weldon. When we went up to Gen. French's room Gen. French gave Gen. P all the information he had of the movements strength & intentions of the enemy. This was his opinion. That all the troops from Suffolk except Corcoran's brigade had been sent or were on their way to Foster that a large quantity of transports, & boats of very light draft in which were mounted mortars & guns of heavy calibre had been prepared & sent to Foster, & that he was preparing another raid of very formidable dimensions, & was very nearly if not quite ready to start.
>
> Last night about midnight he received a telegram from Gen. Evans, that Capt. Whitford (by the way one of our very best scouts) who had gone himself to spy, & to see one of his spys, reported the Yankees 50,000 strong & just setting out on their expedition, which he said was to Wilmington. All this is between you & I as it was a confidential conversation. Which now is the point at which the Yankees are aiming I can not tell.[14]

The Confederate reaction to the reports of General Foster's impending expedition had been immediate. On 1 January, Secretary Seddon had informed General Lee of a large concentration of transports at Hampton Roads and of the threat of a major invasion of North Carolina. Fearing that the point of attack might be Wilmington, the secretary then alerted General Beauregard, at Charleston, urging that he render all possible assistance to General W. H. C. Whiting at Wilmington. Beauregard's reply was favorable although he feared the real point of attack might be Weldon, not Wilmington. Major General Gustavus W. Smith, whose overall command included the Department of North Carolina, urged General French, in command of that department, to transfer his headquarters from Petersburg to Weldon or Rocky Mount and to concentrate all his forces in that general area. "I am endeavoring to obtain additional troops from General Lee's army for service in North Carolina," he informed French, "and will probably know by to-night or to-morrow morning the result of my efforts, and I shall thereupon return to North Carolina."[15]

General Foster was indeed organizing an expeditionary force, but not for the invasion of North Carolina. Although a closely guarded secret, the defenses of Charleston Harbor would be the point of attack, not Wilmington or Weldon. Men and transports were being assembled at Beaufort and Morehead City, but it would be weeks before the invading force reached its South Carolina base of operations on Hilton Head Island. Rumors about the size of the expeditionary force and the number of transports and naval vessels were highly exaggerated. These exaggerations, however, served a useful purpose. The Confederates were obviously kept in the dark as to the time, place, and magnitude of any probable Federal attack. With comparatively limited forces available for the protection of the Carolinas, to strengthen one point meant weakening another.

The Federal command faced the same problem. It, too, had comparatively limited forces with which to engage in offensive operations without unduly exposing its bases at Suffolk and in eastern North Carolina. So, during the winter months of 1863, the contending forces south of the James did little more than react to rumors, thrusts, and counterthrusts. It was greatly to the advantage of the North to weaken Lee's forces before Richmond and to disrupt food production in eastern North Carolina. Of necessity, Confederate strategy was designed to hold the enemy in check at existing bases and to intercept his forays wherever possible.

The disparity in numbers was not nearly so great as rumored and was indicative of the ineffective intelligence operations on both sides. For instance, the number of Federal troops in the Department of Virginia (Major General John A. Dix commanding) was reported at 22,787 officers and men present for duty in December 1862. Not included in these figures were the brigades of Generals Orris S. Ferry, Henry W. Wessells, and Francis B. Spinola, totaling 9,474 officers and men, which had been transferred to the Department of North Carolina. In that department (Major General John G. Foster commanding) there were 21,917 officers and men present for duty in December 1862, including 10,343 under the command of Generals Wessells (First Division) and Henry M. Naglee. Because the brigades transferred to North Carolina were replaced by seventeen new regiments, it is reasonable to assume that the Federal departments of Virginia and North Carolina consisted of more than 50,000 men available for duty in early 1863, approximately 30,000 of whom were stationed in the Norfolk-Suffolk area and 20,000 in the vicinity of New Bern.[16]

To counter this threat from eastern Virginia and south of the James, the Confederates could muster only about half the number. On 20 December 1862, following General Foster's raid on Kinston and Goldsboro, the field return of troops commanded by Major General G. W. Smith at Goldsboro totaled 11,992 present for duty, consisting principally of Clingman's, Junius Daniel's, Joseph R. Davis's, Evans's, and Pettigrew's brigades. The return of troops stationed in the Richmond-Petersburg area, under the command of Major General Arnold Elzey, reflected 10,054 present for duty on 20 December 1862. At about the same time, the number of available troops in the District of the Cape Fear, Brigadier General W. H. C. Whiting commanding, totaled only 7,131.[17] Not only were the Confederates seriously outnumbered but they were forced to spread their thin ranks so as to protect widely scattered areas of strategic importance, and, at the same time, be in a position to concentrate quickly against a threatened attack at any given point.

This situation explains Harry's movements during the next several weeks, as well as the character of his letters, for uncertainty was the order of the day. The men never knew what the next day would hold, although the monotony of camp routine was seldom broken by the expectation of immediate contact with the enemy. Such rumors were generally false and gave rise to fretful impatience, especially to one of Harry's temperament. And then, too, the cheerless, comfortless nature of Confederate encampments, in the dead of winter, in eastern North Carolina, was not calculated to inspire a positive and hopeful outlook.

On 6 January 1863, he wrote to his father that he had been ordered to Goldsboro, then to Rocky Mount, and then to Weldon. He was sent to Garysburg and expected to go to Rocky Mount. On 11 January, believing that the loss of the *Monitor* and the *Passaic* had changed the enemy's point of attack from Wilmington to Weldon, Harry was again entreating his father to do something about the plantation. Clearly exasperated, he accused his father of "apathy amounting almost to indifference" and chided him accordingly: "How you, whose judgment is ordinarily so clear, can shut your eyes to these facts I can not understand. Had you only acted when I wanted you to, you would have had a plantation all ready & your cotton all moved. You say Gen Smith advises you to move, Gen Pettigrew does the same, & everybody whose judgment is worth anything do the same, & yet you do nothing. . . . You confine yourself to stating what a devil of a quandary you are in, instead of getting out in a devil of a hurry."[18]

A few days later, from his headquarters at Magnolia, in a letter to his mother, Harry indicated the scattered positions of Confederate troops defending eastern North Carolina. On 2 February, Harry relayed to his father the confidential information given to him by General Pettigrew that the enemy had "moved 40,000 of his troops to the coast leaving only 10,000 in New Berne, that he was preparing those on the coast, who were mostly stationed at Beaufort-Morehead City & etc., for sea. A dispatch from Whiting states that 5 steamers & 17 schooners had passed New River bound Southward."[19]

A week later, somewhat dispirited, Harry advised his mother that his application for a fifteen-day leave had been declined. "If nothing turns up in a few days," he emphasized, "I shall urge my application in person. I have no doubt myself that the Yankees have gone South, probably to attack Savannah; if this proves to be so I do not know of a more suitable time to apply. But nous verrons." Harry had reason to be bored with the inactivity of camp life; he explained:

> I have not written more frequently myself, for of late I have had the blues & did not wish to inflict any of my ennui upon you. We are located, as you have heard me forcibly describe it, in the most God forsaken land which can be conceived of. We are without any of the comforts of a stationary camp & exposed to the disagreeable privations of an active campaign without any of the stirring excitements which usually alleviate the tedious monotony. If I were in camp or able to get the books, I should commence reviewing some of my mathematical studies & read over some of the latin authors. A few hours a day devoted to Calculus & Virgil would perhaps relieve me somewhat.[20]

On the same day, Harry also wrote his father expressing surprise to learn that he had gone to Richmond on a "transaction," presumably to get his "Northern funds off at par." Harry concurred with the idea but was seemingly more interested in what his father proposed to do with the funds. He had a suggestion:

> It seems to me it would be a capital plan to buy negroes, & in buying I would buy boys & girls from 15 to 20 years old & take care to have a majority of girls. The increase in the number of your negroes by this means would repay the difference in the

amount of available labor. . . . If you can secure enough negroes now to plant a huge cotton crop, if there is any likelihood of peace, you might make a vast amount of money. I would not be surprised to see negroes in 6 mos. after peace worth from 2 to 3000 dollars.[21]

For the first time in months Harry appeared to feel at ease about the safety of Thornbury. The building of fortifications at Weldon, coupled with the distribution of Confederate forces in eastern North Carolina, must have reassured him that the authorities in Richmond were indeed concerned. Harry's reference to the purchase of young Negro slaves as breeding stock, however, poses the question of his sensitivity to human values. Of course, such a suggestion was in keeping with traditional practice, but coming from a young man of recognized character, whose letters from the age of fourteen attested to his Christian faith, compassion, and sense of fairness, it would be less surprising if he had attempted to discourage his father from investing in slave property. He must have considered the odds for peace favorable and the speculative opportunity to make a fortune considerable. Obviously he was not bothered by President Lincoln's Emancipation Proclamation.

Harry soon received a ten-day leave and repaired to Raleigh for a visit with his mother. In a note to his father, who was probably at Thornbury, Harry said, "I do not think there is any danger at present to be apprehended from the Yankees."[22]

If camp life in eastern North Carolina was filled with monotony in the early part of 1863, the same could not be said for the political situation in the state capital. The legislature was considering the so-called ten-regiment bill, which Governor Vance had proposed in his first message to the General Assembly on 17 November 1862, with the intent of creating a reserve force of ten thousand volunteers available for duty in North Carolina. If the Confederate government could not supply sufficient protection, the state would not be left completely defenseless.

The intent of this legislation was either misunderstood or deliberately misconstrued by the public, for considerable controversy developed, particularly involving the Virginia press. The existing political rivalry between the Conservatives and the Secessionists or Destructives within the state of North Carolina was fanned into heated editorial exchanges. The *Richmond Enquirer* joined the fray with a series of articles, one of which asked the Conservatives "'whether there was any lurking hope of a restoration or reconstruction?'" suggesting "that while they are pretending to battle for independence, they are meditating treason." The *Richmond Examiner*, recognizing the situation in the eastern part of the state as being "perilous," took issue with the *Enquirer* in support of North Carolina's ten-regiment bill.[23]

The increasingly strained relations between the authorities in Raleigh and Richmond were undoubtedly a manifestation of the deep apprehension in both capital cities. Eastern North Carolina was not alone in being subjected to constant harassment by the enemy. Eastern Virginia was in much the same position, and, moreover, the capture of Richmond would always be the primary target of Federal strategy. Yet the safeguarding of strategically significant eastern North Carolina was as vital to the security of Richmond as it was to that of Raleigh, for one of the most important lifelines to the Confederate capital was the Wilmington and Weldon Railroad. Governor Vance was acutely aware of this situation when he sent a special message to the General Assembly on 21 January. Perhaps of greatest concern to the governor was the "inefficient execution of the conscript law and the alarming increase of desertion in the army." Recognizing that desertion was not a crime in North Carolina, Vance pointed out that citizens who shielded deserters from arrest were not subject to punishment. As a consequence, he declared, large numbers of deserters were concealed in many parts of the state and "depredate upon the citizens near them." He believed that "a little prudent legislation" could put an end to "this state of things, ruinous alike to the discipline of our army and the morals of our people." His recommendation, subject to the consent of appropriate military authorities, was "to give absentees from the army without leave, by proclamation, thirty days in which they may return to duty free of punishment, and after that time to make them liable for the delay, to the severest penalties of the law."[24]

The same day that Governor Vance sent this special message to the legislature, there appeared an advertisement in the *North Carolina Standard* offering "Two Thousand and Forty Dollars Reward" for the "apprehension and delivery" of sixty-six named deserters, forty-two of whom were from Wilkes County. It was signed "James B. Jordan, Adj't., Headqrs. 26th Regt. N.C. Troops, Garysburg, N.C., Jan 16th, 1863, By command of Col. H. K. Burgwyn, Jr."[25] A week later, on 28 January, Vance issued his proclamation on desertion.[26]

In spite of the governor's efforts, both then and later, North Carolina became an attractive refuge for deserters. The swamps of eastern North Carolina, with their proximity to the Virginia battleground, and the mountains to the west, where strong Union sentiment prevailed, provided natural havens for the lawless. Operating in bands, generally referred to as "buffaloes" and "bushwhackers," they terrorized entire neighborhoods.[27] James Cathcart Johnston, the Pettigrews' friend, was one of the victims. At Hayes, his plantation home near Edenton, he was forced to take the oath of allegiance. In a pathetic letter to a friend in Raleigh he admitted that "the greater portion of us took the oath of allegiance to Bartholomew's Government—of my case you know all. I want you if you please to write me a letter and tell me how we are looked upon by the Government. I want to go up the Country to see my friends. I want to go to Raleigh. I would like to see you; find out if you please if by taking the oath I have forfeited my commission as Lieut. Coln. of the Militia. I have done nothing more than I have been compelled to do."[28]

CHAPTER 18

MY COMPLIMENTS TO

MISS ANNIE DEVEREUX

It was not until 1 February 1863 that General Foster's expedition reached its secret destination at Hilton Head, South Carolina. On that day, ten thousand infantry with six hundred artillery arrived safely. Major General David Hunter, commanding the Department of the South, reported that he welcomed Foster's "thorough acquaintance with the harbor and its defenses."[1] On 9 February, General Foster dispatched a confidential note to General Naglee, second in command of his Eighteenth Army Corps, in which he emphasized the necessity of keeping the command distinct because the force might be recalled to North Carolina in the event of an attack on New Bern. This was also the wish of the Secretary of War Stanton. "Of course, in my absence, after the opening of the operations," Foster concluded, "you will be second in command only to myself of the operating force."[2]

Thus was born the final phase of the long-planned expedition against Charleston, which was destined to end in failure and would add nothing to the credit of those involved. Command of the Eighteenth and Tenth corps was the question at issue. Foster was determined that the former should remain under his command and not be merged with the Tenth under that of David Hunter. Believing that this disposition of command was thoroughly understood, Foster left for Fort Monroe to obtain additional heavy guns and ammunition. From there, on 13 February, he advised General Halleck that he had reconnoitered the coast from Charleston to the Ogeechee and requested permission to come to Washington to report on his findings.[3]

Foster may have gone to Washington, but he did not return to South Carolina. Fearing that he might lose command of the Department of North Carolina, Foster left his subordinate, Brigadier General Henry M. Naglee, to bear the brunt of the offended Hunter's acrimonious protests. On 5 March, Naglee was relieved from duty for insubordination. On 15 March, he wrote General Foster that he considered Hunter's conduct "outrageously indecent, uncivil, illegal, and despotic in the extreme." On 23 March, Hunter demanded of

Halleck how he could be held accountable when "thus saddled with pro-slavery generals in whom I have not the least confidence, and who were encouraged by orders from Washington to protest against my authority."[4]

The long-awaited assault on Charleston was to be a joint expedition of the army and navy, with Rear Admiral S. F. DuPont in command of the naval operations, but it was the navy that steamed in from the sea to challenge Fort Sumter on 7 April. The following day, Admiral DuPont sent a sad message to General Hunter: "I attempted to take the bull by the horns, but he was too much for us. These monitors are miserable failures where forts are concerned; the longest was one hour and the others forty-five minutes under fire, and five of the eight were wholly or partially disabled." On 15 April, Hunter advised Halleck that the expedition had returned safely to Port Royal Harbor "without the loss of a man or a pound of stores."[5]

Thus ended a fruitless expedition that had been in the planning stage since well before the turn of the year. Originally intended for Wilmington, it was ordered to cooperate in the attack on Charleston after the *Monitor* sank off Cape Hatteras and it was learned that the ironclads could not cross the bar at Smithville, thirty miles below Wilmington. That the expedition had been plagued from the beginning with endless delays, occasioned by bad weather, faulty equipment, and frustrated leadership, was no more a novel experience for the Union side than it was for the Confederacy. If nothing else, however, it had served the purpose of creating alarm and confusion along the coast of the Carolinas in the winter of 1863, to which the Confederate high command was forced to address itself.

When it became apparent that the Federal flotilla was moving down the coast, coupled with the appearance of Burnside's old Ninth Corps in Hampton Roads about mid-February, two divisions of General Longstreet's corps were moved into a protective position near Richmond. On 25 February, Longstreet was formally placed in command of the Department of Virginia and North Carolina, which extended from Richmond to the Cape Fear River. This department, in reality, included the Department of Richmond (General Elzey commanding), the Department of Southern Virginia (under Major General Samuel G. French), and the Department of North Carolina, to which the ailing D. Harvey Hill had been assigned.[6]

Perhaps the best example of General Hill's critical mood and bombastic temperament at that time is to be found in the exhortation to his forces, delivered at Goldsboro on 25 February, in which he vilified "able-bodied skulkers," claimed that cavalry commands "who permit themselves to be surprised deserve to die," and promised that "the war will end before July" if the enemy could be checked "everywhere for the next sixty days."[7] This extraordinary message undoubtedly received mixed reactions. Colonel Harry Burgwyn, writing to his mother from "camp near Goldsboro," was unimpressed.[8] Having only recently returned from a visit home, he apparently was in no mood for the general's bombast. "I have got the blues," Harry admitted, "and find camp intensely uninteresting & most disagreeably monotonous. . . . We it appears are to remain here until that most definite period 'further orders' shall arrive; thereafter it is highly probable that we will march in the 'direction of somewhere' & prepare 'at a moments notice' to fight the enemy 'at nowhere.'"[9]

Harry was not far off the mark. An offensive plan of operations was in the works but in the end would avail little primarily because of the general nature of the operations and lack of coordination in command. While still at Magnolia, General French had instructed General Pettigrew to operate in the counties of Washington, Martin, and Tyrrell, as well as adjacent areas, for the purpose of gathering supplies, protecting the people, and encouraging them to plant their crops in the spring. On 14 February French ordered Pettigrew to "assume command of forces at Greenville and Rainbow bend and defend the Tar and Roanoke rivers" and to extend operations as necessary.[10] No sooner did Longstreet and Hill assume their new commands, however, than they immediately started laying plans for an offensive. On 23 February Hill wrote a long letter to Secretary of War Seddon outlining weaknesses in the defenses at Wilmington and insisting upon more guns of heavy caliber. "As soon as the movement begins at Charleston," he emphasized, "I want to threaten New Berne, Washington, and Plymouth, and possibly Morehead City, in order to keep Hunter from getting re-enforcements from this State." In addition to the heavy guns, Hill insisted, "we need another brigade of infantry to harass the Yankees, to detain their troops from Charleston, to protect the planting interest in the rich counties of the east, and to bring out supplies and conscripts; we need an efficient brigade of cavalry to keep the Yankees close shut up in their fortifications."[11]

Shortly thereafter, Longstreet suggested to Hill that they attempt to cut the New Bern garrison off from the coast. On 1 March Longstreet acknowledged Hill's letter, stating that "your views are almost precisely those that I wrote you two or three days ago. I do not know that I expressed the idea that a forward movement would be a diversion in favor of Charleston, but I had it in my mind." He would order Whiting to send four thousand men as reinforcements to bring Hill's force up to about fifteen thousand and urged him to move quickly.

The next day Longstreet ordered Whiting to send half of his force and as many more as could be spared to reinforce Hill. Whiting meanwhile wrote Hill suggesting that because of the Yankees' failure to surprise Charleston, they would probably attack a weaker point, which he expected to be Wilmington. Therefore, he needed more troops at Wilmington. Clearly, Whiting was in no mood to accept Longstreet's order to divide his command when General Foster might show up any day at the mouth of the Cape Fear. "So far from considering myself able to spare troops from here," he remonstrated, "I have applied for and earnestly urged that another brigade be sent here immediately."[12] While Longstreet was calling upon Whiting for more men to bolster Hill's forthcoming expedition, the latter was calling for at least one of Whiting's three Whitworth guns. Whiting, however, rejoined: "The Whitworth guns are all we have to depend on to keep the blockaders at such a distance as will enable the steamers to run the blockade. One is at [Fort] Caswell, one at Fort Fisher, and one about 5 miles above [Fort] Fisher, on the beach. We have now four British and one Confederate steamer in port daily expecting to leave, and several steamers are expected to arrive. We have had an engagement with the enemy over each one of these vessels, the enemy's sloops of war fiercely attacking the forts while their smaller vessels attempt to cut off the steamers."[13]

If Federal strategy had been designed to confuse, it was a resounding success in some quarters. With Burnside's old Ninth Corps at Hampton Roads, and with Foster's expedition seemingly stalled at Hilton Head, the rumor mill was rife with speculation. Would Burnside strike north or south of the James? Would Foster abandon his attack on Charleston, especially now that the general had returned to New Bern? Was Wilmington indeed the ultimate point of attack? Longstreet believed it "possible that disaffection in the ranks of the enemy [the Foster-Hunter controversy] may force him to make some such effort."[14]

It is evident that confusion reigned in the coastal regions of Virginia and the Carolinas. Only General Lee seemed to have a balanced, objective view of the situation. To Longstreet, on 3 March, he observed, "The enemy's positions in North Carolina have always appeared to me to be taken for defense, and if driven from them they can easily escape to their gunboats. Unless therefore they will come out into the country I do not know how you can advantageously get at them. . . . But except to draw provisions from North Carolina at this distance I do not see that you can accomplish much." On 7 March Lee provided Longstreet with more specific observations. He still expected the Yankees to attack Charleston. He estimated that a Union force of about twenty-one thousand had been sent to Newport News and advised Longstreet to be "prepared for all emergencies."[15]

Still in winter quarters at Fredericksburg, Lee was clearly concerned about the possibility of any movement in his rear against Richmond. Although seven of General Joseph Hooker's ten corps were quartered between Falmouth, near Fredericksburg, and Aquia on the Potomac, the Federals at Newport News and Suffolk were fully capable of mounting strong reconnaissances in the James River area. And the Wilmington and Weldon Railroad, at Weldon, would always be a prime target. General Lee believed that the enemy, "by a systematic propagation of falsehood, has been able to deceive us, and that the report of troops from Newport News going to North Carolina was purposely spread to conceal their movement west."[16] His correspondence at this time indicates a strong disinclination for the troops in North Carolina to become heavily engaged with the enemy, for the spring campaign in Virginia was about to begin. Reconnaissances in force, yes, foraging for much needed commissary stores, yes, but not at the expense of Richmond's safety. The Army of Northern Virginia was on the threshold of another challenge on the Rappahannock. It could not further deplete its strength to assist North Carolina, and the troops in that state must be available if Hooker threatened.

The recent command changes in the Department of Virginia and North Carolina had created considerable apprehension among the Federal authorities. Immediate efforts were made, therefore, to ascertain the strength and disposition of the Confederate forces. On 2 March Foster advised General Halleck that an ironclad being constructed on the Roanoke was nearly completed and that he was preparing a reconnaissance toward Wilmington. From Fort Monroe, on 6 March, Major General John A. Dix reported to Halleck that a "reconnaissance on the Blackwater puts the enemy's force at 20,000." Three days later, Dix confirmed the report that there were twenty thousand Confederates on the Blackwater. In addition, "There is a large force at Petersburg and Drewry's Bluff. Very few troops at Richmond."[17]

On 11 March Foster reported to Halleck that reconnaissances had been made in several directions "to catch certain guerrillas . . . and to break up a smuggling trade in corn and forage." Information derived from these scouting reports, according to Foster, indicated that thirty-eight thousand rations were being issued daily from Goldsboro to troops "within drawing distance," in all probability including those forces at Goldsboro, Kinston, Tarboro, Kenansville, and possibly on the Roanoke River. On 12 March Dix received two urgent messages from Suffolk stating that an attack on that place was expected.[18]

It was in this atmosphere, charged with uncertainty and misinformation, that General Hill was hastily preparing his expedition against New Bern. Almost until the day of the attack, however, Harry Burgwyn was in ignorance of either the purpose or destination of the projected movement. His correspondence in early March reveals little of his usual impatience and enthusiasm for action. A winter of monotonous camp life had left him feeling bored. He had just returned from a pleasant visit to Raleigh; he had "the blues"; and he may have fallen in love. On 4 March, in a letter to his mother, he mentioned for the first time the name of Annie Devereux, to whom he had sent some apples. He had asked one of his men who was going on furlough to the mountains to bring back a bushel of apples to be sent to his mother. He requested her, "If they should turn up at your house, please select a dozen of the finest & send them, with my compliments, to Miss Annie Devereaux."[19]

Harry did not have much longer in which to reflect quietly upon home and loved ones. Five days later, his regiment left Goldsboro and reached Kinston in early afternoon the following day. He immediately wrote his father that his regiment had been ordered to prepare six days' rations and would leave the following day, but he did not know the destination or object. He was again suffering from diarrhea.[20]

While Harry was pondering his destination, General Hill was issuing orders to Harry's brigade commander, James Johnston Pettigrew, to "take all the rifled guns in your own Brigade, Daniel's & the reserve Artillery & the Whitworth gun from Wilmington (if arrived) & move with your Brigade to the neighborhood of Barrington's Ferry," where he was to engage the enemy. Hill divulged that "there is to be a combined movement from the James to the Cape Fear & you are to begin it. Upon your success depends very much the success of the whole scheme."[21]

The distance from Goldsboro to Barrington's Ferry was only fifty-seven miles, but the obstacles were many. Heavy rains made many stretches of the roads all but impassable. Bridges broke under the weight of the guns, and it was not until Friday evening, 13 March, that the infantry was in position to attack. The artillery was detained until later. The plan of attack, as outlined by Pettigrew, was for the Twenty-sixth North Carolina, assisted by Captain John N. Whitford's Rangers, to "capture or drive in the enemy's pickets and

. . . to carry the work." Pettigrew then planned "to intrench his 20 pounders and drive away the gunboats and the enemy from his intrenchments in front of New Berne." According to his report, "The first part of this programme was excellently well carried out; 3 of the enemy's pickets were captured; the bridges within the enemy's lines were repaired."[22]

The attack opened soon after daylight on Saturday, 14 March. According to Harry Burgwyn:

> The plan was for our Brigade to go [to] Barrington's Ferry, immediately opposite New Berne, take the fort there & then drive off or sink the Yankee gunboats, then shell & if possible dismount the guns on the Yankee intrenchments at New Berne while Daniel attacked it in front. To do this we had infantry & smooth bored artillery enough to take the Fort but to sink the shipping & etc. we had 4 twenty pdr. Parrot guns & 5 or 6 light rifled guns. These proved perfectly incompetent to damage the boats. One of the twenty pdr. Parrots exploded killing & wounding 3 men, & the men who manned the others were distrustful in firing them. Besides the gunboats kept so far off that the light rifles could scarcely reach them & it was perfectly casual where or whom they hit. As the guns could not damage the boats there was no necessity to storm the Fort.
>
> My Rgt. was in front & was to do the storming. After driving in the pickets I advanced within from 450 to 600 yds of the Fort & remained there 6 hours all the time being shelled upon almost a level plateau by the miserable gunboats. They had a man in the masthead who would direct their fire & they burst their shells amongst us, over us, & in front of us, with wonderful precision & yet wonderful little loss. I lost 17 men. My Rgt acted under this trying fire most admirably. Gen. Pettigrew was highly pleased. After we were ordered to withdraw, which we did under this fire, I had the roll called & not a man was absent improperly. The fire was exceedingly severe.[23]

General Pettigrew, in describing the engagement, admitted making a mistake when he "decided to display my force, demoralize them by a heavy fire, and demand a surrender, thus saving my own men and not unnecessarily killing theirs." In demanding surrender of the Federal garrison early on the morning of the fourteenth, which was declined pending consultations with General Foster, Pettigrew provided invaluable time for the gunboats lying on the other side of the river to be towed into position for returning the fire.[24] General

Foster reported that "the Navy gunboats were . . . towed to position by tugs, and, assisted by a battery of rifled guns on this side of the Neuse, compelled General Pettigrew to withdraw his artillery and infantry, merely remaining in a threatening position till this A.M., when he finally retired." Pettigrew's light rifled guns had proved ineffective at long range against the Federal gunboats, and his four twenty-pounders were "worse than useless." Half of their shells "burst just outside the guns," he reported. Those that did not burst "turned over in the air and were perfectly harmless to the enemy. At length the axle of one of these guns broke and it became unserviceable. Then another burst, wounding 3 men, 1 of them mortally."[25]

Once it was evident that he could not counter the artillery fire from the river, Pettigrew concluded that he had no option but to withdraw. He decided not to try to carry the work, even though convinced that the Twenty-sixth could have done so, because he did not want to risk losing men sixty miles from hospitals. Nothing in Harry Burgwyn's correspondence indicates that he opposed the withdrawal, but he was pleased with the steadfast courage of his men under fire. A week later he expressed the opinion that "Gen. Hill could have taken New Berne if he had collected the artillery in his department, instead of expecting 4 twenty pdr. Parrot guns to do the work of twenty."[26]

On 15 March General Foster reported to Halleck that "the enemy are retiring from an attack on this town, which was intended to have been strong, but was feeble, very feeble." In a later message Foster correctly assessed the outcome of the engagement: "The whole affair, meant to be effective and strong, was ineffective and weak, inflicting no damage and accomplishing no object."[27]

Hill unquestionably failed before New Bern. Neither Daniel nor Pettigrew had succeeded in penetrating its defenses, and the cavalry under General Beverly H. Robertson, operating south of the Trent River, was ineffective. Hill could have undoubtedly concentrated his artillery to better advantage, but that which he had was inadequate for the purpose. Furthermore, much of his ammunition was defective, and General Whiting had failed to send up the Whitworth gun from Wilmington, which might have saved the situation for Pettigrew. But even in failure, Harry Burgwyn was proud of the manner in which his own regiment stood its ground under prolonged and heavy artillery fire.

The attack on New Bern was nothing more than a reconnaissance in force. But to Colonel Harry Burgwyn it proved to be a testing ground for the Twenty-sixth North Carolina and its command. Only two weeks earlier, Louis G. Young, aide-de-camp to General Petti-grew, had submitted to headquarters his inspection report on the Twenty-sixth North Carolina. In the light of Harry's known pride in his regiment, this critical review of the ten companies under his command, about three months before Gettysburg, provided an inter-esting assessment for the record. The men were evaluated on the basis of discipline, instruction, military appearance, arms, ammuni-tion, equipment, clothing, and officer capability. Young summarized his review of Harry's regiment as follows:

> Companies "H" & "K" I consider the finest in the Regiment. The material of which they are composed is most excellent, and with strict attention on the part of the officers the men could be made soldiers of a very high class. Company "I" is the most indifferent Company in the Regiment, but not so bad as to be reported for its deficiencies. The esprit de corps of all the Companies, save Co "I", seems to be good.
>
> The Regiment is better informed & more practised in the skirmish drill than any I have yet inspected, but greater perfec-tion in this respect is most desirable, for the regiment is com-posed for the most part of active young men well fitted to make very effective light troops.
>
> Many of the Companies have some muskets & some rifles. I would suggest that they be armed as far as practicable with the same kind of weapons. The men are as clean as they can well be under the circumstances. As you see from my report the cleanliness of the guns is very much neglected.[28]

Shortly thereafter, the Twenty-sixth North Carolina was cited for bravery and for the manner in which it withstood enemy shelling—indicative of superior training, discipline, and leadership. And yet, except for its participation in the Seven Days' battle, the Twenty-sixth could not be classed among the veteran regiments, seasoned by months of intensive campaigning and battle engagement.

In the meantime, several more weeks of marching and counter-marching lay ahead for the regiment—and under the most trying cir-cumstances. The early spring weather in eastern North Carolina had provided nothing but rain, and, until the Army of the Potomac com-mitted itself on the Rappahannock, the Confederate command would continue to appear hesitant and indecisive. Should Longstreet attack the Federal garrison at Suffolk? Should Lee send more troops to Gen-eral Hill in North Carolina? Could any of these moves be made without weakening the Army of Northern Virginia on the eve of another spring campaign? These were matters of grave concern to General Lee and to the authorities in Richmond, but, given the strength and seeming ubiquity of the enemy, they had little choice but to counter Federal moves, reconnoiter in force, and gather food supplies pending the next major thrust of the Army of the Potomac.

During the week following the abortive expedition against New Bern, Lee, Longstreet, and Hill were in almost constant communication about the situation in North Carolina. The question was whether the divisions of Major General John B. Hood (in camp near Richmond) and Major General George E. Pickett (in camp near Petersburg) should be used to bolster Hill's operations in North Carolina or be held in readiness to support Lee at Fredericksburg. Their correspondence reflects the military problems facing the Confederate leadership in the Department of Virginia and North Carolina during the winter of 1863. It also reveals how these problems were magnified by the temperamental nature of some of those involved in the command structure.[29]

As early as mid-February, when Pettigrew's brigade was moved to the vicinity of Greenville, the purpose was to gather supplies and protect the people so they could plant their crops. When Lee made it clear to Longstreet that his primary objective was to gather "all the forage and subsistence" possible from North Carolina, he was only reemphasizing what had been expressed policy for weeks. Longstreet, on the other hand, took the position that it was a matter of prime necessity "to keep the enemy out of North Carolina." He was in favor of crushing the enemy detachments in eastern Virginia and North Carolina even if Lee were forced to fall "as far back as the South Anna at least." Longstreet felt that his own forces were inadequate, but Lee was convinced that the enemy forces between the Roanoke and the Tar rivers were "feeble." Leaving aside the question of subordination to higher command, Longstreet was exceedingly deliberate in executing the assigned objectives of his first semi-independent command.[30]

D. H. Hill, who had replaced General French in charge of the Department of North Carolina, was not in good health during this period, and his correspondence attests to his occasional ill-tempered nature. On 18 March, he urged Pettigrew to "threaten your timid cavalry with death if they give false information again. . . . I have been torturing my brain to devise a system by which our cavalry can be got under fire. Can you help me?" In another communication to

Pettigrew, he wrote, "I wish you would send a written statement in regard to your defective ammunition to be forwarded to Sec. War. There is treachery in the Ordnance Department."[31]

It is difficult to determine whether Hill ever developed any clear-cut plan of action for the upcoming siege of Washington. If so, it was not reflected in the informal, almost daily instructions delivered to Pettigrew. During the five days between 17 and 22 March, Hill sent six dispatches—all characterized by elements of doubt and indecision about whether to watch, threaten, or capture Washington in an effort to protect General Richard B. Garnett during his foraging expedition.[32]

This week of indecision following the encounter at New Bern is best described by Julius Lineback, who was a reluctant participant in the almost aimless to-and-fro movements between Greenville and Tranter's Creek (near Washington) in response to General Hill's directions. On Sunday, 15 March, the Twenty-sixth bivouacked for the night at Swift Creek. Lineback recorded:

> About midnight, we were aroused under an order to march towards Greenville. . . . We marched rapidly until ten o'clock when we were within eight miles of Greenville, having marched some twenty-three miles. . . . Apparently the hurry was over as we remained at this place until Tuesday morning [17 March] when we marched on to the town. . . . On Wednesday morning we left this place, our course being toward Washington. . . . As usual there were various guesses as to the object of this move. We were to attack Washington. The attention of the enemy was to be distracted from a train of 200 wagons going after corn, etc. . . . At Tranter's Creek we stopped for the night [18 March]. . . . We had expected to go further but the roads were practically impassable for artillery and we made no further advance. . . . Monday [23 March] there was some picket firing in our front but did not lead to any serious fighting. General Hill was expected to arrive. About 10 o'clock we left this place and taking a different route from the one we came and marching rapidly, we arrived at Greenville about 3 P.M.[33]

From Greenville, that same day, Harry Burgwyn provided his mother with a vivid account of the march from Tranter's Creek: "I did not then expect to leave so soon," he wrote, "but this morning I got an order to move in 20 minutes towards this place, ergo I am here now. We have had a very hard time & in our march today the men had literally to wade & tramp through mud nearly all the time. Not a man but what had to wade nearly thigh deep. One single place was 75 to 100 yds wide & 2 or 3 feet deep."[34]

In a letter to his father, written the day before from Tranter's Creek, Harry expressed decided opinions about an attack on Washington. Although Pettigrew seemed to oppose such an attack, "if I were Gen Hill I should most assuredly attack Washington, but I would collect such a force of artillery as to soon sink their gunboats & shell their fortifications so severely that they could not show their heads above the parapet." But in a letter the following day, Harry's thoughts were not on military matters. He was sending a man to Raleigh and with him a box of sardines and a Yankee's canteen, both of which he had taken from a "Yankee picket who fled in haste to Barrington's Ferry." He asked his mother to give the box of sardines to Miss Annie Devereux "with my compliments" and to tell her that he hoped "before very long to send her something better from Yankeedom in return for her lemons."[35]

Anne ("Annie" or "Nan") Lane Devereux was the daughter of Major John and Margaret Mordecai Devereux, Jr. She was the eldest of eight children. Before the war, the family had always spent the winter at Runiroi Meadows, their plantation home on the Roanoke in Bertie County, and the summer months at their home in Raleigh known as Will's Forest. During the war years, however, they lived at Will's Forest year-round, and it was undoubtedly here that Harry came to see her during his infrequent furloughs. The two were distantly related through the Pollock family, and Harry's grandfather, John Fanning Burgwyn, enjoyed a close and affectionate relationship with his Devereux kin. Although Harry's father had some unpleasant litigation with Annie's grandfather, Thomas Pollock Devereux, in the early 1840s, he had always maintained cordial relations with his son John Devereux. He once described John's wife Margaret as "a sweet lovely looking person, charming expression, and very young for a mother of six children."[36] Harry was naturally attracted to Will's Forest when home on leave, especially when Margaret's equally lovely daughter was there to greet him.

Annie Devereux, born on 10 October 1843, was two years younger than Harry. It is likely that their romance flowered in the winter of 1863, for descendants of both families have long believed that they became engaged at that time and planned to be married following the war. For them, that day never came. Harry's nephew, the late Honorable W. H. S. Burgwyn, recalled in 1974: "Although he [Harry] never married we have always understood that he intended to marry a young lady in Raleigh who never married herself—a distant relative

Will's Forest (courtesy of Laura Jones Millender)

of his, Miss Annie Devereux. That, however, we only know from what we have heard others state, of course. I knew her well and I know she never married. I also know she wore mourning all her life, and I have been told she never wore anything but mourning after he was killed."[37] The late Dr. Alfred Mordecai, a half-nephew of Annie Devereux, possessed family correspondence attesting that "Aunt Annie was engaged to Harry Burgwyn & I have heard Mother tell often of his charm & bravery, tho I never heard Aunt Annie mention him—I guess her hurt went too deep."[38]

Annie Devereux never forgot Harry's mother, whom she apparently visited on many occasions. In February 1873, she spent three weeks with the Burgwyns in Richmond.[39] They corresponded frequently, and "Miss Annie" remembered Anna in many thoughtful ways.[40]

CHAPTER 19

BACK TO VIRGINIA

On Sunday, 29 March, Harry Burgwyn noted in his daily journal that his regiment had "rested a day or two" after returning to Greenville from Tranter's Creek and that within the past several days Ransom's brigade had been moved to Kinston, Kemper's to Goldsboro, Garnett's to Greenville, and Daniel's to a place near Greenville. "Behold us then," wrote the colonel, "again ready to start upon another expedition the object of which everyone thinks is Washington, N.C."[1]

Only the day before, satisfied that Washington would be the point of attack, Harry was genuinely concerned when he wrote his mother: "I think as soon as the river falls we will cross to attack Washington. I find great fault with the way in which our movements are managed. Everything has pointed towards Washington. First, Garnett's Brigade came down here, stayed long enough for the enemy to find out that he was here. Then, Pettigrew's Brigade went down to Tranter's Creek, stayed there long enough for the Yankees to find out that we were there, & then we all come back here, wait until Gen. Hill comes, then until a Whitworth gun can come from Wilmington, & then all hands start off to *surprise* the enemy."[2]

On Monday night, 30 March, Harry recorded in his journal that his regiment had left Greenville. They were only two and a half miles from Washington and encountered a regiment that had already been in battle.[3] Harry had every reason to be apprehensive, for the enemy had indeed been alerted to the Confederate movement. Early in the morning of the day the Twenty-sixth North Carolina was en route to Washington, General Foster, with several members of his staff, had arrived there from New Bern. Foster found a garrison of approximately twelve hundred men, consisting of eight companies of the Forty-fourth Massachusetts Volunteer Militia, eight companies of the Twenty-seventh Massachusetts Volunteers, two companies of the First North Carolina (Union) Volunteers, and one company of the Third New York Artillery, supported by three gunboats, the *Commodore Hull*, the *Eagle*, and the *Louisiana*. He examined the works immediately, gave the necessary orders for strengthening them, and then sent out one company of the Forty-fourth Massachusetts on reconnaissance, supported by a few cavalrymen and one piece of artillery. It was this unit that was met by the Forty-seventh North Carolina about halfway between Washington and the crossroads where the regiment was camped. At the same time, Foster dispatched one company of the First North Carolina (Union) Volunteers, with one twelve-pounder Wiard, to occupy Rodman's Point, on the south side of the Pamlico about a mile and a half downriver. This company succeeded in landing at the point and erecting an earthwork for its fieldpiece, but its men were driven back to their boats that night and forced off the beach the next morning by the right wing of the Forty-seventh North Carolina.[4]

Harry recorded in his journal the events of Tuesday, 31 March, as the Confederate siege lines were forming around Washington. Before daybreak his regiment relieved the Forty-seventh on picket near Washington. They spent a quiet day repairing bridges and reconnoitering. Although there were Yankee gunboats nearby, they did not open fire on the troops.[5]

By Wednesday morning, 1 April, Pettigrew's brigade was rapidly completing its investment of Washington on the south side of the Pamlico. Artillery was now in place at Rodman's Point. Fort Hill, built earlier by the Confederates to protect Washington from an attack by water, was also in Pettigrew's possession. Harry had divided his regiment into two parts. Four companies were stationed at Rodman's Point and the remainder at the Grist farm on the Washington road. He was then ordered to report to Colonel Leventhorpe, commanding the Eleventh North Carolina, and marched at sunrise, Thursday, 2 April, toward Blounts Creek. "Not meeting him at his camp," Harry noted, "I went down to Fort Hill. While there a Yankee boat opened fire upon the Fort. 4 shots were fired while I was there none of which did any damage. Took up camp about 2 P.M. some 4 miles above Blount's Mill in supporting distance of Col. Leventhorpe at the Mill or [of] Major Richardson (52nd N.C.T) in charge of the pickets at the river shore."[6]

On Friday afternoon, 3 April, Harry was ordered by General Pettigrew to take eight companies of his regiment and one smoothbore six-pounder to scout beyond Blounts Creek. He left immediately and hurried ahead of his regiment to Mauls Point, where the Yankee fleet was lying. There he counted eleven steamers and six sailing vessels, all out of range. His command bivouacked that night "at an old church where the Core and Maul Point roads intersect." On Saturday they returned to camp and remained until the following Thursday.[7]

During this interim Harry wrote to his father that he was "surprised that you had not received my letter concerning the recommendation which Gen. Hill & Gov. Vance had forwarded to Richmond. I wrote you immediately upon the receipt of your letter stating my intention to accept the position if offered me if I could have a proper understanding with Gen. Hill concerning the time & authority to be allowed me." Although Harry did not specifically say so, he had been recommended for promotion to a brigadier generalship.[8]

In the meantime, across the river to the north, General Garnett had approached Washington from the west to complete its encirclement. On 2 April, from his headquarters command post two miles from the town, he advised General Hill that his forces were "in front of and below the town," deeming "these the best positions to threaten the enemy and prevent his escape." His battery of four smoothbores was "from half to three-quarters of a mile from the enemy's works. I have not yet opened," Garnett reported, "because the guns are partially concealed, and the Yankees can concentrate on my artillery from ten to twelve guns of superior metal, some, if not all, rifled pieces. It is impossible to contend successfully with smooth-bores against guns intrenched and of superior range." If an investment of the town was to be followed by an attack, Garnett would have to take the lead. But he, like Colonel Harry Burgwyn, was satisfied that the Confederates were too deficient in long-range artillery to make a sustained attack.[9]

General Foster had no sooner arrived in the beleaguered town of Washington than all hands were put to work to strengthen the fortifications. The next two days, 31 March–1 April, would be critical for the Federals. Failing in his attempt to establish a battery on Rodman's Point, Foster was issued a summons by General Hill to surrender the town. He refused and dispatched a schooner to New Bern requesting reinforcements.[10]

Outnumbered and surrounded, the Federal garrison holed up in Washington faced an unpromising situation. During the first six days three expeditions up the Pamlico for the relief of Washington were planned and abandoned. And yet a few miles below the town there lay a large Federal flotilla of gunboats, steamers, and schooners, mounting considerable firepower and supporting twenty-five hundred infantrymen. They had been unable to move because of a combination of wind, water, and "Bluff."[11]

About this time, from his headquarters ten miles below Washington on the south side of the river, Harry was reasonably optimistic. The Federal fleet had been kept at bay, although one gunboat had slipped past.

He had heard that the enemy was advancing from New Bern, but "we have very considerable advantage in position if they land below the mouth of Blounts Creek. . . . I think Gen Hill is determined to take Washington now. He can do it if he collects sufficient heavy artillery. Until now we have relied entirely on the game of Bluff. Only think of a fleet, carrying from 20 to 30 heavy guns, brought to a complete standstill for 4 or 5 days by one 12 pd Whitworth & one 10 pd Parrot."[12]

The situation within the enemy's works, however, was beginning to brighten. On 8 April a correspondent for the Forty-fourth Massachusetts Volunteer Militia wrote: "Our chief ground of hope for release, in the case the rebel attack is longer deferred, is in the arrival of forces from Newbern, or from Suffolk overland. General Foster was looking for aid from General Dix yesterday. Of course the aid did not arrive—and it never does." But two days later, the correspondent was more hopeful: "Last night two schooners from Newbern, loaded with ammunition and forage, passed the blockade, and arrived here safely. Those in charge of the vessels inform us that a large force of infantry is on the way by land from Newbern."[13] The writer was unaware that this relieving column of some five thousand infantry, commanded by Brigadier General Francis Barrett Spinola, had been turned back at Blount's Mill only the night before. A lawyer and politician, without benefit of military training or service, Spinola had been appointed a brigadier general on 2 October 1862 simply because he had organized a brigade of four regiments.[14] Although third in command at New Bern, he was thrust into the role of leading the two expeditions, first by water and then by land, for the relief of Washington. Both efforts failed.

That same night Spinola wrote to his senior commander at New Bern. He had left Little Swift Creek at nine that morning, marched fifteen miles to Blounts Creek, found the enemy in an "almost impregnable" position at the mill dam, engaged him for about two hours, and, at 5:00 P.M., abruptly turned back. He explained that he "was obliged to return," because of the imminent presence of Pettigrew's troops as well as a large Confederate army further on.[15]

Colonel Harry Burgwyn was at Blounts Creek. On Thursday, 9 April, he wrote in his daily journal:

> Gen Pettigrew held them in check in front, Gen Hill would pounce down upon their rear. I never knew a more pusilanimous effort. They advanced very rapidly with many promises of sleeping in Washington that night & etc. & after a little skirmish, for it amounted to little more, they retreated in great

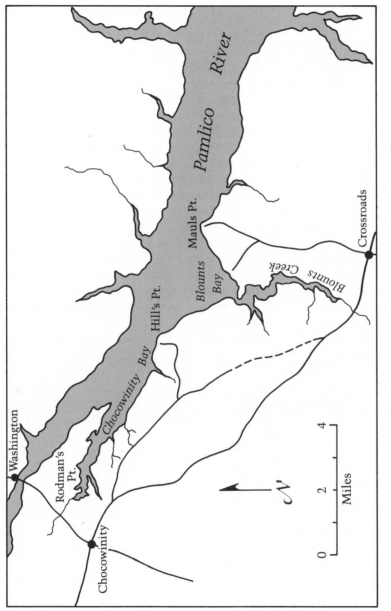

Siege area around Washington, North Carolina, south of the Pamlico River

haste & trepidation. They had about 19 Rgts of Inf. & 22 pieces of Artillery. As well as we can find out they lost a Colonel killed whom they called one of their best men & probably 30 or 40 men killed & wounded: we had only one killed & some one or two wounded.[16]

About the time that General Spinola was attempting to relieve Washington, the final moves of the winter campaign in the Southeast were being made. On both sides, the strategy had developed slowly during the winter and early spring. The Federals were determined to breach the defenses of Charleston and to disrupt the Confederate supply lines in eastern North Carolina. For their part, the Confederates had no choice but to defend Richmond, Charleston, and other strategic points at all costs. In the general theater of operations between Richmond and Charleston, however, neither side enjoyed a preponderance of strength. For that reason, the Federals could not venture far from their bases, and the Confederates could not spread their defending forces too thin. Although each planned and campaigned actively, neither had much to show for its efforts by the end of April—just before the opening of the spring campaign on the Rappahannock.

Nonetheless, as April began, the unfolding drama was rapidly approaching a climax. The long-awaited assault on Charleston, which ended in failure, took place on the afternoon of 7 April. The failure at Charleston immediately posed a problem for North Carolina: would Wilmington or New Bern be the next point of attack? Longstreet was concerned about the concentration of Federal forces in eastern Virginia. Getting much needed supplies of food and forage from the eastern counties of Virginia and North Carolina was a hazardous undertaking, with the Federals strongly poised in the Norfolk-Suffolk area and at New Bern.

If General Hill committed himself too heavily at Washington, protection of the Wilmington and Weldon Railroad at Goldsboro could be jeopardized. Therefore, when Hill invested Washington, his troop deployment was determined by potential threats to Greenville, Kinston, and Goldsboro from the Federal forces at New Bern. He required assistance from Longstreet, which would weaken the latter's ability to defend Petersburg or mount a major offensive across the Blackwater River against Suffolk. Furthermore, General Lee, standing in front of Hooker at Fredericksburg, could not afford to have either Longstreet or Hill heavily engaged as he prepared to meet a new onslaught against Richmond.

It is in the context of these interrelated responsibilities that the quality of information furnished the authorities assumes significance. False rumors, misstatements of fact, misunderstandings, misinterpretation, and delays in transmission all played some role in shaping the success or failure of any given strategy.

General Foster was still in Washington, daily strengthening its defenses. His mission was clear—to raise the siege. He seemed to be unencumbered by doubt, indecision, or conflicting directives. On 30 March he had boldly sailed up the Pamlico and cast his lot with the beleaguered garrison. Nearly two weeks later, he was about to make another bold decision. On the night of 13 April, the steam transport *Escort*, "with hay bales placed on her guards and decks as a protection," ran the batteries and safely reached Washington. On board were the Fifth Rhode Island Volunteers and "a plentiful supply of ammunition and commissary stores." As she passed the batteries, sixty shots were fired at her, but none hit the target. That same night two small schooners also ran the blockade and brought in additional supplies of ammunition and commissary stores.[17]

The following day Foster decided to leave Washington. "Regarding everything as safe in the town, and the re-enforcements and men, with the supplies of ammunition and provisions, as ample until I could raise the siege," he later reported, "I determined to run the blockade and place myself at the head of the relieving force in order to insure more efficiency in its conduct. I therefore embarked on board the *Escort* for the purpose of running the batteries at night, but the pilot could not distinguish the necessary marks to proceed by and therefore waited for the daylight." At dawn on 15 April, the *Escort* got under way and successfully ran the batteries. Although shot at one hundred times and struck forty times, she passed the Rodman's and Hill's Point batteries without suffering material damage. That same day General Hill abandoned the siege of Washington and started his withdrawal.[18]

On 21 April, from his headquarters at Adams Bridge in Greene County, Harry Burgwyn appraised the Washington expedition:

> Gen Hill, as I wrote you, started from Greenville trusting almost entirely to two 12 pd. Whitworth guns to whip the Yankee gunboats, & either sink them or make them surrender, & then to keep off, by their aid, any reinforcements from reaching Washington by water.
>
> I do not know whether he intended to take the place or not. If its capture was his object, his mistake was first: not providing

adequate means. He had no commissary, or Qt.Master, or Ordnance officer, & the troops were therefore subject to a great many more inconveniences than they should have been. He did not provide any reserve train of ammunition & various other necessary articles. Secondly he set out without any definite plan. He should either have made up his mind to storm the place at once, or he should have been prepared to undertake a regular siege. In the 1st case all the troops should have been silently & quickly carried upon the north side of the river, & the town itself attacked the morning after we had left Greenville. In the 2nd place, he should have had a very large siege train with plenty of ammunition.

It is an absolute fact that we were out of ammunition the very first day of the siege. Our guns & ammunition came in by driblets, a gun to day & 50 rounds of ammunition to morrow, then a rumor that another gun was on its way. Two or three days would elapse & then perhaps the gun itself would make its appearance. The grand fault was the absence of any definite plan. It seemed to me that Gen. Hill relied upon circumstances & events to suggest ideas & plans. I think he has lost the confidence of the people entirely, & to a very great extent of the army.[19]

On 23 April General Hill provided his explanation of the failure at Washington. In a letter to General Pettigrew, he, too, blamed the lack of ammunition, asserting, "I think that more treachery than stupidity exists in the Ordnance Department."[20]

All that was accomplished by the ill-fated siege of Washington was the gathering of food supplies. The day that Hill lifted the siege, General Garnett sent him a dispatch advising that his last train had just arrived from the Pungo. "It brings up," Garnett reported, "65 barrels of corn and about 8,000 pounds of bacon. Of this lot 2,000 pounds came from Hyde. Captain Swindell, who sent agents into Hyde, reports that most of the bacon remaining in that country is in the hands of persons who have taken the oath of allegiance, and they will not sell it unless it is impressed."[21]

For Harry Burgwyn the last days of April were not unlike many other days during the previous several weeks, filled with seemingly endless rumors, generally conflicting, and almost always followed by alerts, marches, and countermarches. On 23 April, back at Hookerton as he had surmised, Harry complained of forced marches as he and his command moved back and forth over the swampy roads of eastern North Carolina in early spring with little to eat and no change of clothing. Noting that his commissary would shortly call at their house in Raleigh, Harry requested that his mother send him some handkerchiefs along with his summer clothing—his "white linen jacket 2 pair of thin drawers & 2 pair of thin undershirts"— reminding her that he would send home by express his winter clothing. Feeling that the advent of spring promised some relief from the daily fare of crackers and dried meat, Harry asked his father to send him his "rifle pistol" so that he could "kill terrapins & bull frogs as a variation to my diet."[22]

There was every indication that Harry approached the spring campaign with confidence. As in the past, he was not reticent in advising his father on plantation matters. "I have heard," he wrote, "that you wanted to sell your cotton. I should be very reluctant to do it were I you. Cotton will be worth $1.50 a pound after the war. If you do sell it, I think I would invest in land & negroes. Why not buy Alveston? I suppose your cotton will bring you from 50 to 70,000 dollars & Alveston could be bought for 200,000. I think negroes will be worth 3 to 4000 dollars after the war."[23]

Whether Harry's confidence in the future of the Confederacy was the product of wishful thinking or born of the conviction that he and the men around him could whip the Yankees every time is difficult to determine. But certain it is that he and the men of the Twenty-sixth North Carolina had great pride in the staying power and fighting ability of their regiment. They were obviously anticipating combat when Harry wrote: "My officers are anxious to purchase a silk Rgt. flag, not a state flag, but a battle flag. Please ascertain what we would have to pay for it, & where it could be made. The health of my Rgt. is remarkably good. On yesterday I had 1020 men present, more I suppose than any Rgt. in the C.S."[24]

Nowhere was Harry's pride in his regiment more meaningfully expressed than in his report to General Pettigrew on "the transactions of my command from the 30th March to the 21st April 1863" in which he concluded: "I take great pleasure Gen'l. in testifying to the uniform cheerfulness & alacrity of my entire command from the time we left Goldsboro, N.C. on the 9th March until the present date. I have not heard a murmur or complaint of any kind whatsoever. Exposed during this period of 6 weeks to all the inclemencies of the weather without a change of underclothing subsisting on meagre rations & called upon to perform arduous marches & much work both officers & men have displayed a fortitude & endurance of hardships which have not been surpassed by any troops during the war."[25]

Hawkeye and Kincian (courtesy Burgwyn family)

On the last day in April Harry wrote to his mother, "I am much of the opinion that we will very soon, perhaps in less than a week, return to Virginia. My idea is that Hooker, if he has not already crossed the Rappahannock, will very soon do so; that then Lee will administer to him a most tremendous thrashing; then cross the Rappahannock above Fredericksburg, turn Hooker's right flank, & call to his aid all the troops or nearly all in Southern Va. & N.C. & S.C. to push right into Maryland & Pennsylvania. So I expect to see Old Virginny once more." With Harry would go his beloved body servant, Kincian.[26]

He did not have long to wait. The next morning his regiment was ordered two miles below Kinston, where it halted in line of battle to intercept a rumored approach of the enemy. After an hour or more, "all of a sudden," Harry wrote his mother, "orders came for us to start this evening for Richmond." He expected that they would stop at Petersburg to wait for Longstreet's troops to reach Richmond. But he added, "We may however go right on to Fredericksburg. However it may be all will be for the best."[27] Harry's train left Goldsboro at

10:00 P.M., Friday, 1 May, and sometime during the night, near Halifax, was involved in a serious accident. "The train containing the right wing of my Rgt.," Harry recorded in his journal, "was stopped to pass the mail train & the one on which I was [riding] stopped some three hundred yards behind it. While we were thus stationary the train with the 11th N.C. ran into us killing one man, mortally wounding another, & severely wounding some 8 or 9 more. We were detained at Halifax till 2 P.M. [Saturday]. Reached Petersburg at 11 P.M. & marched rapidly through the town & took the cars for Richmond."[28]

During this enforced layover at Halifax for part of the day on Saturday, 2 May, Harry and his brigade commander, James Johnston Pettigrew, shared a noon meal together at the Willie Jones house in Halifax. Although both officers anticipated early action in Virginia, neither knew of General Lee's daring maneuvers to thwart General Hooker's advance on Richmond, nor, as they rested on Saturday, 2 May, that Stonewall Jackson was, at that very moment, marching around Hooker's right flank to his greatest and last victory. Jackson was mortally wounded that evening.

Pettigrew and Burgwyn did not reach Richmond until five the next morning and immediately received orders to proceed to the "Fred[er]icksburg] R.R. Bridge over the North Anna River & protect it to the last extremity." It was not until Monday morning, 4 May, that Harry "heard the glorious news that Gen. Lee had entirely defeated the Yankees near Chancellorsville, but our joy was dashed by the news that Gen. Jackson was severely wounded." At the same time, he learned that "the Yankee Cavalry which was at Ashland did not exceed 450 men: also that after proceeding to Hanover C.H. they returned towards Louisa C.H. passing within 2 & a half miles of this place." The next day Harry noted in his journal that "we have very little reliable information from Stoneman & his cavalry. A portion of them skirted Richmond crossed the Chickahominy & went out by the White House." By 6 May hundreds of wounded Confederates were passing through Hanover Junction en route to Richmond. "I see a good many of my friends who are wounded," Harry recorded, "& from what I can hear this has been the most terrific fight of the war. The Yankees are said to have fought very well but our troops to have fought desperately."[29]

On Friday, 8 May, Harry wrote to his mother about the great victory at Chancellorsville:

Our army has not suffered so much as I thought at first, & our victory is certainly of a very decisive character. Added to the fact that from 30 to 40,000 of Hooker's men go out [termination of enlistment] within the next fortnight, I hope this battle will puzzle the Abolition government not a little. The first dispatches which went to the North & Europe will unquestionably claim a great victory [Union]. The fact of their taking Marye['s] heights will be heralded to the world as a great & decisive triumph. . . . I saw 2,000 prisoners march past here today. 2,000 more will come tomorrow, & a like number the next day. Then they will come down in smaller detachments. A good proportion are foreigners. From what I can learn from them few if any of the men, whose times are now expiring will reenlist. They say Lincoln made them a big speech asking them to enlist, but it was "nary go."[30]

The battle of Chancellorsville was a "glorious victory" for Southern arms. Although outnumbered almost three to one, Lee had never wavered in his calm determination to stand at Fredericksburg and fight it out on the Rappahannock line. It was there that the fateful campaign of 1863 was opened; and it was there, in tandem with the peerless Jackson, that General Lee fashioned "the master-piece of his military life." They were pitted against Major General "Fighting Joe" Hooker, who had succeeded Burnside in command of the Army of the Potomac on 26 January. According to one historian, Hooker was "an immense braggart," had been fiercely critical of McClellan's campaigns, and had "predicted certain capture of Richmond under his own leadership."[31] His plan of attack was masterful, but he failed utterly against the combination of Lee and Jackson.

On Saturday, 9 May, Harry was in a reflective mood when he noted in his journal: "1260 more Yankee prisoners passed down the Rail Road this morning. I watched them as they filed past & could not help contrasting their good uniform[s] & shoes with our ragged & dirty uniform[s]. They were physically a stout set of men quite as much so as ours but they evidently lacked the spirit & courage which our men possess. Under Divine guidance the skill of our leaders & the courage of our soldiery has gained us so many victories. A dreadful report that Gen. Jackson is doing badly reached us today. May God spare the old hero to lead us on to victory again."[32]

But Harry's fervent hope would not be realized. Jackson died the following day. In the end, there was nothing left for General Lee but to express the same fervent hope, as he wrote his brother Charles Carter Lee, that "Jackson's spirit 'will be diffused over the whole Confederacy.'"[33] The battle of Chancellorsville was unquestionably a monumental victory for the South, but the death of Jackson was an irreparable blow. This costly victory was made no less so by the comparative losses of the two armies. Although Lee's total casualties were approximately forty-five hundred less than those of Hooker, the South could ill afford the loss of almost thirteen thousand men, including a heavy toll of general officers.[34] In the long run, "the skill of our leaders & the courage of our soldiery," as Harry hopefully believed, would not suffice to counter such frightful attrition in victory after victory.

Although dealt a shattering blow, Hooker had not been destroyed. The Army of the Potomac was still intact and still a menace to Richmond, so Lee could lose little time in reorganizing and strengthening the Army of Northern Virginia. This task would occupy the remainder of the month of May. In the meantime, Harry and his Twenty-sixth North Carolina remained in position at or near Hanover Junction to protect both the railroad and the bridge over the North Anna. His letters and daily journal entries during this period provide insight into his view of the progress of the war, future strategy, the spirit of Lee's army, conditions within the ranks, and his own future ambitions.

On 10 May, in one of his infrequent letters to his sister Maria, Harry appealed for her assistance in procuring a new flag for his regiment:

> The Confederate Congress having in the plenitude of their legislative wisdom, determined to change our flag, & having absolutely settled its final character, I am very desirous of testifying my appreciation of its beauty by procuring one of silk for my Rgt.
>
> The officers of the Rgt. are perfectly willing to subscribe any amount to purchase the material, but it is not to be found. Can you not therefore, among your many female acquaintances, & among my many feminine admirers, find some one sufficiently enthusiastic in her admiration & withal sufficiently patriotic to devote her dress to the sacrifice? . . . The red silk should be of the deepest crimson color, & the blue very prominent.[35]

A few days later, Harry was evidently concerned about a possible enemy attack. In a long letter to his father, he commented upon the defenseless nature of Richmond during the recent battle of Chancellorsville:

> This latter place can never be left as defenceless as during the recent battle. There was one portion of the memorable Sunday when not a single soldier was in the city. During the evening

the 11 N.C. Rgt. of our Brigade came in. It is an actual fact that some Yankee cavalry rode with impunity within 3 miles of the City. You can not conceive the excitement in town. The Israelites were loudly appealed to & the guarding of both Yankee prisoners & our own was entrusted to boys raked & scraped together.[36]

On 19 May, "somewhat anxious about Vicksburg," Harry wrote his mother that in the event Vicksburg should fall, "our proper policy would be to concentrate all the Army of the west & the troops on our coast with the Army of Northern Va. & strike out North. . . . I believe the adoption of this policy would end the war in 6 months."[37] Two days later, when referring to the Army of Northern Virginia as "our Army of the Potomac," and after providing his father with estimates of General Lee's new strength, Harry seemed convinced that Hooker's demoralized forces did not have a chance and that Lee could whip "anything in Yankeedom":

Gen Lee is upon the point of advancing to attack Hooker. He is gathering his forces & everybody believes with an eye single to whipping Hooker. That he will do this I have no doubt in the world. When the achievements of our Army of the Potomac are written by an impartial historian I believe they will compare favorably with those of the Romans or of Napoleon's Old Guard. From what I can understand Lee did not have a man over 48,000 at the late battle of the Wilderness [Chancellorsville] & the Yankees did not have less than 130,000.

A great many troops have gone on to Gen Lee since the battle & he is now much stronger than before the fight came off. . . . Thus you see Gen Lee will have from 27,500 [33,500] to 37,500 reinforcements. Call his force before the battle at (in round numbers) 50,000 men & his losses 5 to 7,000. The slightly wound[ed] have already returned to duty. His force now would be from 70,500 [76,500] to 82,500 say in round numbers 80,000 men. These are effective men, all present for duty. . . . Hooker's army will not be in as good a condition as it was before the fight for 6 months to come. . . . Taken all these things into consideration my opinion is that 6 weeks will find Gen Lee's army in Maryland. . . . My opinion is that Gen Lee will be quiet until about the 1st of June.[38]

On 28 May, still preoccupied with the fate of Vicksburg, weary with war, and deeply disconsolate, Harry confessed to his mother:

God alone knows how tired I am of this war, & He alone knows when it will end. I am sure that no day in my life will be hailed by me with the same degree of delight as that on which I hear the blessed tidings of peace assured. You have no idea how exhausted everything is. We get nothing but commissary salt meat to eat & a messenger whom I have had yesterday & to day in search of a shoat or mutton has just returned & reports that he can only find one half grown, half starved mutton. . . . It would not be so bad I suppose but that so many troops are now camped around here. I suppose 12,000 men are in this immediate vicinity, & the locusts of old never searched a country with one half of the devouring ferocity that these men display to anything fresh to eat.[39]

Between 10 and 28 May, Harry made no daily entries in his journal but summarized this period in a general statement, probably entered on 28 May. Focusing primarily on the larger theaters of operation, he concluded:

Our affairs are everywhere in the East in the most prosperous condition. In the South West they appear to be less satisfactory. I can not understand why it is but upon that zone of operations we appear to get along much worse than here. The Pa. Inquirer received in Richmond yesterday says that Vicksburg has been taken & blazes the announcement in the most terrifically huge type. Aint it a wonder we dont give right up before such huge capitals. No one here gives the least credit to what it says & an abiding faith is felt that the Lord will give our leaders the skill & our men the courage to weather this storm also. We look upon the situation as critical in the extreme but are hopeful of the final result.[40]

The following day, Sunday, 31 May, Harry wrote a long letter to his father. It concerned a matter of great personal importance. Earlier in the spring Harry had been led to believe that he was being considered for promotion to brigadier general and that Governor Vance and General D. H. Hill had actively supported his candidacy. Hill was now in command of the Department of Southern Virginia and North Carolina, so Harry thought he would be able to effect the promotion if he wished to. He asked his father to make tactful inquiries about the matter. Noting that in the battles around Fredericksburg, North Carolina had suffered heavier losses than any other state, yet "not one of her sons has been promoted in consequence," he felt that "our

State is systematically slighted by the Presdt & his advisers." Referring directly to the idea of his own promotion, he wrote:

> It is moreover a cardinal point with me never to lose an opportunity. I cannot say that I have any expectation of promotion now or very soon, but during the summer in all probability I will be engaged in some of the great battles which will undoubtedly occur in this state, & after one of these the time would be favorable for pressing the claims which now we merely call attention to. In case of promotion I shall make every effort to be transferred to N.C. both because an opportunity for distinction is much greater there than in a large army & because any success will be much more appreciated & will conduce much more to my future success & perhaps political influence should the end of the war find me in the land of the living.
>
> I do not believe Gen. Pettigrew will be promoted soon. He has done nothing to deserve it & he appears to hold himself too much aloof from everybody. To be sure he has a very fine Brigade, but everybody in the Brigade knows that he is not entitled to one particle of the credit for it. To the Rgt. commanders, & the good material, & to these causes alone, is the excellence of the Brigade owing. For instance Gen. P. has never come to my camp but once or twice since I have been in the Brigade. He has never reviewed the Brigade but once & he holds himself as much aloof as if he were a Mj. General. His Headquarters now are over 2 miles from my camp & although we receive orders by couriers enough to keep us continually bothered he personally judges of nothing & personally does nothing.[41]

CHAPTER 20

AND NOW I MUST BID YOU GOOD BYE

By 1 June, as Harry had predicted, it was evident that a major Confederate movement was imminent. On 5 June he wrote his mother:

We are still stationary though expecting to receive orders at any moment. It appears that we are on an important movement & all the troops will probably be required at the front. I know no more than you what movements are on foot but something important is expected. Some think Gen Lee is going to threaten Washington & draw Hooker's force away from Fredericksburg & then take up the old Manassas position during the summer. He will thus deliver the Valley of the Rappahannock from the enemy & be able to graze his stock upon the grass of Fauquier & Loudoun Counties. He has received very considerable reinforcements since the late battle & his whole army is in most excellent condition. Hood's Division joined him very soon after the battle of the Wilderness or Chancellorsville & is now said to be at Raccoon Ford on the Rapidan.

The whole Army of Northern Va. as it is called is now divided into three Army Corps; commanded by Lt. Gens Longstreet [1st Corps], A. P. Hill [3d Corps] & Ewell [2d Corps]. Our Brigade [Pettigrew's] has been assigned to Gen Heath's [Heth's] Division A. P. Hill's Corps. The other Brigades of our Division are Archer's—Walker's & Cook's Brigade which may perhaps now be in N.C. but which from what I have just told you must be under orders to come to this state. The other Divisions of our Corps are Pender's & R. H. Anderson's formerly my old Division around Richmond. I think that our Corps is now on the extreme right below Fredericksburg some distance though I am not positive even of this. I feel almost certain that we will leave here pretty soon. . . . Continue to direct your letters to Hanover Junction until you hear from me that we have left. Then direct them to Richmond but put the Brigade (Pettigrew's) Division (Heath's) & Corps (Hill's) in plain letters. The irregularity of the mails now is a constant & just reproach to our authorities.[1]

On 6 June, Harry's regiment was ordered to Fredericksburg. They arrived there about two the following afternoon "& were immediately put into position in the 2nd line of battle. We found our corps in line of battle & some Yankees on this side of the river, estimated at from 13 to 15 Rgts. They were shelling Marye's Heights but we were not replying. They ceased after a while & everything is quiet. No one expects that the Yanks will attack us here. The bulk of our army is up at Culpepper where Gen Lee himself is." On 10 June his brigade was detached from Henry Heth's division and moved down the river road below Hamilton's Crossing. He was still thinking about the possibility of a promotion, although he did not intend to press for it, believing that "if the campaign in Virginia is as active as it promises to be there will be sufficient vacancies & sufficient opportunities."[2]

Writing to his father on 15 June, Harry expressed surprise at discovering that morning that the Federal army had left its position near Fredericksburg.

In the same letter he again urged his father to consider buying young Negroes as an investment for the future.[3] These repeated suggestions indicate that even in mid-1863, Harry still expected the Confederacy to triumph or, at least, slavery to survive. Since the day General Lee assumed field command, had not the Army of Northern Virginia won incredible victories? Within twelve months Lee had thwarted McClellan before Richmond, driven the hapless Pope back on Washington, fought McClellan to a draw at Sharpsburg, delivered a crushing blow to Burnside at Fredericksburg, and, most recently, dramatically outmaneuvered Hooker to win a "glorious victory" at Chancellorsville.

And yet, considering his intelligence and understanding, one wonders if he must not have had occasional misgivings about the ultimate fate of the Confederacy. Although the Army of Northern Virginia had been almost uniformly victorious since the battle of First Manassas, Harry must have realized what attrition in men and matériel would do to its future effectiveness. In spite of Confederate victories, the Yankees seemed to linger and keep coming back for more—and always stronger. Their manpower and matériel seemed inexhaustible. But there were other theaters of conflict and other Confederate armies. Harry had followed their fortunes with keen interest, particularly in the Southwest. All was not well in that sector, and May of 1863 found him deeply concerned about the fate of Vicksburg.

There the Yankees had been no less persistent than in other theaters. The Union navies under David G. Farragut and David Porter had all but succeeded in gaining control of the Mississippi from Cairo to New Orleans. Only Port Hudson and Vicksburg stood in their way. And now Grant had crossed the river below Vicksburg in an effort to capture the city from the east. By 14 May James B. McPherson's and William T. Sherman's Corps of Ulysses S. Grant's army had occupied Jackson after General Johnston's withdrawal to the north with his small Confederate force of twelve thousand. On 16 May General John C. Pemberton, marching out from Vicksburg, attempted to form a junction with Johnston but was intercepted by Federal forces at Champion's Hill, about midway between Jackson and Vicksburg. The hill changed hands three times in heavy fighting, but by late afternoon Pemberton was forced to fall back on Vicksburg. Three days later, Grant made his first assault on Vicksburg but failed to penetrate the works at any point. On 22 May the Federals launched a heavier and more sustained attack along a three-mile line but again were repulsed with heavy losses. The deep ravines over which the men had to charge to reach the heavily defended fortifications made the attempt almost suicidal. That was Grant's last assault, and the siege of Vicksburg had begun.[4] As for Grant's likelihood of success, Harry Burgwyn probably shared the view of his moderate friends, who believed "we will eventually save the place & drive Grant off without however, any very decisive victory."[5]

But the euphoria of the moment, following the victory at Chancellorsville, was such that Harry and others "in well informed quarters" felt that "if Vicksburg should fall our proper policy would be to concentrate all the Army of the west & the troops on our coast with the Army of Northern Va. & strike out North. . . . I believe the adoption of this policy would end the war in 6 months."[6] This view indicates that he still believed the South would eventually win her war for independence but that victory could come within a matter of months if the Confederacy should mount a major invasion of the North.

General Lee also contemplated the possibility and even necessity of an early termination of the war, through negotiation if need be, for he knew the Confederacy's supply of men was diminishing, giving the North an increasing advantage. He urged President Davis to consider negotiating a peace should the North propose terms.[7] Even the *Richmond Enquirer* editorialized, "It surely must be plain at last that this is to be a war of extermination. Sooner or later we have to accept it upon this footing."[8] These words suggest despair, especially coming from the *Richmond Enquirer*, known for its strongly partisan, secessionist views. And it is singular that this editorial was reprinted, in full and without criticism, in the *North Carolina Standard*, long an editorial adversary of the *Enquirer*. Their editorial exchanges were frequent and caustic; W. W. Holden, editor of the *Standard* and a self-proclaimed conservative, was tireless in his denunciation of the Democrats or secessionists, whom he labeled the "destructives." Almost from the beginning of the war, Holden had been an uncompromising critic of the Confederacy. He constantly hammered away at the theme of "a rich man's war and a poor man's fight." Although he did not openly advocate disloyalty, the net result of his persistent badgering of the Confederate government and the Democrats was to encourage disaffection at home and desertion in the ranks. By mid-1863, the seeds of disaffection were being persistently nourished throughout the South by conscription, mounting casualties, the burning of cotton, impressment, privation, hunger, and a sense of abandonment in some quarters. For these reasons, Holden may have welcomed the editorial from the *Richmond Enquirer* for publication in North Carolina. The despairing tone undoubtedly suited his purposes and would soon be put to good use.

Perhaps the greatest concentration of disloyal elements and organized resistance to the Confederacy was in the mountain areas of South Carolina, Georgia, and Alabama, eastern Tennessee, western North Carolina, and southwestern Virginia. Here the people were relatively poor and fiercely independent. They had little in common with the plantation South, and some Unionists were in open rebellion even before the end of 1861. It was about this time that the secret Order of the Heroes of America is believed to have been conceived for the purpose of organizing the disloyal elements in eastern Tennessee and the border counties of North Carolina. When Holden became actively identified with the order is not known, but within weeks after the *Enquirer* editorial was reprinted, the Order of the Heroes of America, with Holden's backing, was promoting peace meetings throughout North Carolina, particularly in the central and western portions. He intended for the meetings to appear spontaneous, but one observer characterized them as having been "issued from the same mint, the common stamp being that North Carolina has not received due justice or credit, that she has done more than her share, and that her people ought to contribute no further."[9]

Governor Vance had been troubled by the problem of desertion ever since the beginning of his administration, and it was becoming increasingly worse—in spite of his proclamation of 28 January, which decreed, in effect, that any soldier, absent without proper leave, who did not return to duty by 10 February, would be "tried for desertion, and upon conviction, be made to suffer death." By May General Lee was forced to advise Secretary Seddon "that the North Carolina troops in his army would soon be greatly reduced unless their desertion could be stopped immediately."[10] Lee also communicated his concern to General Pettigrew, who dispatched to Governor Vance letters sent to soldiers from home inducing them to desert. Pettigrew accompanied the letters with an appeal:

> General Lee telegraphs me that men from our State are deserting every day carrying off guns and ammunition. I fear the thing has gone to such an extent that requires the axe to be laid to the root of the tree. . . . A certain class of soldiers is influenced by this condition of public opinion. They are told, as you see by the letters, that they can desert with impunity: that the militia officers will not do their duty; that they can band together and defy the officers of the law, while their comrades are fighting the enemy. . . . The great majority of my brigade would shoot a deserter as quick as they would a snake, but our place is here and not in the rear.[11]

The problem of disloyalty in North Carolina was undoubtedly exacerbated by Chief Justice Richmond M. Pearson's belief that the conscription law was unconstitutional. As a consequence, he was not known to have refused a writ of habeas corpus "to secure the release of conscripts, deserters, or anyone accused of disloyalty." Governor Vance may have unwittingly contributed to the problem. An avowed believer in the writ, he refused to bring any pressure upon the courts and declared that he was bound by his oath to sustain Pearson, thereby providing a cloak of security to deserters and to men like Holden and his followers who favored peace at any price. Vance and Holden would later sever political relations. Holden would challenge Vance for the governorship the following year and be virtually destroyed politically when the treasonable purposes of the Order of the Heroes of America were exposed.[12]

Disloyalty in North Carolina probably was not much worse than in some of the other Confederate states, but publicly it was more pronounced. Early in the war President Lincoln had selected North Carolina as a likely candidate for reconstruction and readmission to the Union, and as the war progressed, thousands of deserters from several states sought refuge in her western mountains. More important, perhaps, the state and Confederate authorities were constantly at odds, and the Davis administration openly "blamed Vance, Holden, Judge Pearson and other Conservative leaders for the 'disaffection' in North Carolina."[13] They, in turn, complained openly and bitterly of unfair treatment by the authorities in Richmond. There would even be talk of the state's desertion of the Confederacy. The proximity of North Carolina to Virginia and the large concentration of Carolinians in the Army of Northern Virginia undoubtedly magnified the growing discontent and sense of estrangement felt by the people of North Carolina.

But there is no evidence, in May and June of 1863, that Harry Burgwyn was concerned with disloyalty within his own command. In his report to General Pettigrew covering the activities of the Twenty-sixth North Carolina during the arduous spring campaign in eastern North Carolina, the colonel had acclaimed the fortitude and endurance of his officers and men. A few days later, after having watched several hundred Yankee prisoners file past on their way from Chancellorsville to Richmond, Harry observed: "They were physically a stout set of men quite as much so as ours but they evidently lacked the spirit & the courage which our men possess."[14] Clearly, Harry had full confidence in the courage and patriotism of his command. Within days, however, this confidence would be put to the supreme test.

On Monday, 15 June, the Twenty-sixth North Carolina, bearing its new Confederate battle flag, left Marye's Heights for the last time as it marched westward to an unknown destination.[15] It must have been during the afternoon of the seventeenth, from his temporary encampment just beyond Culpeper, that Harry wrote his last letter:

My last letter was written to father from Fredericksburg. We (our Division) left Fredericksburg at 3 P.M. on Monday the 15th & marched that day about 9 miles: Camping some 2 miles from Chancellorsville. Left our bivouac at half past 3 the next morning & marched about 18 miles camping 12 miles from this place. We left our bivouac again at 4 A.M. this morning & reached Culpepper C.H. about 10. We are now bivouacing some 2 miles from the C.H. cooking rations & preparing to start on another tramp [illegible] tomorrow.

The day we left Fred[sbg] an order came round for every single trunk to be sent to the rear. Mine had to go with the rest. I sent it to Richmond by my sutler with instructions to express it to Raleigh. My name was on the cover in the largest sort of letters. I directed the sutler to be certain to take a receipt for it. So please look out for it at Raleigh. Today another order has come round for a rigid inspection of baggage which is to be reduced to the minimum prescribed by law. We probably will leave here by daylight in the morning & in the direction either of Leesburg or Winchester. We are ordered to have 3 days cooked rations in haversacks & 3 days more in the wagons. I suppose the division supply train will carry one or two days more. All this preparation means in my opinion a movement upon the largest scale.

Ewell's Corps took Winchester & captured a large amount of stores & trains & etc. I can give you nothing but reports from there. It is reported that he captured from 5 to 30,000 prisoners from 11 to 30 pieces of artillery & from ⅔ to all of his wagon train. The bulk of our army is now either there or preparing, in my opinion, to cross into Maryland. Of course we know & hear nothing here. But I judge by the fact that Gen Lee has now a larger army than he ever had before. From what I can understand he has about 90,000 effective men not counting what troops he may have had in the valley. He has a very large cavalry force, included in the above, of from 10 to 12,000 effective men & just as much of the very best artillery as can be managed. When 3 days rations will carry us to Winchester, why therefore would we be supplied with 6 or 7 days. We can march with the rations which we now have some 120 or 150 miles which would carry us some 60 or 80 miles into Maryland. It is possible that Gen Lee may be able to get 10,000 more troops in the valley which would give him a total of 100,000 effective men & no Yankee army can whip that when handled by Lee. He has completely deceived Hooker thus far. Lee is certainly making a very bold movement, but I think he will strike a tremendous & a successful blow.

When we left Fredericksburg one division was left, but I suppose that has already left. I doubt if the great battle takes place in Virginia. I think it will occur in Maryland. After we leave here I suppose that the difficulty of getting letters to the rear will prevent my writing except at long intervals. I shall have to be very guarded in my language lest some Yankee might get hold of my letter. Heaven only knows how when or where I will hear from you. Recollect to direct your letters to Richmond Va. & put Pettigrew's Brigade—Heth's Division—Hill's Corps. I suppose that once in a while I may be able to get a letter from there. I wish I could give you more news, but you have no idea how difficult it is to hear anything definitely & to get reliable information.

Troops are continually passing in every direction & going it appears in the most opposite directions & yet they all have one common aim one common destination. If my conjecture is correct about Maryland I think Gen Lee will cross the Potomac at two or three places. I have no idea that Gen Lee expects to stop in Maryland. I think he will essay Pennsylvania. His army is admirably organized & officered & has the most implicit confidence in him. The men are all in good spirits & the whole army expects to go into Pennsylvania. We have had little or no rain which makes the roads exceedingly dusty & a hot sun makes a long march the most disagreable thing conceivable. We lie down at night upon a single blanket & have a biscuit or two & piece of ham for each meal.

And now I must bid you good bye. What will be the result of the movement now on foot God alone can tell. I hope to be able to do my duty to the best of my ability & leave the result to His infinite wisdom & justice. What ever may be my own fate I hope to be able to feel & believe that all will turn out for the best. With my love to all I am Ever your Most Affectionate Son.[16]

It was appropriate that Harry's last letter should have been addressed to his mother, for a special bond existed between the two. From the time he had first gone off to school, his letters had consistently mirrored their deep mutual affection. Harry appreciated her love of learning and was sensitive to her tastes and desires. It was to her that he opened his heart before battle, and it was to her that he reported afterward—as though always seeking to justify her pride and confidence in him. Unquestionably, his mother's approval was Harry's guiding light in life, and his subsequent death in battle fulfilled his determination to be the noblest of sons. The concluding paragraph in this last letter to his mother would prove sadly prophetic.

By 17 June, Lee's strategy for invading the North was clearly unfolding. Ewell (Second Corps) had already crossed into the valley, routed Robert H. Milroy at Winchester, forced Daniel Tyler out of Martinsburg, crossed the Potomac at Shepherdstown, and was well on his way into Maryland. To mask this movement west of the Blue Ridge, Longstreet (First Corps) had moved north along the east side of the mountains, turned west through Ashby's Gap, and then north along the east bank of the Shenandoah River, where he had positioned himself to guard the passes through Ashby's and Snicker's gaps. General Anderson's lead division of A. P. Hill's Third Corps followed Longstreet's line of march out of Culpeper on the seventeenth. This division would be followed by Henry Heth's and William Dorsey Pender's divisions on succeeding days, all bearing west through Chester Gap into the valley, and then north along Ewell's general line of march through Charlestown and Shepherdstown into Maryland. Longstreet would later bear north through Berryville and Martinsburg, crossing the Potomac into Maryland at Williamsport.[17]

To prepare for this bold movement, much had been accomplished in a short period of time. After the death of Jackson, General Lee believed it essential to reorganize the Army of Northern Virginia. For some time he had felt that a corps of thirty thousand men was too large for one commander to handle, the First Corps (Longstreet) and Second Corps (Jackson) each having about that number of men. On 20 May he suggested to President Davis that Ewell be placed "in command of three divisions of Jackson's Corps, to take one of Longstreet's divisions, A. P. Hill's division, and form a division of Ransom's, Cooke's, and Pettigrew's brigades, and give the corps thus formed to A. P. Hill."[18]

Although not complete, this general plan of reorganization was formally announced within a few days. About the same time, field returns for the Army of Northern Virginia disclosed 67,858 men and officers present in the two corps, 8,193 in Stuart's Cavalry Division, and 5,503 in all artillery commands, making a total of all arms present of 81,568 (including fourteen general staff personnel).[19] Because reorganization entailed enlargement as well as reassignment of forces, it was here that Lee encountered considerable difficulty, particularly in North Carolina. If he was to assume the offensive and force Hooker off the Rappahannock line, additional strength would be required for his own army as well as for the defense of Richmond. From General D. H. Hill, in command of the department from the James to the Cape Fear River, Lee had requested "every man he could spare," believing that Hill had more than adequate forces for the protection of southside Virginia and eastern North Carolina. To this request Hill turned a deaf ear. In frustration, Lee appealed to the president to relieve him of control over Hill's department.[20]

Even without Hill's troops, Lee's army was relatively strong and its morale high. For his adversary north of the Rappahannock, the situation was different. The Army of the Potomac was still strong, but the crushing defeat suffered at Chancellorsville had left its mark. Although Hooker had apparently lost the confidence of some of his commanders, he early indicated his determination to resume the offensive. On 13 May he advised President Lincoln that his movements had been delayed by the withdrawal of many "of the two-years' and nine-months' regiments," but that his marching force of infantry was about eighty thousand strong and he hoped to commence his movement the following day. His primary concern at the moment was whether Longstreet was being retained for the defense of Richmond. If not, and if Longstreet had joined Lee, he would need a reserve infantry force of twenty-five thousand. Hooker considered the combination of the two as "much superior, besides having the advantage of acting on the defensive, which, in this country, can scarcely be estimated."[21]

Lincoln's response was immediate and to the point, clearly indicating that he would be entirely satisfied if Hooker did nothing more than put his own army in good condition again and keep the enemy at bay. "Still, if in your own clear judgment you can renew the attack successfully," the president concluded, "I do not mean to restrain you. Bearing upon this last point, I must tell you that I have some painful intimations that some of your corps and division commanders are not giving you their entire confidence. This would be ruinous, if true, and you should therefore, first of all, ascertain the real facts beyond all possibility of doubt."[22]

Hooker had also incurred the displeasure of General Heintzelman by suggesting that the twenty-five-thousand-man reserve force might be drawn from the troops in and around Washington and Baltimore. Heintzelman, commanding the forces at Washington, was of the decided opinion that no more troops could be spared. General Halleck strongly supported Heintzelman. He was not about to weaken the defenses of Washington in view of the uncertainties of the moment. Halleck expected Lee to maneuver in such a way that his intentions would be known only after he had struck. Halleck also argued that Hooker's force already heavily outnumbered Lee's. But Halleck admitted that Hooker reported directly to the president and did not inform him of his movements.[23] Responsibility for this failure to coordinate at the highest level of military authority was obviously Lincoln's. This must have been impressed upon him, for he shortly advised Hooker that "I now place you in the strict military relation to General Halleck of a commander of one of the armies to the general-in-chief of all the armies. I have not intended differently, but as it seems to be differently understood, I shall direct him to give you orders and you to obey them."[24]

While the Federal high command was bickering, Lee had dared and accomplished much. Morale was high, but, in the opinion of a noted historian, he was embarking upon his fateful march to Gettysburg with "two untried corps commanders, three of the nine divisions under new leaders, seven freshly promoted brigadier generals of infantry, six infantry brigades under their senior colonels, a third of the cavalry directed by officers who had not previously served with the Army of Northern Virginia, the artillery redistributed, the most experienced of the corps commanders [Longstreet] inflated with self-importance, above all, Jackson's discipline, daring, and speed lost forever to the army."[25]

Although the protection of Washington was obviously of primary concern, with the debacle of Second Manassas still fresh in memory, General Hooker's immediate reaction was to attack the enemy's rear as soon as he learned that Lee was moving westward from his old position on the Rappahannock. Believing that Lee had "it in mind to cross the Upper Potomac, or to throw his army between mine and Washington," Hooker advised Lincoln that he thought the best action would be to attack Lee's rear. Lincoln responded that if Lee was north of the Rappahannock, Hooker should not cross to the south of the river: "I would not take any risk of being entangled upon the river, like an ox jumped half over the fence and liable to be torn by dogs front and rear, without a fair chance to gore one way or kick the other." Halleck supported Lincoln by suggesting to Hooker "another contingency not altogether improbable—that Lee will seek to hold you in check with his main force, while a strong force will be detached for a raid into Maryland and Pennsylvania."[26]

On 10 June, emboldened by a successful Federal cavalry raid that had caught Stuart and his troopers by surprise near Brandy Station, Hooker again raised the question of crossing the Rappahannock and attacking the enemy in his rear. If Lee should make the contemplated raid into Maryland with a heavy force, Hooker suggested to Lincoln that there would be no "serious obstacle to my rapid advance on Richmond." In his usually cryptic style, Lincoln replied: "If left to me, I would not go south of Rappahannock upon Lee's moving north of it. . . . I think Lee's army, and not Richmond, is your sure objective point. If he comes toward the Upper Potomac, follow on his flank and on his inside track, shortening your lines while he lengthens his. Fight him, too, when opportunity offers. If he stays where he is, fret him and fret him." Asked by the president whether he agreed with his reply to Hooker, Halleck responded, "I do so fully."[27]

Paradoxically, Hooker was both impetuous and indecisive. It is not surprising that he did not enjoy the full confidence of his staff, and he must have sorely tried the patience of President Lincoln. His avoiding the appropriate chain of command and communicating directly with the president, rather than through the general-in-chief, H. W. Halleck, only exacerbated his problems. On 16 June General Hooker was clearly perturbed when he conceded that he did not enjoy Halleck's confidence and that "so long as this continues, we may look in vain for success, especially as future operations will require our relations to be more dependent upon each other than heretofore." [28]

It was following this message that Lincoln told Hooker that he would direct Halleck "to give you orders and you to obey them." But from then until 27 June, when he was relieved of command of the Army of the Potomac, Hooker's situation only worsened. Perhaps the crowning blow to his credibility came in his dispatch to General Halleck on 24 June, when he declared, "If the enemy should conclude not to throw any additional force over the river [Potomac], I desire to make Washington secure, and, with all the force I can muster, strike for his line of retreat in the direction of Richmond." Hooker concluded, "I request that my orders be sent me to-day, for outside of the Army of the Potomac I don't know whether I am standing on my head or feet." [29]

In light of this situation, Lee could not have selected an adversary better suited to his strategy. Although news of Lee's moves was reasonably accurate and timely, Hooker seemed never able to accept the fact that Lee was indeed bent upon a major invasion of the North— not just a raid—until it was almost too late. Hooker, however, was not to blame for the failure of the president and of the general-in-chief to coordinate their own policy actions and to establish a more efficient command structure.

CHAPTER 21

ROADS TO GETTYSBURG

It was still dark on the morning of 18 June when the Twenty-sixth North Carolina filed out of Culpeper on its way to the Shenandoah Valley.[1] Thus began the first of ten grueling days for Harry Burgwyn's command on the long march to Gettysburg. A. P. Hill's Third Corps was the last of Lee's army to pass into the valley. R. H. Anderson's division had left Culpeper on the seventeenth. Heth's division, with the Twenty-sixth North Carolina in the lead, followed the next day, and Pender's division brought up the rear on the nineteenth.

The Army of Northern Virginia was now clearly committed to an invasion of the North, its ultimate destination still unknown. Its purpose was to draw Hooker's army away from the Rappahannock, encourage the growing peace movement in the North, and gather as many provisions and supplies as possible. Lee had earlier conceded the risks inherent "in taking the aggressive with so large an army in its front, intrenched behind a river, where it cannot be advantageously attacked. Unless it can be drawn out in a position to be assailed," he wrote Secretary Seddon, "it will take its own time to prepare and strengthen itself to renew its advance upon Richmond, and force this army back within the intrenchments of that city. This may be the result in any event," he concluded; "still, I think it is worth a trial to prevent such a catastrophe."[2]

By 18 June Lee had succeeded in drawing the enemy away from his entrenchments on the Rappahannock and creating near panic in Maryland and Pennsylvania. On 15 June Governor Andrew G. Curtin of Pennsylvania had called out the militia and issued an urgent call for volunteers, claiming that the state capital was threatened. The next day, Secretary Stanton wired Curtin that "troops for your aid are to be forwarded speedily from the States of Maine, Massachusetts, Rhode Island, Vermont, New Jersey, and New York." It was A. G. Jenkins's cavalry raid into Pennsylvania that had sounded the alarm and created such consternation. General Darius N. Couch reported from Harrisburg that a mounted force of twelve to fifteen hundred had been seen at Chambersburg. Secretary Stanton urgently inquired whether any other rebel force had been seen in Pennsylvania. And General Hooker, far to the east at Fairfax Station, wired that "from all reports here, we might conclude that he [the enemy] covered all Western Pennsylvania and Maryland, or that he was not there at all."[3]

Uncertainty also prevailed at General Lee's headquarters. He did not know whether Hooker was moving toward Harpers Ferry or into Maryland by crossing the Potomac farther down the river. Longstreet's Corps still guarded the west side of the passes through the Blue Ridge, and Stuart's cavalry roamed to the east, always with a protective eye on Ashby's and Snicker's gaps. With Ewell well advanced into Maryland, Lee was obviously concerned lest the enemy "force a passage through the mountains" and cut Ewell off from the rest of the army. It was with this possibility in mind that he wrote Ewell: "I very much regret that you have not the benefit of your whole corps, for, with that north of the Potomac, should we be able to detain General Hooker's army from following you, you would be able to accomplish as much, unmolested, as the whole army could perform with General Hooker in its front."[4]

As the rear of Lee's army reached Berryville, anxiety for the safety of Richmond mounted. On the twenty-first, Arnold Elzey, in command of the city's defenses, claimed to be reliably informed that the enemy had twenty thousand men at Yorktown and intended to march on Richmond. On that same day, Secretary Seddon must have gained little comfort from a message from General D. H. Hill reporting that in his area there were only three regiments of cavalry to guard a three-hundred-mile front.[5] It must have been clear to Seddon that little support could be expected from south of Richmond.

Monday, 22 June, was a day of rest for Harry Burgwyn's regiment[6] but not for the general-in-chief of the Federal high command in Washington. Striving for a better-coordinated defense structure for Washington and Baltimore against the mounting threat from the south, Halleck advised Hooker that all of the Eighth Corps and of the Middle Department east of Cumberland were being placed under his command.[7]

For General Lee, 22 June was a critical day of decision. Fearing that General Hooker might "steal a march on us" by crossing the Potomac without Confederate knowledge, Lee addressed a fateful dispatch to his trusted cavalry commander, J. E. B. Stuart: "If you find that he [Hooker] is moving northward, and that two brigades can guard the Blue Ridge and take care of your rear, you can move with the other three into Maryland, and take position on General Ewell's right, place yourself in communication with him, guard his flank, keep him informed of the enemy's movements, and collect all the supplies you can for the use of the army. . . . All supplies taken in Maryland must be by authorized staff officers for their respective departments—by no one else. They will be paid for, or receipts for the same given to the owners."[8]

Lee's instructions to Stuart implied the dual responsibility of guarding Ewell's right flank and gathering supplies. Stuart's later actions suggest that he interpreted too literally the dual nature of his responsibility by failing to guard Ewell's right as he should have done. For Lee had specifically instructed him to maintain communication with Ewell and keep the latter informed of the enemy's movements. From General Lee's point of view there can be no doubt that his instructions emphasized primarily the protection of Ewell's right, only secondarily the collection of supplies. The same day, Lee wrote Ewell of his instructions to Stuart.[9] The Army of Northern Virginia would obviously need subsistence in enemy territory, but Lee could not have intended that it be deprived of the protective "eyes and ears" of cavalry.

On the following day, with particular concern for the safety of Richmond as well as for his own advantage, General Lee suggested to President Davis that at least some of the troops in North Carolina and those under Beauregard should be moved to Virginia to divert the enemy and protect Richmond.[10]

The invasion of the North had clearly begun, and there was ample evidence that the Confederates had crossed, and were crossing, the Potomac in force. From the Federal signal officer, atop Maryland Heights, came an alarming message: "Enemy have not yet crossed, but are encamped 2 miles south of Shepherdstown, on the Charlestown road. Are in force in Charlestown. A large camp can now be seen southeast of and near Berryville. Enemy have left Sharpsburg, in direction of Hagerstown. Sharpsburg is 2 miles from Shepherdstown." From Harrisburg, the same day, came news that "a force of the enemy's cavalry occupy Chambersburg." But from Fort Monroe, Virginia, the news was more encouraging. On 23 June General Dix advised Halleck that he had moved "a considerable force" up the York and would land at the White House the following day.[11]

The movement was obviously to threaten Richmond and to divert the Army of Northern Virginia from its intended invasion. This strategy of diversion was similar, of course, to General Lee's plan for stationing a force at Culpeper to threaten Washington while he was north of the Potomac. But there would be no material diversions. Both major armies were now on the march, groping for one another as they moved northward across the Potomac on opposite sides of

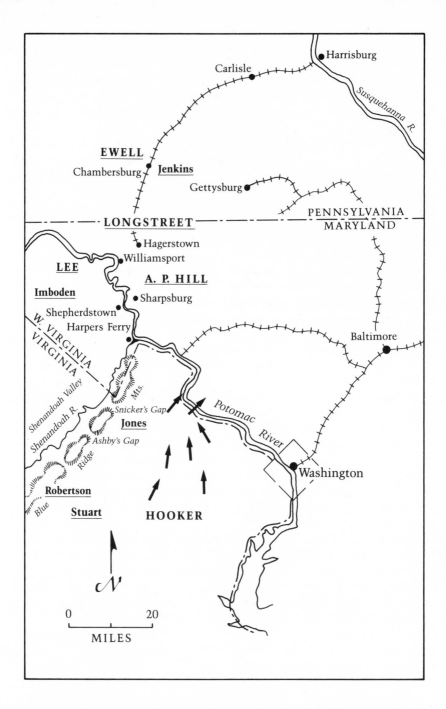

Gettysburg campaign, situation on 24 June 1863 (Civil War Atlas, adaptation, courtesy Department of History, U.S. Military Academy)

the mountains. The answer to when and where they would meet was not far off in point of time and distance.

Colonel Harry Burgwyn led his men across the Potomac, just below Shepherdstown, early Thursday morning, the twenty-fifth. The colonel's faithful bandsman and diarist, Julius Lineback, later wrote:

> We made an early start again, Sam still being sick and I not at all well. The Colonel ordered that in future as we were going into camp, we should play, "The Campbells Are Coming" and "The Girl I Left Behind Me" when leaving. Soon we came to the Potomac river, which was pretty wide and halfthigh deep. Taking off our shoes, socks, pants and drawers, we made a comical looking set of men. . . . We passed thru Sharpsburg at 12 and saw but two persons that showed themselves to be rebel sympathizers. Beyond the town was a church [Dunkard] that bore traces of the battle that was fought about it last fall. After a hard day's march we stopped about 5 o'clock within half a mile of Hagerstown.[12]

Having been ordered by General Lee on 21 June to take Harrisburg, Ewell had moved expeditiously in getting his three divisions into Pennsylvania. By the twenty-fifth, Jubal Early was at Greenwood on the Chambersburg pike, only a few miles west of Gettysburg and the divisions of Robert E. Rodes and Edward Johnson were with Ewell in the vicinity of Chambersburg. With his entire army now north of the Potomac it was natural that Lee's correspondence should reflect uneasiness and concern. From his headquarters on the south bank of the river across from Williamsport, he wrote two long letters to President Davis on the twenty-fifth. Both peace and war were on his mind as he reflected upon the peace movement at the North, the exposed position of Richmond to the south, and the exposed position of his own army because he had been compelled to abandon his communications. He urged that Beauregard's army be stationed at Culpeper to threaten Washington and thus divert Federal attention from his own invasion. The authorities in Richmond, however, their judgment strongly influenced by their insecurity, wanted additional protective forces stationed at Richmond—not at Culpeper. Secretary of War Seddon was convinced that Richmond was in imminent danger.[13]

General Lee's strategy was sound, and, if implemented earlier, might have averted the battle of Gettysburg. But as he worked in his headquarters "opposite Williamsport," it was too late. He had committed his entire army to the invasion. It was 25 June, and General Hooker was in the act of making his own commitment. To General

John F. Reynolds, now commanding the First, Third, and Eleventh Corps, and presently crossing the Potomac at Edwards' Ferry, Hooker sent detailed instructions.[14]

Unbeknownst to General Hooker, the Confederate cavalry was also put in motion on 25 June. "At 1 o'clock at night, the brigades with noiseless march moved out. This precaution was necessary on account of the enemy's having possession of Bull Run Mountains, which in the daytime commanded a view of every movement of consequence in that region. Hancock's corps occupied Thoroughfare Gap."[15] Thus did General J. E. B. Stuart later report the initial movement of his cavalry command as he swung east and to the rear of Hooker on his march to the Potomac.

That Pennsylvania was Lee's objective was now clearly evident. Governor Curtin reacted with a defiant proclamation calling for sixty thousand men. The governor, of course, was looking primarily to Hooker for relief, but the Confederates were already in Pennsylvania, and Hooker's men were only then crossing into Maryland. The race was on. After crossing the Potomac at Edwards' Ferry, advance units of Hooker's army moved swiftly to protect their left from possible enemy flank attacks through the passes of the Catoctin Mountains and South Mountain. By the twenty-sixth, advance cavalry and infantry units were reporting to headquarters from Frederick City and Middletown, Maryland.[16]

On Saturday, 27 June, Julius Lineback was more concerned about food, cooking, and camp chores than the proximity of battle when noting his recollections of regimental activities:

> Last night it was my turn to cook and it was 2 o'clock by the time I could lie down. It may seem strange that it should take so long to cook, but everything had to be prepared. Wood had to be cut and carried in and it was green, too, and did not burn well. Then one had to wait for the wagons to come in with the cooking "tools" and rations, and the latter had to be issued.
>
> At 4 we were up again and soon on the road. We passed thru Waynesboro, Quincy, Funkstown, Greenwood and Fayetteville. The bands were ordered not to play while passing thru any town in Pennsylvania. All along the road I tried to buy some of that standard Pennsylvania product, apple butter, but without success. Some of the others were more fortunate. Alec got on the good side of an old lady by talking German with her and wheedled her out of some "lat werg." It was impossible for the officers to keep the men from "flanking" to some extent, but

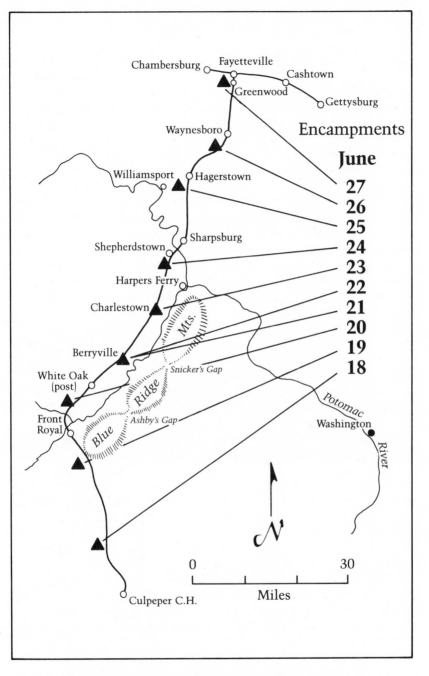

Chambersburg ○   Fayetteville
                    ● Greenwood ○   ○ Cashtown
                    Greenwood
                                          ○ Gettysburg

Waynesboro ○
            ▲

Williamsport ○   ○ Hagerstown
                  ▲

                 ○ Sharpsburg
Shepherdstown ○
              ▲

Harpers Ferry ○
Charlestown ○
            ▲   Mts.

Berryville ○
           ▲   Snicker's Gap

White Oak ○
(post)   Ridge
        ▲
                   Ashby's Gap
Front
Royal ○   Blue
      ▲

        ▲

        ▲
○ Culpeper C.H.

Encampments

June

27
26
25
24
23
22
21
20
19
18

Potomac
Washington ●
                River

N

0   30
|————————————|
      Miles

Gettysburg campaign, line of march of the Twenty-sixth
North Carolina Regiment

upon the whole there was less depredating than might have been expected. We were halted about 1 o'clock and the men were ordered to clean themselves up as well as possible, washing their clothes, etc. For quite awhile we have been doing our own cooking, the negro we brought with us from North Carolina having left us and gone to the Yankees, as we supposed. We now had a man from Co. D. Wake County, detailed to cook for us, thus relieving us of much work and drudgery.[17]

General Lee shared Lineback's observation that "there was less depredating." Pursuant to the issuance of General Orders No. 72 on 21 June, establishing strict regulations for procuring supplies in enemy territory, the general issued another order on 27 June from his headquarters at Chambersburg. Commending his troops for their conduct, he told them: "It must be remembered that we make war only upon armed men, and that we cannot take vengeance for the wrongs our people have suffered without lowering ourselves in the eyes of all whose abhorrence has been excited by the atrocities of our enemies, and offending against Him to whom vengeance belongeth, without whose favor and support our efforts must all prove in vain."[18]

This aspect of the war was apparently of little concern to General Hooker as he moved about his headquarters on the morning of 27 June. His concern was whether he had the numerical strength to cope with General Lee. At 9:00 A.M., from his headquarters at Poolesville, Maryland, Hooker advised Halleck that his headquarters would be at Frederick that night, that three of his corps were at Middletown, one at Knoxville, two at Frederick, with the remaining corps arriving there that night. "That there may be no misunderstanding as to my force," he added, "I would respectfully state that, including the portions of General Heintzelman's command, and General Schenck's, now with me, my whole force of enlisted men for duty will not exceed 105,000. . . . I state these facts that there may not be expected of me more than I have material to do with."[19]

Only the day before, he had suggested to Halleck the propriety of abandoning Maryland Heights, adding, "It must be borne in mind that I am here with a force inferior in numbers to that of the enemy, and must have every available man to use on the field." Halleck declined to approve the abandonment of the heights "except in case of absolute necessity." So, en route to Frederick, Hooker stopped by Maryland Heights to see for himself. From there he wired Halleck, "I have received your telegram in regard to Harper's Ferry. I find 10,000 men here, in condition to take the field. Here they are of no earthly account. . . . They are but a bait for the rebels, should they return." Halleck received this message at 2:55 P.M. Five minutes later, he received a second message from Hooker. It read: "My original instructions require me to cover Harper's Ferry and Washington. I have now imposed upon me, in addition, an enemy in my front of more than my number. I beg to be understood, respectfully, but firmly, that I am unable to comply with this condition with the means at my disposal, and earnestly request that I may at once be relieved from the position I occupy." At eight that evening Halleck advised Hooker that he did not have the power to relieve him from command and had referred his dispatch to the president.[20]

In the meantime, Halleck wrote Major General George G. Meade: "You will receive with this the order of the President placing you in command of the Army of the Potomac. . . . You will not be hampered by any minute instructions from these headquarters. Your army is free to act as you may deem proper under the circumstances as they arise. You will, however, keep in view the important fact that the Army of the Potomac is the covering army of Washington as well as the army of operation against the invading forces of the rebels. . . . In fine, General, you are intrusted with all the power and authority which the President, the Secretary of War, or the General-in-Chief can confer on you, and you may rely upon our full support."[21]

It was not until 7:30 on the night of 27 June that the commander of the pontoon train at Edwards' Ferry could report that the last of the Federal troops were crossing over into Maryland. They included General John Sedgwick's Sixth Corps, followed shortly thereafter by General Alfred Pleasanton's cavalry command. They would be greeted by a new commander of the Army of the Potomac, who had little time in which to marshal his forces. Only this army stood between Washington, Baltimore, Philadelphia, and the relentless pressure of the invader. At this moment, Rodes's and Johnson's divisions of Ewell's corps were at Carlisle. They had already requisitioned and sent back a train loaded with ordnance and medical stores and, in addition, had collected and sent back nearly three thousand head of cattle.[22] General Early's division left Mummasburg on the morning of the twenty-seventh, headed for York. That night a deputation from York surrendered the town, which was occupied without opposition the next morning. Longstreet's First Corps now occupied Chambersburg, and A. P. Hill's Third Corps, which came up on the twenty-seventh, was encamped along the Chambersburg pike between Greenwood and Fayetteville.

Only General Stuart was far removed from the scene of impending action. His line of march on the twenty-seventh carried him past Wolf Run Shoals, to Fairfax Station, where Wade Hampton had a spirited encounter with Scott's Nine Hundred, and then to Dranesville late in the afternoon. There he found the campfires of Sedgwick's Sixth Corps still burning. By midnight, Stuart succeeded in crossing the Potomac at Rowser's Ford in spite of almost insuperable difficulties.

Sunday, 28 June, dawned warm and clear. The Army of Northern Virginia had penetrated Yankee territory in good order. Encountering surprisingly little opposition in its march through western Virginia and Maryland, it was now poised to strike at the heart of Pennsylvania. On this bright Sunday, General Lee had every reason to be proud of his army. It had performed well under trying circumstances and had left few marks of an invader in its wake. Depredations had been kept to a minimum, and the morale of the men was high. This was a far cry from the army's experience during the Maryland campaign in September 1862. It was a war-weary Army of Northern Virginia that had been catapulted into Maryland immediately following Second Manassas. Morale was low and straggling was high. During the seventeen days leading up to the battle of Antietam, Lee's army dwindled from fifty-five to thirty-five thousand men. But the story was different in the campaign of 1863, which was to culminate in the battle of Gettysburg.

Although General Lee was justifiably proud of his command, he had ample reason for concern on Sunday, 28 June. True, his advance into Pennsylvania had caused panic throughout the North; but he was far from home base—his communications abandoned, his army scattered, the position and direction of the enemy unknown to him, and Stuart's cavalry command completely out of touch. The Army of Northern Virginia was dangerously exposed, and only a fortuitous circumstance would save it from embarrassment. Lee had counted upon Stuart's placing himself on Ewell's right, guarding his flank, and maintaining close communication with the corps commander. But there was no word from Stuart.

Nor was there any word from President Davis, to whom Lee had written on 23 June, urging that General Beauregard be given immediate command of a diversionary threat against Washington. In fairness to Davis, however, this request was not received until the night of the twenty-eighth. Although it was too late, the president was not favorably disposed to the plan, and he did not put it into effect.

But where was Stuart? Following closely on Hooker's heels, Stuart's command had crossed the swollen Potomac at midnight on 27 June, moving rapidly so as to join Lee in Pennsylvania as speedily as possible. Rockville was soon occupied. This community lay astride the direct wagon road and line of communication between the city of Washington and Hooker's army. Stuart's men proceeded to tear down miles of telegraph lines. A long train of wagons was sighted, pursued, and captured, netting 125 of the "best United States model wagons and splendid teams," together with nearly 400 prisoners, many of whom were officers. Because this effort scattered his leading brigade, Stuart determined not to threaten the defenses of Washington but to continue on the march and to cut the Baltimore and Ohio Railroad that night.[23]

Under any other circumstances, the capture of the wagon train and the cutting of the rail artery to the enemy would have been highly meritorious, but any actions that delayed or compromised Stuart's primary responsibility for protecting Ewell's right and keeping him posted on the enemy's movements were contrary to specific orders. General Stuart was indeed running late. He was out of touch with his own army. Now heavily encumbered with the captured wagon train, his command would be subject to still further delays.

In the meantime, the Army of the Potomac had gained a new commander. General George G. Meade accepted the appointment with humility. That night, one of Longstreet's trusted scouts brought in a report that "the enemy had passed the Potomac, and was probably in pursuit of us." As Longstreet later recalled, "The scout was sent to general headquarters, with the suggestion that our army concentrate east of the mountains, and bear down to meet the enemy."[24] It is important that this intelligence came from a scout, not from General Stuart. Thus was Lee alerted to the enemy's approach and to how little time he had in which to concentrate his scattered command.

Lee and Longstreet were headquartered near each other about three-quarters of a mile east of Chambersburg on the Gettysburg pike. Whether they discussed this report later is not known, but Lee would act swiftly the next day in anticipation of the enemy's approach. Sunday, 28 June, must have ended on a somber note for the general, for he carried the sole burden of ultimate responsibility. There is reason to believe that others shared this sense of impending conflict. In camp a few miles east of Lee's headquarters, Colonel Harry Burgwyn had attended a religious service conducted by his chaplain, the Reverend Mr. Wells. Julius Lineback was deeply impressed by what he observed on that occasion:

> During the day our chaplain, Rev. Mr. Wells, preached a very forceful and appropriate sermon on the text, "The harvest is passed, the summer is ended and we are not saved." Jer. 8–20.

This was the last sermon that many men were to hear on earth. God grant that some souls were led to consider and turn to Him who is ready to receive them, even in this eleventh hour. In speaking about this sermon afterward in our tent someone remarked: "Did you notice Col. Burgwyn during the preaching? He seemed to be deeply impressed. I believe we are going to lose him on this trip." Sadly prophetic words they were, fulfilled much sooner than any of us had the remotest idea.[25]

Monday, 29 June, was another day of uncertainty. Neither Lee nor Meade knew the precise position of the other, but both now realized that a confrontation was inevitable. Learning that the Federal army was advancing, Lee immediately directed his entire command to concentrate at Gettysburg. General Ewell, with Rodes's and Johnson's divisions, supported by Jenkins's cavalry, was at Carlisle preparing to advance on Harrisburg when he received orders from Lee "to join the main body of the army at Cashtown, near Gettysburg."[26]

Jubal Early's division of Ewell's corps was in the vicinity of York, having occupied that town without opposition on the morning of the twenty-eighth. Early had immediately dispatched Gordon to Wrightsville in an effort to secure both ends of the bridge over the Susquehanna between Wrightsville and Columbia. This vital railroad bridge, one mile and a quarter in length, was only lightly defended. Before Gordon could cross, however, the local militia had set it ablaze. Therefore, Early could only make destructive raids on other bridges in the area and levy on the people. Requisitions in York netted the Confederates between twelve and fifteen hundred pairs of shoes, a thousand pairs of socks, a thousand hats, three days' rations, and $28,600 in money. It was not until the evening of 29 June that Early received instructions "to move back, so as to rejoin the rest of the corps on the western side of the South Mountain."[27]

On the morning of the twenty-ninth, Longstreet was ordered to move part of his command to Greenwood, about seven miles east of Chambersburg on the Gettysburg turnpike. Pickett's division was to be left to guard the rear until relieved by John D. Imboden. A. P. Hill's Third Corps, consisting of the divisions of Anderson, Heth, and Pender, and supported by five battalions of artillery under command of Colonel R. L. Walker, was encamped on the turnpike near the village of Fayetteville, about six miles east of Chambersburg. That same morning, Hill was directed to move his corps east along the turnpike "in the direction of York, and to cross the Susquehanna, menacing the communications of Harrisburg with Philadelphia, and to cooperate with General Ewell, acting as circumstances might require." Accordingly, General Heth's division was set in motion that afternoon for Cashtown, a small village at the eastern end of the pass through South Mountain, and only eight miles from Gettysburg.[28]

The entire Federal army, now concentrated in the vicinity of Frederick, Maryland, lay between Lee and his cavalry corps, which had been delayed and heavily encumbered by its capture of the Federal wagon train on Sunday, 28 June. As soon as the train could be secured, Stuart headed due north in order to cut the Baltimore and Ohio Railroad, one of the main supply lines to the enemy. His men marched all night and reached the railroad soon after dawn. Cutting the railroad was important, but spending most of the day in the hope of intercepting trains meant another costly delay. Stuart realized the need for haste and for reporting the enemy's movements, as well as rejoining the army. But it was not until late in the afternoon of the twenty-ninth that the head of Stuart's column reached Westminster. There, after a brief skirmish with Federal cavalry, he camped for the night.[29]

But the enemy's cavalry had taken possession of the direct road between Stuart's position and Gettysburg. To gain Lee's flank, Stuart had no choice but to take a longer, more northerly route around the Federal line of march before belatedly turning toward Gettysburg. He had performed yeoman service in disrupting enemy communication and transportation lines, but the loss to the enemy would prove far less than that to the Army of Northern Virginia, for General Lee now had to maneuver against an adversary without knowledge of the latter's movements and disposition of forces.

Sunday, 28 June, had been a day of restful anticipation for that part of Lee's army encamped in the vicinity of Chambersburg and Carlisle, but it was a day of dark foreboding in the North. And it was on this day, in an atmosphere tense with excitement and alarm, that General Meade assumed command of the Army of the Potomac. Meade's first task was to ascertain the position and strength of his several corps before putting them in motion. This done, marching orders for the following day were quickly issued from his headquarters at Frederick.

By Monday morning, the twenty-ninth, General Meade was prepared to outline his plans for intercepting the Army of Northern Virginia. He knew Lee's army was in the general vicinity of Chambersburg, but he was still in doubt as to Lee's ultimate objective. His strategy allowed for the possibility that Lee might advance upon Baltimore or cross the Susquehanna in the direction of Philadelphia.

Unfortunately, his dispatch to Halleck containing his plan did not reach its destination. It was found on the body of a soldier, presumably the courier, who was killed on 30 June, near Glen Rock. This dispatch is significant because it helps to explain why Meade was not able to hold his "force well together" so as to fall "upon some portion of Lee's army in detail." That he would encounter Lee at Gettysburg the next day evidently had not crossed his mind that Monday morning. At the time, based upon available information, he was justified in assuming that Lee might conceivably head for Baltimore or cross the Susquehanna. Therefore, he wrote, "While I move forward, I shall incline to the right" in order "to get between his main army and that place [Baltimore]."[30] At the same time, he could not be unmindful of his responsibility for protecting Washington. Obviously, if Meade inclined to the right, he would have to spread his forces so as to present a reasonably solid front to Lee and, at the same time, provide cover for the roads leading to Frederick and Washington.

Had he known that his cavalry would make contact with Lee the following day, he probably would have arranged his forces differently. But with the information available to him, Meade's plan made sense, for Rodes and Johnson were still at Carlisle and Early at York. In fact, that same morning, Secretary Stanton received a telegram from Philadelphia reporting that "rebels are marching on Philadelphia in large force, and also on points on the Philadelphia, Wilmington and Baltimore Railroad." In the meantime, General Pleasanton issued orders to his three cavalry divisions, the disposition of forces being so designed as to protect the army's flanks and rear.[31]

By the evening of 29 June, the Army of the Potomac had largely completed its first major movement under the direction of its new commander. The First and Eleventh Corps were now at Emmitsburg; the Second Corps, delayed three hours in starting, was at Union but short of its destination, Frizellburg; the Third Corps was at Taneytown, although, at 7:00 that night, its wagon train was stopped at Middleburg, delaying all behind it; the Fifth Corps, following in the wake of the Second Corps, was at Liberty but short of its destination, Union; the Sixth Corps was encamped short of New Windsor but directed to move the following morning and occupy the railroad at Westminster; the Twelfth Corps was at Woodsborough in early evening but delayed far short of Taneytown.[32]

General Pleasanton's cavalry corps, more mobile and less encumbered with huge trains than the infantry, reached its assigned positions on the twenty-ninth in good order. The First (William Gamble's) and Second (Thomas C. Devin's) brigades of John Buford's First

Division moved without incident from Middletown, via Boonsborough, Cavetown, and Monterey Springs, to their encampment near Fairfield. Buford's reserve brigade, under Brigadier General Wesley Merritt, was detached and took position at Mechanicstown. David McM. Gregg's Second Division moved on Westminster, "covering the country toward York and Carlisle by reconnaissances and patrols." Judson Kilpatrick's Third Division moved directly to Hanover by way of Littlestown. It was probably a unit of Gregg's division that "obstinately disputed" Jeb Stuart's approach to Westminster in late afternoon on 29 June.[33]

CHAPTER 22

GETTYSBURG—MORNING

OF THE FIRST DAY *

Unknown to the participants, Tuesday, 30 June, would be the last day given to either army for maneuvering independently of the other before their unexpected encounter at Gettysburg. Each now knew that the other was nearby, but neither realized that the morrow would bring on an engagement of frightful intensity, lasting three days, and later would be generally considered the turning point of the war. Neither Lee nor Meade was prepared for such an eventuality, but the armies seemed predestined to converge on Gettysburg, as if drawn by an irresistible force. In retrospect, as one studies the course of their movements north into Pennsylvania, Lee by way of the Cumberland Valley and Meade in parallel fashion along the east side of South Mountain, it was almost inevitable that they should meet at Gettysburg once Lee turned eastward from Chambersburg.

Ten different roads radiated from the town of Gettysburg, the county seat of Adams County. Laid out in 1780 by James Gettys, for whom it was named, Gettysburg had prospered as a marketplace for the rich agricultural region it served; but in 1860 it was still a relatively unknown rural community with a population of only about two thousand inhabitants. Its cultural resources included the small Pennsylvania College and the Lutheran Theological Seminary. Otherwise, its importance lay in its location. The turnpikes from Pittsburgh to Philadelphia and Baltimore intersected at Gettysburg, and in 1858 the Hanover Branch Railroad was extended from Hanover to Gettysburg (Susquehanna, Gettysburg, and Potomac Railway), pro-

---

* This and the succeeding two chapters on the first day at Gettysburg are not designed to provide a detailed account of all the fighting that swirled along the ridges and in the valleys north and west of the town throughout the day, but rather to focus upon that portion of the battlefield lying west of Gettysburg and south of the Chambersburg pike. For it was here, in McPherson's woods, that the battle of Gettysburg began, and it was from these same woods later in the afternoon that the Twenty-sixth North Carolina drove Meredith's Iron Brigade in the deadliest engagement of the war, leading to the withdrawal and concentration of all Union forces on the ridges immediately south and east of Gettysburg.

viding a rail connection with the Northern Central at Hanover Junction, thirty miles distant. Gettysburg's military significance, however, lay in the road system radiating from its center. And it was this characteristic that favored Lee initially, once he decided to concentrate his forces in front of Meade.[1]

From his headquarters at Taneytown on 30 June, General Meade was not yet prepared to commit himself. Now led to believe that Lee's operations on the Susquehanna were no longer offensive in nature, although enemy movements indicated an advance from Chambersburg to Gettysburg, Meade was prepared for offense or defense as required or to let his troops rest. Therefore, his orders for the day retained roughly the same positions as held by his troops the day before, with the exception of a greater concentration on his left in the vicinity of Emmitsburg and the extension of his right to Manchester. He also placed General Reynolds in command of the three corps in the vicinity of Emmitsburg—the First (now under Doubleday), the Third (Sickles), and the Eleventh (Howard). Although Meade seemed hesitant, his moving Reynolds closer to Gettysburg and urging all corps commanders to prepare for action indicated his readiness for battle should it occur.[2]

General Reynolds was preparing for the possibility of having to play a defensive role. On the morning of the thirtieth, he moved the First Corps to within five miles of Gettysburg, where he placed two divisions behind Marsh Creek—one on the road to Gettysburg and the other on the road from Fairfield to the Chambersburg road at Moritz Tavern. The other division, with the reserve batteries, was stationed on the road to Chambersburg behind Middle Creek. Reynolds suggested to Meade's chief of staff that if the army was forced to fight a defensive battle near Gettysburg, the area north of Emmitsburg covering the plank road to Taneytown should be occupied.[3]

At some point during the day, Reynolds reported that the enemy had appeared at Fairfield, on the road between Chambersburg and Emmitsburg. Meade responded by ordering Daniel Sickles to move the infantry and artillery of the Third Corps to Emmitsburg immediately. In his reply to Reynolds, Meade told him that in the event of an attack he was to fall back to Emmitsburg and Meade would send reinforcements to him.[4]

General Meade clearly was relying primarily on his cavalry as the two great armies groped for one another on 30 June. In a communication to Pleasanton, Meade's adjutant urged the importance of obtaining reliable information on the presence, strength, and movements of the enemy, emphasizing the necessity of preventing the Confederates from concentrating their forces either on Meade's right in the vicinity of York, especially between him and the Susquehanna, or on his left toward Hagerstown and the passes below Cashtown. Pleasanton responded by exhorting his men to distinguish themselves as they had at previous engagements.[5]

Judson Kilpatrick's response from Hanover contained the gratifying news that he had encountered Stuart's cavalry and had cut it in half. One portion was in the woods on the east side of the road from Hanover to Baltimore, the other on the west side of the road from Hanover to Littlestown. Although he did not know its size, he knew that a large Confederate force was on the way from York. He surmised that the enemy was concentrating at Gettysburg.[6]

But from General John Buford, who had reached Gettysburg, came a startling series of communications: "I entered this place to-day at 11 A.M. Found everybody in a terrible state of excitement on account of the enemy's advance upon this place. He had approached to within half a mile of the town when the head of my column entered. His force was terribly exaggerated by reasonable and truthful but inexperienced men." That night Buford informed Pleasanton that A. P. Hill's corps was massed back of Cashtown, nine miles away. Confederate cavalry was on the road from Cashtown, and it was rumored that Ewell was crossing the mountains from Carlisle.[7]

Buford's intelligence was well founded. Hill had advanced to within a short distance of Gettysburg, and the three divisions of Ewell's corps were moving in the direction of Gettysburg—Rodes and Johnson from Carlisle, and Early from York. Following a thorough reconnaissance by Jenkins's cavalry, Rodes's division had eagerly anticipated an attack on Harrisburg when word was received from General Lee on the twenty-ninth, ordering Ewell's corps to join "the main body of the army at Cashtown, near Gettysburg." Accordingly, Rodes's division was pointed toward Gettysburg, not Harrisburg. After an arduous twenty-two-mile march across the mountains, by way of Petersburg, the division bivouacked for the night at Heidlersburg about twelve miles northeast of Gettysburg. Edward Johnson's division left Carlisle on the twenty-ninth and took the longer route through Shippensburg and Green Village before turning southeast to Scotland and Gettysburg. As a consequence, Johnson did not arrive in time to participate in the action of 1 July.[8]

It was not until the evening of the twenty-ninth that Early received instructions to rejoin his corps "on the western side of the South Mountain." At daylight the following morning he put his command in motion. That night he encamped within three miles of Heidlersburg and rode over to visit with General Ewell, who had accompanied Rodes's division on the march from Carlisle. There he learned that the corps was to concentrate at or near Cashtown—Rodes by way of Middletown and Arendtsville, and Early by way of Hunterstown and Mummasburg.[9]

The last day of June was not a good day for Jeb Stuart. While the rest of Lee's army was converging upon Gettysburg, Stuart, still encumbered with the captured wagon train and badgered by Judson Kilpatrick's cavalry division, was slowly making his way northward along Meade's right flank. Longstreet's First Corps, on the other hand, easily covered the seven miles between Chambersburg and Greenwood on the Gettysburg turnpike. Leaving Pickett at Chambersburg to guard his rear, Longstreet's other two divisions under Lafayette McLaws and Hood reached Greenwood about two in the afternoon and encamped for the night. General A. P. Hill's Third Corps was also moving east along the turnpike, but in front of Longstreet. On the twenty-ninth, Hill had moved General Heth's division to Cashtown. Pender's division was directed to follow on the thirtieth and R. H. Anderson's on 1 July.[10] Heth's division was destined to make the first contact with the enemy at Gettysburg.

Heth later reported that on 30 June he ordered Pettigrew to "take his brigade to Gettysburg, search the town for army supplies (shoes especially), and return the same day. On reaching the suburbs of Gettysburg, General Pettigrew found a large force of cavalry near the town, supported by an infantry force. Under these circumstances, he did not deem it advisable to enter the town, and returned, as directed, to Cashtown." According to Major John T. Jones of the Twenty-sixth North Carolina, the brigade did not return to Cashtown on the night of 30 June but "was on picket on the turnpike road leading from Chambersburg to Gettysburg, about half way between Cashtown and the latter place."[11]

The presence of the Federal cavalry in Gettysburg was obviously a surprise to Pettigrew. His superiors in Cashtown, however, received the news with apparent disbelief. That Colonel Harry Burgwyn shared his commander's concern there can be little doubt. Julius Lineback's account of the regiment's activities on the thirtieth lends credence to the belief that the men of the Twenty-sixth North Carolina had every reason to suspect that hostilities were imminent:

> 30th. There was some rain during the night. Orders were issued for the men to leave their knapsacks and those not able to

make a forced march to remain in camp. This order was ominous of trouble, and Colonel Burgwyn gave us permission to remain in camp if we preferred doing so. We decided to remain. The men left at 6:30 A.M., going in the direction of Gettysburg. Some of the officers had given us charge of their tents, and we moved them to the wagon camp near Cashtown, a quarter of a mile away. The enemy was reported to be in heavy force at Gettysburg.

At 2 o'clock we heard that General Pettigrew, who had been making a reconnaissance in force, had taken some prisoners, who said that Hooker had been reinforced by Meade. . . . Our troops, in coming in contact with a small portion of the enemy, had quite a little brush, but being under orders not to bring on a general engagement, fell back, followed by the enemy. Artillery was moving forward constantly, while the rain was falling nearly all day. Before the night the wagons went to the regiment and issued rations. . . . Our brigade was in lead of the division, the Twenty-sixth Regiment having gone on picket for the night.[12]

This was to be Harry Burgwyn's last night in camp. It is likely that he bivouacked with his command east of Cashtown on the road to Gettysburg. What his thoughts were on the eve of the first day at Gettysburg we can have no idea, for his last known letter was written on 17 June. But if his previous voluminous correspondence with his parents has any significance, it lies in the completely candid spirit in which he addressed them. His ideas about war and peace, conduct of military operations, the strengths and weaknesses of those in command, his future aspirations all regularly claimed Harry's attention.

The battle of Gettysburg began early on the morning of 1 July. It lasted for three days. It proved to be the greatest battle ever fought on the American continent. There can be no doubt that it was a pivotal victory for the North and probably the turning point of the Civil War. But such broad interpretations of the significance of the battle of Gettysburg were not recognized at the time. To General Meade, it represented a victory that drove the enemy from northern soil. For this "crowning victory" Meade lavished praise upon "the heroic bravery of the whole army, officers and men."[13] The victory was won at great cost, however, and it was a cautious Meade who pursued a still dangerous foe as Lee made his difficult and long-delayed withdrawal across the Potomac.

Although Lee was disconsolate over the outcome at Gettysburg, it is doubtful that he considered it the shattering blow to the Confederate cause that it later proved to be. As Lee reported shortly afterward, he probably required "more of his men than they were able to perform. . . . Owing to the strength of the enemy's position and the reduction of our ammunition, a renewal of the engagement could not be hazarded, and the difficulty of procuring supplies rendered it impossible to continue longer where we were."[14] Although he did not realize it, Lee's invasion of Pennsylvania altered or delayed any Federal plans for attacking Richmond. The capital of the Confederacy would not again be seriously endangered until the beginning of Grant's campaign the following spring.

That the great battle of Gettysburg was stumbled into adds a fascinating dimension to that pivotal encounter. Because Stuart had failed to keep him informed of the enemy's position, Lee had not learned of Meade's whereabouts until the night of 28 June. On 30 June, Pettigrew's brigade of Heth's division, not expecting to find the enemy, had approached Gettysburg and then withdrawn upon finding Buford's cavalry in force. Pettigrew had complied with Lee's order not to bring on a "general engagement." And yet, still disbelieving "that any portion of the Army of the Potomac was up," A. P. Hill again ordered Heth to Gettysburg early on the morning of 1 July, with not the slightest hint that a general engagement was about to ensue.[15] General Meade was equally in the dark. Having placed General Reynolds in command of three corps in the vicinity of Emmitsburg, Meade was moving hesitantly toward Gettysburg. As late as 30 June, however, both he and Reynolds were thinking primarily of fighting a defensive battle south of Gettysburg.

So it was that the battle of Gettysburg began in the early morning hours of 1 July. It had rained off and on the day before, and the first day of July was greeted by an overcast sky with wisps of fog clinging to the lowlands. It promised to be hot and sultry as the advance units of two great armies moved toward Gettysburg, the Federals from the south and southeast and the Confederates from the west and north. They were only a few miles apart as they commenced their fateful march. Neither commander would be present for this first day's encounter. General Meade, at his headquarters at Taneytown fourteen miles away, would not arrive at the scene of action until after midnight on 2 July. General Lee had spent the night of 30 June at Greenwood and would not arrive on the outskirts of Gettysburg until late in the afternoon of the first day of battle. The events of that day, therefore, occurred without the knowledge or guidance of the commanding generals. As the day progressed, the outcome was determined largely by the men and officers on the field. The contending forces fought at a time and place they had not intended.[16]

General Lee was in a pleasant frame of mind as he rode along the turnpike in the direction of Cashtown on the morning of the first. By noon Lee reached Cashtown, where he met briefly with A. P. Hill, commander of his Third Corps, and Major General Richard H. Anderson, whose division was being held in reserve. Neither could enlighten Lee on the extent of the fighting ahead. Hill was visibly ill and could only add that Heth had gone forward with instructions not to bring on an engagement until the rest of the army came up. After a brief pause Lee and his staff moved rapidly eastward in the direction of the heavy firing.[17] It was about two o'clock, "and the battle was raging with considerable violence," when the general reached "the crest of an eminence [Herr Ridge] more than a mile west of the town."[18]

Later that afternoon Lee approached Seminary Ridge overlooking Gettysburg almost three-quarters of a mile to the east. Along a two-mile front the enemy had been routed and was in full retreat, fleeing through the town to the safety of Cemetery Hill and Cemetery Ridge, which lay just to the south of Gettysburg. Behind Lee to the west lay McPherson's Grove, Oak Ridge, the railroad cut, and the Chambersburg pike, which had witnessed bloody fighting both in the morning and in the afternoon. The Federals had fought a stubborn holding action all day, but the timely arrival of Rodes's and Early's divisions of Ewell's Second Corps from the north between two and three in the afternoon, supported by Heth's renewed offensive from the west at about the same time, had proved their undoing. There was simply no withstanding such a concerted attack by superior forces, and the Confederates had won the day by the time General Lee reached the vicinity of the Lutheran Theological Seminary on Seminary Ridge. The first day's battle had been fought without his knowledge and direction and in spite of his expressed will.

At nine that morning, Henry Heth, in command of Hill's lead division, was "ignorant what force was at or near Gettysburg, and supposed it consisted of cavalry, most probably supported by a brigade or two of infantry." When he ordered Brigadier General James J. Archer's Third Brigade and Brigadier General Joseph R. Davis's Fourth Brigade to advance at 5:00 A.M., the object, as he later wrote, was "to feel the enemy, to make a forced reconnaissance, and determine in what force the enemy were—whether or not he was massing his forces on Gettysburg."[19] The reconnaissance encountered unexpectedly strong resistance.

Although both sides seemed drawn irresistibly into this protracted and bloody conflict, each had hoped for a defensive position of its own choosing. Meade had certainly not chosen Gettysburg, and Lee would have undoubtedly preferred a position closer to the protective folds of South Mountain. His youthful but ailing corps commander, A. P. Hill, probably played the decisive role on that fateful day. Hill refused to believe that the Federals were at or near Gettysburg in force, in spite of Pettigrew's encounter the day before. That same night, when asked by Heth if he had any objection to his going to Gettysburg the next day to "get those shoes," Hill's laconic reply was, "None in the world." This thoughtless response, which led to Heth's precipitate action, "took the control of affairs out of the hands of the commanding general of the army." [20]

The Federals, although committed to a defensive strategy, were also on the move early on the morning of the first, but for a different reason. General Buford had kept them posted. They knew that General Lee's forces were concentrating in the Cashtown-Gettysburg area. Meade was preparing to assume the defensive south of Gettysburg, but he was also intent upon feeling out the strength of the enemy. To this end, the First and Eleventh corps were ordered to Gettysburg on the morning of the first under the command of Major General John F. Reynolds. Should Reynolds find himself "in the presence of a superior force," he was instructed "to hold the enemy in check, and fall slowly back." [21]

Riding at a fast pace ahead of his troops, Reynolds reached Gettysburg about nine o'clock. There, in company with Buford, he surveyed the field from the cupola of the Lutheran Theological Seminary building. From this vantage point on Seminary Ridge the plight of Buford's hard-pressed cavalry units was plainly evident. Also clearly visible was the terrain surrounding Gettysburg. A few hundred yards to the west, and parallel to Seminary Ridge, lay McPherson's Ridge. Both ran in a north-south direction, but north of the Chambersburg pike the name of Seminary Ridge gave way to Oak Ridge, and the direction of McPherson's Ridge inclined to the northeast. The two joined at Oak Hill a little over a mile north of the pike. About nine hundred yards west of McPherson's Ridge, crossing the Chambersburg pike at right angles, ran Herr's Ridge (named for Herr's Tavern situated at the intersection of a small road and the turnpike). Between the two ridges meandered Willoughby Run, a small, shallow stream that witnessed the opening battle at Gettysburg.

To the east, about three-quarters of a mile away, Reynolds had a clear view of Gettysburg, bordered on the north by a broad plain through which converged the roads from Mummasburg, Carlisle, and Harrisburg. Just above and to the south of the town rose Cemetery Hill. Extending southward from it ran Cemetery Ridge, which terminated at the Round Tops about two miles distant. From his position in the cupola Reynolds could see that the two ridges, Seminary and Cemetery, were roughly parallel and about one mile apart. The rolling country in between was crossed diagonally by the road from Emmitsburg as it approached Gettysburg from the southwest.[22]

But Reynolds's hurried visit with Buford provided little time for general observation. He quickly ascertained that Buford's dismounted cavalrymen had been fighting a skillful delaying action for two hours before making their stand on McPherson's Ridge. Without immediate support, their gallant defense must soon yield to the Confederate onslaught. To his trained eye it was also apparent that the heights around Gettysburg must be held at all costs. Time was of the essence. Orders were immediately dispatched instructing Abner Doubleday and Oliver O. Howard to hasten to the front, with Major General Howard's Eleventh Corps to follow in reserve position to the First. Reynolds wrote to Meade: "The enemy is advancing in strong force, and I fear he will get to the heights beyond the town before I can. I will fight him inch by inch, and if driven into the town I will barricade the streets, and hold him back as long as possible."[23]

The lead elements of the First Corps were not long in arriving. At about nine o'clock, Brigadier General Lysander Cutler's Second Brigade of Brigadier General James S. Wadsworth's First Division reached the N. Cordori farm buildings, which were located on the east side of the Emmitsburg road about a mile south of Gettysburg. General Reynolds was there to meet them. He had ridden out to hasten their deployment. The Second Brigade was followed immediately by Captain James A. Hall's Second Maine Battery of six three-inch guns and shortly thereafter by Brigadier General Solomon Meredith's First Brigade. Cutler's brigade was the first to be deployed. Reynolds personally directed the placement of Hall's Battery on the western crest of McPherson's Ridge between the railroad cut and the Chambersburg pike. Cutler accompanied three of his regiments to their position north of the cut and to the right of the battery. Reynolds ordered the other two regiments of Cutler's brigade, the Ninety-fifth New York and the Fourteenth Brooklyn, into position just south of the pike to protect Hall's left flank. He then rode off to hurry Meredith's First Brigade (Iron Brigade) into position on the left of his line.[24]

It was about this time that the initial crisis of the day developed. No sooner were Cutler's men deployed into line of battle north of the pike than the Confederates of Davis's brigade came into "easy musket range." South of the pike, Archer's men were charging up the western slope of McPherson's Ridge just as the lead regiment of Meredith's Iron Brigade, the Second Wisconsin, was mounting the slope from the east. Reynolds was waiting for the men of the Second as they neared the crest. As they rushed past, he shouted, "Forward men, forward for God's sake and drive those fellows out of those woods." Reynolds turned in his saddle to see whether supports were coming up. Suddenly there was a heavy exchange of gunfire with the enemy. Reynolds was seen to sway and then fall from his horse. He had been struck behind the right ear, probably by a stray ball, and killed almost instantly. It was about 10:15 on the morning of the first that this brave and intrepid leader was struck down, but not before he had probably set the stage for a Union victory at Gettysburg.[25]

Thus was battle joined. The die had been cast when Reynolds reached the field. His few, hurried moments with Buford, the evident massing of Confederate troops from the west, the magnificent delaying action of Buford's thin blue line as it had stubbornly yielded ground from the west, and the defensive capability of Cemetery Ridge, anchored by prominent elevations at both ends, could mean only one thing to the perceptive mind of the courageous Reynolds. The high ground before the town must be held until relief could come up. From that moment his actions were geared to battle. He had momentarily considered the possibility of withdrawing to the protective elevations of Cemetery Ridge south of the town, but instinct directed otherwise. He must fight to maintain the lines already established by Buford and await developments. Howard's Eleventh Corps must also hasten to the front, for the strength of the enemy demanded "an immediate showdown."[26]

In bringing on "a general engagement," Reynolds was to Meade what A. P. Hill was to Lee, with one notable exception. Hill had inadvertently but arbitrarily committed Lee to battle the night before with little knowledge of the enemy's actual position. Reynolds committed Meade to the defense of Gettysburg the following morning by his alert and perceptive reaction to the military situation as he found it. What might have been the outcome of the first day's battle had Reynolds lived to direct it is idle to speculate. Major General Doubleday had just arrived on the field and was instructed by Reynolds to "hold on to" the Hagerstown road on the Union left only moments before being struck down.[27]

Doubleday was now senior in command. His precarious position was no less enviable than Reynolds's had been, for urgent decisions had to be made under extreme pressure. Later events would demonstrate that Doubleday was equal to the task. He was quick to note that McPherson's Grove (a triangular-shaped wood with its base bordering Willoughby Run for about three hundred yards and its apex resting on the eastern crest of McPherson's Ridge about eight hundred yards distant) afforded a strong defensive position for the Union line south of the Chambersburg pike.[28]

Meredith's Iron Brigade, with the Sixth Wisconsin having been left in reserve at the seminary, reached the grove none too soon. The Second Wisconsin, followed in echelon from right to left by the Seventh Wisconsin, the Nineteenth Indiana, and the Twenty-fourth Michigan, entered the woods just as Archer's Confederates were charging to the crest of the ridge from the opposite direction. A fierce, close-quarter battle ensued. The Seventh Wisconsin immediately joined the fray. The Nineteenth Indiana and the Twenty-fourth Michigan, following a wooded ravine to the left, suddenly closed in on the Confederate right flank. The Twenty-fourth Michigan even succeeded in crossing Willoughby Run and overlapping the enemy's right and rear.

Archer's command, consisting of five regiments, the Seventh Tennessee, the Fourteenth Tennessee, the Fifth Alabama battalion, the Thirteenth Alabama, and the First Tennessee, extended south in that order from the Chambersburg pike to beyond McPherson's Grove. Outflanked, with the right of his line now crumbling in the face of a heavy crossfire, Archer suddenly found himself in an untenable position. His entire line gave way. Swept back across the run, Archer was captured along with an undetermined number of his men. For a relatively brief encounter, it was a severe blow. Archer was succeeded by Colonel B. D. Fry, who withdrew what was left of the command to Herr Ridge about a thousand feet to the west. The Iron Brigade, clearly the victor, withdrew to the east of Willoughby Run and took position in the grove on the west side of McPherson's Ridge.[29]

Meanwhile, north of the Chambersburg pike, the Confederates under General Davis suffered much the same fate, but in a different sequence. Davis's brigade was concentrated north of the railroad cut as its three regiments, the Forty-second Mississippi, the Second Mississippi, and the Fifty-fifth North Carolina (from right to left), advanced to the attack from the west. Cutler's Union brigade, which had just been rushed onto the field from the southeast, was hastily deployed. Three of its regiments were placed north of the cut, two just south of the Chambersburg pike, and Hall's Second Maine Battery between the railroad cut and the pike. The 147th New York, which anchored Cutler's left on the north side of the cut, was supported on its right by the Fifty-sixth Pennsylvania and the Seventy-sixth New York. The Fourteenth Brooklyn and Ninety-fifth New York were aligned on Cutler's extreme left south of the pike.[30]

Although the Confederate assault was momentarily checked, the Fifty-fifth North Carolina succeeded in flanking the Seventy-sixth New York on Cutler's right. The brigade commander was thus caught between the enfilading fire of the Carolinians on his flank and the pressure of the Mississippians on his front. Part of the Seventy-sixth New York managed to change front to the north to meet this critical situation, but to no avail. Recognizing that Cutler's entire command north of the pike was in jeopardy, General Wadsworth ordered the brigade back to the shelter of Seminary Ridge. The Seventy-sixth New York and Fifty-sixth Pennsylvania retired in reasonably good order, but Wadsworth's command to withdraw never reached the men of the 147th New York. Its commanding officer, Lieutenant Colonel Francis Miller, was shot in the throat at the moment he received the message. This order was never transmitted to his successor, Major George Harney.[31]

The 147th and the Maine battery were left in a dangerously exposed position. The full weight of the Confederate attack was now directed at this Union remnant north of the pike. Having no instructions to the contrary, Major Harney held his ground as long as possible against the combined pressure of the Second Mississippi and the Fifty-fifth North Carolina on his right and rear. Heavy losses soon forced the New York regiment to give way, but not before permitting Hall's Second Maine Battery to retire in relative safety, temporarily losing only one gun in the process.[32] This brave stand also provided precious time for the Fourteenth Brooklyn and Ninety-fifth New York on the extreme left of Cutler's line to change front and come to the aid of Harney's beleaguered forces.

The arrival of Meredith's Iron Brigade south of the pike had relieved these troops somewhat from the necessity of holding the open ground between the pike and McPherson's Grove. It was their change of front to the north, and obvious threat to Davis's right flank as he pursued the retreating Federals eastward, that suddenly altered an apparent Confederate victory. Sensing this new danger to their right, units of the Second and Forty-second Mississippi regiments paused in their pursuit, changed front to the south, and sought safety in the railroad cut as they faced the Federal units concentrating along the pike not two hundred yards distant.[33]

Shortly thereafter, the Sixth Wisconsin of the Iron Brigade, which had been held in reserve at the seminary, came up in time to join the Fourteenth Brooklyn and the Ninety-fifth New York in a fierce charge upon the cut. Under ordinary circumstances this deep trench would have provided an excellent defensive position, but the Confederates had not reckoned on being caught in an enfilading fire from two companies of the Sixth Wisconsin, which had succeeded in making their way to the eastern end of the cut. Shot at from front and flank, several hundred men of Davis's shattered brigade were forced to surrender. Some few escaped from the western end of the cut.[34]

"In this critical condition," Davis later reported, "I gave the order to retire, which was done in good order, leaving some officers and men in the railroad cut, who were captured, although every effort was made to withdraw all the commands."[35] Davis was a bit too sanguine in his official report. His brigade had been so severely damaged that Heth hesitated to bring it into action any more that day. Later in the afternoon, however, the brigade did assist John M. Brockenbrough in the final attack on Doubleday south of the pike.[36]

Following the forced withdrawal of the Confederates about 11:00 to 11:30 A.M., the heavy fighting on both sides of the Chambersburg pike temporarily subsided. At five that morning they had started out from Cashtown on their eight-mile march to Gettysburg with Davis on the north side of the pike and Archer on the south. The object, according to Heth, was "to feel the enemy" and to determine whether or not he was concentrating his forces at Gettysburg. At first, only Buford's cavalrymen stood in the way. During the night of 30 June, Buford had posted vedettes on the Chambersburg pike about four miles west of Gettysburg to observe Heth's skirmish line and to employ delaying tactics at every opportunity. It was not until 8:00 A.M. that Colonel William Gamble, commanding Buford's First Cavalry Brigade, was informed that his pickets were being driven in by a strong enemy force. He was promptly instructed by Buford to form a battle line on McPherson's Ridge immediately in his front. Armed with Sharps rapid-firing carbines, and supported by Lieutenant John H. Calef's battery of horse artillery (Battery A, Second U.S.), these dismounted cavalrymen held the Confederates in check until shortly after 10:00 A.M., when relieved by the advance elements of the First Corps under the command of General Doubleday.[37]

It was at this point that the Confederates must have realized that they had marched blindly into a major engagement. Almost within the hour, on both sides of the Chambersburg pike, they were repulsed and driven back on Herr Ridge, leaving Meredith's Iron Brigade firmly implanted in the grove on McPherson's Ridge south of the pike and Cutler's brigade in a more exposed position north of the pike. Buford's courageous delaying action, Reynolds's early presence on the field, his immediate determination to fight, and the arrival of Wadsworth's First Division of the First Corps all seemed so perfectly timed as to appear to have been predetermined. And then, shortly after 11:00 A.M., the remaining divisions of Doubleday's First Corps arrived on the field. Fighting having subsided, Doubleday directed Brigadier General John C. Robinson to hold his Second Division in reserve at the seminary and "to throw up some slight intrenchments." He divided Brigadier General Thomas A. Rowley's Third Division into two parts, deploying Colonel Roy Stone's Second Brigade on the western crest of McPherson's Ridge between the grove and the Chambersburg pike and Colonel Chapman Biddle's First Brigade on the eastern crest of the ridge slightly to the left and rear of the Iron Brigade stationed in the grove.[38]

The subsequent arrival of the Eleventh Corps fitted a similar pattern of fortuitous timing. General Howard, riding ahead of his troops, was in sight of Gettysburg when news was brought to him that the battle had started. It was then 10:30 A.M. He rode immediately into town to reconnoiter. About an hour later he learned of Reynolds's death. Now the ranking officer on the field, Howard proceeded to Cemetery Hill, where he established his headquarters and selected a strong reserve position for Brigadier General Adolph von Steinwehr's Second Division and three batteries of artillery. The First Division (Brigadier General Francis C. Barlow) and the Third Division (Major General Carl Schurz) of the Eleventh Corps preceded von Steinwehr's division into Gettysburg and were directed into position north of the town by General Howard. Steinwehr did not reach his position on Cemetery Hill until about 2:00 P.M.[39]

Up until noon, the Federals had met the exigencies of the first day in masterful and resolute fashion. Thrown into battle on the run, they had succeeded in driving the Confederates back on Herr Ridge and stabilizing their own position on McPherson's Ridge. As fast as reinforcements had come up they had been deployed in anticipation of a renewed offensive by the enemy. They had little time, for the Confederates were about to strike simultaneously from the north and the west. The lull in battle that had settled over the field shortly before noon lasted only long enough for the Federals to regroup and to get more men and batteries into position.

In the morning fight, although the numbers of men engaged had been about evenly divided between the opposing forces, the Confederates had enjoyed superior artillery capability.[40] But they had nothing with which to counter the magnificent role played by Buford's cavalry. Furthermore, the South had no senior officers on the field at the time to match the performance of the Union commanders. Reynolds and Doubleday had determined to make a stand at Gettysburg and had undoubtedly inspired a will to win not found among their adversaries during those early morning hours. After all, General Heth's troops were on "reconnaissance" and still under orders not to bring on a general engagement. And yet, as events were later to reveal, it was the determination of Reynolds to stand and fight on the morning of that first day, and Doubleday's decision to hold his position on McPherson's Ridge as long as possible, that were to figure so largely in the ultimate Federal victory at Gettysburg two days later.[41]

Casualties that morning had been heavy on both sides. Certainly the Confederate brigades of Archer and Davis had suffered severely and were to be of little service for the balance of the day. For their part, the Federals had sacrificed heavily in establishing their positions on McPherson's Ridge. North of the Chambersburg pike, for example, the Seventy-sixth New York lost 234 officers and men out of 370 engaged, the 147th New York, 220 out of 380 engaged, and Hall's Second Maine Battery 22 men killed and wounded in addition to 34 horses. South of the pike, where Meredith's Iron Brigade was stationed, the Second Wisconsin suffered 116 casualties (38 percent) in its head-on collision with Archer.[42] But the Iron Brigade was not seriously hurt in the morning fight and would make a desperate stand in McPherson's Grove later in the day. Clearly, the fighting qualities of the men and the timely arrival of reinforcements had carried the morning for the Union defenders. It would be a different story in the afternoon, however, for two divisions of Ewell's corps were rapidly approaching Gettysburg from the north.

Earlier that morning, while accompanying Major General Robert Emmett Rodes's Third Division on its march from Heidlersburg toward Cashtown, General Ewell had received word from A. P. Hill that he was advancing on Gettysburg. Ewell immediately pointed Rodes's column in the direction of Gettysburg by turning south on the Middletown road. He ordered Early, who had been following him by way of Hunterstown, to advance directly on the Heidlersburg road. Ewell then notified Lee of his movements and, in reply, was urged not to bring on a general engagement "till the rest of the army came up." By the time Ewell received Lee's message, however, it was too late to avoid an engagement because Rodes's division was already in contact with the enemy.[43] Preceded by Lieutenant Colonel Thomas H. Carter's battalion of light artillery, Rodes's large division of some 8,125 effectives had veered off to the right as it approached Gettysburg on the Carlisle road and proceeded south about a mile along a wooded ridge before reaching Oak Hill.[44]

This commanding elevation, about a mile north of the Chambersburg pike, afforded an excellent vantage point for enfilading Doubleday's (First Corps) entire line running north-south along Oak Ridge and McPherson's Ridge. Carter lost little time in putting his artillery into action. Two batteries, posted on the southern crest of Oak Hill, directed their fire southward against the right flank of Doubleday's line, and the other two, posted on the southeastern crest of Oak Hill, pounded away at the advance units of Howard's Eleventh Corps as they moved into position on the plain north of the town.[45]

Carter's fire apparently caught the enemy by surprise, for, at the time, as later reported by General Rodes, there were "no troops facing me at all." But before he could make his dispositions, large bodies of the enemy (Eleventh Corps) began to appear on the plain in front of Gettysburg, and almost simultaneously part of the First Corps facing A. P. Hill to the west "changed position so as to occupy the woods on the summit of the same ridge [Oak or Seminary] I occupied." Rodes was referring to the wooded area that extended northward from the railroad along the summit of the ridge to the point where the Mummasburg road crossed the ridge at the base of Oak Hill.[46]

Since his arrival on the field, General Howard had lost little time in deploying his Eleventh Corps of some ninety-five hundred effectives. He was aware that the Federal right might soon be threatened, for Colonel Thomas C. Devin, commanding Buford's Second Cavalry Brigade, had been alerted earlier that morning to enemy movements along the road leading into Gettysburg from the north. Posted on McPherson's Ridge to the right of Gamble's First Brigade, and north of the Chambersburg pike with his right resting on the Mummasburg road, Devin had not been directly involved in the morning battle. Exposed to heavy fire from the enemy's batteries on Herr Ridge, however, he had been ordered to "retire gradually." About the same time, his skirmishers east of the Mummasburg road were driven back by advance elements of the enemy approaching the town from the direction of Heidlersburg. It was here, according to his later report, that Devin succeeded in holding "the rebel line in check for two hours until relieved by the arrival of the Eleventh Corps."[47]

CHAPTER 23

AFTERNOON IN McPHERSON'S GROVE

General Heth, encamped on the night of 30 June near Cashtown, could not have heard the shot that opened the battle of Gettysburg on the morning of 1 July. Harry Burgwyn probably did. The Twenty-sixth North Carolina had been the lead regiment of Pettigrew's brigade on the abortive expedition to Gettysburg the day before. Returning toward Cashtown rather than risk a general engagement, the Twenty-sixth was left on picket duty on the west side of Marsh Creek, which crossed the Chambersburg pike a little over four miles from the village.[1] Harry undoubtedly remained with his men during the night of 30 June.

That same evening an advance picket of the Eighth Illinois picket squadron of Buford's cavalry came up and took position on the pike at a blacksmith's shop just east of the bridge over Marsh Creek. Early the following morning these Union pickets observed a cloud of dust in the vicinity of Cashtown. Archer's and Davis's brigades of Heth's division were moving eastward on the turnpike with Archer in the lead. "As the enemy in gray neared the stone bridge across Marsh Creek," it was later recounted, "an officer, riding at the head of his column, halted by the stone coping to allow his men to pass. Lieutenant Marcellus E. Jones, of Wheaton, Illinois, in command of the Eighth Illinois picket-line, standing in the pike, took the carbine of Sergeant Shafer, raised it to his shoulder, aimed at the officer sitting on his horse, and fired 'the first gun at Gettysburg.'" The time was about 7:30 A.M.[2]

Archer's men filed across the bridge. As his skirmishers deployed south of the pike, firing immediately broke out between the picket lines. The advance picket of Union cavalrymen then withdrew beyond the blacksmith's shop to a ridge slightly to the east and joined its squadron, which was being held in reserve. Here the men dismounted and, leading their horses, fought a stubborn delaying action for the next couple of miles. Davis's brigade followed Archer in much the same manner except that his men turned left after crossing the bridge and moved eastward along the north side of the pike. Immediately confronting them were the picket squadrons of the Twelfth Illinois and Third Indiana, which were posted on the ridge to

the right of the Eighth Illinois squadron. The record does not indicate that the Federal pickets north of the pike offered much resistance to the advancing Confederates in Davis's brigade.[3]

Alerted earlier that the Confederates were marching on Gettysburg from the vicinity of Cashtown, General Buford had ordered
Gamble's First Brigade, about sixteen hundred strong, to take position on the western crest of McPherson's Ridge, with Devin's Second
Brigade on about the same line just north of the railroad cut. Calef's
battery was posted between the two and astride the turnpike. The
Yankee cavalrymen and gunners were to give an extraordinarily good
account of themselves before being relieved by the First Corps shortly
after 10:00 A.M. From the time that Archer's men crossed the bridge
at Marsh Creek they were continuously engaged, first by the Yankee
skirmishers and then by Buford's main line as they penetrated the
thick underbrush bordering Willoughby Run. Even then, it is doubtful that either Archer or Davis considered the engagement anything
more than a sharp brush with a determined cavalry outpost. It is improbable that they would have crossed the run and charged up the
western slope of McPherson's Ridge with such reckless abandon had
they known that the First Corps was moving rapidly across the eastern crest of the ridge to intercept them.[4]

To the men involved, however, the resulting engagement must
have resolved all doubt, for the Confederates had been routed and
Archer captured. So crippled were the two brigades that neither
would play an active role in the gathering storm that threatened to
unleash its fury all along the line as the noon hour passed. Heth's
division was now effectively reduced to Colonel John M. Brockenbrough's brigade of seventeen hundred Virginia troops and General
Pettigrew's North Carolinians numbering approximately two thousand effectives.[5] These troops were comparatively fresh. Having followed Davis and Archer on the march eastward from Cashtown and
Marsh Creek earlier that morning, they had encountered no enemy
resistance until taking position behind the Confederate batteries
just west of Herr Ridge. Here they were exposed to random fire for
about half an hour before being ordered forward several hundred
yards, where they were halted in a wooded area. Subsequently, three
brigades of Pender's division came up in support of Heth, taking their
position behind the Confederate artillery. Brigadier General Edward L. Thomas's brigade of this division was held in reserve north of
the pike in support of the batteries. It would see no action that day.[6]

The woods beginning about a quarter of a mile south of the Chambersburg pike followed a southerly course along the eastern slope of

Herr Ridge, extending almost to the Hagerstown road. Running roughly parallel to Willoughby Run, this wooded area ranged anywhere from five to eight hundred yards west of the stream.[7] The timber provided welcome shade and excellent cover for the men in gray as they deployed in line of battle along a three-quarter-mile front, with Brockenbrough on the left, Pettigrew in the center, and Archer on the far right. The latter's depleted forces would assist in protecting the Confederate right from the enemy's cavalry, but Davis's shattered brigade on the extreme left, north of the pike, would do little more than remain in reserve and collect stragglers. The major burden of the impending battle would be borne primarily by thirty-seven hundred men in the two brigades of Heth's division, attacking along a half-mile front. They would be supported by three brigades of Pender's division numbering about forty-two hundred effectives.[8]

The late morning lull in the fighting had afforded both sides an opportunity to bring up reserves and establish battle lines. Across the way, on the east side of Willoughby Run and hardly half a mile distant, Doubleday had moved swiftly to consolidate the First Corps's position following the bloody repulse of Archer and Davis. Cutler's Second Brigade of Wadsworth's First Division was retained north of the pike to protect the right flank of the corps. As in the morning, the Sixth Wisconsin of Meredith's Iron Brigade was held in reserve near the seminary.[9] Colonel Roy Stone's Second Brigade of Rowley's Third Division arrived on the field about 11:30 A.M. and was deployed on the western crest of McPherson's Ridge, with its right (149th Pennsylvania) resting on the Chambersburg pike and its left (150th Pennsylvania) connecting with the right of the Iron Brigade (Seventh Wisconsin).[10] The 143d Pennsylvania was placed initially in the center of the line. With the exception of the Sixth Wisconsin, Meredith's entire brigade was stationed in McPherson's Grove, anchored on the right by the Seventh Wisconsin and on the left by the Nineteenth Indiana. The Twenty-fourth Michigan and the Second Wisconsin, in that order, occupied the center of the grove to the right of the Nineteenth Indiana.[11]

Colonel Chapman Biddle's First Brigade of Rowley's division was deployed about the same time along the eastern crest of McPherson's Ridge to the immediate left and rear of the woods occupied by Meredith. Leaving the 151st Pennsylvania temporarily in reserve at the seminary, the three remaining regiments of Biddle's brigade were posted in the following order: the 142d Pennsylvania on the right, the Eightieth New York (Twentieth New York State militia) in the center, and the 121st Pennsylvania on the left. Cooper's battery was stationed between the 142d Pennsylvania and the Eightieth New York. Gamble's cavalrymen occupied the ground between Biddle's left and the Hagerstown road. Thus deployed, Biddle's line lay in open fields facing west. With three of his brigades posted on McPherson's Ridge south of the pike and one (Cutler) north of the pike, General Doubleday wisely chose to hold the two brigades of Robinson's Second Division in reserve at the seminary.[12]

Although these troop dispositions were made during the lull in battle, all was not quiet along Willoughby Run. In taking their position, Stone's skirmishers had to advance across an open field. They were met by "a hot fire from the enemy's skirmishers concealed behind a fence." Without stopping to return the fire Stone's men rushed the enemy and drove the gray line from the fence. At the same time, they were greeted by fire from two of the Confederate batteries posted on the opposite (Herr) ridge. This was a harbinger of things to come, for Stone's pivotal position between the grove and the pike would shortly subject his men to intense enemy pressure on both front and flank.[13] Biddle reached his position on the ridge south of the grove after going through a series of maneuvers which involved crossing and recrossing Willoughby Run near the enemy.[14] After finally taking position, Colonel Theodore B. Gates (Eightieth New York) was ordered to advance a company of skirmishers to a brick house and stone barn an eighth of a mile forward and across the valley. This advance position would later be reinforced and would cause considerable discomfort to the Confederates.[15]

By 1:00 P.M., in the sweltering heat of a humid July day, the lines of the opposing forces on both sides of Willoughby Run were now clearly drawn. From a defensive standpoint, the First Corps's position on McPherson's Ridge could not be considered particularly strong. Facing west, the brigades of Stone, Meredith, and Biddle did enjoy some advantage of elevation and particularly the natural protection afforded the Iron Brigade, which was centered in the heavily wooded grove. But the Federal position along the ridge was an easy target for the Confederate gunners on Herr Ridge and Oak Hill a mile to the north. Furthermore, the left of Biddle's line, lying in the open fields, was largely unprotected. Gamble's cavalry, operating in the vicinity of the Hagerstown road, would neutralize Archer on the extreme right of the Confederate line, but the right of Pettigrew's attacking column (Fifty-second North Carolina) would not have much difficulty in later flanking Biddle's left and forcing his withdrawal.[16] From the outset, however, the right flank of the Federal line would be subjected to even greater pressure. Attacked almost simultaneously by Rodes from the north and Brockenbrough from the west, Stone's Pennsylvanians would display rare courage and skill in fighting on two fronts before finally yielding to overwhelming numbers.

On balance, however, the forces that were about to converge on the slopes east of the run in the initial encounter were not too unevenly matched. The three Federal brigades numbered about forty-five hundred effectives, the two Confederate brigades of Brockenbrough and Pettigrew approximately thirty-seven hundred.[17] The reserve strength of Pender (forty-two hundred effectives) would later convert the stubborn resistance of the First Corps into a rout when the Federals attempted to establish a second position on Seminary Ridge, but the two brigades of Heth's division, particularly Pettigrew's brigade, would bear the brunt of the initial Confederate assault. The battle in and around the grove on McPherson's Ridge developed into a fight to the finish with no quarter sought or given. At the outset, neither Archer nor Davis could give any support to Pettigrew, and Brockenbrough's weak brigade would not add much strength to the left of the Confederate line. Pettigrew's brigade thus found itself pitted directly against an adversary strongly posted on the ridge, about equal in numbers, and just as determined to defend Northern soil as the Southerners were to prove their ability to whip "anything in Yankeedom."

When the battle south of the Chambersburg pike actually began is not clear, but the Federal right (Stone) resting on the pike was first drawn into the conflict by Rodes's threat to its flank from the north. In a later report, Colonel Stone provided a dramatic account of the developments that led to a concerted drive by the enemy that would virtually envelop his command. Between noon and one o'clock Rodes's division opened heavy fire, causing Cutler's brigade to fall back to Seminary Ridge.

> This made my position hazardous and difficult in the extreme, but rendered its maintenance all the more important. I threw one regiment (One hundred and forty-ninth, Lieutenant-Colonel Dwight commanding) into the road, and disposed the others on the left of the stone building, to conceal them from the enfilading battery. My line thus formed a right angle facing north and west. Soon after, as the enemy's infantry was developed in heavy force upon the right, I sent another regiment (One hundred and forty-third, Colonel Dana) to the right of the One hundred and forty-ninth.

At about 1:30 p.m. the grand advance of the enemy's infantry began. From my position I was enabled to trace their formation for at least 2 miles. . . . Their line being formed not parallel but obliquely to ours, their left first became engaged with the troops on the northern prolongation of Seminary Ridge. The battalions engaged soon took a direction parallel to those opposed to them, thus causing a break in their line and exposing the flank of those engaged to the fire of my two regiments in the Chambersburg road. . . . A heavy force was then formed in two lines parallel to the Chambersburg road, and pressed forward to the attack of my position.[18]

By 2:00 P.M., as the battle raged north of the pike, the men of the First Corps still had not been challenged from the west. But the blow would soon fall. Meredith's Iron Brigade, now rested and strongly posted in the grove, was ready for the attack. This battle-hardened brigade of Westerners had gained an enviable reputation for stamina and courage. Only a month earlier it had become the First Brigade of the First Division of the First Corps, thus giving it the honor of carrying the divisional colors. Added to this distinction was the brigade's unique dress. All other troops in the army wore the regular forage caps, but every man in the Iron Brigade wore a large black hat, described as "tall, black, bell-crowned, and wide brimmed, sported black feathers worn with a flourish, and had the left brim turned up and secured to the side with an eagle, the seal of their country." It was indeed a "badge of honor."[19]

The Twenty-fourth Michigan was the newest regiment in the brigade. Having been recruited the previous summer and assigned to the brigade in October 1862, its reception had been anything but cordial. A false rumor had spread that the Twenty-fourth was composed of "bounty men," which revolted the veterans who had early volunteered to fight for their country without benefit of bounty. For months, the men from Michigan were ostracized. But in May 1863, they were finally accorded the privilege of exchanging their forage caps for the famous black hats. The Twenty-fourth was now truly a part of the Iron Brigade. Morale was never higher.[20] At Gettysburg, on the afternoon of 1 July, it would be given a chance to prove its worth.

Following the rout of Archer that morning, the Iron Brigade was justifiably confident as it took up its new position in McPherson's Grove. But the position of the Twenty-fourth was somewhat awkward and was a matter of grave concern to its commander, Colonel

Henry A. Morrow. The left of his line joined the right of the Nineteenth Indiana in the low ground near Willoughby Run. His right was bent back along the ridge to connect with the left of the Second Wisconsin, resulting in a concave line, which could impede full firepower. Morrow tried repeatedly to convince his superiors that the position of his line was untenable, but to no avail. The peremptory response was simply that "the position was ordered to be held, and must be held at all hazards."[21]

Subsequent developments would justify Morrow's concern. Biddle's brigade, positioned to the left and rear of Meredith, was several hundred yards up the ridge behind the Nineteenth Indiana, leaving the latter immediately exposed to a flanking movement by the advancing Confederates. The Twenty-fourth Michigan would also be exposed to an enfilading fire from the left as it was valiantly seeking to withstand a ferocious frontal assault by the left of Pettigrew's line. Before the engagement began, the 151st Pennsylvania, Lieutenant Colonel George F. McFarland commanding, was brought up from its reserve position near the seminary and placed in line to the right of the 142d Pennsylvania. As McFarland later described it, "The position of the regiment was now such that a little more than one-half of its left wing extended beyond the strip of woods on the ridge directly west of the seminary." Unwittingly, his men, and those of the Twenty-fourth Michigan, would be so situated as to receive the concentrated fury of the impending attack.[22]

Across the way, the Confederates were preparing to advance. Shielded by the woods, the extreme right of their line (Archer) extended about a quarter of a mile beyond the Federal left, but Archer's brigade, now under the command of Colonel B. D. Fry, would not participate in the attack because of Gamble's successful diversionary tactics.[23] Once in position, the Fifty-second North Carolina of Pettigrew's brigade would be on the right flank of the Confederate line. This regiment, Colonel James K. Marshall commanding, would be supported on its left by the Forty-seventh North Carolina (Colonel George H. Faribault), the Eleventh North Carolina (Colonel Collett Leventhorpe), and the Twenty-sixth North Carolina (Colonel Harry Burgwyn, Jr.), in that order. With the possible exception of the Twenty-sixth, which had received its "baptism of fire" in the Seven Days' battle, none of Pettigrew's regiments could be considered battletried. Since Pettigrew formally took command of his brigade on 18 August 1862, he had been largely confined to "surveillance and containment" exercises in southeastern Virginia and eastern North Carolina. But this role of "arduous but less conspicuous service" had fashioned a strong, well-disciplined brigade in which the spirit and morale of the men were high.[24] In the engagement to come, now just minutes away, these men from North Carolina would display a courage and a determination under intense fire rare in the annals of military history.

While in the woods the regiments of Pettigrew's brigade were "in line by echelon" with the Twenty-sixth North Carolina in advance. To its right and rear was the Eleventh North Carolina, followed by the Forty-seventh and Fifty-second North Carolina, respectively. According to one observer, "This made the Confederate troops appear to the enemy's vision, as in several lines of battle, whereas there was only one line of battle, and as the fight progressed, these regiments came up successively and formed one single line in the attack."[25]

If any regiment deserved the honor of taking the lead position, it was the Twenty-sixth North Carolina. In active service for almost two years, the regiment had had little turnover of manpower except for the customary attrition resulting from illness and battle. When the twelve-month volunteer enlistment terms began to expire in the spring of 1862, almost all of the men of the Twenty-sixth had reenlisted for the duration.[26] Furthermore, the command structure of the regiment had been carefully developed from the very beginning. Of the ten company commanders present at Gettysburg, six had come up through the ranks since the regiment was organized in August 1861. This was true of the three field commanders, Colonel Harry Burgwyn, Lieutenant Colonel John R. Lane, and Major John T. Jones, and other regimental officers.[27] The Twenty-sixth was a large regiment. As recently as 31 May, Harry had proudly written his father: "I now command nearly as many men as most of our Brig. Generals. My Rgt. numbers 1090 men & officers 'present' & very nearly 1250 all told. But few of our brigades are very much larger now than that."[28]

But a month later, on the eve of the first day of the battle, Captain J. J. Young, the regimental quartermaster, could list as present for duty only a total of 885.[29] Sickness, furloughs, and the long march from Virginia had undoubtedly taken their toll. Even then, the Twenty-sixth was considered a huge regiment by any standard. As distinctive as its size, however, was its esprit de corps. During their year in service together, Colonel Vance and Lieutenant Colonel Burgwyn had instilled a sense of mission that had proved invaluable, but it was Harry Burgwyn who had, from the outset, demanded strict adherence to military discipline, insisted upon rigorous training, and imparted a cohesive, regimental will to stand and fight whatever the sacrifice. His men had never failed him, and Harry had never failed to justify their confidence in him. Years after the war, in referring to the battle of Blount's Mill (9 April 1863), one observer was remembered as having said of the colonel: "My father thought him the bravest man he ever saw. He said that he had seen him apparently as cool amid flying shell as if battles were any ordinary occasions."[30]

In Lieutenant Colonel Lane and Major Jones, Harry could not have had two finer officers. Both were admirable men and exceptional leaders. Lane was a fighter and, like Burgwyn, an excellent drill master and strict disciplinarian.[31] He had enlisted as a private in one of the companies (probably Company E) from Chatham County in May 1861. The following December he was promoted to captain and was commended for bravery at the battle of New Bern on 14 March 1862. In October of that year he was promoted to lieutenant colonel.[32] In the same month Captain John T. Jones was promoted to major. At that time, Harry said of these two young officers: "The courage of both Lane & Jones has been often tried, & never failed. I have every confidence in them in that respect. Lane also, though greatly deficient in education, is exceedingly attentive & hard working, & I think I can educate him to fill his post very well."[33] His words were prophetic. Before the end of that first day at Gettysburg, all three would share the honor of commanding the Twenty-sixth North Carolina.

They led good men and good soldiers. Only a few weeks earlier Lane had boasted, somewhat facetiously, that his boys "were noted for fighting, dirt and begging. They didn't mind asking for anything they wanted, and as they were always ready to fight they didn't have much time to devote to their toilet."[34] Forty years later, in an address delivered on the battlefield at Gettysburg, Lane spoke with deep pride and emotion of the men with whom he had fought and bled on that hot afternoon of 1 July 1863. Proclaiming that "a finer body of men never gathered for battle," he explained why they were such good soldiers:

> In the first place, the soldiers came of good blood. I do not mean that their parents were aristocrats—far from it; many of them never owned a slave. They were the great middle class that owned small farms in central and western North Carolina. . . . These boys had grown up on the farm and were of magnificent physique. . . . These men, many of them without much schooling, were intelligent, and their life on the farm and in the woods had taught them to be observant and self-reliant. . . . Every

man of them had been trained from boyhood to shoot a rifle with precision. General Pettigrew, observing the deadly execution of their muskets on this field, remarked that the 26th shot as if shooting squirrels. . . .

These men were patriots; they loved their country, they loved liberty. Their forefathers had fought the British at King's Mountain and Guilford Court House. . . . Now every man of them was convinced that the cause for which he was fighting was just; he believed that he owed allegiance first to his home and State. . . . Finally these men had native courage—not the loud-mouthed courage of the braggart—but the quiet, unfaltering courage that caused them to advance in the face of a murderous fire. The men of this regiment would never endure an officer who cowered in battle. They demanded in an officer the same courage they manifested themselves; they would endure no domineering, they would suffer no driving. At this time the men had come to understand and to trust the officers, the officers the men, and like a mighty, well-arranged military engine it was ready with one spirit to move forward. That noble band of men, God bless them! God bless them![35]

These, then, were the men who had been waiting in the woods since midmorning. As the hours slowly passed they watched with growing impatience as the enemy steadily reinforced his position in the grove and along the ridge that lay hardly half a mile distant. If there had been any monotony during the long wait, in spite of the sporadic shelling, it was relieved by some Federal sharpshooters stationed on the roof of an old farmhouse to the right and front of the regiment. Colonel Burgwyn ordered an end to the annoyance. Lieutenant J. A. Lowe, Company G, volunteered for the assignment and soon silenced the intruders, whom he spotted behind a chimney. But where was Hill? Time was wasting and still Pender's light division had not come up. Burgwyn was visibly agitated and complained that "we were losing precious time."[36] Pender's delay in getting into support position was undoubtedly occasioned by the shift of Lane's brigade from the left to the extreme right of Pender's line. It was about this time that part of Daniel's North Carolina brigade of Rodes's division began to challenge Stone's Pennsylvania "Bucktails," who protected the open ground on Doubleday's right flank just south of the turnpike.[37]

Whether Burgwyn had earlier communicated his sense of urgency to General Heth is not known, but about 2:00 P.M., seeing that Rodes

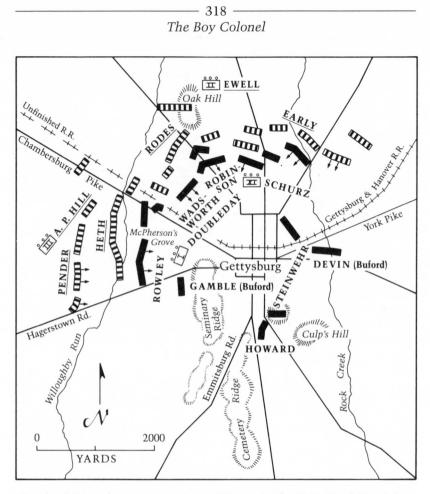

Battle of Gettysburg, situation at 2:30 P.M., 1 July 1863 (Civil War Atlas, adaptation, courtesy Department of History, U.S. Military Academy)

was heavily engaged, Heth went to Lee and requested permission to attack. Lee was still not prepared to bring on a general engagement without Longstreet. Only upon learning that Early was coming up on Rodes's left did the commanding general finally order Heth to press forward to the attack. The time was approximately 2:30 P.M. [38] As later recalled by Lieutenant Colonel Lane, "General Ewell's corps had come up on our left and engaged the enemy. Never was a grander sight beheld. The lines extended more than a mile, and directly visible to us. When the battle waxed hot, now one [of] the armies would be driven, now the other, while neither seemed to gain any advantage. The roar of artillery, the crack of musketry and the shouts of the combatants added grandeur and sublimity to the scene. Suddenly about 2 p.m. there came down the line the long awaited command 'Attention.' The time for this command could not have been more inopportune. Our line had inspected the enemy and we knew the desperateness of the charge we were to make." [39]

Having lived through that heroic charge, though severely wounded, Lane never forgot the courage and fortitude that sustained the men of the gallant Twenty-sixth as they charged, in the face of a withering fire, through the wheatfield, across Willoughby Run, and into McPherson's Grove. There, the Iron Brigade waited to contest every foot of the way. It was literally do or die for these brave lads from North Carolina. They died by the score. Forty-five minutes after the 800 charged across the wheatfield, only a bare remnant emerged in triumph from the grove on the east side of McPherson's Ridge. Behind them lay 584 killed and wounded. [40]

It is little wonder that "tears gathered in the heart and rose to the eyes" of Colonel Lane whenever he spoke of the deeds and daring of the remarkable Twenty-sixth North Carolina at Gettysburg: "What a magnificent body of men it was! I see them now. In the center with the first glow of youth on his cheek, was the gallant Col. Harry King Burgwyn. His eye was aflame with the ardor for battle. Near him was his Lieutenant Colonel [John R. Lane], commanding the right, and Major John T. Jones, commanding the left. These officers had put their souls into the training of the soldiers and were now waiting the issue of battle with full confidence in their courage and proficiency." [41]

The Confederates had been impatient to engage the men in blue before they could reinforce their position on McPherson's Ridge, and the Federals had also watched with growing apprehension the movement of troops and the buildup of Confederate strength along Herr Ridge. Colonel William W. Robinson, commanding the Seventh Wisconsin, reported to General Meredith: "Early in the afternoon columns of infantry were seen moving to our left, evidently with the intention of turning our left. Also heavy columns were being massed in our front. This information I sent to the general, and the order I received was to hold the position at all hazards." Major John Mansfield, commanding the Second Wisconsin on the immediate left of the Seventh Wisconsin, concluded that the Confederates were attacking with two lines of infantry: "We remained in position some two hours or more, when the enemy were discovered emerging from the timber beyond the field we had just left, in two lines, with a heavy line of skirmishers. The front line of the enemy, with skirmishers, advanced directly to the front, while the second line advanced obliquely to the left."[42]

Colonel Henry A. Morrow, commanding the Twenty-fourth Michigan, reported that "the enemy advanced in two lines of battle, their right extending beyond and overlapping our left." Morrow was concerned because he felt that the left of his line, curving down the slope to join the right of the Nineteenth Indiana, was in an untenable position. General Meredith offered no relief, simply replying that the position "must be held at all hazards." Colonel Chapman Biddle, commanding the First Brigade of Rowley's Third Division, stationed to the immediate left and rear of Meredith, also emphasized that "between 2 and 3 p.m. a large body of them [Confederates], amounting to a division or more, advanced in two lines toward us."[43]

In reality, what Biddle and others saw was not "a division" advancing "in two lines," but Pettigrew's brigade emerging from the woods in echelon as it extended its line to the right. Brockenbrough's brigade was stationed on Pettigrew's left. When Heth gave the order to advance, Brockenbrough's brigade filed out of the woods on a slightly oblique course to the left in order to confront Stone's Second Brigade of Rowley's Third Division in the open fields between the grove and the Pennsylvania turnpike. The Twenty-sixth North Carolina, to the right of Brockenbrough and on the left of Pettigrew's line, advanced obliquely down the slope, across the wheatfield, and into the grove, where it encountered the Iron Brigade. Pettigrew's other regiments fanned out to the right between the grove and Biddle's left.

The combination of these moves apparently conveyed the impression that the Confederates were advancing in two lines with greatly superior numbers. Actually, Pettigrew's brigade of 2,000 faced Biddle's brigade of 1,422 and Meredith's brigade of perhaps 1,300 (not including the Sixth Wisconsin). Brockenbrough's 1,700 effectives were pitted against Stone's 1,312 Pennsylvanians.[44] If there was any great disparity in numbers, it was near the turnpike, where Stone was subjected to attack on two fronts—by Brockenbrough's Virginians from the west and by Daniel's North Carolinians from the north.

When Brockenbrough crossed Willoughby Run he was challenged immediately by a strong skirmish line posted four hundred yards in front of Stone's position. As the Virginians slowly worked their way up the ridge, as if to engage the Pennsylvanians in a frontal assault, they drifted to the right to avoid a small quarry that lay midway between the pike and the grove. Entering the woods to the left of the Twenty-sixth North Carolina, Brockenbrough's men immediately became engaged with the Seventh Wisconsin. The extent to which the brigade took shelter in the woods below the crest of the ridge or remained in the open is not clear. But certainly the full force of the brigade was never brought to bear on Stone's front.

Brockenbrough had been ordered to advance only after Stone had become heavily engaged with Daniel, whose brigade was attacking from the north. Stone had ordered two of his three regiments, the 149th Pennsylvania and the 143d Pennsylvania, to change front to meet this challenge to his right. Only the 150th Pennsylvania was left in its original position facing west although, at one point, its right wing was turned to join the left of the 149th in repulsing Daniel's third attempt to drive the Pennsylvanians out of the railroad cut. Because Stone was able to concentrate so much strength on his right (north), with no more than one regiment protecting his front (west), the force of Brockenbrough's attack was evidently blunted either by the division of his forces or by his failure to press a frontal assault.[45]

It was about this time that A. M. Scales's brigade of Pender's division advanced in support of Brockenbrough. "We pressed on," the general later reported, "until coming up with the line in our front (presumably Brockenbrough), which was at a halt and lying down. I received orders to halt, and wait for this line to advance. This they soon did, and pressed forward in quick time. That I might keep in supporting distance, I again ordered an advance, and, after marching one-fourth of a mile or more, again came upon the front line, halted and lying down. The officers on this part of the line informed me that they were without ammunition, and would not advance farther. I immediately ordered my brigade to advance. We passed over them, up the ascent, crossed the ridge, and commenced the descent just opposite the theological seminary."[46]

Scales's North Carolinians were about midway between the eastern crest of McPherson's Ridge and the seminary when they suddenly encountered a devastating fire from the enemy's batteries. It was about 4:15 P.M. To Scales's right was Abner Perrin's brigade, also of Pender's division. Both came over the ridge about the same time. Immediately in their front, along the western edge of the woods surrounding the seminary, Doubleday had assembled what remained of the shattered First Corps following its long and valiant holding action on the ridges west and northwest of Gettysburg. These men were making their last stand behind the light entrenchments hastily prepared by Gabriel Paul's brigade earlier in the afternoon. In their immediate support were concentrated "twelve guns in so small a space that they were hardly 5 yards apart." But it was Lieutenant James Stewart's Battery B, Fourth United States, just north of the turnpike that caused such havoc. Lieutenant James Davison, commanding the left half of Stewart's battery between the railroad cut and the pike, had swung his six twelve-pounder bronze Napoleons into a position where he could pour a deadly enfilading fire into the left of the Confederate ranks at a distance of not over one hundred yards.[47]

As Scales described the slaughter: "Here the brigade encountered a most terrific fire of grape and shell on our flank, and grape and musketry in our front. Every discharge made sad havoc in our line, but still we pressed on at a double-quick until we reached the bottom, a distance of about 75 yards from the ridge we had just crossed, and about the same distance from the college, in our front. . . . Our line had been broken up, and now only a squad here and there marked the place where regiments had rested." With one exception, every field officer in the brigade had been disabled, including General Scales. Colonel William L. J. Lowrance succeeded Scales in command. That evening, the colonel found his men in a "depressed, dilapidated, and almost unorganized condition, numbering in all about 500."[48]

Perrin's brigade, on the right of Scales, also suffered severely from the enfilading fire but continued to advance. When within about two hundred yards of the seminary, the brigade suddenly received "the most destructive fire of musketry I have ever been exposed to," Perrin later reported. "We continued to press forward, however, without firing," he added, "until we reached the edge of the grove. Here the Fourteenth Regiment was staggered for a moment by the severity and destructiveness of the enemy's musketry. It looked to us as though this regiment was entirely destroyed." It was then that Perrin realized he was "without support either on the right or left." Scales was at a standstill on his left and rear, and General Lane's brigade on the right was not in sight, having come up on the south side of the Hagerstown (Fairfield) road. Only through the skillful handling of his four regiments was Perrin able to outflank and finally rout the enemy from his positions behind the obstructions in the grove and on both sides of the seminary.[49]

Pender's light division, in its supporting role to Heth, was spread out for about a mile between the Chambersburg pike and the Hagerstown road. The arrangement of brigades was such that Perrin was in the middle of the line, moving in direct support of Pettigrew's brigade, with Scales on the left in support of Brockenbrough and Lane on the right supporting Archer. Because Archer was effectively pinned down by the diversionary tactics of Gamble's cavalrymen, and Lane had crossed to the south side of the Fairfield road to flank Doubleday's left,[50] it fell to Perrin and Scales to mount the final assault that drove the shattered remains of Doubleday's First Corps back on Cemetery Ridge.

But it was Pettigrew's brigade that broke the back of the Federal resistance on McPherson's Ridge. By the time Heth's division had "become closely engaged with the enemy," Perrin's brigade had moved through an open field for about a mile on the west side of Herr Ridge. There it took position and remained until about 3:00 P.M. Perrin was again ordered forward. This time he advanced about half a mile and "came close upon General Heth's division pressing the enemy." Perrin's brigade "remained in this position probably until after 4 o'clock," he later reported, "when I was ordered by General Pender to advance, and to pass General Heth's division should I come up with it at a halt, and to engage the enemy as circumstances might warrant. I soon came up with and passed Brigadier-General Pettigrew's brigade, the men of which seemed much exhausted by several hours' hard fighting."[51] But among the "exhausted" there lay perhaps as many as a thousand Confederates dead or wounded. They lay the thickest in McPherson's Grove, on the left of Pettigrew's line, where the casualties of the Twenty-sixth North Carolina exceeded those of the rest of the entire brigade. There had been heavy fighting all along the line, but, from right to left, regimental casualties mounted progressively as proximity to the grove narrowed.[52]

Pettigrew's attack was executed with precision. Each of his four regiments fought with courage and determination, and each carried the field in its front against an equally determined adversary. On the far right, the Fifty-second North Carolina delivered a devastating blow to the enemy once it reached the point where it could enfilade the left of the 121st Pennsylvania (Lieutenant Colonel Alexander

Biddle commanding). In advancing to the attack, however, the Fifty-second was challenged on its right by a body of the enemy's cavalry. Although under heavy fire, Colonel Marshall skillfully formed his regiment in square to meet this menace and, with the aid of a company detached for the purpose, succeeded in driving the horsemen from his flank. To one of his men who fought on that day, "the losses in the brigade were appalling, and those of the Fifty-second Regiment were heavy."[53] As for the 121st Pennsylvania, Major Biddle succinctly reported: "As the enemy's forces appeared over the crest of the hill, we fired effectually into them, and, soon after, received a crushing fire from their right, under which our ranks were broken and became massed together as we endeavored to change front to the left to meet them. . . . The regiment, broken and scattered, retreated to the wood around the hospital. . . . We now have almost exactly one-fourth of our force and one commissioned officer besides myself."[54]

As the Forty-seventh North Carolina drove forward on the left of the Fifty-second, it was "met by a furious storm of shells and canister." Pressing on through the wheatfield to the accompaniment of the wild and eerie rebel yell, the men had pierced two of the enemy's lines "when suddenly a third line of the enemy arose forty yards in front, as if by magic, and leveled their shining line of gun barrels on the wheat heads." Although caught by surprise, one witness later reported, "the roar of our guns sounded along our whole line. We had caught the drop on them. . . . The earth just seemed to open and take in that line which five minutes ago was so perfect." It was then that a stirring drama unfolded, admired by friend and foe alike. As observed by this same witness: "A Federal officer came in view and rode rapidly forward bearing a large Federal flag. The scattered Federals swarmed around him as bees cover their queen. In the midst of a heterogeneous mass of men, acres big, he approached our left, when all guns in front and from right and left turned on the mass and seemingly shot the whole to pieces. This hero was a Colonel [Chapman] Biddle, who (if he were otherwise competent) deserved to command a corps. It was with genuine and openly expressed pleasure our men heard he was not killed."[55]

It was the combined attacks of the Fifty-second and Forty-seventh North Carolina regiments that so effectively turned the left wing of the Federal line, exposing Cooper's battery and forcing its withdrawal. As Colonel Gates later explained: "The enemy soon after advanced two very strong lines of infantry, and, driving in our skirmishers . . . moved rapidly on our lines. Their line extended the front of two regiments beyond our left flank, completely enfilading our line, and pouring a terrible fire into our front and left flank. We held the position until the artillery was removed, and then fell back slowly behind a barricade of rails, some eighth of a mile in our rear."[56] But before the artillery (Cooper's battery) was removed, it had severely punished the Twenty-sixth North Carolina, "especially while charging across Willoughby Run, and reforming thereafter."[57] Because the Twenty-sixth was the first of Pettigrew's regiments to come to grips with the enemy across the run, having such a short distance to cover in its advance, Cooper's battery had sufficient time to pour a deadly enfilading fire into its ranks before being forced back by the right of Pettigrew's line. The Eleventh North Carolina, in echelon to the right of the Twenty-sixth, was undoubtedly exposed to much of this same fire.

CHAPTER 24

SO NOBLE & SO GLORIOUS

From the moment the Twenty-sixth and the Eleventh North Carolina regiments advanced to the charge, they were destined for a fearful encounter. The field in their front sloped gently down to the narrow ravine through which coursed Willoughby Run. As Major John T. Jones of the Twenty-sixth later recalled: "In our front was a wheat field about a fourth of a mile wide; then came a branch [Willoughby Run], with thick underbrush and briars skirting the banks. Beyond this was again an open field with the exception of a wooded hill [McPherson's woods] directly in front of the Twenty-sixth Regiment, about covering its front."[1] Under the cover of this wooded hill lay four regiments of the Iron Brigade, ready and waiting. According to General Doubleday, "These woods possessed all the advantage of a redoubt strengthening the centre of the line and enfilading the columns should they advance in the open spaces on either side. I deemed the extremity of the woods which extended to the summit of the ridge, to be the key of the position, and urged that portion of Meredith's [Iron] Brigade—the western men assigned to its defence—to hold it to the last extremity."[2]

The Eleventh faced the open hillside just south of this grove. Its forward movement would carry it past the edge of these woods, flanking the left of the Nineteenth Indiana, and on up the hill where it would confront the right wing of Biddle's brigade. But within the space of approximately four hundred yards, the forward movement of the Twenty-sixth would propel it into the bloodiest engagement of the entire war. Its record on that hot, sultry afternoon, indeed that of the entire brigade, would sustain the axiom that "fighting regiments leave a bloody wake behind them; retreating regiments lose few men."[3]

Just minutes before the charge, Lieutenant Colonel Lane was suffering from severe nausea. He told Colonel Burgwyn that he might be forced to request permission to go to the rear. Burgwyn's immediate response was: "'Oh, Colonel, I can't, I can't; I can't think of going into this battle without you; here is a little of the best French brandy which my dear mother gave me and asked me to take with me in battle; it might do me good.' I took a little of it under the circumstances," Lane later recalled, "though I had not drunk any during the war, and, I may add, neither had Col. Burgwyn. In a few minutes I was somewhat relieved and said: 'Col. Burgwyn, I can go with you;' with his usual politeness he replied: 'Thank you, Colonel, thank you.' Continuing the conversation, he said: 'Colonel, do you think that we will have to advance on the enemy as they are? Oh, what a splendid place for artillery, why don't they fire on them!' He saw and realized the very decided advantage their position gave them over us."[4]

Neither knew the strength of the enemy hidden in the forest on the opposite hillside, but each sensed that a frightful journey lay ahead. Lane recounted the events years later:

> All the men were up at once and ready, every officer at his post, Col. Burgwyn in the centre, Lieut. Col. Lane on the right, Major Jones on the left. Our gallant standard bearer Mr. J. B. Mansfield, at once stepped to his position—four paces to the front, and the eight color guards to their proper places. At the command 'Forward March!,' all to a man stepped off, apparently willingly and as proudly as if they were on review. The enemy at once opened fire, killing and wounding some, but their aim was rather too high to be effective. All kept the step and made as pretty and perfect line as regiment ever made, every man endeavoring to keep dressed on the colors. We opened fire on the enemy. On, on we went, our men yet in perfect line, until we reached the branch [Willoughby's Run] in the ravine. Here the briers, reeds and underbrush made it difficult to pass. There was some crowding in the center, but the right and left crossed the branch where they struck it. The enemy's artillery [Cooper's battery] on our right got an enfilade fire. Our loss was frightful. But our men crossed in good order and immediately were in proper position again, and up the hill we went firing now with better execution.[5]

The first line of battle was in the ravine. As described by Major Jones of the Twenty-sixth: "When nearing the branch referred to [Willoughby Run], the enemy poured a galling fire into the left of the brigade from the opposite bank, where they had massed in heavy force." Colonel Henry A. Morrow, commanding the Twenty-fourth Michigan, reported that the Confederates advanced in two lines of battle. He ordered his men not to fire until they were at close range.

Nevertheless, "Their advance was not checked, and they came on with rapid strides, yelling like demons." The Confederates overpowered the Nineteenth Indiana, striking on both flanks. Morrow's left was then exposed to an enfilading fire and was forced to fall back.[6]

This new, fall-back position of the Federals was referred to as the "second line" by combatants on both sides. It was probably near the western crest of McPherson's Ridge, only a short distance up the slope from the run. Here, in the middle of the grove, the Twenty-fourth Michigan fought desperately, but the Twenty-sixth North Carolina would not be denied. As Lane later recalled: "The engagement was becoming desperate. It seemed as if the bullets were as thick as hailstones in a storm. At his post on the right of the regiment and ignorant as to what was taking place on the left, Lieut. Col. Lane hurries to the centre. He is met by Col. Burgwyn, who informs him 'it is all right in the centre and on the left; we have broken the first line of the enemy.' The reply comes: 'We are in the line on the right, Colonel.'"[7]

Another Confederate witness to this bitter, almost hand-to-hand struggle recalled:

> We advanced on; about half way up the hill we encountered another line—where a desperate engagement took place 'twas there I first became aware of our heavy loss—by Capt. Louis G. Young of Gen'l J. Johnston Pettigrew's staff (who was riding cooly along in rear of my Company) ordering me to close my Company (B) to the right to the Colours—and when I looked to right (where Company F should have been there was only two or three men all the rest were killed or wounded) I saw Col. H. K. Burgwyn advancing toward me with the Colours in his hands (Capt. McReary [McCreery] of Gen'l Pettigrew's staff [had] just been killed trying to advance them)—Col. Burgwyn ask me *quickly* if Company B could not furnish a man to carry the Colours—I ordered private Frank Hunneycut [Honeycutt], Company B from Union County to him. Col. Burgwyn gave Hunneycut the Colours and told him to advance—but the poor fellow only advanced a few steps till he was shot dead.[8]

The intensity of the fighting was such that allowances must be made for seeming contradictions in eyewitness accounts; yet it is remarkable that so few evident contradictions appear in the recollections of those caught in this maelstrom. Colonel Lane recounted the next few moments:

At this time the colors have been cut down ten times, the color guard all killed or wounded. We have now struck the second line of the enemy where the fighting is fiercest and the killing the deadliest. Suddenly, Captain W. W. McCreery, Assistant Inspector General of the Brigade, rushes forward and speaks to Col. Burgwyn. He bears him a message. "Tell him," says General Pettigrew, "his regiment has covered itself with glory today." Delivering these encouraging words, Capt. McCreery, who has always contended that the 26th would fight better than any other regiment in the brigade, seizes the fallen flag, waves it aloft and advancing to the front, is shot through the heart and falls, bathing the flag in his life's blood. Lieut. George Wilcox of Company H, now rushes forward, and pulling the flag from under the dead hero, advances with it. In a few steps he also falls with two wounds—not fatal—in his body.

The line hesitates; the crisis is reached; the colors must advance. The gallant Burgwyn leaps forward, takes them up and again the line moves forward. Returning again from the right Lieut. Col. Lane sees Col. Burgwyn advancing with the colors. At this juncture, a brave private, Franklin Honeycutt, of Company B, takes the colors and Burgwyn turns to hear from the right. Col. Lane says: "We are in line on the right." Col. Burgwyn delivers Pettigrew's message to Lieut. Col. Lane. At that instant he falls with a bullet through both lungs, and at the same moment brave Honeycutt falls dead only a few steps in advance.

Then indeed was our situation desperate. The flag is down, the line is halting, the enemy are strengthening their line and firing upon our men with murderous effect, and more than all the youthful commander has fallen, and all the responsibility falls upon the shoulders of his successor. Bowing by the side of the fallen youth, Lieut. Col. Lane stops for a moment to ask: "My dear Colonel, are you severely hurt?" A bowed head and a motion to the left side and a pressure of the hand is the only response; but he looked as pleasant as if victory were on his brow.[9]

Lieutenant T. J. Cureton of Company B wrote of the critical moment in the charge when Colonel Burgwyn was shot down:

The Colours lay on the ground a few seconds, and Lieut. Blair and myself both run to pick them up (Col. Burgwyn and Cap-

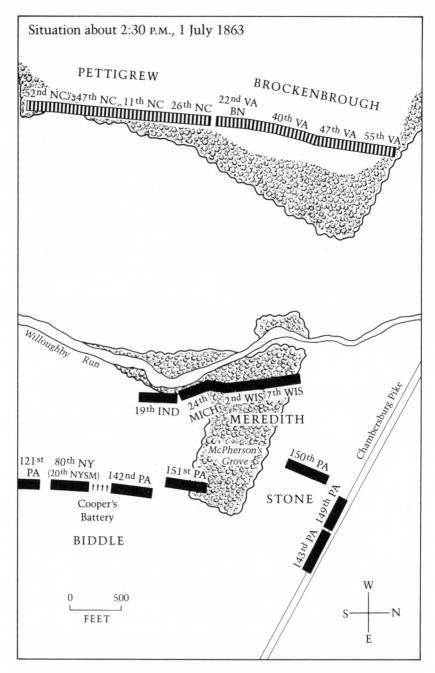

Situation about 2:30 P.M., 1 July 1863

PETTIGREW

BROCKENBROUGH

52nd NC 47th NC 11th NC 26th NC 22nd VA BN 40th VA 47th VA 55th VA

Willoughby Run

Chambersburg Pike

19th IND 24th MICH 2nd WIS 7th WIS

MEREDITH

McPherson's Grove

121st PA 80th NY (20th NYSM) 142nd PA 151st PA 150th PA

††††

Cooper's Battery

STONE 149th PA

143rd PA

BIDDLE

0   500
FEET

W
S — — N
E

Battle of Gettysburg, charge of Heth's division, afternoon, 1 July 1863 (adaptation: J. B. Bachelder, troop position maps [Gettysburg National Military Park] and official regimental records)

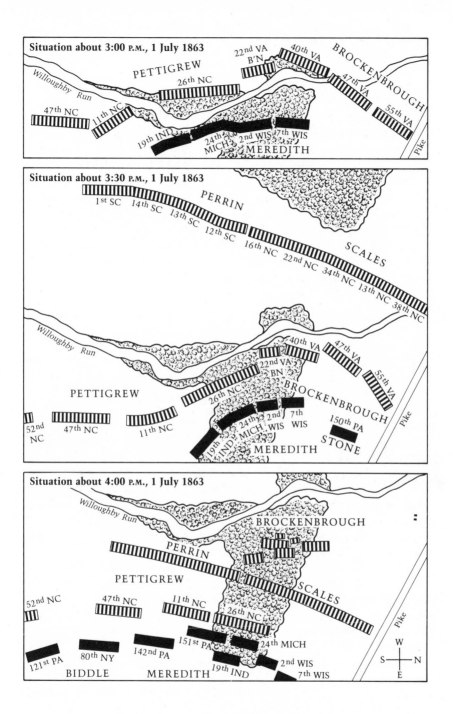

Situation about 3:00 P.M., 1 July 1863

Situation about 3:30 P.M., 1 July 1863

Situation about 4:00 P.M., 1 July 1863

tain Wilson [Company B] were both shot down at that fire besides many others] but Blair got them first, and started to advance with them—when I heard the voice of Lieut. Col. J. R. Lane say Blair give me them Colours—Blair handed them to him—as he did so—He [Blair] remarked you will get *tyred* of them—Col. Lane took the Colours and advanced quickly to the front and as he did so gave the command 26th follow me—He looked back (like Lot's wife) and fell as limber as a rag—I thought killed *dead*—but not so—but badly wounded—in the back of head coming out at his mouth—we raised a cheer—the Yankee line gave way—we charge to the top of the Hill where we found another line which we charged—they gave way and run into the town. Just then our support (Pender's Division) came up and relieved us.[10]

It was near the top of the hill, on the eastern crest of the ridge, that the Twenty-fourth Michigan was finally driven from the woods. This defiant regiment had taken its third position beyond a slight ravine but still could not withstand the unrelenting pressure of the Twenty-sixth North Carolina. "We had inflicted severe loss on the enemy," reported Colonel Morrow, "but their numbers were so overpowering and our own losses had been so great . . . that scarcely a fourth of the forces taken into action could be rallied." To the left of the Twenty-fourth Michigan, as it fought along the line of its third position, stood the 151st Pennsylvania. This regiment, struck almost simultaneously by the Twenty-sixth and the Eleventh North Carolina regiments, suffered frightful losses. Lieutenant Colonel George F. McFarland of the 151st Pennsylvania later reported that despite the heavy fire, "the regiment held its ground and maintained the unequal contest until the forces both on my right and left had fallen back and gained a considerable distance to the rear."[11]

The Second Wisconsin was stationed to the immediate right of the Twenty-fourth Michigan. It, too, suffered at the hands of the Twenty-sixth North Carolina but not to the extent of the Twenty-fourth Michigan and the 151st Pennsylvania. The Seventh Wisconsin, defending the right flank of the Iron Brigade, was probably more engaged with Brockenbrough's command than with elements of the Twenty-sixth North Carolina. As Colonel Robinson later summarized the situation: "In a short time the enemy advanced into the wood in our front, lay down behind the crest of the hill and behind the trees, and opened a galling fire. . . . The troops on our right [Stone] had fallen back; the Twenty-fourth [Michigan] and Nineteenth [Indiana], on the left of the brigade, were being badly cut up by superior numbers; the Second and Seventh were keeping up a rapid fire upon the enemy in front, but, I think, without doing him much injury, as he was protected by the hill and timber. He was rapidly gaining ground on our left."[12] From these accounts it is evident that the bitterest fighting in McPherson's Grove took place between the center and the area bordering the southern edge of the woods. This was where the concentrated fury of the Twenty-sixth North Carolina had been brought to bear.

It was just as the Iron Brigade was being driven out of the woods on the eastern crest of the ridge that Perrin's brigade of Pender's division moved up to relieve Pettigrew. His weary brigade was ordered to fall back, but the men of the Twenty-sixth never received the order. They were busily taking ammunition from the enemy's dead and were about to advance when Perrin's men came charging through. The remnant of the Twenty-sixth "followed on, and assisted in driving the enemy from the heights [Seminary Ridge] on the edge of the town. They then halted."[13]

Years later, Lieutenant Cureton recalled:

Just at the Top of the Hill—at the edge of the Town—we were ordered to Halt and Stacked arms at the female Seminary— while "Pender" pursued the enemy with the "Rebel shout of Victory" through the town. The sun I think was 2 [illegible] Hours High when we "Haulted." The men and officers of [the] 26th Regt. were Completely exhausted in Climbing that Hill through the woods under such circumstances—but the writer recollects going to the Seminary—and talking to the Girls who were in the Basement of the Seminary which above appeared to be filled with the enemy's wounded—and How scared the Girls were—until I assured them we were "Southern Soldiers" and did not war on women, and that they would be protected. Then "woman like" they all wanted to talk at *once*. The enemy had the Yellow Flag flying from the Building.

After remaining there a short time we were ordered back to the woods near the place where we started to make the charge from—going over the same ground—then it was we saw the Sickening Horrors of War—a great many of our wounded had not yet been carried to the Hospital. The Enemy's dead and wounded lay mixed with their [our] wounded crying piteously—for water—which we freely gave what [we] had—our dead were lying where they had fallen—but the "Battlefield

Robbers" had been there plundering the "dead." They seemed to have respected neither the enemy's or our own dead—Colonel Burgwyn had not been long dead having bled to death—his last words (I was informed by one of the ambulance corps that saw him die) "I know my gallant Regiment will do their duty—where is my sword."[14]

The night of Wednesday, 1 July 1863, would never be forgotten by those who survived the slaughter in McPherson's woods. The coolness of evening, drifting slowly up the gentle slopes of Herr Ridge from the bottomland along Willoughby Run, would afford some relief to the weary, but there would be no stillness during that long night. The air was rent by the piteous cries of the wounded, many still lying in the fields and woods, pleading for water, for succor of any kind, and even perhaps for the ultimate relief that only death could afford. And none had suffered more than the men of the Twenty-sixth North Carolina. Out of the approximately eight hundred who had been engaged in that bitter fight with Meredith's Iron Brigade and the 151st Pennsylvania, hardly more than two hundred were able to make their way back to the narrow woods on Herr Ridge. Although victorious, the Twenty-sixth was virtually destroyed. Yet many of its survivors, along with the bandsmen and others detailed to hospital duty, spent the long night in search of the wounded and in carrying off the dead.[15]

Julius Lineback would recall years later that "as our wounded men came in, we helped the surgeons with them until 11 o'clock at night, when I was so thoroly tired I could do no more, and lay down for a little rest. At 3 o'clock [A.M.] I got up and resumed the task of doing what I could for the men. While we had been thus engaged," he continued, "we were sent for to come to the regiment and play for the men. Our brigade surgeon, Dr. Warren, sent Sam [Captain Sam Mickey] with a note to Col. Marshall, who was in command of the brigade, Gen. Pettigrew having charge of the division, as Gen. Heath had been slightly wounded, saying that the musicians could not well be spared, as there were so many wounded men needing attention."[16] Lineback quoted from Captain Mickey's diary:

> On reaching the brigade I gave the note to Capt. Grewer, who took it to Col. Marshall, who approved it. While Capt. Grewer was with Col. Marshall, at his headquarters, I walked over on the hill where our men had met the Yankees the day before. Pettigrew's brigade had charged thru two fields and a narrow strip of woods, down grade all the way, to a small branch, where

they were in thirty steps of the enemy, who were said to have had three lines of men firing into our ranks. . . . While there I saw many wounded Yankees, and about five hundred dead on the hill, and wondered how any of our men had escaped. On returning to the hospital, I found Col. Burgwyn's grave under a tree, in a large field, near a stone house, and Capt. Wilson's and Capt. McCreery's graves near by. After returning to the hospital, having walked four or five miles, and being on my feet since 3 a.m., I felt like resting.[17]

Two days later, the following letter from one of Harry's friends was started on its long journey southward:

Captain Young has undertaken to give you the sad news of your son's death but I can not let the opportunity pass without expressing my deep sympathy with his bereaved parents & family, as well as testifying to the gallant & soldier's way in which he met his death. He was one of 11 shot bearing the Colours of his regt. & fell with his sword in his hand & cheering on his men to victory—the ball passed through the lower part of both lungs & he lived about 2 hours—among his last words he asked how his men fought & said they never would disgrace him. He died in the arms of Lt. Young bidding all farewell & send love to his mother father sisters & brothers.

It was my painful privilege to assist Capt. Young to inter his body under a walnut tree about one mile west of the town on the north side of the turnpike road—75 yds. N.E. of a medium sized stone farm house, which has a large yellow barn on the opposite side of the road. There are several graves under the tree but his is directly east of the tree with the head strait towards it. I have given this description that in case none of us should ever return & this reached you, you might still recover his remains. I can not attempt to offer consolation to friends so bereaved but can only mourn with them the loss of one of my most cherished friends. His death, however, was so noble & so glorious that it was all a soldier could desire.[18]

It is not known precisely when Harry's family learned of his death. At least two letters were written and mailed by two of his fellow officers on or about 3 July,[19] but by 13 July these had not been delivered, for on that day Harry's father telegraphed a family friend in Richmond, Mary W. Barney, inquiring about the fate of his son. The same day she replied by letter, saying, "Dr. Barney left the city this morning for Winchester and Martinsburg—he will make all possible enquires about your son, the Col., and inform you as soon as possible. . . . Your telegram is this moment received, and it grieves me that I can say nothing to relieve your horrid doubts, but I trust to be able, very soon, to send you a cheering telegram."[20]

To this slight ray of hope was added still another bit of encouragement. It, too, came from Richmond, under date of 13 July, from Samuel Melton: "No official report—the Dispatch Correspondent at Martinsburg reports the Rumor in today's papers—a lady at Staunton who knows Col. Burgwyn received the information in such a way as to lead her to believe it. I have not doubted the report but several of the officers reported as killed proved to be unhurt and I hope it may be so in this case—will telegraph as soon as I can hear further." The following day, 14 July, Mary Barney undertook the sad duty of informing Harry's father: "Mr. Young Quartermaster of Twenty sixth (26th) NCR writes that Col. Burgwyn fell on Wednesday while bearing the flag died two hours after Col. Hoke here wounded believes it true."[21]

It must have been about this time that the family heard directly from Captain Young. Whether the following letter arrived in Raleigh before Mary Barney's telegram is not known, but it confirmed their worst fears:

> I feel it my duty to communicate the painful & melancholy intelligence to you of the death of your son, Col. H. K. Burgwyn, who was killed nobly fighting for his country, July 1st 1863. He was shot through both lungs & died an easy death. I have buried him as well as possible under a walnut tree on the turnpike leading from G[ettysburg] to Chambersburg, 2 miles from the former place in a field about 100 yds. from the road. I have all his effects & will carefully guard them, his horses & Kincheon [Kincian or Kinchen] until I get a chance to send them off. I would like very much to send them immediately but being in the enemy's country it is impossible.
>
> His loss is great, more than any of us can imagine to his country. To me it [is] almost stunning & [to] the whole regiment. We gained a great victory the 1st of the month the enemy loosing [sic] it is said 12,000 but though ours was not a fourth so large, his [death] made it great. Poor Kincheon takes it bitterly enough. The Col., Col. Lane, Capt. McCreery & 8 others were shot down with our colors. Capt. McCreery was instantly killed, Col. Lane seriously if not mortally wounded. The regt.

went in 800 strong & came out with but 250 men. The fighting yesterday & today has been terrible & will continue tomorrow I suppose. Gen. Pettigrew is in command of our Division, Maj. Jones of our brigade. This will give you an idea of the frightful loss of the officers.[22]

Still deeply saddened by Harry's loss to the regiment, Captain Young again wrote the family several days later. This time it was to tell them of the faithful Kincian's proposed journey southward with Harry's two horses and some personal effects in his care—and, more meaningfully, to convey to his sorrowing parents something of the love and abiding respect in which their son was held by all with whom he had lived and fought. The following letter is both a testimonial and a memorial to one of unblemished character and courage:

I have concluded to send Kincheon off towards home as some of my wagons will go to Winchester tomorrow, though I am fearful to do so yet for somebody might possibly take both horses from him. This however they will have to do by force if at all for I never saw fidelity stronger in any one. But taking everything into consideration I fear to keep him longer, for we may advance & he fall into the hands of the enemy & there is now every prospect of a great battle again so I will start him off. He will take both horses, the Col's clothes, except his best uniform suit which is in the medical wagon & cannot be reached & a pair of shoes. The Col's. arms, both spy glasses, pocketbook & a couple of memoranda books, both shot through by the more than cruel ball that deprived the Confederacy of one of her brighter ornaments, his watch & tooth brush I have fearing Kincheon might loose [sic] them or they be forcibly taken away from him. I will preserve them faithfully & send or bring to you if nothing happens.

There was in the pocketbook $135, one hundred & thirty-five dolls. I give $95 ninety-five of it to Kincheon, leaving $40 forty in my possession. If anything should happen to me, I hereby state that Col. Burgwyn was last paid by me to May 31st 1863. There is due him, one month & one day from the Confederacy. I will pay up his mess bill & other debts if any, I suppose there are none else, which we will arrange hereafter.

The death of one so young, so brave, so accomplished, with every prospect of being at no distant period one of our greatest men has filled all with sadness & sorrow. His fall is universally regretted but in his regt. now reduced to less than 200 all are filled with the greatest sorrow.

In some way I have ever felt uneasy whenever he went into battle & always cautioned him to be cautious. My forebodings, alas, have proved too true & I have lost one of my best friends. I can truly say, the death of Gen. Lee himself I would have preferred. But all mortal that is lovely has to fade away, but his example ought ever to be a shining light to his relatives & friends left behind. Their loss is great but I hope & believe it is his eternal gain.

Everything has been quiet since the 3 days' fight, but this evening everything is astir on our lines. Our army is in line of battle & ere this reaches you you will doubtless hear of another great battle. Please inform me when Kincheon arrives safely for I shall feel a good deal of anxiety until I hear he is safe.[23]

Shortly thereafter the family received another letter, this time from one of Harry's closest friends, who was also at Gettysburg. Recognizing from his own personal experience "how dearly sadly welcome is every item concerning those we have loved & lost, & how we preserve as precious treasures the remembrances of the last acts & appearances on earth," young W. E. Taylor, Jr. (Company C, Garnett's Battalion of Artillery), was evidently moved by a deep sense of understanding and compassion when he wrote:

I was with H[arry] up to Gettysburg, seeing & conversing with him nearly every day; he was in good health & spirits. On that fatal day while passing to the front to go into position, I learned that he had been hit, but it was impossible then to look for him as I expected every minute to be engaged. The next morning as soon as possible I got permission & started, but found his remains surrounded by many of his sorrowing regiment. Every-[thing] that could be done had been attended to before I arrived, & all I could do was to cut off a lock of hair for his mother, & see his remains properly buried. His body was enclosed in a box & buried at a proper depth, & in a place reasonably secure from disturbance. I attended to the last & took notes of the place, so that if I can be of any service to you I am at your command at any time.

H[arry] was very much beloved by all his men & officers, & respected for his courage & competency by all who knew him; & I have great reason to believe that Genl. Pettigrew thought him one of his best officers. I made enquiries of all who could have any knowledge on the subject, & all agreed that he suffered but little, & died quietly in full possession of all his faculties. When I saw him, his face was as calm & placid as if he were asleep, with no contortion or appearances of pain about any of the features. I hope & believe that he passed quietly & resignedly to another world.

Several color-bearers had been shot down & the regiment was faltering when he seized the colors & with a cheer led the men on to Victory, but he was too prominent a mark & he fell shot thro' the body. He lived only about two hours breathing last in the arms of an aide of Gen'l Pettigrew. I earnestly desired & tried to be with him, but I could not leave my post which was in front.

I believe I knew & loved Harry as well as anyone outside of his family & his loss was a severe blow to me, but I almost fear to attempt to relieve their great grief, but I have written, hoping.

Seemingly as if to apologize for having failed to convey the true depth of his heartfelt sentiments, young Taylor concluded with an earnest plea for understanding: "I sincerely hope, Sir, that however I may have worded it, you will believe that my heart is in this letter, & that I have done what I believe would have been most consonant to my parents' feelings had I died in my country's cause."[24]

AFTERWORD

One cannot conclude this story of the life of Harry Burgwyn without further reference to those whose lives were intertwined with his. Much has been written about the long war years but little about those who were left to contend with the desolation and despair of a shattered land. The Burgwyns would fare much better than most, for they were neither homeless nor without means. But the death of their beloved Harry was not the end of their sorrows. And somehow, Anna, the lady from Boston, always strong in resolve and Christian commitment, would emerge triumphant in the end. The few miscellaneous letters extant, interlaced with her cryptic diary notations, tell the story.

Four months after Harry's death his father was stricken with paralysis. In June 1864, young Will was seriously wounded at Cold Harbor. He was sent home to convalesce, and Anna met him at Garysburg on his way to Thornbury, 5 June 1864. A few days later, Anna's father-in-law, John Fanning Burgwyn, died in Raleigh at Will's Forest, the home of John Devereux. On 1 August, George Pollok, Anna's third son, was in Petersburg under General Ransom.[1] By 19 September, Will was sufficiently recovered to return to his regiment, but within a matter of days he was taken prisoner at Chaffin's Bluff. He was soon able, however, to assure his mother that "although his haversack had been shot off & several balls had passed through his clothes, he had escaped unhurt & was well treated." On 27 October, George Pollok left for Camp Lee to join the cadets of VMI for temporary field service.[2]

On 13 December 1864, the Burgwyns journeyed from Raleigh to Thornbury, where they must have spent a forlorn Christmas. As the new year unfolded, only Will's return to Raleigh as a paroled prisoner on 6 March served to brighten an otherwise despairing time for the Burgwyn family. Anna later remarked upon the failure of the "conference for cessation of hostilities at Fortress Monroe Feb 6th 1865," the evacuation of Richmond and Petersburg "by our forces April 4th 1865," and Henry's removal of "his people to Elwood April 10th 1865."[3]

Thereafter, the situation in North Carolina deteriorated rapidly, as reflected in Anna's notes:

Gen'l Joe John[ston's] forces were retreating through Raleigh during the entire day Ap[ril] 11th 1865. Heard of the surrender of Gen'l Lee same date.

Moved all my family & what I could of my furniture to Major John Devereux Ap[ril] 12th 1865.

Gen'l Sherman's army occupied Raleigh April 13th 1865. The town had surrendered. A guard was sent to protect us, & Gen'l Barry was to take a room at Major Devereux['s].

News of the assassination of President Lincoln reached Raleigh April 17th 1865.[4]

On 12 June, Henry King Burgwyn petitioned President Andrew Johnson for permission to take the amnesty oath prescribed in the president's proclamation of 29 May 1865. Henry declared that before John Brown's raid, "he was a devoted friend to the Union of the States and never encouraged the slightest disaffection to the Union." It was only after this event that he had come "to the conclusion that it was better for the two sections of the country—free & slave—to live apart under two different governments, allied to each other offensively & defensively against all foreign countries. He was led to believe," Burgwyn added, "that such separation might & would take place without war: for he was fully convinced that each state had a right to secede from the others." For these reasons he became "an advocate for a separation of the states, which he truly thought would be productive of greater peace, tranquility & prosperity of both sections." He had not changed his mind until the middle of the war. After admitting that he had been in error but now regarded the question "as forever settled against the right of secession," Burgwyn asserted that all of his slaves (about 150 before the termination of the war) were now freedmen and that his real estate and other property, after satisfying the mortgages and other bond debt, might be worth no more than twenty thousand dollars. The same day (12 June), he requested Governor Holden to approve the inclusion of his property in the amnesty, but, on the following day, the governor recommended that "this application be suspended."[5]

But General John Schofield was more accommodating. From his headquarters in Raleigh, on 13 June, he issued an order allowing the Burgwyns to go to Boston. Anna would be on her way home, back to her beloved Boston to the warmth and understanding of her old friends and relatives. It must have been with a deep sense of relief that she recorded: "Subrented the house we had occupied in Raleigh to Mrs. Winder & left for Thornbury on our way to Boston,

Mass., June 18th 1865.—Henry concluded an arrangement with Mr. Randolph to take charge of his Plantation & business June 19th 1865.—Left Thornbury for Boston, June 22nd 1865.—Took the steamer at Norfolk for New York June 25th 1865. Henry, Maria, Alveston, Collinson & self formed the party. Arrived in Boston & took rooms at Mrs. Putnam's in Pemberton Square, June 27th 1865."[6]

Anna and her family would not return to North Carolina until October of the following year. In the meantime, Alveston and Collinson entered the Boston Latin School on 1 September 1865, and Henry sailed from New York for Europe a few days later. It was on 16 October that Captain Drennan brought to Anna Harry's diary, which he had found on the battlefield at New Bern in March 1862. Will spent Christmas with his mother at Mrs. Putnam's and left Boston to return to Chapel Hill on 2 January 1866.[7]

Henry returned from Europe on 27 August. Anna joined him in New York, and together they reached Boston on 2 September. Before the end of the month, Henry, in company with his son Collinson, was on his way to North Carolina. Anna, with the rest of her family, followed on 2 October, arriving at Thornbury two days later.[8] It has never been clear why Henry left his family in Boston and spent almost a year abroad. Having suffered two strokes, the latest in May 1865, he must have had some compelling reason for traveling alone to Europe. In his petition to President Johnson he had emphasized that "these attacks, & especially the last, have almost wholly destroyed his physical strength & very greatly impaired the energies of his mind."[9] Whether his brother Tom or sister Emily was in Europe at the time is not known. Nonetheless, Henry's interest in art was unimpaired, for he purchased copies of several fine Italian paintings, some ancient Chinese porcelains, a collection of French clocks, and a variety of Italian furniture that had formerly belonged to such distinguished names as the Bianchi, Mantua, Contarini, and Pisaro families. These works of art and furniture were acquired at a total cost of 12,418 francs, on which Henry paid down about a third in gold, leaving a balance owing of 8,369 francs.[10] They were shipped to New York and sold at auction the following year.

The auction was held at Leeds' Art Galleries at the southwest corner of Twelfth Street and Broadway on 30 May 1867. The catalog of "Articles of Furniture and Vertu" being offered for sale claimed: "The following articles now offered for Sale, were all purchased by a gentleman who passed the last year in Europe, selected by himself, exclusively, for his own use; but being unable to secure a house, is about to return to Europe. He had every advantage in selection, and is confident from the altered state of things in Venice and Italy, they cannot be replaced now."[11] The success of the auction is not known, but to none did "the altered state of things" apply more than to Henry King Burgwyn. The war years had left him heavily in debt. While in Europe the euphoria of travel might have led him to believe that, upon his return, he could liquidate his plantation holdings, satisfy his creditors, and have sufficient funds with which to buy a house and live comfortably in a city such as Richmond, for on 1 November 1866 he and his family went to the Exchange Hotel in Richmond, where they took rooms for the winter. But serious financial difficulties lay immediately ahead, and, in mid-December, to compound the problem, a disastrous fire destroyed the cotton gin, grist mill, and stored cotton at Thornbury.[12]

In the years before the war, Henry and his brother Tom had relied heavily upon credit in developing their two outstanding plantation systems, Thornbury and Occoneechee Wigwam. Their indebtedness had greatly worried their father, and it was not until 1856 that John Fanning Burgwyn grudgingly conceded that the "worldly concerns" of his sons were improving. But only "with due care, caution, prudence, *economy* & good management," he was constrained to add, would they "be enabled to surmount the difficulties which have so long enthralled them."[13] The extent of their indebtedness when the war broke out is not known, but at war's end Henry doubted that his estate was worth more than $20,000 after satisfying all creditors.[14] Now physically handicapped and neither mentally nor emotionally prepared to labor under the burden of protracted ill fortune, he had no alternative but to liquidate as best he could before bankruptcy enveloped him.

Henry did attempt to farm his plantation in 1867. On 5 February he proposed to McIlwaine and Company a renewal of their former business arrangement whereby the factor would advance necessary operating funds against ninety-day acceptances supported by crop liens. In this instance, Burgwyn said that he would pledge his cotton and wheat crops (600 acres in cotton and 250 acres in wheat) from which he hoped to realize better than $50,000.[15] There is no evidence that he succeeded in effecting this arrangement, and certainly he spent little, if any, time at Thornbury during the year. He and Anna spent the summer in Boston and did not return to Richmond until after mid-September. And on their infrequent visits to Northampton County in 1867, the members of the family regularly stayed at Cypress plantation.[16]

As the year 1867 drew to a close every effort was apparently being made to sell the Burgwyn holdings in order to satisfy creditors. Anna and Henry were at the Cypress plantation the latter part of November and on the twenty-third of that month put up Alveston plantation for sale, "but not a bid made for it." On 28 December Henry's son Will went to North Carolina armed with a power of attorney from his father "to arrange his business." On 10 January 1868 Henry accompanied the governor of Virginia on a visit to Thornbury because the latter "talked of purchasing it." After about a week there, the governor decided not to make the purchase, and the Burgwyns returned to Richmond on the sixteenth. On 12 February 1868 they succeeded in selling Cypress plantation, but apparently it was too little and too late, for, on the twentieth of that month, "Henry filed a petition in Bankruptcy."[17]

Shortly before this Anna had received a letter from James Read, a longtime friend and confidant of the Greenough family, in response to a letter she had written seeking his advice on matters of great moment to her. Read suggested that "the condition of Mr. Burgwyn[']s affairs make it very desirable . . . that he should go into Bankruptcy, & it would be well to do so with as little delay as possible." He thought that rather than take a house in Richmond, one alternative Anna had mentioned, they would do better to move to the Boston area and remarked that he was pleased to read of "your determination, that for yourself & family, to live within your income, & to pay everything as you go along."[18]

Earlier in the month Read had clarified for Anna the conditions of a real estate trust, established for her benefit by General Sumner, in which the proceeds of sale "were to be invested in a 'healthy situation at the South'—for you during your life, & the life of Mr. Burgwyn, then to go to Wm. H. Sumner Burgwyn [their son and namesake of the general]." Read emphasized, however, that if Anna wanted to invest the proceeds in the Boston area it would be necessary to "get the parties interested in Genl. Sumner's estate to agree to a change," a likelihood, he added, that "might not be very easy."[19] In any event, he felt that $9,000 to $10,000 could be realized from the sale of the property. Because money was "very scarce in Richmond," Anna had earlier indicated that she could "get a good estate for 25 to 30 pct. off for cash down," and if she did not occupy the property, it could be rented at a price to net her 6 percent. Read replied that this would not be a good arrangement; she should hope to net 10 percent should she buy property to rent. Nor did he recommend purchasing a house "unless you intend it for your own purposes & comfort." Should she find a house she wished to buy, Read offered to "advance ten thousand, say 10,000 dollars in payment of the same, but *be sure* not to purchase unless the House is satisfactory for *your use* & the situation all right."[20]

From these letters it is apparent that James Read was a loving and faithful friend. He was almost fatherly in his concern for Anna's well-being. She apparently acquired a house in Richmond during the summer of 1869, for in late August, Read felt that she had not allowed enough for alterations and repairs. "It is your home," he insisted, "& it seems to me that the estimates are very small. I never expected that you would go into the House without laying out *double* the amount you have named, & I have always supposed it would exceed 'two thousand dollars.'"[21] A week later, on 1 September, Anna and her family moved into their house at 301 East Main Street.[22]

It would be her home for the remainder of her years. The future pattern of her life would be relatively free of the heartaches and uncertainties that had characterized the war years and their immediate aftermath—and, indeed, the antebellum period at Thornbury. Her oldest child, Maria, was now married and living in Richmond.[23] Her youngest son, Collinson, graduated from the Boston Latin School that summer and enrolled at Harvard College in the fall. Her third son, George Pollok, was married to Emma Wright Ridley of Southampton County, Virginia, on 27 May 1869, and her second son, Will, graduated from the law school at Cambridge that summer. Only Alveston, two years older than Collinson and unwell, would soon drop out of school and go to work.[24] Until Christmas 1874, when her diary book was abruptly concluded, Anna's notes generally refer to family, friends, travels, and visits, largely centered around Richmond and Boston.

Her first grandchild, Henry King Burgwyn Baker (named for her beloved son Harry), was born at her home in Richmond on 20 September 1869. Anna learned of the death of her friend and adviser, James Read, on 29 December 1870. Reverend Cameron F. McRae, first married to Henry King's oldest sister, Julia, died in August 1872. Mrs. William H. Sumner, Anna's stepfather's third wife, died 16 November 1872. All of Anna's children and John McRae (Julia and Cameron McRae's only son) were with her during Christmas of 1872. And Annie and Meta Devereux "came to visit us Feb 1st & remained until Feby. 20th 1873." Later that year Anna learned of the death of her dear Mary Ann (Madie) on 16 August 1873. But soon followed a happy notation: "Heard of the birth of a daughter to Emma & George who was to be named for me March 18th 1874." And finally, and perhaps much to the chagrin of James Read had he been alive, Anna re-corded: "Moved with my family to the Ballard House where we had taken rooms for the winter Nov 2nd 1874 & Mrs. Garland rented & took possession of my house Nov 7th 1874."[25]

Anna also kept a daily journal. On Tuesday, 19 October 1886, she wrote: "As soon as my room was in order took down my journal[s] to have them put by themselves in a trunk & sent to the attic to give me more room in my wardrobe."[26] Only one of these journals has survived. It covers the last year of Anna's life, from Thursday, 13 May 1886, to Wednesday, 6 April 1887—just six days before her death at the home of her son, Colonel W. H. S. Burgwyn, in Henderson, North Carolina.[27] Unwittingly, it serves as an autobiographical memorial to a rare lady; for it is nothing more than a daily record of her activities, of visits with friends, of news from the children and grandchildren and of events of the day—with no evidence of sadness or of self-pity.

A sense of Christian resignation seems to pervade the whole. Anna's daily activities were dutiful with respect to her family as well as to her friends and community; yet she reflects upon the serenity of spirit that comes with the rising and the setting of the sun, enabling her to adjust to the new and not sorrow for the old. Her "new" home at 301 East Main Street had long since replaced Northampton County and Raleigh as her principal place of residence. For it was here that her first grandchild, Harry Burgwyn Baker, was born on 20 September 1869 and where her late husband had died on 2 February 1877.[28]

But the cherished memories of her dear Harry never faded:

Saturday, July 10th [1886], Richmond.
Bright and beautiful after the rain. . . . When I went to break-fast I found a box in my parlor left by Express & which con-tained a worsted shawl as a gift from Annie Devereux. It was very kind in her to remember me in this way & I shall doubtless find it a most useful addition to my wardrobe & always wear it with pleasure as she made it for me.[29]

Wednesday, Oct 13th [1886], Richmond.
My Birthday & Minnie & Mr. Baker came to my room early with good wishes & a framed Photograph of my son Harry taken in his uniform when he was at the V.M.I. & of my grand-son Harry taken in his uniform as a Cadet there. It was a very unexpected gift & nothing could have pleased me so much.[30]

Monday, Dec 20th [1886], Richmond.

Rec'd a paper from Will containing Governor Vance's speech delivered in Boston at the ——. He alluded to dear Harry's gallantry & death & the carnage of his Regiment at Gettysburg.[31]
Thursday Feb 3rd [1887], Richmond.
Then went & selected a new frame for dear Harry's portrait.[32]
Friday, Feb 25th [1887], Richmond.
The anniversary of my last parting with dear Harry.[33]

Undoubtedly Anna's saddest memory was of that day long ago when she and Henry had stood prayerfully by as Harry's remains were lowered to their final resting place. That day was 9 June 1867,[34] and the grave site was in Raleigh, at the Oakwood Cemetery. For four years his body had rested almost where he had fallen, in an unmarked, unattended grave at the foot of a walnut tree in faraway Pennsylvania. Now, at long last, Harry was home again, where he could forever rest in the company of other fallen comrades and in the land that he loved and had so bravely defended. His epitaph bears the mark of Anna's deep faith and spiritual resignation:

HENRY KING BURGWYN
COL. 26th REGT. N.C.T.
AGED 22 YEARS
FELL AT GETTYSBURG, JULY 1, 1863
THE LORD GAVE
AND
THE LORD HATH TAKEN AWAY[35]

APPENDIX

Only the darkness of night could still the battle that had begun so unceremoniously in the early morning hours of 1 July. As twilight settled over the ridges and meadows surrounding Gettysburg, a deep sense of relief, mingled with fear and apprehension, must have been felt by friend and foe alike, for that long, hot, and humid July day had witnessed one of the bloodiest and most intensive battles of the war. It was a battle that had begun by accident and would probably prove to be the most decisive conflict of the three-day Gettysburg engagement. The general engagement that neither Lee nor Meade wanted had ended in an apparent victory for the South. Yet in the succeeding two days, the fruits of final victory would elude Lee. As the exhausted men waited out the night in fitful slumber, as others roamed the fields and woods in search of the dead and wounded, as Longstreet's divisions marched eastward on the Chambersburg pike, and as Meade's forces converged on Cemetery Ridge, everyone must have sensed that the greatest battle of the war had indeed begun.

On the first day at Gettysburg, the Union men, many of them Pennsylvanians, were determined to stand and die in defense of their native soil. And the men under Lee were equally determined to win yet another victory. It was a proud and defiant army from the South that had converged on Gettysburg. But it was hardly prepared for the fighting that took place in the open fields and along the wooded ridges surrounding the little town. As the fighting grew in intensity throughout the day it was characterized by almost continuous attacks, counterattacks, and flanking movements, with the heaviest fighting concentrated on the northern end of Oak Ridge, near the crossing of the Mummasburg road, in the vicinity of the turnpike and railroad cut between McPherson's Ridge and Seminary Ridge, and in McPherson's Grove and immediately south of it.

It was in these three areas that bitter, almost hand-to-hand fighting occurred, and it was here that both sides suffered severe losses. And none suffered more than the troops from North Carolina. In Rodes's division, of the sixteen regiments and one battalion that fought north of the pike in the vicinity of Oak Ridge on the afternoon of the first, twelve regiments and one battalion were North Carolina troops. The other four regiments were Alabama troops in

O'Neal's brigade. In the magnificent attack on McPherson's Ridge on the same afternoon, only two Confederate brigades led the charge against units of Doubleday's First Corps. They consisted of four North Carolina regiments in Pettigrew's brigade of two thousand men and three Virginia regiments and one Virginia battalion in Brockenbrough's brigade of seventeen hundred men.[1] They would later be supported by ten North Carolina and five South Carolina regiments in Pender's division. Of the forty-six regiments and three battalions that fought on the ridges west and northwest of Gettysburg on the morning and afternoon of the first, twenty-seven regiments and one battalion were from the Old North State.[2] If the Confederates were victorious on 1 July, no little credit was due the troops from Carolina. Many an intrepid soul was crowned with glory on that hot and humid July day, but none more so than the gallant Colonel Harry Burgwyn, commander of the immortal Twenty-sixth North Carolina Regiment.

Late in the afternoon of the day following, the bandsmen of the Twenty-sixth and Eleventh North Carolina regiments were ordered to lay aside their duties at the field hospital and report to Colonel Marshall (Fifty-second North Carolina), who now commanded Pettigrew's brigade. As Captain Mickey later remembered, "This was about six o'clock [P.M., 2 July]. Both bands played together for some time, heavy firing going on meanwhile, tho not in our immediate neighborhood. Our playing seemed to do the men good, for they cheered us lustily. We got back to the hospital sometime after dark. . . . We learned some time afterwards, from northern papers, that our playing had been heard by the enemy, amid the noise of the cannon, and that they had supposed with wonder that we were in the midst of the fight."[3]

That same evening the sadly depleted ranks of Pettigrew's brigade were moved about a mile to the right and stationed in the woods in the rear of their batteries facing the enemy's works on Cemetery Ridge.[4] Still greater sacrifice lay in store for them the following day, for this brigade would be in the front and left-center of the Pettigrew-Pickett charge. These North Carolinians would be posted on the front line of Pettigrew's division, flanked by Fry's brigade (Archer) on the right and by Davis and Mayo (Brockenbrough) on the left. Two brigades of Pender's division, Lane and Scales (commanded by Colonel W. L. J. Lowrance), would be in support. Pickett's division would be formed to the right of Pettigrew. There would be forty-seven regiments in the attacking column of these two divisions, including nineteen from Virginia and fourteen from North Carolina, numbering about fifteen thousand men in all.[5] In this final battle of the Gettysburg campaign, the Twenty-sixth North Carolina, which had been virtually destroyed in the first day's engagement, would be able to muster only about two hundred men capable of making the charge. Of this number, perhaps no more than seventy would make it to the "Angle" and back.[6]

As one of those intrepid few who made it back, Lieutenant Cureton of Company B (the Waxhaw Jackson Guards) later described the charge:

> The enemy's artillery did not open on us till we got within about half mile of the works. . . . But our lines crossed the lane [Emmitsburg road] in splendid order when about two hundred yards from their works the musketry opened on us. . . . Our brave men pressed quickly forward and [when] we had reached within about forty yards of the works our regiment had been reduced to a skirmish line . . . but still they kept closing to the colours. We were still pressing quickly forward when a cry came from the left and I look[ed] and saw the right regiment of Davis' Mississippi Brigade—our left regiment—driven from the field as if chaff before a "whirl wind." The entire left of the line was gone. . . . The writer and some other officers tried to form our men in the lane where they were somewhat protected by the road and would have succeeded but a line of the enemy had [been] thrown outside of the works to [the] left, and were quickly advancing down the fence capturing every man they could find. . . . The writer made his way back [to] the artillery . . . but before he reached the artillery or starting point he ran up with a solitary man on foot. When he looked at him it was Gen'l J. Johnston Pettigrew—three (3) horses had been killed under him in the charge that day and, now wounded in the arm, wearied, was making his way out on foot. I promptly asked him if I could assist him. He thanked me, offered me his unwounded arm, and I assisted him up the steep little hill to the artillery. . . . By night we had a pretty good skirmish line, and the gallant old 26th Regiment had sixty-seven muskets and three (3) officers present on the night [of] July 3rd 1863 of the eight hundred and fifty carried in the fight July 1st 1863.[7]

Colonel William F. Fox, authority on Civil War casualties, wrote: "At Gettysburg, the 26th North Carolina . . . went into action with an effective strength which is stated in the regimental official report as 'over 800 men.' They sustained a loss, according to Surgeon-

General Guild's report, of 86 killed and 502 wounded; total, 588. In addition there were about 120 missing, nearly all of whom must have been wounded or killed; but, as they fell into the enemy's hands, they were not included in the hospital report. This loss occurred mostly in the first day's fight. . . . This loss of the 26th North Carolina, at Gettysburg, was the severest regimental loss during the war."[8]

Colonel Fox's study revealed further that out of twenty-seven Confederate regiments with 134 or more losses, twelve were from North Carolina. In Pettigrew's brigade the Twenty-sixth North Carolina ranked first with 708 losses, the Eleventh North Carolina ranked fourth with 209 losses, the Forty-seventh North Carolina ranked fifteenth with 161 losses, and the Fifty-second North Carolina ranked nineteenth with 147 losses, bringing the total brigade casualty figure to 1,225.[9]

The losses of the Twenty-sixth North Carolina were so staggering at Gettysburg, with a casualty rate of over 88 percent, that each of its ten companies was obviously subjected to severe sacrifice. For example, based upon muster rolls taken the day before the battle and sixty days later, the following statistics tell a frightful story of carnage:

Company A went into action with 92 men and lost 11 killed and 66 wounded on the first day; and on the third day, 1 killed (Captain Wagg) and 10 wounded and missing, for a total of 88.

Company E took into battle 82 men on the first day and lost, killed and mortally wounded, 18, and wounded, 52. Of the 12 men available for duty on the third day, only two escaped injury or capture.

Company F, according to Captain R. M. Tuttle, went into battle with three officers and 88 muskets. Every man was killed or wounded; 31 were killed or died of wounds and 60 were wounded. There were three sets of twin brothers in this company. "At the close of battle, five of the six lay dead on the field."

In Company G, out of 91 present for duty, 12 were killed and 58 were reported wounded or missing.

In Company H, out of 78 present for duty, 17 were killed and 55 wounded.

Company K was reported to have recrossed the Potomac at Falling Waters with 16 men, "having crossed that river in June on the way to Gettysburg with 103, rank and file."[10]

Colonel John R. Lane, Twenty-sixth North Carolina Regiment, Pettigrew's Brigade, CSA, and Colonel Charles H. McConnell, Twenty-fourth Michigan, Meredith's Iron Brigade, USA, at Gettysburg, on the fortieth anniversary of the battle

In a letter to Dr. George C. Underwood, dated 30 September 1889, Colonel Fox observed: "I took great pains to verify the loss of the Twenty-sixth North Carolina at Gettysburg, for I am inclined to believe that in time this regiment will become as well known in history as the Light Brigade at Balaklava."[11] The glorious record of the Twenty-sixth must have been foremost in the colonel's mind when he added these final words to his long and authoritative study on Civil War casualties: "The bloody laurels for which a regiment contends will always be awarded to the one with the longest Roll of Honor. Scars are the true evidence of wounds, and the regimental scars can be seen only in the record of its casualties."[12] This quotation was incorporated in the concluding paragraph of Underwood's history of the Twenty-sixth North Carolina. And to it Underwood appended yet another: "The men of the Twenty-sixth Regiment would dress on their colors in spite of the world."[13]

But it was left to the brigade commander, General Pettigrew, to summarize the magnitude of the Twenty-sixth's heroic charge up the wooded slopes of McPherson's Ridge on the bloody afternoon of 1 July. In less than a week before his own fatal wounding at Falling Waters on 14 July, Pettigrew wrote Governor Vance:

> Knowing that you would be anxious to hear from your old regiment, the Twenty-sixth, I embrace an opportunity to write you a hasty note. It covered itself with glory. It fell to the lot of the Twenty-sixth to charge one of the strongest positions possible. They drove three, and we have every reason to believe, five regiments out of the woods [works] with a gallantry unsurpassed. Their loss has been heavy, very heavy, but the missing are on the battlefield and in the hospital. Both on the first and third days your old command did honor to your association with them and to the State they represent.[14]

NOTES

CHAPTER 1

1. James M. Drennan to H. K. Burgwyn, 15 September 1865, Burgwyn Family Papers, Southern Historical Collection, University of North Carolina Library, Chapel Hill, N.C.; hereinafter referred to as Burgwyn Family Papers.

2. Anna Greenough Burgwyn, Diary Book, 1863–74, in the possession of John Alveston Burgwyn Baker, Richmond, Va.

3. John R. Lane, "Address at Gettysburg," copied from *Raleigh News and Observer*, 5 July 1903, p. 5, John Randolph Lane Papers (#411), Southern Historical Collection, University of North Carolina Library, Chapel Hill, N.C.

4. Robert K. Krick, *Lee's Colonels: A Biographical Register of the Field Officers of the Army of Northern Virginia* (Dayton, Ohio: Press of Morningside Bookshop, 1979), p. 65. According to this study, at the time he was elected lieutenant colonel on 27 August 1861, at the age of nineteen, Harry Burgwyn was the youngest officer of this field grade rank in what later became the Army of Northern Virginia.

5. *Five Points in the Record of North Carolina in the Great War of 1861–5* (Report of the Committee appointed by the North Carolina Literary and Historical Society, 1904, and issued by the North Carolina Historical Commission), pp. 73–79.

6. Kenneth M. Stampp, *The Peculiar Institution: Slavery in the Ante-Bellum South* (New York: Vintage Books, 1956), pp. 30, 132–40.

7. Burgwyn Family Papers.

8. Ibid.

9. Despite the statutes, however, one of New Bern's leading citizens, William Gaston, a Catholic, was elected to and served in both state and federal offices. Furthermore, a Jew, Jacob Henry, had served in the General Assembly from neighboring Carteret County.

CHAPTER 2

1. Anna Greenough to William H. Sumner, 25 May 1838, Burgwyn Family Papers.

2. Anna Greenough Burgwyn to her mother, 4 December 1838, ibid.

3. See William H. Sumner, *A History of East Boston* (Boston: J. E. Tilton, 1858), pp. 269–70, 224, 226; Alfred A. Doane, comp., *The Doane Family* (Boston, 1902), pp. 1–18.

4. Sumner, *East Boston*, pp. 288–89.

5. *Appleton's Cyclopaedia of American Biography*, 6 vols. (New York: Appleton, 1888), 2:9–11.

6. William L. Saunders VI, ed., *The Colonial Records of North Carolina*, 10 vols. (Raleigh: State of North Carolina, 1888), p. 896. For more detail on the Greenough-Burgwyn family connections, see Archie K. Davis, "The Boy Colonel: The Life and Times of Henry King (Harry) Burgwyn, Jr.," typescript, 3 vols., 1:27–64, North Carolina Collection, University of North Carolina Library, Chapel Hill; North Carolina State Archives, Raleigh; New Bern–Craven County Public Library, New Bern, N.C.; Northampton County Memorial Library, Jackson, N.C.; Salem Academy and College Library, Winston-Salem, N.C.; Virginia Historical Society Library, Richmond; Virginia Military Institute Library, Lexington, Va., United States Military Academy Library, West Point, N.Y.

7. Anna to her mother, 7 December 1838, Burgwyn Family Papers.

8. Anna to her mother, 14 January 1839, ibid.

9. Anna to her mother, 25 January, 10 February 1839, ibid.

10. Anna to her mother in the form of a four-day journal, 1–4 January 1839, ibid.

11. Anna to her mother, 26 December 1838, ibid.

12. Anna to her brother, 26 December 1838, ibid.

13. Anna to General Sumner, 31 December 1838, ibid.

14. Anna to her mother, 12 March 1839, ibid.

15. Anna to her mother, 15 February 1839, ibid.

16. Anna to her mother, 4 February 1839, ibid.

17. Anna to her mother, 2 April 1839, ibid. George William Bush Burgwyn, younger brother of John Fanning Burgwyn, was the planter of the family and lived at the Hermitage, near Wilmington, N.C., a large plantation formerly owned by his father, John Burgwin.

18. Anna to her mother, 4 February, 6 March 1839, ibid.

19. The Loring-Greenough House in Jamaica Plain was built about 1760 by Commodore Joshua Loring, taken over by the state in 1779 under the Act of Confiscation and sold at auction, and purchased by the widowed Ann Doane on 5 April 1784, five weeks before her marriage to David Stoddard Greenough. The property remained in the family until 1924, when the Jamaica Plain Tuesday Club acquired it. See Eva Phillips Boyd, "Jamaica Plain by Way of London," *Old-Time New England*, 49 (Spring 1959): 85–103.

20. Anna to her mother, 9 February 1840, Burgwyn Family Papers.

CHAPTER 3

1. Anna to her mother, 9 May 1840, Burgwyn Family Papers.

2. Anna to her mother, 23 April 1840, ibid.

3. Anna to General Sumner, 27 December 1840, ibid.

4. Henry King Burgwyn Typescript Diaries, 1840–42, P.C. 515.1, North Carolina Department of Archives and History, Raleigh.

5. Anna to Jane Greenough, 27 October 1841, Burgwyn Family Papers.

6. Katherine M. Jones, *The Plantation South* (Indianapolis: Bobbs-Merrill Co., 1957), p. 48.

7. Henry King Burgwyn Typescript Diaries, 1844–48.

8. Ibid.

9. Josephine L. Harper, reference archivist, State Historical Society of Wisconsin, in letter of 13 August 1975, writes: "Burgwyn was one of the two first purchasers in the South excluding Virginia."

10. William T. Hutchinson, *Cyrus Hall McCormick*, 2 vols. (New York: Century, 1930), 1:199.

11. Ibid., pp. 417–19, 373–74.

12. Henry King Burgwyn Diaries, 1842–44, in possession of John Burgwyn, Jackson, N.C.

13. Ibid.

14. Ulrich Bonnell Phillips, *Life and Labor in the Old South* (Boston: Little, Brown, 1929), pp. 254–55.

15. Henry King Burgwyn Typescript Diaries, 1844–48, 3, 16 January, 7, 19, 29 March, 8 April 1848.

16. Henry Wilkins Lewis, *Northampton Parishes* (Jackson, N.C.: Henry W. Lewis, 1951), pp. 46–48.

17. Ibid., pp. 50, 57–58.

18. Ibid., pp. 60, 55.

19. Margaret Devereux, *Plantation Sketches* (Cambridge, Mass.: Privately printed at Riverside Press, 1906), pp. 18–19.

20. Lewis, *Northampton Parishes*, p. 55.

21. The Burgwyn house at Hillside plantation burned on 1 September 1849. The family rented quarters in nearby Jackson, pending construction of a new house to be known as Thornbury. They moved to Thornbury on 24 January 1853 (Anna Greenough Burgwyn, Diary Book, 1847–61, in the possession of John Alveston Burgwyn Baker, Richmond, Virginia). Thornbury was named for a village in Gloucestershire, England. It was at St. Mary's Church in Thornbury, about ten miles north of Bristol, that Harry's great-grandparents were married on 27 April 1782. Their first son, John Fanning Burgwin, was born at the Grove, a rented property near Thornbury, on 14 March 1783. He was baptized at St. Mary's Church. Later, after coming to America in 1801, John Fanning changed the spelling of his surname to Burgwyn. See Davis, "Boy Colonel," 1:47–55.

22. John Fanning Burgwyn Typescript Diary, 1855–56, P.C. 564.1, North Carolina Department of Archives and History, Raleigh.

23. Kenneth M. Stampp, *The Peculiar Institution: Slavery in the Ante-Bellum South* (New York: Vintage Books, 1956), p. 396.

24. John Fanning Burgwyn Typescript Diary, 1855–56.

25. See Davis, "Boy Colonel," 1:130–33.

26. Henry King Burgwyn Typescript Diaries, 1842–44.
27. John Fanning Burgwyn Typescript Diary, 1855–56.
28. Ibid.
29. Ibid.

CHAPTER 4

1. Referred to as Marianne (Mary Ann Smith) by Anna but as Madie by the children, she came to the Burgwyns from New England shortly after they moved to the Roanoke and remained with the family for years.
2. Burgwyn Family Papers.
3. Letters to his mother, 14 December, 30 November 1856, 25 January, 4 April 1857, ibid.
4. Letter to his mother, 14 December 1856, ibid.
5. Letter to his mother, 28 March 1857, ibid.
6. Letter to his mother, 14 December 1856, ibid.
7. James C. Dobbins to Henry Burgwyn, 10 February 1857, ibid.
8. Letter to his father, 13 March 1857, ibid.
9. Anna Greenough Burgwyn, Diary Book, 1863–74, in the possession of John Alveston Burgwyn Baker, Richmond, Va.
10. Letter to his mother, 25 August 1857, Burgwyn Family Papers.
11. Minutes of meeting 19 September 1856, quoting extract from minutes of the Executive Committee, Board of Trustees, assembled in Raleigh on 13 September 1856, University of North Carolina, Faculty Minutes, 1856–85, Southern Historical Collection, University of North Carolina Library, Chapel Hill.
12. Letter of President Swain, 19 September 1856, ibid.
13. Henry Francis Jones, Diary Book, #3019, Southern Historical Collection.
14. Archibald Henderson, *The Campus of the First State University* (Chapel Hill: University of North Carolina Press, 1949), pp. 149, 116.
15. Elizabeth Anne Barber, "Henry Harrisse at the University of North Carolina, 1853–1856," #3494, Southern Historical Collection.
16. Ibid.
17. Ibid.
18. UNC Faculty Minutes, 1856–85.
19. University Student Records, Scholarship 1852–68, 9043, vol. S-11, Irregulars, 1857–8, Irregulars 1858–9, Southern Historical Collection. See also Davis, "Boy Colonel," 1:181.
20. Letter to his mother, 11 October 1857, Burgwyn Family Papers.
21. Letter to his mother, 31 October 1857, ibid.
22. Autograph album of a student at the University of North Carolina, member of class of 1859, Southern Historical Collection, Addition to 3129.
23. Philanthropic Society Treasurer's Book, 1856–59, Southern Historical

Collection, 9008, vol. S–72, p. 372; see also 9008, vol. 14, p. 237, for date of initiation, 18 September 1857.

24. Letter to his mother, 13 September 1857, Burgwyn Family Papers.

25. Letter to his father, 7 March 1858, ibid. Harry's admonition was apparently heeded, for "H.K.B. sold the Level Plantation [Alveston] to Gen'l Persons for thirty thousand dollars Oct. 6th, 1858" (Anna Burgwyn, Diary Book, 1847–61, in the possession of John Alveston Burgwyn Baker, Richmond, Va.).

26. Letter to his mother, 27 March 1859, Burgwyn Family Papers.

27. Ibid.

28. Letter to his mother, 27 March 1859, ibid. It bears the same date as that appearing on the letter referred to in note 27 above. A comparison of the texts indicates that the first letter was probably dated incorrectly.

29. Ibid.

30. University Student Records, Scholarship, 1849–66, 9043, vol. 10, June 1859, Southern Historical Collection.

31. Anna Greenough Burgwyn, Diary Book, 1847–61.

32. Ibid.

CHAPTER 5

1. H. K. Burgwyn, Sr., to Col. Francis H. Smith, 8 July 1859, Letter Book, Preston Library, Virginia Military Institute, Lexington, Va.

2. H. K. Burgwyn, Sr., to Col. Francis H. Smith, 8 August 1859, ibid.

3. Harry to Col. Francis H. Smith, 10 September 1859, ibid. Maria survived her illness. She left Stribling Springs on a stretcher, 13 October 1859, and arrived at Thornbury a week later (Anna Greenough Burgwyn, Diary Book, 1847–61, in possession of John Alveston Burgwyn Baker, Richmond, Va.).

4. Order No. 193, 1st Order Book, VMI, 1857–60, p. 131, Preston Library.

5. Order No. 198, p. 136, ibid.

6. Order No. 203, p. 139, ibid.

7. Order No. 236, p. 161, ibid.

8. Anna Greenough Burgwyn, Diary Book, 1847–61.

9. Order No. 237, 1st Order Book, pp. 161–62.

10. Order No. 239, p. 164, ibid.

11. General Order No. 1, p. 168, ibid.

12. General Order No. 4, p. 169, ibid.

13. Order No. 237, pp. 161–62, ibid. See also Lenoir Chambers, *Stonewall Jackson*, 2 vols. (New York: Morrow, 1959), 1:294.

14. Chambers, *Stonewall Jackson*, 1:295. The ubiquitous Ruffin would later be credited with possibly firing the first shot on Fort Sumter and participating in the battle of First Manassas. He committed suicide upon the demise of the Confederacy.

15. William Kauffman Scarborough, ed., *The Diary of Edmund Ruffin*, 2 vols. (Baton Rouge: Louisiana State University Press, 1972), 1:362–68.

16. Ibid., pp. 264, 337.

17. John Fanning Burgwyn, Typescript Diary, 1855–56, P.C. 564.1, North Carolina Department of Archives and History, Raleigh.

18. Anna Greenough Burgwyn, Diary Book, 1847–61.

19. Order No. 2, 1st Order Book, p. 180.

20. Commandant's Delinquency Reports, 1859–1918, 27 vols., vol. 1, 1859–63, p. 23, Preston Library.

21. Letter to his mother, 3 June 1860, Burgwyn Family Papers. This is the first letter extant during Harry's first year at VMI.

22. Letter to his father, 17 June 1860, ibid.

23. Letter to his mother, 29 June 1860, ibid.

24. The original report, dated 10 July 1860, is among the Burgwyn Family Papers; see also 1st Order Book, p. 227. H. W. Hunter ranked first in the class with a point score of 1100.8; Harry Burgwyn ranked second with a point score of 1088.1.

25. Letter to his mother, 9 September 1860, Burgwyn Family Papers.

26. Order No. 65, 1st Order Book, pp. 213–15.

27. Order No. 66, p. 216, ibid.

28. Letter to Maria, 10 June 1860, Burgwyn Family Papers.

29. Letter to his mother, 12 August 1860, ibid.

30. Letter to his mother, 24 August 1860, ibid.

31. Letter to his mother, 20 August 1860, ibid.

32. Letter to his mother, 9 December 1860, ibid.

33. Letter to his mother, 15 December 1860, ibid.

34. Letter to his father, 22 December 1860, ibid.

35. H. K. Burgwyn, *Considerations Relative to a Southern Confederacy* (Raleigh, 1860), pp. 30–33, North Carolina Collection, University of North Carolina Library, Chapel Hill.

36. Ibid., pp. 4–7.

37. Ibid., pp. 9–12.

38. Ibid., p. 15.

39. Letter to his father, 22 December 1860, Burgwyn Family Papers.

40. Noble J. Tolbert, ed., *The Papers of John Willis Ellis*, 2 vols. (Raleigh: North Carolina Department of Archives and History, 1964), 1:210.

41. Ibid., lxxxiii. See *North Carolina Standard*, 8 June 1859.

42. Ibid., lxxxii. See *North Carolina Standard*, 15 June 1859.

43. Ibid., p. 331.

44. Ibid., 2:349.

45. Ibid., pp. 387–92. The acceptance speech was delivered before the Democratic State Convention at Raleigh on 9 March 1860.

46. Ibid., p. 470.

47. Ibid., pp. 513–15.

48. Ibid., p. 473. This indictment of W. W. Holden is highly significant. As editor of the *North Carolina Standard* Holden had long been an ardent and articulate champion of Southern rights. As spokesman for the Democratic party he had served its interests faithfully and well. He had aspired to the

governorship in 1858, but Ellis was selected as the Democratic nominee. Holden dutifully supported Ellis's candidacy then and again in 1860. In 1858 and 1859, when vacancies occurred in the U.S. Senate, Holden was overlooked in favor of Thomas L. Clingman, formerly a Whig, and Thomas Bragg. Failure to receive the endorsement of the party in support of his political aspirations must have been keenly disappointing to Holden, but he remained faithful. In 1860, though partial to the ad valorem tax, he supported the Democratic leadership in opposition. In the presidential election of that year he first supported Douglas and later shifted to Breckinridge. "After the election of Lincoln," according to Sitterson, "he became one of the strongest Unionists in the State." Recognizing the strength of the pro-Union sentiment in North Carolina, and the party division between the slaveholders and nonslaveholders, he was probably convinced that the majority of the people were opposed to secession. In that event he chose to be their spokesman. For a thorough explanation of Holden's complete change in philosophy, see Joseph Carlyle Sitterson, *The Secession Movement in North Carolina* (Chapel Hill: University of North Carolina Press, 1939), n. 78, pp. 162–64.

49. Tolbert, ed., *Papers of John Willis Ellis*, 2:473, 475.

50. Ibid., pp. 530–31.

51. Ibid., p. 529n. Robert N. Gourdin (1812–94), graduate of South Carolina College, lawyer, and member of the mercantile firm of Gourdin, Mathiessen and Company of Charleston, S.C.

52. Ibid., p. 541.

53. Ibid., pp. 546–47.

54. Ibid., p. 476.

CHAPTER 6

1. Jennings C. Wise, *The Military History of the Virginia Military Institute from 1839 to 1865* (Lynchburg, Va.: J. P. Bell, 1915), pp. 126–27.

2. Ibid., pp. 128–32.

3. Ibid., pp. 132–33.

4. Letter to his father, 11 January 1861, Burgwyn Family Papers.

5. Forts Johnston and Caswell, near Smithville (now Southport), were taken possession of on 9 January, but not by Governor Ellis. This action had been taken by "a few fanatics" in Wilmington in the mistaken belief that Federal troops were on their way to garrison these and other Southern forts. Governor Ellis immediately ordered the forts restored to the U.S. authorities and wrote President Buchanan accordingly. See *The War of the Rebellion: A Compilation of the Official Records of the Union and Confederate Armies* (Washington, D.C.: U.S. Government Printing Office, 1880; rpr., Gettysburg: National Historical Society, 1972), Ser. 1, 1:474–76, 484–85; hereinafter referred to as *Official Records*.

6. Henry to Anna Burgwyn, 15 February 1861, Burgwyn Family Papers.

7. Henry to Anna Burgwyn, 18 February 1861, ibid. Since December, both

houses of Congress had been futilely engaged in a last-minute effort to find some acceptable compromise. Unhappily, the positions of the extremists on both sides were not negotiable. Their differences were irreconcilable because neither side genuinely wanted to compromise. Those who sponsored compromise proposals were sincerely motivated, but all such proposals were doomed to failure from the start. For a full discussion of these compromise efforts, see Allan Nevins, *The Emergence of Lincoln: Prologue to Civil War, 1859–1861*, 8 vols. (New York: Charles Scribner's Sons, 1950), 2:385–413.

8. During this time it is believed that Henry King Burgwyn, Sr., was serving as a military aide to Governor Ellis, at least on an unofficial basis. Nothing has been found in the records to indicate that he held an official position with the administration.

9. Henry to Anna Burgwyn, 23 February 1861, Burgwyn Family Papers.

10. Henry to Anna Burgwyn, 25 February 1861, ibid.

11. Joseph Carlyle Sitterson, *The Secession Movement in North Carolina* (Chapel Hill: University of North Carolina Press, 1939), pp. 206–8, 211.

12. Ibid., pp. 214, 216–20.

13. Ibid., p. 223.

14. *North Carolina Standard*, 2 March 1861.

15. For a lengthy and detailed account of H. K. Burgwyn's views on the economic indispensability of slavery, the viability of an independent Southern Confederacy, and the dependency of European nations upon the South for cotton, see the *State Journal*, 5 December 1860, open reply to letter of B. F. Moore in the *Raleigh Register* of 20 October.

16. Letter to his mother, 3 March 1861, Burgwyn Family Papers.

17. Letter to his mother, 10 March 1861, ibid.

18. Letter to his father, 14 March 1861, ibid.

19. Letter to his father, 23 March 1861, ibid.

20. Letter to his mother, 1 April 1861, ibid.

21. Noble J. Tolbert, ed., *The Papers of John Willis Ellis*, 2 vols. (Raleigh: North Carolina Department of Archives and History, 1964), 2:608.

22. Ibid., pp. 609, 611–12.

23. Ibid., p. 612.

24. *Official Records*, Ser. 1, 1:486.

25. Order No. 60, 2nd Order Book, beginning 1 January 1861, VMI, pp. 40–42, Preston Library, Virginia Military Institute, Lexington, Va.

26. Letter to his father, 19 April 1861, Burgwyn Family Papers.

27. Order No. 63, 2nd Order Book, pp. 43–44.

CHAPTER 7

1. Letter from Maj. R. E. Colston, 19 April 1861, Burgwyn Family Papers.

2. Jennings C. Wise, *The Military History of the Virginia Military Institute from 1839 to 1865* (Lynchburg, Va.: J. P. Bell, 1915), pp. 142–44.

3. Letter to his father, 23 April 1861, Burgwyn Family Papers, with post-

script: "Excuse writing and mistakes as I have had only 5 hours sleep in the last two days & worked at the artillery 4 hours last night."

4. Ibid., probably written in late April.

5. Charles D. Walker, *Virginia Military Institute Memorial* (Philadelphia: J. B. Lippincott, 1875), p. 75. On 26 April 1861 Jackson was promoted to colonel in the Virginia Volunteers and left immediately for Harpers Ferry. See Wise, *Military History of the Virginia Military Institute*, p. 151.

6. Burgwyn Family Papers. Both letter and resolution dated 22 May 1861.

7. Letter to his mother, 21 May 1861, ibid. Harry was staying at the home of George W. Rives near Jefferson. In a postscript, he characterized the men of this area "as the best rifle shots in the State."

8. Letter to Maria Burgwyn, 27 May 1861, ibid.

9. Letter to his father, 28 May 1861, ibid. Across the top of the page is written, "Don't let anybody know of this if we fail to secure it."

10. Letter to his mother, 2 June 1861, ibid.

11. H. K. Burgwyn, Jr., Journal of Events from August 27, 1861, ibid.; hereinafter referred to as Journal.

12. Weymouth T. Jordan, Jr., comp., *North Carolina Troops, 1861–1865: A Roster*, 9 vols. (Raleigh: North Carolina Department of Archives and History, 1975–), 5:106.

13. Ibid., pp. 117–236.

14. This hypothesis is strongly supported by the recollection of his nephew, Judge W. H. S. Burgwyn of Woodland, N.C. In a taped interview with the writer on 8–9 July 1974 Judge Burgwyn recalled: "When I was a little boy I stayed in Captain Robards' home in Henderson. . . . The Captain liked to talk about the war. One night he was talking to me about Colonel Burgwyn and asked me if I was kin to him. I told him I was his nephew. Well, he said he was the first man who ever gave me a military order in my life, at Garysburg, North Carolina, and he was a fine looking man but he was very strict. And he had a slight impediment in his voice. He would say 'forward mollop' instead of saying 'forward march,' but Mr. Robards said he got so he could say it perfectly before he left there." See Burgwyn Family Papers, 14:13–14.

15. Walker, *Virginia Military Institute Memorial*, pp. 75–76.

16. Burgwyn Family Papers.

17. Archibald Henderson, *North Carolina: The Old North State and the New*, 2 vols. (Chicago: Lewis, 1941), 2:223.

18. *North Carolina Standard*, 10 January 1861.

19. Noble J. Tolbert, ed., *The Papers of John Willis Ellis*, 2 vols. (Raleigh: North Carolina Department of Archives and History, 1964), 2:547–50.

20. Ibid., p. 563, 1:337–38.

21. Ibid., 2:562. Lee was a graduate of West Point but currently serving as professor of the Charlotte Military Institute.

22. Ibid., pp. 567, 573.

23. Ibid., p. 581.

24. Ibid., pp. 584, 604, 612. This order was never filled. On 12 April, the day that Fort Sumter was fired upon, Secretary of War Cameron advised Ellis

of the delay but added: "The Superintendent of the Arm[o]ry has been instructed to make the issue to your State at the earliest possible moment (ibid., pp. 607–8). Obviously, "the earliest possible moment" was too late.

25. Ibid., pp. 678–80.

26. Ibid., pp. 689–90.

27. Ibid., pp. 694–96.

28. Ibid., pp. 697–99.

29. Even W. W. Holden was outraged; see *North Carolina Standard,* 20 April 1861.

30. Tolbert, ed., *Papers of John Willis Ellis,* 2:700–701.

31. Ibid., pp. 702–3.

32. Ibid., p. 704.

33. Ibid., p. 705.

34. R. D. W. Connor, *North Carolina: Rebuilding an Ancient Commonwealth, 1854–1925,* 2 vols. (Chicago: American Historical Society, 1929), 2:175–77.

35. *Appleton's Cyclopaedia of American Biography,* 6 vols. (New York: D. Appleton, 1888), 4:231. Martin, a West Point graduate, class of 1840, was born in Elizabeth City, N.C., 14 February 1819, and died in Asheville 4 October 1878.

36. Connor, *North Carolina,* 2:175.

37. Tolbert, ed., *Papers of John Willis Ellis,* 2:759.

38. Ibid., p. 769.

39. Ibid., p. 654; also see p. 634, n. 155. Whiting, a native of Mississippi, graduated from West Point in 1845. Resigning from the U.S. Army on 20 February 1861, he joined the Confederate Service with the rank of major. He was responsible for developing Fort Fisher, N.C., the strongest fortress in the Confederacy. A major general, he was severely wounded and captured when Fort Fisher fell on 15 January 1865 (see also *Appleton's Cyclopaedia of American Biography,* 6:484).

40. Walter Clark, *North Carolina Regiments, 1861–65,* 5 vols. (Raleigh: State of North Carolina, 1901), 1:18.

41. Tolbert, ed., *Papers of John Willis Ellis,* 2:851.

42. *Official Records,* Ser. 1, 4:580–87.

43. Virgil Carrington Jones, *The Civil War at Sea: The Blockaders* (New York: Holt, Rinehart, and Winston, 1960), p. 385.

44. Naval History Division, Navy Department, *Civil War Naval Chronology, 1861–1865* (Washington, D.C.: U.S. Government Printing Office, 1971), pp. 1, 23–24.

45. George C. Underwood, *History of the Twenty-sixth Regiment of the North Carolina Troops in the Great War 1861–'65* (Goldsboro, N.C.: Nash Brothers, 1901), pp. 1–2.

46. Lane later became lieutenant colonel of the Twenty-sixth when Burgwyn was promoted colonel upon the resignation of Zebulon Vance in August 1862. Lane was at Burgwyn's side when the latter was killed at Gettysburg. He was severely wounded but recovered and served with distinction as colonel of the Twenty-sixth until the end of the war.

47. Underwood, *History of the Twenty-sixth Regiment*, pp. 2–3.

48. Ibid., p. 4. Vance had been notified of his election on 26 August. At that time he was serving as captain of Company F of the Fourteenth North Carolina Infantry. This company was organized in Buncombe County under the banner name of "Rough and Ready Guards." Vance had enlisted as a private but was quickly elevated to captain (Glenn Tucker, *Zeb Vance: Champion of Personal Freedom* [New York: Bobbs Merrill, 1965], pp. 109–11).

49. Journal, p. 1, Burgwyn Family Papers.

50. Ibid., p. 3.

51. Ibid., pp. 4–5.

52. Ibid., p. 7.

53. G.P. 154, 16 September 1861, Governors Papers, Henry Toole Clark, North Carolina Department of Archives and History, Raleigh.

54. John G. Barrett, *The Civil War in North Carolina* (Chapel Hill: University of North Carolina Press, 1963), p. 32.

55. Clark's letter to the Senate, 7 September 1861; resolution of House of Commons, 3 September 1861; resolution of the Senate, 4 September 1861, all in Governors Papers, Henry Toole Clark.

56. McRae to Courts, 14 October 1861, ibid.

57. L. O'B. Branch to Clark, 10 September 1861, ibid., estimating the cost of quartermaster's supplies for a cavalry regiment, consisting of ten companies of one hundred privates and noncommissioned officers each, $198,000, not including clothing, arms, and accoutrements.

58. Dimmock to Clark, 19 September 1861, ibid.

59. Vance to Clark, 18 September 1861, ibid.

60. Journal, pp. 8–12, Burgwyn Family Papers.

61. *Official Records*, Ser. 1, 4:573–79.

62. Letter to W. N. H. Smith unsigned but presumed to have been written by H. K. Burgwyn, Sr., Burgwyn Family Papers.

63. Letter to his father, 26 December 1861, ibid.

64. *Official Records*, Ser. 1, 4:611.

65. Ibid., pp. 659–60.

66. Governors Papers, Henry Toole Clark.

CHAPTER 8

1. Letter to his father, 26 December 1861, Burgwyn Family Papers.

2. Letter to his mother, 3 January 1862, ibid.

3. Camp Wilkes was the second camp of the Twenty-sixth on Bogue Banks, the first having been Camp Burgwyn. Camp Vance, near Carolina City on the mainland, was established as the regiment's winter quarters during Harry's absence.

4. Journal, 23 January 1862, Burgwyn Family Papers.

5. *Harper's Weekly: A Journal of Civilization*, 16 November 1861, pp. 721–22.

6. Douglas Southall Freeman, *R. E. Lee: A Biography*, 4 vols. (New York: Charles Scribner's Sons, 1934), 1:600.

7. Lenoir Chambers, *Stonewall Jackson*, 2 vols. (New York: Morrow, 1959), 1:401–3.

8. Freeman, *Lee*, 1:606–9.

9. *Harper's Weekly*, 21 December 1861, p. 802.

10. Ibid.

11. Ibid., p. 803.

12. *Raleigh Register*, 25 December 1861.

13. *Illustrated London News*, 30 November 1861, p. 541.

14. Walter Clark, *North Carolina Regiments, 1861–65*, 5 vols. (Raleigh: State of North Carolina, 1901), 1:7.

15. *Raleigh Register*, 19 October 1861.

16. Letters to his mother, 8, 9 January 1862, Burgwyn Family Papers.

17. *Official Records*, Ser. 1, 9:352–53.

18. Ibid., pp. 355–56.

19. Ibid., pp. 356–57. This account appears to be reliable, for the violent storms off Hatteras in mid-January did play havoc with Burnside's fleet. A number of ships were lost, including the *Louisiana*, the *City of New York*, the *Grapeshot* (a floating battery), the *Zouave*, and the *Pocahontas*. The casualties were undoubtedly high. See John G. Barrett, *The Civil War in North Carolina* (Chapel Hill: University of North Carolina Press, 1963), pp. 70–73.

20. *Official Records*, Ser. 1, 9:358–60.

21. Ibid., p. 360.

22. Ibid., pp. 362–63.

23. Ibid., p. 364.

24. George B. McClellan, *McClellan's Own Story: The War for the Union* (New York: Charles L. Webster, 1887), pp. 228, 237–38.

25. Edward A. Pollard, *The Lost Cause* (New York: E. B. Treat, 1866), pp. 215–16. Pollard was editor of the *Richmond Examiner* during the war.

26. George C. Underwood, *History of the Twenty-sixth Regiment of North Carolina Troops in the Great War, 1861–'65* (Goldsboro, N.C.: Nash Brothers, 1901), p. 6.

27. Letter to his father, 19 January 1862, Burgwyn Family Papers.

28. Journal, pp. 20–21, ibid.

29. Letter to his mother, 18 February 1862, ibid.

30. Letter to his father, 19 February 1862, ibid.

31. Letter to his father, 26 February 1862, ibid.

32. Glenn Tucker, *Zeb Vance: Champion of Personal Freedom* (New York: Bobbs Merrill, 1965), p. 117.

33. Letter to his father, 11 January 1862, Burgwyn Family Papers.

34. Letter to his father, 1 February 1862, ibid.

35. Letter to his mother, 8 February 1862, ibid. During the day of 7 February, the Federal fleet succeeded in passing through the Roanoke Marshes Channel at the lower end of Roanoke Island. By midnight, approximately ten

thousand of Burnside's troops were safely ashore without opposition. The main Confederate defenses consisted of a fortified line extending east-west across the narrowest part of the island to the swamps on each side (supposedly impenetrable) and three forts to the northwest, Fort Bartow, Fort Blanchard, and Fort Huger. The battle began about eight o'clock on the morning of the eighth. Realizing that a frontal attack on the fortified line would be costly, the Federals flanked the position by successfully penetrating the undefended extremities of the line. By noon the battle was over and the Confederates in full retreat. By nine o'clock that night the U.S. flag "floated over every battery." That afternoon, the Confederate fleet, having expended all its ammunition, had retired to Elizabeth City, twelve miles up the Pasquotank River. On 10 February, it was trapped and destroyed by a Federal flotilla of thirteen vessels. Only the C.S.S. *Beaufort* escaped to Norfolk by way of the Dismal Swamp Canal. See Barrett, *Civil War in North Carolina*, pp. 74–87. Had the fortified line across the island been extended through the swamps, as earlier recommended by General D. H. Hill, the battle of Roanoke Island might have turned out differently, according to Barrett (note p. 80).

36. Letter to his mother, 15 February 1862, Burgwyn Family Papers.

37. Daniel Harvey Hill, *Bethel to Sharpsburg*, 2 vols. (Raleigh: Edwards & Broughton, 1926), 1:185–95. For her ultimate defense, Roanoke Island had two North Carolina regiments, Colonel H. M. Shaw's Eighth North Carolina (568 men), Colonel J. V. Jordan's Thirty-first North Carolina (475 men), and General Wise's legion under Lieutenant Colonel Frank P. Anderson (450 men). General Wise said of these troops, "They were undrilled, unpaid, not sufficiently clothed and quartered, and miserably armed." (Ibid.)

38. Ibid., p. 192.

39. Letter to his father, 19 February 1862, Burgwyn Family Papers.

40. Letter to his father, 24 February 1862, ibid. The use of a bodyservant by well-to-do Confederate officers was not uncommon. Such a servant was either a family slave or a hired man. His duties generally included cooking for his "master" and caring for his camp equipage and horses. During his service Harry had at least three different servants, George, William, and Kincian (Kinchen); the latter was his best and faithful to the end.

41. Letter to his mother, 26 February 1862, ibid.

42. Letter to his father, 26 February 1862, ibid.

43. Letter to his father, 4 March 1862, ibid.

44. Letter to his father, 12 March 1862, ibid.

45. Letter from H. K. Burgwyn, 22 February 1862, Governors Papers, Henry Toole Clark, G.P. 157, North Carolina Department of Archives and History, Raleigh.

46. *Official Records*, Ser. 1, 9:369.

47. Ibid., p. 370.

48. Ibid., pp. 370–71.

49. Letter to his mother, 12 March 1862, Burgwyn Family Papers.

CHAPTER 9

1. Glenn Tucker, *Zeb Vance: Champion of Personal Freedom* (New York: Bobbs Merrill, 1965), pp. 121, 118.

2. *Official Records of the Union and Confederate Navies* (Washington, D.C.: U.S. Government Printing Office, 1898), Ser. 1, 7:110.

3. *Official Records*, Ser. 1, 9:242–43.

4. Ibid., pp. 261–62.

5. Letter to his mother, 17 March 1862, Burgwyn Family Papers.

6. *Official Records*, Ser. 1, 9:242.

7. Walter Clark, *North Carolina Regiments, 1861–65*, 5 vols. (Raleigh: State of North Carolina, 1901), 2:537.

8. Daniel Harvey Hill, *Bethel to Sharpsburg*, 2 vols. (Raleigh: Edwards & Broughton, 1926), 1:222.

9. Clark, *North Carolina Regiments*, 2:427, 653; 1:363.

10. *Official Records*, Ser. 1, 9:262.

11. Hill, *Bethel to Sharpsburg*, 1:223.

12. *Official Records*, Ser. 1, 9:255.

13. Letter to his mother, 17 March 1862, Burgwyn Family Papers. The three companies of the Twenty-sixth, B, E, and K, were pushed across the swamp and placed under Burgwyn's command at two o'clock Friday morning (*Official Records*, Ser. 1, 9:255). The two companies of dismounted cavalry were companies A (Captain Hays) and K (Lieutenant William A. Graham, Jr.) of the Nineteenth N.C., Colonel S. B. Spruill (ibid., p. 252). The single independent company was under Captain MacRae, and the two guns of Captain Brem's battery under Lieutenant A. B. Williams (Hill, *Bethel to Sharpsburg*, 1:223).

14. Clark, *North Carolina Regiments*, 2:537–42; see also *Official Records*, Ser. 1, 9:244.

15. *Official Records*, Ser. 1, 9:252. According to Captain William A. Graham, the Nineteenth, "with the first eight regiments of infantry, the Ninth North Carolina (First Cavalry), the Tenth Regiment (First Artillery) and the Thirty-third Regiment of infantry, comprised what was originally known as 'State Troops.'" They enlisted "for the war," and their officers were appointed by the governor. The so-called "Bethel" regiment was the only one to enlist for six months. See Clark, *North Carolina Regiments*, 2:79.

16. Hill, *Bethel to Sharpsburg*, 1:223; see also *Official Records*, Ser. 1, 9:244.

17. Hill, *Bethel to Sharpsburg*, 1:219–20.

18. 26 March 1862, *Official Records*, Ser. 1, 9:241.

19. Letter to his father, 26 February 1862, Burgwyn Family Papers. Company C of the Nineteenth North Carolina arrived from Washington at 2 A.M. on the fourteenth, and the Twenty-eighth North Carolina arrived too late on the fourteenth to reach the battlefield. Branch undoubtedly had attempted to bring up reinforcements at the last minute, but too late. See *Official Records*, Ser. 1, 9:245.

20. Clark, *North Carolina Regiments*, 2:310–11.

21. *Official Records*, Ser. 1, 9:201–2, 208, 212, 221, 219.

22. Ibid., pp. 231, 197.

23. *Official Records, Navies*, Ser. 1, 7:111.

24. *Official Records*, Ser. 1, 9:212.

25. Ibid., p. 221. In this report, Reno undoubtedly referred to the two Confederate twenty-four-pounders that were brought to the brickyard but not mounted in time.

26. Ibid., pp. 233–34.

27. Clark, *North Carolina Regiments*, 2:311–12.

28. *Official Records*, Ser. 1, 9:244; see also p. 224.

29. Ibid., p. 226.

30. Ibid., pp. 226, 238.

31. Ibid., p. 235. For full details of the battle of New Bern, with illustrations, see Davis, "Boy Colonel," 2:407–49.

32. *Official Records*, Ser. 1, 9:244–45.

33. Clark, *North Carolina Regiments*, 2:314–16.

34. *Official Records*, Ser. 1, 9:255–56.

35. Years later, in writing the history of the Thirty-fifth North Carolina, Captain W. H. S. Burgwyn (younger brother of Harry Burgwyn) wrote that the regiment's poor showing at the battle of New Bern was attributable to poor leadership. See Clark, *North Carolina Regiments*, 2:595.

36. *Official Records*, Ser. 1, 9:245.

37. Ibid., p. 264.

38. Ibid., p. 265.

39. *Official Records, Navies*, Ser. 1, 7:112.

40. *Official Records*, Ser. 1, 9:246.

41. Ibid., p. 245.

42. Letter to his mother, undated (obviously 15 March 1862), Burgwyn Family Papers.

43. All telegrams are in Burgwyn Family Papers.

44. Letter to his mother, 17 March 1862, ibid. The trunks were never found. If they were left in his tent, they were undoubtedly looted. Since everything he possessed was in the trunks, it is likely that his Journal of Events was in one of them, for it was recovered by a Yankee and returned to his family after the war.

45. Second letter to his mother, 17 March 1862, ibid. On the second page of this letter Harry drew a crude map of the battlefield area and route of retreat. Although not drawn to scale, it graphically depicts his predicament as he retreated down the "Road of the County" in the direction of New Bern only to find the Yankees ahead of him. He then veered off in the direction of the "2nd Bridge" over the Trent River to find that in flames. Trapped, his only recourse was to attempt a crossing of Brice's Creek.

CHAPTER 10

1. George B. McClellan, *McClellan's Own Story: The War for the Union* (New York: Charles L. Webster, 1887), pp. 244–45.

2. *North Carolina Standard*, 22 March 1862.

3. *Official Records*, Ser. 1, 4:573–79.

4. Letter to his father, 18 March 1862, Burgwyn Family Papers.

5. Letter to his father, 20 March 1862, ibid.

6. W. G. Lewis to William Battle, 20 March 1862, Battle Family Papers, Southern Historical Collection, University of North Carolina Library, Chapel Hill.

7. W. G. Lewis to Kemp Battle, 1 April 1862, ibid. The reference as to the exact time when the Thirty-third Regiment was sent into action is important, for the news account, as reported in the *State Journal*, 26 March 1862, stated: "In the meantime, for an hour and a half had now elapsed . . . Gen. Branch had ordered up five companies of his reserve (Avery's) under Lieutenant Colonel Hoke." And again, "In the meantime Gen. Branch had ordered forward Col. Avery with the other companies of the reserve." But to Major Lewis the term "in the meantime" obviously did not accurately reflect the fact that his men were ordered into action "about fifteen minutes after the engagement opened."

8. J. F. Shaffner to Carrie L. Fries, 3 April 1862, Southern Historical Collection.

9. Frontis W. Johnston, ed., *The Papers of Zebulon Baird Vance*, 1 vol. to date (Raleigh: North Carolina Department of Archives and History, 1963–), 1:128–30.

10. Walter Clark, *North Carolina Regiments, 1861–65*, 5 vols. (Raleigh: State of North Carolina, 1901), 2:398.

11. Julius A. Lineback (Leinbach), "Extracts from a Civil War Diary," *Winston-Salem Sentinel*, 13 June 1914–3 April 1915, Southern Historical Collection, University of North Carolina Library, Chapel Hill. Julius A. Lineback always spelled his name *Lineback*, the anglicized version of the German *Leinbach*. The separate versions still prevail.

12. *People's Press*, 17 January 1862, Moravian Archives, Winston-Salem, N.C. Branding this article as "unjust," the editors of the *Press* stoutly defended the loyalty of Forsyth County by defining political conservatism as being against lynch law, vigilance committees, test oaths, and gag laws but not against the Confederate government.

13. *People's Press*, 28 March 1862.

14. Joseph Carlyle Sitterson, *The Secession Movement in North Carolina* (Chapel Hill: University of North Carolina Press, 1939), pp. 211–29.

15. *Official Records*, Ser. 1, 9:244.

16. W. G. Lewis to Kemp Battle, 1 April 1862, Battle Family Papers.

17. *Official Records*, Ser. 1, 9:269–70.

18. Hugh Talmadge Lefler and Albert Ray Newsome, *The History of a*

Southern State: North Carolina, 3d ed. (Chapel Hill: University of North Carolina Press, 1973), p. 475. North Carolina also led in the number "returned from desertion." But its proportion of deserters was about one-fifth and in line with "the general average for both northern and southern armies."

19. Lineback, "Extracts from a Civil War Diary," p. 9.

20. *People's Press*, 28 March 1862.

21. Official report of J. J. Young, Acting Quartermaster, 26th Regiment NCT, approved by Colonel Z. B. Vance, dated 31 March 1862, Civil War Collection, Box 53, Department of Archives and History, Raleigh.

22. *State Journal*, 26 March 1862.

23. Ibid., 22 March 1862.

24. *Western Sentinel*, 28 March 1862, Moravian Archives, Winston-Salem, N.C.

25. Douglas Southall Freeman, *R. E. Lee: A Biography*, 4 vols. (New York: Charles Scribner's Sons, 1934), 2:5–6.

26. *Harper's Weekly*, 29 March 1862. "If he can fight as well as he writes," concluded the editor of *Harper's Weekly*, "the Army of the Potomac will win imperishable glory."

27. John G. Barrett, *The Civil War in North Carolina* (Chapel Hill: University of North Carolina Press, 1963), p. 108. See also *Official Records*, Ser. 1, 9:445–51.

28. *Official Records*, Ser. 1, 9:450, 455.

29. Ibid., pp. 453–55.

30. Ibid., pp. 455–56.

31. Letter Book of Governor Henry Toole Clark, pp. 287–88, North Carolina Department of Archives and History, Raleigh.

32. Ibid., p. 299. The C.S.S. *Nashville*, not the *Southwick*, arrived at Wilmington, N.C., shortly thereafter. On 28 April, Governor Clark notified General French that he was sending for "the arms brought by the Nashville for North Carolina." It was not until 15 May, in a letter to General Lee, that Clark clarified the situation. According to the governor, "North Carolina owned 1760 Enfield Rifles of the cargo of the 'Southwick' and 1500 of them arrived in the Nashville at Wilmington and were immediately turned over to Gen'l. Holmes—the balance [of] 260 I heard indirectly had arrived in Charleston but I can get no intelligence who received that portion" (ibid., p. 304).

33. Ibid., pp. 302–3, 307.

CHAPTER 11

1. *Official Records*, Ser. 1, 9:458–61, 465.

2. Glenn Tucker, *Zeb Vance: Champion of Personal Freedom* (New York: Bobbs Merrill, 1965), p. 119; Julius A. Lineback (Leinbach), "Extracts from a Civil War Diary," *Winston-Salem Sentinel*, 13 June 1914–3 April 1915, p. 9, Southern Historical Collection, University of North Carolina Library, Chapel Hill.

3. Tucker, *Zeb Vance*, p. 119; Lineback, "Extracts from a Civil War Diary," p. 9.

4. Lineback, "Extracts from a Civil War Diary," p. 9.

5. Letters to his father, 20, 23, 30 March 1862, Burgwyn Family Papers.

6. Letter to his father, 1 April 1862, ibid.

7. *Official Records*, Ser. 1, 9:375–76, 378–79.

8. Letters to his father, 6, 7 April 1862, Burgwyn Family Papers.

9. Frontis W. Johnston, ed., *The Papers of Zebulon Baird Vance*, 1 vol. to date (Raleigh: North Carolina Department of Archives and History, 1963–), 1:132–33.

10. Letter to his father, 22 April 1862, Burgwyn Family Papers.

11. Letters to his mother, 26 April 1862, and to his father, 28 April 1862, ibid.

12. Letter to his father, 7 May 1862, ibid.

13. Letter to his mother, 11 May 1862, ibid. Earlier, Harry had interceded with Governor Vance on behalf of his brother but to no avail. On 1 May he wrote William that there was little chance of his getting the adjutancy of the Twenty-sixth because there were many other applicants (letter to his brother William, 1 May 1862, ibid.).

14. *Harper's Weekly*, 22 March 1862, p. 178.

15. Joseph E. Johnston, *Narrative of Military Operations, during the Late War between the States* (New York: D. Appleton, 1876), p. 117.

16. Ibid., pp. 111–16; see also Douglas Southall Freeman, *R. E. Lee: A Biography*, 4 vols. (New York: Charles Scribner's Sons, 1934), 2:32–35.

17. Freeman, *Lee*, 2:43–49.

18. Ibid., pp. 58–59.

19. Ibid., pp. 60–61.

20. G. F. R. Henderson, *Stonewall Jackson and the American Civil War*, 2 vols. (London: Longmans, Green, 1898), 1:270, 265, 279–89.

21. Ibid., pp. 290–301. Although Ashby had attempted a thorough reconnaissance, the intelligence picked up in Winchester turned out to be erroneous.

22. *Official Records*, Ser. 1, vol. 12, pt. 1, p. 379.

23. Ibid., pt. 3, p. 16.

24. Ibid., pp. 848, 853, 857.

25. Ibid., pp. 859, 863.

26. Ibid., p. 38.

27. Ibid., p. 872.

28. Ibid., pp. 875–76.

29. Ibid., pp. 877–78.

30. Henderson, *Stonewall Jackson*, 1:347, 349–72.

31. Ibid., 1:385–86.

32. *Official Records*, Ser. 1, vol. 12, pt. 1, p. 702.

33. Ibid., pp. 704–7.

34. Letter to his father, 20 May 1862, Burgwyn Family Papers.

35. Walter Clark, *North Carolina Regiments, 1861–65*, 5 vols. (Raleigh:

State of North Carolina, 1901), 1:180; 2:545, 679, 498. Verified by checking the regimental histories of the brigades mentioned. See *Official Records*, Ser. 1, 9:460, for listing of brigades and regiments under command of Major General T. H. Holmes on 19 April 1862.

36. *Official Records*, Ser. 1, vol. 11, pt. 3, p. 559.

37. Letter Book of Governor Henry Toole Clark, p. 327, North Carolina Department of Archives and History, Raleigh.

CHAPTER 12

1. Douglas Southall Freeman, *R. E. Lee: A Biography*, 4 vols. (New York: Charles Scribner's Sons, 1934), 2:60–61.

2. Ibid., pp. 63–65.

3. G. F. R. Henderson, *Stonewall Jackson and the American Civil War*, 2 vols. (London: Longmans, Green, 1898), 1:211–13.

4. Joseph E. Johnston, *Narrative of Military Operations during the Late War between the States* (New York: D. Appleton, 1876), p. 132.

5. Freeman, *Lee*, 2:74.

6. Edward A. Pollard, *The Lost Cause* (New York: E. B. Treat, 1866), p. 281.

7. Johnston, *Narrative of Military Operations*, p. 143.

8. Clyde Norman Wilson, Jr., "Carolina Cavalier: The Life of James Johnston Pettigrew" (Ph.D. dissertation, University of North Carolina, 1971), pp. 342–47; see also Fries and Shaffner Family Papers, #4046, Southern Historical Collection, University of North Carolina Library, Chapel Hill.

9. Freeman, *Lee*, 2:78–80. This was the first time that the term "Army of Northern Virginia" was used in its own orders. According to Freeman, "Lee, and Lee alone," had so styled it in previous references (ibid., p. 77).

10. Ibid., pp. 80–83.

11. Henderson, *Stonewall Jackson*, 1:441–46. On the afternoon of 6 June, in a fierce rear-guard cavalry engagement some three miles south of Harrisonburg, the daring Turner Ashby was killed in action. His horse had fallen under him, and he was leading a charge on foot when shot through the heart.

12. Ibid., pp. 449–52; see also *Official Records*, Ser. 1, vol. 12, pt. 3, pp. 358–61.

13. Henderson, *Stonewall Jackson*, 1:453–56.

14. Ibid., pp. 459–63.

15. Ibid., pp. 464–65.

16. *Official Records*, Ser. 1, vol. 12, pt. 1, pp. 714–15; see also Henderson, *Stonewall Jackson*, 1:466–72.

17. Henderson, *Stonewall Jackson*, 1:472–73.

18. *Official Records*, Ser. 1, vol. 12, pt. 1, p. 716.

Clara Strayer, a young woman who lived at Bogota, across the river from the battlefield, was an eyewitness to Frémont's reprehensible action. "With the aid of a glass" she had watched the battle as it progressed. "At first," she later wrote, "we saw every movement of the enemy but as the battle progressed—the view was somewhat obscured by the smoke. By 10 o'clock (as Jackson intended), the battle was over & Fremont who soon after showed himself on the hill above us, saw only the smoking bridge at Port Republic and the hearse-like ambulances as they bore off the *dead & wounded, upon which he fired although* the *yellow flag was displayed* from what was *then* the *Fletcher,* now the Lynnwood house. A rifled shell passed about 15' feet from the S.West corner of this house and another fell *through* the 'roof of a cabin' on the upper edge of the orchard, within two feet of old Uncle Daniel, who had for years been on the 'retired list.' He yelled lustily as though being 'worse scared than hurt,' as the shell did not *explode. *[Tho' it broke through both table & floor]"

Following the battle, Frémont's men invaded Bogota. They "poured in at every door," according to Clara Strayer. "Such clanking of sabers; ransacking of presses; trying to break open doors, I never saw. They came into our chamber when I remarked 'this is a ladies chamber & as such will be respected by *gentlemen.'* The leader, a big huffy Dutchman replied—'Yeh! Yeh! if *dere be any Dutch gentlemen!* Come boys, lets go [to] town.'" But the Yankees met their match when they descended upon "the *Bee House* where they were met by a *bayonet* charge, not of Six hundred but Six thousand & were completely routed for the time" (manuscript by Clara Strayer, 9 February 1880, in the possession of Mrs. Margaret Lilly of Bogota, Port Republic, Va.).

19. *Official Records,* Ser. 1, vol. 12, pt. 1, p. 716.

20. Letter to his mother, 18 June 1862, Burgwyn Family Papers.

21. Letter to his father, 19 June 1862, ibid.

22. *Official Records,* Ser. 1, vol. 11, pt. 3, pp. 587, 589.

23. Ibid., p. 590; Freeman, *Lee,* 2:97–99.

24. *Official Records,* Ser. 1, vol. 11, pt. 3, p. 602.

25. Ibid., p. 607.

26. Ibid., p. 610. The Second Brigade under the command of Brigadier General Robert Ransom, Jr., consisted of the Twenty-fourth, Twenty-fifth, Twenty-sixth, Thirty-fifth, Forty-eighth, and Forty-ninth North Carolina regiments.

27. Letter to his father, 22 June 1862, Burgwyn Family Papers.

28. Journal of Lieutenant Colonel Burgwyn preceding and following the battle of Richmond from 26 June to 3 July 1862; hereinafter referred to as Burgwyn Journal, 14 July 1862. For complete verbatim account, see Davis, "Boy Colonel," 2:584–602.

29. Henderson, *Stonewall Jackson,* 2:12–13; see also *Civil War Atlas* (West Point, N.Y.: U.S. Military Academy, 1941); R. L. Dabney, *Life of Lieutenant General Thomas J. Jackson,* 2 vols. (London: James Nisbet, 1866), 2:174–75.

30. *Official Records,* Ser. 1, vol. 11, pt. 2, p. 19.

31. Freeman, *Lee,* 2:108–10, 112–13, 116; see also Henderson, *Stonewall Jackson,* 2:11, 14.

32. Freeman, *Lee,* 2:110–11; see also Henderson, *Stonewall Jackson,* 2:16.

33. Freeman, *Lee,* 2:111–14; see also Henderson, *Stonewall Jackson,* 2:116–17.

34. Freeman, *Lee,* 2:112, 115–16, 120; see also Henderson, *Stonewall Jackson,* 2:14–17; *Official Records,* Ser. 1, vol. 11, pt. 2, p. 499.

35. Henderson, *Stonewall Jackson,* 2:16.

36. Freeman, *Lee,* 2:122; see also Dabney, *Life of Jackson,* 2:178.

37. Freeman, *Lee,* 2:122–35, 139–41.

38. *Official Records,* Ser. 1, vol. 11, pt. 2, pp. 19–20.

39. Burgwyn Journal, 14 July 1862, Burgwyn Family Papers. For other references to the Twenty-sixth North Carolina during the night and early morning hours of 25–26 June, see Davis, "Boy Colonel," 2:588, n. 435.

40. Henderson, *Stonewall Jackson,* 2:31–35; see also Dabney, *Life of Jackson,* 2:179–83.

41. Henderson, *Stonewall Jackson,* 2:35–38.

42. Ibid., pp. 38–42.

43. Ibid., pp. 42–51.

44. Burgwyn Journal, 14 July 1862, Burgwyn Family Papers.

45. Henderson, *Stonewall Jackson,* 2:52.

46. Henderson, *Stonewall Jackson,* 2:55–57.

47. Ibid., pp. 56–59.

48. Ibid., pp. 58–60.

49. Burgwyn Journal, 14 July 1862, Burgwyn Family Papers.

CHAPTER 13

1. Allan Nevins, *The War for the Union,* 8 vols. (New York: Charles Scribner's Sons, 1960), 2:139–44.

2. Walter Clark, *North Carolina Regiments, 1861–65,* 5 vols. (Raleigh: State of North Carolina, 1901), 5:467.

3. *Official Records,* Ser. 1, vol. 11, pt. 2, pp. 502–6.

4. Clark, *North Carolina Regiments,* 1:12.

5. John G. Barrett, *The Civil War in North Carolina* (Chapel Hill: University of North Carolina Press, 1963), p. 129.

6. *Official Records,* Ser. 1, vol. 11, pt. 3, pp. 252–53.

7. Ibid., pp. 237, 270–71, 294, 300, 305.

8. Barrett, *Civil War in North Carolina,* pp. 129–30.

9. Letter Book of Governor Henry Toole Clark, pp. 365–369, 384–85, North Carolina Department of Archives and History, Raleigh.

10. Ibid., pp. 386–87.

11. Ibid., pp. 389–90.

12. Ibid., pp. 393–94.

13. Ibid., p. 391.

14. Hugh T. Lefler and Albert R. Newsome, *The History of a Southern State: North Carolina*, 3d ed. (Chapel Hill: University of North Carolina Press, 1973), pp. 466–67. The Conservative party leadership consisted of most of the state's prewar leaders (mainly old-line Whigs and Democrats loyal to the Union) such as William A. Graham, Zebulon B. Vance, William W. Holden, George E. Badger, John M. Morehead, and Jonathan Worth. The Confederate party leadership consisted principally of original secessionists, including Weldon N. Edwards and Governor Ellis.

15. *North Carolina Standard*, 6 August 1862.

16. Lefler and Newsome, *History of a Southern State*, p. 467.

17. Glenn Tucker, *Zeb Vance: Champion of Personal Freedom* (New York: Bobbs Merrill, 1965), p. 154.

18. Letters to his mother, 11 July 1862, and to his father, 22 June [July] 1862, Burgwyn Family Papers.

19. Letters to his father, 26 July 1862, and to his mother, 27 July 1862, ibid.

20. Lenoir Chambers, *Stonewall Jackson*, 2 vols. (New York: Morrow, 1959), 2:98, 91, 99.

21. Burgwyn Journal, 14 July 1862, Burgwyn Family Papers.

22. Nevins, *The War for the Union*, 2:180–88.

23. *North Carolina Standard*, 20 August 1862.

24. Ibid., 30 July 1862.

25. Ibid., 13 August 1862.

26. Ibid., 20 August 1862.

27. Robert C. Black III, *The Railroads of the Confederacy* (Chapel Hill: University of North Carolina Press, 1952), map in back of book.

28. *North Carolina Standard*, 27 August 1862.

29. J. Jones to Harry Burgwyn, 11 August 1862, Burgwyn Family Papers.

30. H. K. Burgwyn, Sr., to Wm. J. Clarke, Colonel Commanding 24th Rgt. N.C.T., 15 August 1862, ibid. The Twenty-fourth was a part of General Robert Ransom's brigade, and Burgwyn probably wrote Colonel Clarke because both were from Craven County and were undoubtedly well known to one another. See Clark, *North Carolina Regiments*, 2:269–77.

31. Clarke to H. K. Burgwyn, 19 August 1862, Burgwyn Family Papers.

32. J. Jones to Harry Burgwyn, 21 August 1862, ibid.

33. J. J. Young to Harry Burgwyn, 22 August 1862, ibid.

34. Letter to his mother, 23 August 1862, ibid.

35. Letter to his mother, 24 August 1862, photostatic copy in possession of his nephew, Judge W. H. S. Burgwyn, now deceased. The signature has been cut out, but Harry's brother, W. H. S. Burgwyn, appended the following handwritten notation: "This signature was cut out Oct. 18, 1909, to be engraved on Col H. K. Burgwyn picture in Biographical History of North Carolina where appears a sketch of Col Burgwyn—mailed to Chas L Van Noppen, Publisher, Greensboro, N.C., Oct. 18, 1909."

36. Letter to his mother, 27 August 1862, Burgwyn Family Papers. Until the transfer of Harry's regiment to Pettigrew's brigade, the brothers had

served together in Ransom's brigade. Willie's regiment, the Thirty-fifth, remained with Ransom's brigade, which was actively involved in the Maryland campaign of 1862 and in the battle of Fredericksburg, 11–12 December 1862. See Clark, *North Carolina Regiments*, 2:600–610.

CHAPTER 14

1. Clyde Norman Wilson, Jr., "Carolina Cavalier: The Life of James Johnston Pettigrew" (Ph.D. dissertation, University of North Carolina, 1971), pp. 42, 62–78, 126, 153–55.

2. Ibid., pp. 101–13, 117–19.

3. Ibid., pp. 239–43, 288–310.

4. Ibid., p. 310.

5. Ibid., pp. 311–20.

6. Ibid., pp. 324–31, 333–36.

7. Ibid., p. 339. See also E. B. Long with Barbara Long, *The Civil War Day by Day* (New York: Doubleday, 1971), p. 186.

8. Wilson, "Carolina Cavalier," pp. 341–44.

9. Ibid., pp. 349–50.

10. Ibid., pp. 351–52.

11. *Official Records*, Ser. 1, vol. 11, pt. 3, pp. 672, 651; see also ibid., Ser. 1, 9:480.

12. Wilson, "Carolina Cavalier," p. 354.

13. Ibid., pp. 342–43, 346–47, 221.

14. Journal of Events, p. 19, Burgwyn Family Papers.

15. Letter to his father, 26 February 1862, ibid.

16. Letter to his mother, 12 March 1862, ibid.

17. Letter to his mother, 16 (?) March 1862, ibid.

18. Letter to his father, 20 March 1862, ibid.

19. Letter to his father, 2 July 1862, ibid.

20. Carey Pettigrew (Jane Carolina North) to her husband, Charles (Johnston's oldest brother), 21 August 1862, Pettigrew Papers, Southern Historical Collection, University of North Carolina Library, Chapel Hill.

21. Walter Clark, *North Carolina Regiments, 1861–65*, 5 vols. (Raleigh: State of North Carolina, 1901), 2:335.

22. Ibid., 4:555–56; see also *Official Records*, Ser. 1, vol. 11, pt. 3, p. 657. Lee regretted that the president had accepted Martin's resignation without his knowledge. "What I wish to know," he requested, "is whether you could not retain your position and duties in the Confederate service in addition to those appertaining to your State office. I would desire that you should be placed in immediate command of the forces within the lines of the State of North Carolina, so that General Hill would be enabled to give the most of his time and attention to the troops in Virginia, and especially those along James River." On 12 August, Lee advised Hill that General Martin's resignation had not been accepted and that "he has been directed by the Depart-

ment to report to you for further orders, and desire you to assign him to the command of the troops in the State of North Carolina" (ibid., p. 673); see also *Official Records*, Ser. 1, 9:480.

23. Pettigrew to his sister, 5 September 1862, Pettigrew Papers.

24. Letter to his mother, 2 September 1862, Burgwyn Family Papers.

25. Harry to Captain J. R. Lane, 3 September 1862, ibid.

26. Letter to his father, 27 September 1862, ibid.

27. Letter to his mother, 2 September 1862, ibid.

28. Letter to his father, 7 October 1862, ibid.

29. Letter to his mother, 14 October 1862, ibid.

30. Letters to his father and mother, 13 September 1862, ibid.

31. Letter to his mother, 23 September 1862, ibid.

32. Letters to William Pettigrew, 23, 29 September 1862, Pettigrew Papers.

33. *Official Records*, Ser. 1, 9:476; ibid., vol. 11, pt. 3, p. 657.

34. Ibid., 9:410.

35. Ibid., pp. 411–13.

36. Ibid., pp. 414–16.

37. Letter to his father, 9 September 1862, Burgwyn Family Papers.

38. Letter to his mother, 18 September 1862, ibid.

39. Letter to his father, 7 October 1862, ibid.

40. Letter to his parents, 3 October 1862, ibid.

41. Ibid.

42. Letter to Pollok Burgwyn, 5 October 1862, ibid.

CHAPTER 15

1. Letter to his father and mother, 3 October 1862, Burgwyn Family Papers.

2. Letter to his father, 19 October 1862, ibid.

3. Letter to his father, 25 October 1862, ibid.

4. Letter to his father, 27 October 1862, ibid.

5. Letter to his father, 1 November 1862, ibid.

6. Letter to his father, 5 November 1862, ibid.

7. Letter to his father, 8 November 1862; see also *Official Records*, Ser. 1, 18:20–22.

8. Letter to his father, 10 November 1862, Burgwyn Family Papers.

9. *Official Records*, Ser. 1, 18:20–22.

10. Letters to his father, 1, 5, 8 November 1862, Burgwyn Family Papers; see also Walter Clark, *North Carolina Regiments, 1861–65*, 5 vols. (Raleigh: State of North Carolina, 1901), 2:336–39. In these and other references to the engagement at Rawls' Mill there are some discrepancies as to numbers, movements, and magnitude, but hardly sufficient to question Harry Burgwyn's intimate knowledge of the event.

11. John G. Barrett, *The Civil War in North Carolina* (Chapel Hill: University of North Carolina Press, 1963), p. 139.

12. *North Carolina Standard*, 12 November 1862.

13. Letter to his father, 19 November 1862, Burgwyn Family Papers.

14. Pettigrew to William Pettigrew, 15 November 1862, Pettigrew Papers, Southern Historical Collection, University of North Carolina Library, Chapel Hill.

15. *North Carolina Standard*, 10 September, 22 October 1862. The governor formally issued the appeal on 15 October 1862.

16. Frontis W. Johnston, ed., *The Papers of Zebulon Baird Vance*, 1 vol. to date (Raleigh: North Carolina Department of Archives and History, 1963–), 1:257–58.

17. *North Carolina Standard*, 26 November 1862.

18. Ibid.

19. Ibid.

20. Ibid.

21. Ibid.

22. Ibid. The Literary Board had made only half of the usual semiannual distributions of the common school fund for the fall of 1861, and none for the spring of 1862.

23. Ibid.

CHAPTER 16

1. Letter to his mother, 8 December 1862, Burgwyn Family Papers.

2. Ibid.

3. *Official Records*, Ser. 1, 21:1052–54.

4. Ibid., pp. 1053–54.

5. Ibid., 18:469, 473, 475.

6. Ibid., pp. 40–41.

7. Ibid., 21:1055–56.

8. Ibid., 18:476–77.

9. Letter,to his father, 11 December 1862, Burgwyn Family Papers.

10. Lenoir Chambers, *Stonewall Jackson*, 2 vols. (New York: Morrow, 1959), 2:270–97; see also Douglas Southall Freeman, *R. E. Lee: A Biography*, 4 vols. (New York: Charles Scribner's Sons, 1934), 2:443–71.

11. *Official Records*, Ser. 1, 18:401–2.

12. Ibid., pp. 457–58, 476–77.

13. Letters to his father, 14 December, and to his mother, 16 December 1862, Burgwyn Family Papers.

14. *Official Records*, Ser. 1, 18:54–56.

15. Ibid., pp. 113, 56.

16. Ibid., pp. 56–57, 113.

17. Ibid., pp. 802–3.

18. Ibid., pp. 803–4, 57.

19. Ibid., p. 117.

20. Ibid., pp. 117–19.

21. Ibid., p. 119.

22. Letter to his mother, 18 December 1862, Burgwyn Family Papers.

23. Letter to his father, 20 December 1862, ibid.

24. *Official Records*, Ser. 1, 18 : 108–9.

25. Ibid., p. 489.

26. Letter to his father, 24 December 1862, Burgwyn Family Papers.

27. *North Carolina Standard*, 31 December 1862.

CHAPTER 17

1. Douglas Southall Freeman, *R. E. Lee: A Biography*, 4 vols. (New York: Charles Scribner's Sons, 1934), 2 : 476–77.

2. *Illustrated London News*, 8 November 1862, p. 487.

3. *Harper's Weekly*, 8 November 1862, p. 706.

4. Varina Jefferson Davis, *Jefferson Davis: A Memoir by His Wife*, 2 vols. (New York: Belford, 1890), 2 : 367–68.

5. *Diary of Gideon Welles*, 3 vols. (Boston: Houghton Mifflin, 1911), 1 : 211.

6. *Illustrated London News*, 22 November 1862, p. 541.

7. *North Carolina Standard*, 26 November 1862.

8. John G. Nicolay and John Hay, *Abraham Lincoln*, 10 vols. (New York: Century, 1890), 6 : 125–26, 164–72.

9. Allan Nevins, *The War for the Union*, 8 vols. (New York: Charles Scribner's Sons, 1960), 2 : 273.

10. *Official Records*, Ser. 1, vol. 19, pt. 2, pp. 709, 718.

11. Ibid., 18 : 814–16.

12. John G. Barrett, *The Civil War in North Carolina* (Chapel Hill: University of North Carolina Press, 1963), pp. 149–50.

13. Letters to his father, 2, 3 January 1863, Burgwyn Family Papers.

14. Letter to his father, 3 January 1863, 6 P.M., ibid.

15. *Official Records*, Ser. 1, 18 : 810–13, 816.

16. Ibid., pp. 499–500.

17. Ibid., pp. 807, 809.

18. Letters to his father, 6, 11 January 1863, Burgwyn Family Papers.

19. Letter to his mother, 23 January 1863, and to his father, 2 February 1863, ibid.

20. Letter to his mother, 8 February 1863, ibid.

21. Letter to his father, 8 February 1863, ibid.

22. Note appended to Anna to Henry Burgwyn, undated, but sometime between 8 and 28 February 1863, ibid.

23. *North Carolina Standard*, 14 January 1863.

24. Ibid., 28 January 1863.

25. Ibid., 21 January 1863.

26. Ibid., 28 January 1863.

27. Hugh Talmadge Lefler and Albert Ray Newsome, *The History of a Southern State: North Carolina*, 3d ed. (Chapel Hill: University of North Carolina Press, 1973), pp. 474–75.

28. Johnston to General H. G. Spruill, 2 February 1863, Pettigrew Papers, Southern Historical Collection, University of North Carolina Library, Chapel Hill.

CHAPTER 18

1. *Official Records*, Ser. 1, 14:394.
2. Ibid., 14:407–8.
3. Ibid., p. 400.
4. Ibid., pp. 420, 428, 431.
5. Ibid., pp. 437, 441–42.
6. Douglas Southall Freeman, *Lee's Lieutenants*, 4 vols. (New York: Charles Scribner's Sons, 1945), 2:467–69.
7. *Official Records*, Ser. 1, 18:894–95.
8. Letter to his mother, 28 February 1863, Burgwyn Family Papers.
9. Ibid.
10. Pettigrew Papers, vol. 17, 1863–64, Southern Historical Collection, University of North Carolina Library, Chapel Hill.
11. *Official Records*, Ser. 1, 18:890–91.
12. Ibid., pp. 898, 902–3, 904–5, 907–8.
13. Ibid., pp. 910–11, 913.
14. Ibid., p. 907.
15. Ibid., pp. 906–7, 911–12.
16. Ibid., pp. 906–7.
17. Ibid., pp. 549–50, 553, 555.
18. Ibid., pp. 556–58.
19. Letter to his mother, 4 March 1863, Burgwyn Family Papers.
20. Letter to his father, 10 March 1863, ibid.
21. Hill to Pettigrew, 10 March 1863, Pettigrew Papers, vol. 17.
22. *Official Records*, Ser. 1, 18:192–95.
23. Letter to his mother, 15 March 1863, Burgwyn Family Papers. See Davis, "Boy Colonel," 3:820–21, "Excerpts from daily journal of Colonel H. K. Burgwyn, Jr.," for an account of his activities, 12–14 March 1863.
24. *Official Records*, Ser. 1, 18:192–95.
25. Ibid., pp. 183–84, 192–95.
26. Letter to his father, 22 March 1863, Burgwyn Family Papers.
27. *Official Records*, Ser. 1, 18:183–84.
28. Young to J. J. Pettigrew, 2 March 1863, Pettigrew Papers, vol. 17, pp. 29–30.
29. *Official Records*, Ser. 1, 18:921–22; see also pp. 923–27, 932–37; Hill to Pettigrew, 22 March 1863, Pettigrew Papers, vol. 17.
30. Freeman, *Lee's Lieutenants*, 2:480–81.
31. Pettigrew Papers, vol. 17, p. 53.
32. Hill to Pettigrew, 17 March 1863; 18 March 1863 [8 A.M.]; 18 March 1863 [11 A.M.]; 19 March 1863, p. 47; 21 March 1863, p. 51; 22 March 1863, 8 P.M., 21 miles from New Berne, p. 51.

33. Julius A. Lineback [Leinbach], "Extracts from a Civil War Diary," *Winston-Salem Sentinel*, 13 June 1914–2 April 1915, Southern Historical Collection, University of North Carolina Library, Chapel Hill.

34. Letter to his mother, 23 March 1863, Burgwyn Family Papers.

35. Letters to his father, 22 March 1863, and to his mother, 23 March 1863, ibid.

36. Beth G. Crabtree and James G. Patton, eds., *Journal of a Secesh Lady* (Raleigh: Division of Archives and History, Department of Cultural Resources, 1979), p. xxvi–xxvii. John Devereux, Jr., was a distinguished North Carolinian. An honor graduate of Yale in 1840, he was forced to forego the practice of law in order to manage a very substantial estate. On 20 September 1861, he was promoted to the rank of major and appointed chief quartermaster of North Carolina. John Devereux's "predominant trait was a genuine love of books, and his wide acquaintance with them, especially with Classic English prose and poetry" (ibid., p. xxvii). Annie, a schoolteacher in adult life, must have shared this interest with her father, for they were credited with having provided Joel Chandler Harris with some of the "myths and legends of the old plantation." In *Nights with Uncle Remus*, the author acknowledged his indebtedness to "Mr. John Devereux, Jr., and Miss Devereux of Raleigh, North Carolina" (Harris, *Nights with Uncle Remus* [New York: Houghton Mifflin, 1881], p. xlii). John Devereux died in 1893 after a long illness. Margaret was forced to sell Will's Forest to settle her husband's estate, but she and Annie continued to live in Raleigh until her own death in 1910.

37. "Reflections of Judge W. H. S. Burgwyn," Woodland, N.C., 8–9 July 1974, pp. 3–4, Burgwyn Family Papers (#1687), vol. 14.

38. Photocopy of letter from Margaret Jones Mackay to her cousin, Dr. Alfred Mordecai, probably written about 1974–75, in possession of writer.

39. Anna Greenough Burgwyn Diary Book, 1863–74, p. 11, in the possession of John Alveston Burgwyn Baker, Richmond, Va.

40. Anna Greenough Burgwyn Journal, May 1886–April 1887, in possession of John Alveston Burgwyn Baker, Richmond, Va.

CHAPTER 19

1. Daily Journal, p. 8, Burgwyn Family Papers.

2. Letter to his mother, 28 March 1863, ibid.

3. Daily Journal, p. 8, ibid.

4. *Official Records*, Ser. 1, 18:212–13; see also James B. Gardner, ed., *Record of the Service of the Forty-fourth Massachusetts Volunteer Militia in North Carolina August 1862 to May 1863* (Boston: Privately printed, 1887), p. 164.

5. Daily Journal, pp. 8–9, Burgwyn Family Papers.

6. Letter to his father, 2 April 1863; Daily Journal, p. 9, ibid.

7. Daily Journal, pp. 9–10, ibid.

8. Letters to his father, 6 April, 31 May 1863, ibid.

9. *Official Records*, Ser. 1, 18:955–56.

10. Gardner, ed., *Record of the Service of the Forty-fourth Massachusetts*, pp. 165, 169; *Official Records*, Ser. 1, 18:213.

11. For a detailed account of the siege of Washington, 30 March–15 April 1863, see Davis, "Boy Colonel," 3:846–86.

12. Letter to his father, 6 April 1863, Burgwyn Family Papers.

13. *"Corporal," Letters from the Forty-fourth Regiment M.V.M.*, a record of the experience of a Nine Months' Regiment in the Department of North Carolina in 1862–3 (Boston, 1863), pp. 96–98.

14. Ezra J. Warner, *Generals in Blue* (Baton Rouge: Louisiana State University Press, 1964), pp. 467–68.

15. *Official Records*, Ser. 1, 18:245–46.

16. Daily Journal, p. 10, Burgwyn Family Papers.

17. *Official Records*, Ser. 1, 18:215.

18. Ibid.

19. Letter to his father, 21 April 1863, Burgwyn Family Papers.

20. Hill to Pettigrew, 23 April 1863, Pettigrew Papers, vol. 17, 1863–64, p. 69, Southern Historical Collection, University of North Carolina Library, Chapel Hill.

21. *Official Records*, Ser. 1, 18:988–89.

22. Letters to his parents, 23 April 1863, Burgwyn Family Papers.

23. Letter to his father, 21 April 1863, ibid.

24. Ibid.

25. Harry Burgwyn to Captain N. C. Hughes, A.A.G., 26 April 1863, ibid.

26. Letter to his mother, 30 April 1863, ibid.

27. Letter to his mother, 1 May 1863, ibid.

28. Daily Journal, p. 13, ibid.; see also *Raleigh News and Observer*, 26 February 1926.

29. Daily Journal, p. 14, ibid.

30. Letter to his mother, 8 May 1863, ibid.

31. Edward A. Pollard, *The Lost Cause* (New York: E. B. Treat, 1866), pp. 377, 372.

32. Daily Journal, p. 15, Burgwyn Family Papers.

33. Douglas Southall Freeman, *R. E. Lee: A Biography*, 4 vols. (New York: Charles Scribner's Sons, 1935), 3:2.

34. Ibid., p. 5; see also E. B. Long with Barbara Long, *The Civil War Day by Day: An Almanac, 1861–1865* (Garden City, N.Y.: Doubleday, 1971), p. 348. The sources disagree about the casualty estimates.

35. Letter to Maria Burgwyn, 10 May 1863, Burgwyn Family Papers.

36. Letter to his father, 14 May 1863, ibid.

37. Letter to his mother, 19 May 1863, ibid.

38. Letter to his father, 21 May 1863, ibid.

39. Letter to his mother, 28 May 1863, ibid.

40. Daily Journal, p. 15, ibid.

41. Letter to his father, 31 May 1863, ibid.

CHAPTER 20

1. Letter to his mother, 5 June 1863, Burgwyn Family Papers.

2. Letters to his mother, 8, 10 June 1863, and to his father, 13 June 1863, ibid.

3. Letter to his father, 15 June 1863, ibid.

4. E. B. Long with Barbara Long, *The Civil War Day by Day: An Almanac, 1861–1865* (Garden City, N.Y.: Doubleday, 1971), pp. 353–56.

5. Letter to his mother, 28 May 1863, Burgwyn Family Papers.

6. Letter to his mother, 19 May 1863, ibid.

7. Douglas Southall Freeman, *R. E. Lee: A Biography*, 4 vols. (New York: Charles Scribner's Sons, 1934), 3:34–35.

8. Article reprinted in *North Carolina Standard*, 13 May 1863.

9. Georgia Lee Tatum, *Disloyalty in the Confederacy* (Chapel Hill: University of North Carolina Press, 1934), pp. 150, 110–21; William T. Auman and David D. Scarboro, "The Heroes of America in Civil War North Carolina," *North Carolina Historical Review* 58 (October 1981): 327–63.

10. *North Carolina Standard*, 28 January 1863; Tatum, *Disloyalty in the Confederacy*, p. 118.

11. Clyde Norman Wilson, Jr., "Carolina Cavalier: The Life of James Johnston Pettigrew" (Ph.D. dissertation, University of North Carolina, 1971), pp. 388–89.

12. Tatum, *Disloyalty in the Confederacy*, pp. 114, 127, 130–32.

13. Hugh T. Lefler and Albert R. Newsome, *The History of a Southern State: North Carolina*, 3d ed. (Chapel Hill: University of North Carolina Press, 1973), p. 475.

14. Report of Colonel H. K. Burgwyn, Jr., to Captain N. C. Hughes, A.A.G., 26 April 1863; Daily Journal, p. 15, Burgwyn Family Papers.

15. Julius A. Lineback [Leinbach], "Extracts from a Civil War Diary," *Winston-Salem Sentinel*, 13 June 1914–3 April 1915, p. 45, Southern Historical Collection, University of North Carolina Library, Chapel Hill.

16. Letter to his mother, 17 June 1863, Burgwyn Family Papers. Subsequent to this date, there are no other letters from Harry known to exist. The last entry in his daily journal is dated 12 June 1863.

17. *Official Records*, Ser. 1, vol. 27, pt. 3, p. 896; ibid., pt. 2, pp. 357–58; see also Department of Military Art and Engineering, U.S. Military Academy, *Civil War Atlas* (West Point, N.Y.: U.S. Military Academy, 1941), p. 75a. Rodes's division of Ewell's Corps crossed the Potomac at Williamsport (*Official Records*, Ser. 1, vol. 27, pt. 2, pp. 546–47).

18. *Official Records*, Ser. 1, vol. 25, pt. 2, pp. 810–11.

19. Ibid., p. 814.

20. Ibid., pp. 832–33.

21. Ibid., p. 473.

22. Ibid., p. 479.

23. Ibid., pp. 499–500, 504–6, 531.

24. Ibid., vol. 27, pt. 1, p. 47.

25. Freeman, *Lee*, 3:15–16.

26. *Official Records*, Ser. 1, vol. 27, pt. 1, pp. 30–32.

27. Ibid., pp. 34–35.

28. Ibid., p. 45.

29. Ibid., pp. 55–56.

CHAPTER 21

1. Julius A. Lineback [Leinbach], "Extracts from a Civil War Diary," *Winston-Salem Sentinel*, 13 June 1914–3 April 1915, p. 49, Southern Historical Collection, University of North Carolina Library, Chapel Hill.

2. *Official Records*, Ser. 1, vol. 27, pt. 3, pp. 868–69, 880–82.

3. Ibid., pp. 169, 167, 186, 181.

4. Ibid., p. 905.

5. Ibid., pp. 910–11.

6. Lineback, "Extracts from a Civil War Diary," p. 49.

7. *Official Records*, Ser. 1, vol. 27, pt. 1, p. 54.

8. Ibid., pt. 3, p. 913.

9. Ibid., pp. 914–15.

10. Ibid., pp. 924–25.

11. Ibid., pp. 276–77.

12. Lineback, "Extracts from a Civil War Diary," p. 49.

13. *Official Records*, Ser. 1, vol. 27, pt. 3, pp. 930–31.

14. Ibid., p. 314.

15. Ibid., pt. 2, pp. 692–93.

16. Ibid., pt. 3, pp. 347–48, 334–39.

17. Lineback, "Extracts from a Civil War Diary," p. 55.

18. *Official Records*, Ser. 1, vol. 27, pt. 3, pp. 942–43.

19. Ibid., pt. 1, p. 59.

20. Ibid., pp. 58–60.

21. Ibid., p. 61.

22. Ibid., pt. 3, p. 354; pt. 2, pp. 439–52.

23. Ibid., pt. 2, pp. 693–95.

24. Ibid., p. 358.

25. Lineback, "Extracts from a Civil War Diary," p. 55.

26. *Official Records*, Ser. 1, vol. 27, pt. 2, pp. 298, 439–52.

27. Ibid., pp. 466–67.

28. Ibid., pp. 357–63, 606–9.

29. Ibid., p. 695.

30. Ibid., pt. 1, pp. 66–67.

31. Ibid., pt. 3, pp. 409, 400–401.

32. Ibid., pp. 395, 398–99.

33. Ibid., pt. 1, p. 914.

CHAPTER 22

1. *Bachelder's Illustrated Tourist's Guide* (Boston: John B. Bachelder, 1873), pp. 6–8.

2. *Official Records*, Ser. 1, vol. 27, pt. 3, pp. 416–17.

3. Ibid., pp. 417–18.

4. Ibid., pp. 419–20.

5. Ibid., pp. 421, 425–26.

6. Ibid., pt. 1, p. 987.

7. Ibid., p. 923.

8. Ibid., p. 924; ibid., pt. 2, pp. 439–52, 545–61.

9. Ibid., pt. 2, pp. 459–73.

10. Ibid., pp. 357–63, 606–9.

11. Ibid., pp. 637–39, 642–44.

12. Julius A. Lineback [Leinbach], "Extracts from a Civil War Diary," *Winston-Salem Sentinel*, 13 June 1914–3 April 1915, p. 55, Southern Historical Collection, University of North Carolina Library, Chapel Hill.

13. *Official Records*, Ser. 1, vol. 27, pt. 1, pp. 118–19.

14. Ibid., pt. 2, p. 309.

15. Walter Clark, *North Carolina Regiments, 1861–65*, 5 vols. (Raleigh: State of North Carolina, 1901), 5:113–32.

16. Warren W. Hassler, Jr., *Crisis at the Crossroads: The First Day at Gettysburg* (University, Ala.: University of Alabama Press, 1970), pp. 19–21.

17. Douglas Southall Freeman, *R. E. Lee: A Biography*, 4 vols. (New York: Charles Scribner's Sons, 1934), 3:66–67.

18. *Official Records*, Ser. 1, vol. 27, pt. 2, p. 348.

19. Ibid., p. 637.

20. Hassler, *Crisis at the Crossroads*, p. 18.

21. George Meade, *The Life and Letters of General George Gordon Meade*, 2 vols. (New York: Charles Scribner's Sons, 1913), 2:31.

22. Hassler, *Crisis at the Crossroads*, pp. 22–24; see also Robert U. Johnson and Clarence C. Buel, eds., *Battles and Leaders of the Civil War*, 4 vols. (New York: Century, 1887–88), 3:272–73; Edwin B. Coddington, *The Gettysburg Campaign: A Study in Command* (Dayton, Ohio: Morningside Bookshop, 1979), pp. 264–66.

23. Hassler, *Crisis at the Crossroads*, pp. 37–38.

24. Coddington, *Gettysburg Campaign*, pp. 267–68.

25. Ibid., p. 269. See also, Hassler, *Crisis at the Crossroads*, p. 40.

26. Jesse Bowman Young, *The Battle of Gettysburg* (New York: Harper & Brothers, 1913), pp. 174–76; see also Coddington, *Gettysburg Campaign*, p. 269.

27. Hassler, *Crisis at the Crossroads*, p. 40.

28. Johnson and Buel, eds., *Battles and Leaders of the Civil War*, 3:273; see also Hassler, *Crisis at the Crossroads*, p. 40.

29. Coddington, *Gettysburg Campaign*, pp. 270–71; see also Donald L.

Smith, *The Twenty-fourth Michigan of the Iron Brigade* (Harrisburg: Stackpole, 1962), pp. 124–27; John M. Vanderslice, *Gettysburg Then and Now* (New York: G. W. Dillingham, 1897), pp. 75–76; *Official Records*, Ser. 1, vol. 27, pt. 2, pp. 646–47.

30. *Official Records*, Ser. 1, vol. 27, pt. 2, p. 649; ibid., pt. 1, pp. 281–82.

31. Ibid., p. 282; see also Hassler, *Crisis at the Crossroads*, pp. 46–47.

32. *Official Records*, Ser. 1, vol. 27, pt. 1, pp. 282, 360.

33. Hassler, *Crisis at the Crossroads*, pp. 47–48.

34. Ibid., pp. 47–49.

35. *Official Records*, Ser. 1, vol. 27, pt. 2, p. 649.

36. Hassler, *Crisis at the Crossroads*, p. 49.

37. Coddington, *Gettysburg Campaign*, pp. 266–67.

38. Hassler, *Crisis at the Crossroads*, pp. 55–57; see *Official Records*, Ser. 1, vol. 27, pt. 1, pp. 289–91, 312–14, 247.

39. Coddington, *Gettysburg Campaign*, pp. 278–80.

40. Hassler, *Crisis at the Crossroads*, pp. 32–33.

41. *Official Records*, Ser. 1, vol. 27, pt. 1, pp. 246–47.

42. Hassler, *Crisis at the Crossroads*, pp. 43, 47, 44, 53.

43. *Official Records*, Ser. 1, vol. 27, pt. 2, p. 444.

44. Hassler, *Crisis at the Crossroads*, p. 86.

45. Ibid., p. 87.

46. *Official Records*, Ser. 1, vol. 27, pt. 2, p. 552.

47. Ibid., pt. 1, pp. 938–39.

CHAPTER 23

1. *Official Records*, Ser. 1, vol. 27, pt. 2, p. 642.

2. John L. Beveridge, "The First Gun at Gettysburg," in Ken Bandy and Florence Freeland, comps., *The Gettysburg Papers*, 2 vols. (Dayton, Ohio: Morningside Bookshop, 1978), 1 : 173–74.

3. Ibid., pp. 174, 172, 175.

4. Ibid., pp. 175–76; see also *Official Records*, Ser. 1, vol. 27, pt. 1, p. 938.

5. Warren W. Hassler, Jr., *Crisis at the Crossroads* (University, Ala.: University of Alabama Press, 1970), p. 150.

6. *Official Records*, Ser. 1, vol. 27, pt. 2, pp. 642, 668–69.

7. James K. P. Scott, *The Story of the Battles at Gettysburg* (Harrisburg: Telegraph Press, 1927), p. 196.

8. Hassler, *Crisis at the Crossroads*, pp. 118–19, 150.

9. Scott, *Story of the Battles at Gettysburg*, p. 204.

10. *Official Records*, Ser. 1, vol. 27, pt. 1, p. 329; see also Hassler, *Crisis at the Crossroads*, pp. 56–57.

11. Scott, *Story of the Battles at Gettysburg*, p. 203.

12. *Official Records*, Ser. 1, vol. 27, pt. 1, pp. 315, 247; see also Hassler, *Crisis at the Crossroads*, p. 57.

13. *Official Records*, Ser. 1, vol. 27, pt. 1, p. 329.

14. Hassler, *Crisis at the Crossroads*, pp. 57–58.

15. *Official Records*, Ser. 1, vol. 27, pt. 1, p. 317.

16. Hassler, *Crisis at the Crossroads*, p. 115.

17. Edwin B. Coddington, *The Gettysburg Campaign: A Study in Command* (Dayton, Ohio: Morningside Bookshop, 1979), p. 287; Hassler, *Crisis at the Crossroads*, pp. 143, 150; Donald L. Smith, *The Twenty-fourth Michigan of the Iron Brigade* (Harrisburg: Stackpole, 1962), p. 139. In these references to the strength of the three brigades of the First Corps south of the pike, Coddington uses the total figure of 4,586 officers and men. Hassler ascribes 1,312 effectives to Stone's brigade and 1,422 to Biddle. Smith considers 1,883 men as the effective strength of Meredith's Iron Brigade. On this basis, the total strength of the three brigades added up to 4,617. On the other hand, *Official Records*, Ser. 1, vol. 27, pt. 1, p. 315, allows for only 1,287 effectives in Biddle's brigade. Using this figure in lieu of Hassler's estimate, the total of the three brigades numbered only 4,482. As for the two opposing Confederate brigades, Hassler assigns 1,700 men to Brockenbrough and 2,000 to Pettigrew.

18. *Official Records*, Ser. 1, vol. 27, pt. 1, pp. 329–30.

19. Smith, *Twenty-fourth Michigan*, pp. 109, 41.

20. Ibid., pp. 40–41, 109–10.

21. *Official Records*, Ser. 1, vol. 27, pt. 1, p. 268; see also Smith, *Twenty-fourth Michigan*, p. 130.

22. *Official Records*, Ser. 1, vol. 27, pt. 1, pp. 327, 173–74.

23. Ibid., pt. 2, pp. 646–47.

24. Clyde Norman Wilson, Jr., "Carolina Cavalier: The Life of James Johnston Pettigrew" (Ph.D. dissertation, University of North Carolina, 1971), p. 355; see also Walter Clark, *North Carolina Regiments, 1861–65*, 5 vols. (Raleigh: State of North Carolina, 1901), 3:88.

25. Clark, *North Carolina Regiments*, 2:348.

26. Glenn Tucker, *Zeb Vance: Champion of Personal Freedom* (New York: Bobbs Merrill, 1965), p. 119.

27. Clark, *North Carolina Regiments*, 2:303–7, 370–73.

28. Letter to his father, 31 May 1863, Burgwyn Family Papers.

29. Clark, *North Carolina Regiments*, 2:371–73. Allowing 10 percent "for extra duty and details," the Twenty-sixth took only about eight hundred muskets into battle on the first day at Gettysburg (ibid.).

30. *Carolina and the Southern Cross*, 1, no. 8 (1913): 1–2.

31. Clark, *North Carolina Regiments*, 2:336.

32. Copied from the *Randolph Tribune* (Asheboro, N.C.), John Randolph Lane Papers, #411, Southern Historical Collection, University of North Carolina Library, Chapel Hill.

33. Letter to his mother, 14 October 1862, Burgwyn Family Papers.

34. *Carolina and the Southern Cross*, 1, no. 8 (1913): 1–2.

35. John R. Lane, "Address at Gettysburg," copied from the *Raleigh News and Observer*, 5 July 1903, pp. 1–2, Lane Papers.

36. Ibid., pp. 2–3. This was probably the E. Harman farm property. See *Official Records*, Ser. 1, vol. 27, pt. 1, p. 317.

37. *Official Records*, Ser. 1, vol. 27, pt. 2, p. 669.

38. Douglas Southall Freeman, *R. E. Lee: A Biography*, 4 vols. (New York: Charles Scribner's Sons, 1934), 3:69–71; see also *Official Records*, Ser. 1, vol. 27, pt. 2, p. 348.

39. Lane, "Address at Gettysburg," p. 3.

40. Ibid., p. 5.

41. Ibid., p. 1. In listing the several companies, Lane inadvertently omitted reference to Company B, Captain William Wilson commanding. Wilson was killed in the charge and was succeeded by Lieutenant T. J. Cureton.

42. *Official Records*, Ser. 1, vol. 27, pt. 1, pp. 279, 274.

43. Ibid., pp. 268, 315; see also Clark, *North Carolina Regiments*, 2:348.

44. Hassler, *Crisis at the Crossroads*, pp. 142–43; see also Smith, *Twenty-fourth Michigan*, p. 139. According to this account, the Iron Brigade (five regiments) lost a total of 1,212 out of 1,883 engaged at Gettysburg.

45. Hassler, *Crisis at the Crossroads*, pp. 103–5, 111, 113; see also John M. Vanderslice, *Gettysburg Then and Now* (New York: G. W. Dillingham, 1897), p. 96; *Official Records*, Ser. 1, vol. 27, pt. 1, pp. 279–80, 330, 332, 335, 346–47.

46. *Official Records*, Ser. 1, vol. 27, pt. 2, pp. 669–70.

47. Hassler, *Crisis at the Crossroads*, pp. 120–21; see also, *Official Records*, Ser. 1, vol. 27, pt. 1, pp. 356–57; Vanderslice, *Gettysburg Then and Now*, pp. 99–100.

48. *Official Records*, Ser. 1, vol. 27, pt. 2, pp. 670–71.

49. Ibid., pp. 661–62.

50. Ibid., p. 665.

51. Ibid., p. 661.

52. Hassler, *Crisis at the Crossroads*, p. 144.

53. Clark, *North Carolina Regiments*, 3:236–39. Reported losses of the Fifty-second for the first and third days were 33 killed on the field, 114 wounded and 169 missing. Colonel Marshall was killed on the third day "within a very short distance of the enemy's lines."

54. *Official Records*, Ser. 1, vol. 27, pt. 1, pp. 323–24.

55. Clark, *North Carolina Regiments*, 3:89–90.

56. *Official Records*, Ser. 1, vol. 27, pt. 1, p. 317.

57. Clark, *North Carolina Regiments*, 2:347–48.

CHAPTER 24

1. *Official Records*, Ser. 1, vol. 27, pt. 2, p. 643.

2. Walter Clark, *North Carolina Regiments, 1861–65*, 5 vols. (Raleigh: State of North Carolina, 1901), 2:349.

3. William F. Fox, *Regimental Losses in the American Civil War, 1861–1865* (Albany, N.Y.: Joseph McDonough, 1898), p. 559.

4. Address of Colonel John R. Lane before the Chatham County Confederate Veterans' Association, Burgwyn Family Papers. A portion was published by the *Chatham Record*, 14 August 1890.

5. John R. Lane, "Address at Gettysburg," copied from the *Raleigh News and Observer*, 5 July 1903, pp. 3–5, John Randolph Lane Papers, #411, Southern Historical Collection, University of North Carolina Library, Chapel Hill.

6. *Official Records*, Ser. 1, vol. 27, pt. 2, p. 643; ibid., pt. 1, p. 268.

7. Lane, "Address at Gettysburg," pp. 3–4.

8. Letter from T. J. Cureton to Colonel J. R. Lane, 15 June 1890, Lane Papers. In several accounts, one finds reference to an unnamed Confederate colonel, astride a mule, coolly urging the boys of the Twenty-sixth on to victory (Smith, *Twenty-fourth Michigan*, p. 130). That person was probably Captain Louis G. Young of Pettigrew's staff.

9. Lane, "Address at Gettysburg," pp. 4–5.

10. Cureton to Lane, 15 June 1890, Lane Papers.

11. *Official Records*, Ser. 1, vol. 27, pt. 1, pp. 268–69, 327–28.

12. Ibid., pp. 279–81.

13. Ibid., pt. 2, p. 643.

14. Cureton to Lane, 27 June 1890, Lane Papers.

15. Ibid. Lieutenant Cureton succeeded to the command of Company B, Twenty-sixth North Carolina, following the death of Captain William Wilson on the first day at Gettysburg. He was wounded on the third day but refused to leave the field.

16. Julius A. Lineback [Leinbach], "Extracts from a Civil War Diary," *Winston-Salem Sentinel*, 13 June 1914–3 April 1915, p. 59, Southern Historical Collection, University of North Carolina Library, Chapel Hill.

17. Ibid.

18. Letter of G. P. Collins to H. K. Burgwyn, 3 July 1863, Burgwyn Family Papers.

19. Collins to Burgwyn, 3 July 1863; and letter from Captain J. J. Young to H. K. Burgwyn, 3 July 1863, ibid.

20. Letter from Mary W. Barney to Henry K. Burgwyn, 13 July 1863, ibid.

21. Telegram from Sam'l W. Melton to H. K. Burgwyn, 13 July 1863; telegram from Mary W. Barney to Henry Burgwyn, 14 July 1863, ibid.

22. Letter from Captain J. J. Young to H. K. Burgwyn, 3 July 1863, ibid.

23. Letter from Captain J. J. Young to H. K. Burgwyn, 11 July 1863, ibid.

24. Letter from W. E. Taylor, Jr., to H. K. Burgwyn, 2 August 1863, ibid.

AFTERWORD

1. Anna Greenough Burgwyn's diary book, 1863–74, p. 1, in the possession of John Alveston Burgwyn Baker, Richmond, Va. Henry Burgwyn was not so handicapped by his stroke that he could not travel. He would make a number

of trips to and from Boston by water, and in September 1865 he sailed for Europe, where he resided for a year before returning home.

2. Ibid., p. 2.

3. Ibid.

4. Ibid., p. 3.

5. Letter from Burgwyn to Andrew Johnson, 12 June 1865, Military Collection, Civil War Collection, Henry K. Burgwyn, North Carolina Department of Archives and History, Raleigh. See H. K. Burgwyn, *Considerations Relative to a Southern Confederacy* (Raleigh, 1860); Anna Greenough Burgwyn's diary book, 1863–74. Burgwyn's petition was supported by letters from Dr. Jeffries, 7 July 1865, for twenty years the family physician in Boston, and from Asa Owen Aldis of St. Albans, Vermont, 31 August 1865, who had been befriended by Burgwyn while visiting in North Carolina just before the outbreak of the war (North Carolina Department of Archives and History, Raleigh).

6. Anna Greenough Burgwyn's diary book, 1863–74, p. 3.

7. Ibid., p. 4.

8. Ibid., p. 5.

9. Letter from Burgwyn to Andrew Johnson, 12 June 1865, Military Collection, Civil War Collection, Henry King Burgwyn.

10. The original list of these accounts, in Henry King Burgwyn's handwriting, is in the possession of his great-granddaughter, Mrs. Frank Hunter, Roanoke Rapids, N.C.

11. The original catalog is in the possession of Mrs. Frank Hunter, Roanoke Rapids, N.C.

12. Anna Greenough Burgwyn's diary book, 1863–74, p. 5.

13. John Fanning Burgwyn Typescript Diary, 1855–56, P.C. 564.1, North Carolina Department of Archives and History, Raleigh.

14. A cursory examination of the records on file in the Register of Deeds office of Northampton County, Jackson, North Carolina, indicates that Henry's brother Tom had liquidated about all of his holdings on the Roanoke River before the outbreak of the Civil War. Henry, on the other hand, sold little property before the war but apparently borrowed heavily, leading to forced sales and foreclosures shortly after the war's end. Some postwar transactions suggest that Henry's obligations were largely to kinsmen and that his son George Pollok was later given the opportunity of assuming some of these obligations and ultimately keeping a part of the Burgwyn properties within the immediate family (Davis, "Boy Colonel," 3 : 1174 n. 47, 1175 n. 52).

15. Matt W. Ransom Papers, Southern Historical Collection, University of North Carolina Library, Chapel Hill.

16. Anna Greenough Burgwyn diary book, 1863–74, pp. 5–7.

17. Ibid., pp. 6–7.

18. Letter from James Read to Anna Burgwyn, 24 January 1868, in the possession of Mrs. Frank Hunter, Roanoke Rapids, N.C.

19. Letter from James Read to Anna Burgwyn, 13 January 1868, ibid.

20. Letter from James Read to Anna Burgwyn, 7 January 1868, ibid.

21. Letter from James Read to Anna Burgwyn, 24 August 1869, ibid.

22. Anna Greenough Burgwyn's diary book, 1863–74, p. 9.

23. Ibid., p. 8. Maria and T. Roberts Baker were married in the Church of the Advent, Boston, Massachusetts, on 28 October 1868.

24. Ibid., pp. 8–9.

25. Ibid., pp. 9, 11, 12.

26. Anna Greenough Burgwyn Journal, May 1886–April 1887, in possession of Anna's great-grandson, John Alveston Burgwyn Baker, Richmond, Va. She had discontinued her diary book in 1874.

27. Obituary notice, *Richmond Dispatch*, 14 April 1887, of the death of Anna Greenough Burgwyn on 12 April 1887.

28. Obituary notice, *Richmond Dispatch*, 5 February 1877, of the death of Henry King Burgwyn at his residence, corner of Third and Main Streets, on 2 February 1877.

29. Anna Greenough Burgwyn Journal.

30. Ibid.

31. Ibid.

32. Ibid. This portrait mentioned in the entry for 3 February 1887 now hangs in the home of Anna's great-grandson, John Alveston Burgwyn Baker, Richmond, Virginia.

33. Ibid. It was on 25 February 1863 that Harry had left his home in Raleigh for the last time. He was returning to his post after a pleasant and relaxing ten-day furlough.

34. Anna Greenough Burgwyn Diary Book, 1863–74, p. 7.

35. Beside him rest the remains of his brother Will (W. H. S.) who died on 3 January 1913.

APPENDIX

1. Warren W. Hassler, Jr., *Crisis at the Crossroads: The First Day at Gettysburg* (University, Ala.: University of Alabama Press, 1970), p. 150.

2. *Official Records*, Ser. 1, vol. 27, pt. 2, pp. 342, 344–45. Other than the North Carolina regiments, there were five regiments and one battalion from Alabama, three regiments and one battalion from Virginia, three regiments from Tennessee, three from Mississippi, and five from South Carolina.

3. Julius A. Lineback [Leinbach], "Extracts from a Civil War Diary," *Winston-Salem Sentinel*, 13 June 1914–3 April 1915, p. 59, Southern Historical Collection, University of North Carolina Library, Chapel Hill.

4. *Official Records*, Ser. 1, vol. 27, pt. 2, p. 643.

5. Douglas Southall Freeman, *R. E. Lee: A Biography*, 4 vols. (New York: Charles Scribner's Sons, 1934), 3:112, 117.

6. Letter from T. J. Cureton to Colonel J. R. Lane, 22 June 1890, John Randolph Lane Papers, #411, Southern Historical Collection, University of

North Carolina Library, Chapel Hill; see also *Official Records*, Ser. 1, vol. 27, pt. 2, pp. 643–46, and Thomas Perrett, "Record of 26th, North Carolina Regiment, at Gettysburg," UDC 5, United Daughters of the Confederacy, North Carolina Division, Papers of Georgia Hicks, North Carolina Department of Archives and History, Raleigh.

7. Letter from T. J. Cureton to Colonel J. R. Lane, 22 June 1890, Lane Papers.

8. William F. Fox, *Regimental Losses in the American Civil War* (Albany, N.Y.: Joseph McDonough, 1898), pp. 555–56.

9. Ibid., pp. 569–70.

10. Walter Clark, *North Carolina Regiments, 1861–65*, 5 vols. (Raleigh, State of North Carolina, 1901), vol. 2, "Twenty-sixth Regiment" by Assistant Surgeon George C. Underwood, pp. 358–60, 371–73.

11. Ibid., p. 360.

12. Fox, *Regimental Losses in the American Civil War*, p. 575.

13. Clark, *North Carolina Regiments*, vol. 2, "Twenty-sixth Regiment" by Assistant Surgeon George C. Underwood, p. 423.

14. Ibid., p. 357, letter dated 9 July 1863.

INDEX